Human Rights *and* Oppressed Peoples

Human Rights *and* Oppressed Peoples

Collected Essays and Speeches

Georg Brandes

Edited and translated by William Banks

THE UNIVERSITY OF WISCONSIN PRESS

The University of Wisconsin Press
728 State Street, Suite 443
Madison, Wisconsin 53706
uwpress.wisc.edu

Gray's Inn House, 127 Clerkenwell Road
London ECIR 5DB, United Kingdom
eurospanbookstore.com

Printed in the United States of America
This book may be available in a digital edition.

Library of Congress Cataloging-in-Publication Data
Names: Brandes, Georg, 1842-1927, author. | Banks, William, 1970- editor, translator.
Title: Human rights and oppressed peoples : collected essays and speeches / Georg Brandes ; edited and translated by William Banks.
Description: Madison, Wisconsin : The University of Wisconsin Press, [2020] | Includes bibliographical references and index.
Identifiers: LCCN 2019011082 | ISBN 9780299324100 (cloth)
Subjects: LCSH: Brandes, Georg, 1842-1927—Political and social views. | Human rights. | Europe—Politics and government—20th century.
Classification: LCC PT8125.B8 A2 2020 | DDC 801/.95092 [B]—dc23
LC record available at https://lccn.loc.gov/2019011082

For all the world's small nations

Contents

Acknowledgments

This book is in one respect the result of a happy accident. Many years ago, while collecting an unrelated Georg Brandes text at the University of Wisconsin Memorial Library, I happened in error to reach for volume 17 of his *Samlede Skrifter*. That volume, as I was pleasantly surprised to discover, begins with a section titled "Undertrykte Folkeslag" (Oppressed Peoples), which contains some eighteen essays and speeches, all of them written in the first years of the twentieth century, on the widest variety of subject peoples, from as far west as the impoverished rural day laborers of Andalusia to the Boxer Rebels of Late Imperial China. A little further browsing that day revealed that there were many more of these, that Brandes's interest in the oppressed peoples of the globe was sustained all the way up to his death in 1927, and that the scope of his engagement would spread ever outward, culminating in his monumental 1922 Christiania address "Imperialism," which is truly planetary in its scope. Like so many with only an incomplete knowledge of the critic's immense oeuvre, I had generally presumed that Brandes, after his fateful encounter with Friedrich Nietzsche in the late 1880s, had largely retreated from the kind of political commitment that had defined the first phase of his career; Brandes after the completion of *Main Currents* in 1890, it is generally said, enters into his mature phase of "aristocratic radicalism," thereafter occupying himself with the long series of relatively apolitical monographs on the *store mennesker* (great men) of world history. Yet here was another side of Brandes that the larger world seemed to have almost entirely forgotten.

Gradually over the course of the following years the plan for this book crystallized; critical to this initial process was the mentorship of B. Venkat Mani, to whom I shall always remain indebted. Still another fortunate coincidence, a chance meeting in Ljubljana between Venkat and Svend Erik Larsen of Aarhus University, ultimately led to an invitation to the Brandes Archive housed there. The initial drafts of the translations were written during my year there as a visiting scholar, with funding provided by the American Scandinavian Foundation and the Lois Roth Endowment. The guidance of the archive's director, Per Dahl, was critical in this first stage of the project; additional support and counsel were generously provided by Karen-Margrethe Simonsen, Mads Rosendahl Thomsen, Jonas Ross Kjærgård, and Rikke Peters.

This book owes much of its form and structure to Amber Rose, assistant acquisitions editor at the University of Wisconsin Press. Her guidance at every stage of the process of publishing this book, my first, was invaluable, indeed sine qua non. My gratitude is also due to the anonymous peer reviewers, to senior project editor Sheila McMahon, and especially to copyeditor Marlyn Miller, whose assiduousness and keen eye contributed immeasurably to improving the quality of this volume.

While Brandes's nineteenth-century Danish prose does not present the same degree of challenge as the German of his good friend Nietzsche, a handful of passages in the text proved to be beyond my hermeneutic capacities. For the resolution of these troublesome turns of phrase I offer my thanks to Randolph Ford, who someday very well might come to understand all the languages of the world. His assistance with decoding Brandes's all but impenetrable Danish renderings of Chinese personal names and place-names was also indispensable.

Essential encouragement and guidance in bringing Brandes into dialogue with the young discipline of human rights history was provided by Julie K. Allen, who has always been and always will remain a model mentor to me.

The critical introduction to the translated texts would, furthermore, be a shadow of its present form without the wise counsel and tireless support of my three most significant interlocutors, James Rushing Daniel, Matthew Nicholas, and Tobias Zürn. My only hope is that I can repay some measure of all they have contributed to this book.

In preparing the annotations for a text as vast and as world-spanning as is Brandes's corpus of political journalism, many good souls have come forward to provide assistance in tracking down the obscurer historical figures discussed by Brandes. The assistance of Jan Nedvêd of the Karlovy Vary Museum was critical in discovering the identity of the unnamed "Oriental Prince" portrayed in the essay "Missionaries"; Trask Roberts's assistance with the French text of Clemenceau's essay on him was also essential; the further efforts of Tania Roy, finally, have helped shed light on this stubbornly enigmatic figure. Michalina Petelska's vast knowledge of Brandes's many Polish associates was essential in identifying the misnamed "Warsaw painter" mentioned in "Introductory Words for the Polish Evening in Copenhagen." Jens Bjerring-Hansen, a fellow member of Team Brandes at the Digital Currents project, provided critical information on the complex publication history of *Main Currents*; his general support of the project in its final phases was also of great value.

Joshua B. Parton's intrepidness was crucial in connecting me with Ann N. Knake of the Jesuit Archives and Research Center.

While the great majority of the material in this book is here published for the first time, small parts of the critical introduction were adapted for my general article "Brandes after *Main Currents*," published by the Digital Currents project at georgbrandes.dk. Additionally, I have delivered guest lectures on various aspects of the book at Aarhus University, Gustavus Adolphus, and the Universities of Minnesota and Washington; my thanks are due, respectively, to Karen-Margrethe Simonsen, Kjerstin Moody, Richard McCormick, and Marianne T. Stecher for these opportunities. Lastly, I have delivered conference papers on Brandes's political journalism at the Yale Conference on Baltic and Scandinavian Studies and at SASS UCLA.

Finally, and most importantly, I offer my deepest gratitude to my family, from whom among so many other things I have learned the meaning of love unconditional. This book would never have passed beyond the stage of a half-formed manuscript were it not for the boundlessness of their generosity, their encouragement, and their never-wavering belief in me.

Note on the Source Texts

Of the thirty-five texts that are presented in this volume, thirty-two initially appeared in print form, while "Armenia and Europe," "Introductory Words for the Polish Evening in Copenhagen," and "Imperialism" were first delivered as public lectures. Almost all were first published in Danish in the radical newspaper *Politiken*, founded in 1884 by the critic's brother Edvard and the politician Viggo Hørup. Many were simultaneously published in other European languages, particularly those works that had been initially requested by foreign editors or activists. "To the Students of Germany" thus appeared in German in the *Freier Almanach deutscher Studenten: Deutschland, Oesterreich, Schweiz* (*The Free Almanac for German Students: Germany, Austria, Switzerland*), while "To the Schoolchildren of Russian Poland" was of course circulated in Polish as well as Danish. Many texts appeared in multiple languages at once; the critic's 1916 "Appeal" for peace talks, for instance, was distributed across Europe in the millions in German and French editions.

Because of his outsize presence in Danish intellectual life, much of Brandes's journalism was reissued in book form, a process he himself oversaw until the conclusion of World War I, after which his major journalistic works were reissued in posthumous editions. And since many of the essays on oppressed peoples were written in relative haste, at the urgent request of those same peoples, the critic often made revisions to the original texts, in effect producing polished "posterity versions" for future readers. Because this volume is intended as a kind of intellectual portrait of Brandes's evolving thinking about the nature of the rights of peoples and of human rights rather than as a historiographic investigation of the contemporary impact of these writings, the translator has used these "final" versions as source texts for the translations. Not only do these versions reflect the critic's more measured thoughts; it was also the intention of their author that they serve as a kind of official historical record.

The first twenty-four texts in this volume are taken from volumes 17 and 18 of his *Samlede Skrifter*, published respectively in 1906 and 1910, and from the follow-up volume *Fugleperspektiv* of 1913. The following nine wartime essays (texts twenty-five through thirty-three) are taken from the four editions of his *Verdenskrigen* (1916–17); the first seven of these have previously appeared in Catherine D. Groth's *The World at War*, published in the United States in 1917. The final two texts of the volume, the monumental 1922 Christiania address "Imperialism" and the 1925 essay "Europe Now," appeared in book form in posthumous collections, the former in *Kulturbilleder* (1932) and the latter in *Georg Brandes: Den mangfoldige* (2005).

Human Rights *and* Oppressed Peoples

Introduction

It was England bade our wild geese go
That small nations might be free.
—"The Foggy Dew"

If the name of the Danish literary critic Georg Brandes (1842–1927) is known outside his native Scandinavia today, it is typically by virtue of the immense impact he exerted on European and even global belles lettres during the more than half century of his activity. Students of comparative literature are generally aware of his essential role in the founding of their discipline, and even more so his work as literary *modernizer*; it was the young critic himself who in a seminal Copenhagen address of November 1871 launched what would come to be called the Modern Breakthrough in Scandinavian letters, that momentous movement that within the span of a decade would catapult the Nordic countries from a cultural backwater into the very center of the world literary system.[1] As the foremost literary critic and mediator of his age, Brandes is also known to contemporary students of continental philosophy for introducing his fellow Dane Søren Kierkegaard and a then still obscure Friedrich Nietzsche to Germany and the larger world.[2] And as an outgrowth of his late 1880s encounter with Nietzsche, one of the more consequential exchanges of ideas of the nineteenth century, Brandes is sometimes remembered for his pivotal role in the outbreak of early modernism in central and northern European literature.[3]

Yet world literary memory can hardly be said to have been kind to Brandes, his name, or his work, which for a number of reasons have been subjected to a near complete process of historical erasure since his death in 1927. In recent years, however, a broad effort by Brandes scholars to "reintroduce" him to the larger world has begun to take shape; new English translations of his key works have appeared, as well as the first English-language monograph in more than a generation.[4] Most ambitiously, a major Danish initiative known as the Digital Currents (DC) project has recently launched, with the intention of publishing new digital editions of Brandes's major work, *Main Currents in Nineteenth-Century Literature* (1872–90, English edition 1906), in Danish, English, French, and German, with new introductory essays and extensive supplementary material for each of the six volumes.[5] This book was conceived as a contribution to this larger effort, albeit with a focus on an aspect of Brandes's work that is very different from his better-remembered literary criticism and history.

In particular, this book is intended to introduce to a broad readership an aspect of Brandes's life's work almost entirely forgotten by the larger world, and indeed largely so in his native Scandinavia as well, namely his quarter century of activity in political journalism. Beginning in the summer of 1900, Brandes issued the first in a long series of essays and speeches in defense of the rights of all those to whom he referred as *undertrykte folkeslag*, that is, all those *oppressed peoples* suffering under the rule of Europe's continental and overseas empires. Brandes's emergence as "international tribune of the rights of peoples" was not without precedent; throughout the 1890s, in fact, Brandes had honed his advocacy skills on the specifically *national* Sønderjylland Question, that is, the fate of the nearly 200,000 ethnic Danes of Schleswig who had come under increasingly repressive German rule since their defeat in the 1864 Dano-Prussian War. At the turn of the century Brandes effectively turned his considerable talents to issues beyond his native land, initially toward the national minority populations of Eurasia and then, near the end of his long life, the many subject nations of overseas colonialism; the arc of Brandes's engagement with oppressed peoples was thus marked by ever-outward expansion, from the national through the European toward the planetary. Within a few short years, Brandes had established himself as one of Europe's preeminent defenders of the rights of subject peoples the world over. Requests for assistance from representatives of oppressed peoples would continue to pour in for the remainder of his life; indeed, in his 1905 essay "Zionism," Brandes would reveal that his advocacy work that year had consumed no less than a quarter of his working life. While he did occasionally evince frustration with the demands of his newfound role, those beseechers whom he turned away number only a handful; as Julie Allen has recently reminded us, during the final months of his life he was still attempting to fulfill his obligations through dictation, having lost the physical ability to write.[6]

I have chosen my words carefully in designating Brandes as an "international tribune of oppressed peoples," as it remains an open question whether Brandes's peculiar form of rights advocacy constitutes what in our time has come to be called specifically *human* rights activism. Yet given how closely Brandes approximates contemporary human rights advocacy, this book also therefore seeks a specific readership among the relatively young subdiscipline of human rights history. Much of the present essay, indeed, involves an effort to provide an answer to this critical question regarding the precise nature of Brandes's thinking and praxis in rights advocacy. In essence I will argue that Brandes, because of historical conditions unique to early twentieth-century Scandinavia, was able to think more boldly and more broadly about a more humane and just world than his contemporaries in much larger and more influential countries. Brandes thus *anticipated* much of the spirit and even the letter of the doctrine of universal human rights that would eventually crystalize in the 1940s. As such, he is wholly deserving of a place within existing narrative structures of the history of this noble idea.

As is well known to contemporary historians, the young subdiscipline of human rights history, after its emergence around the turn of our new century, soon split into two opposing camps. On one side is what might be termed the "expansive" school of human rights history, represented by such seminal studies as Paul Gordon Lauren's *The Evolution of Human Rights: Visions Seen* (1998), Micheline Ishay's *The History of Human Rights: From Ancient Times to the Globalization Era* (2004), Lynn Hunt's *Inventing Human Rights: A History* (2007), and Peter N. Stearns's *Human Rights in World History* (2012). These works generally place the genesis of universal human rights proper in the 1940s, as signaled by the 1948 UN Declaration of Universal Human Rights. More importantly, they are all in general agreement in acknowledging the existence of a concrete *prehistory* of human rights, key moments in this gradualist and evolutionary narrative including (among many others) the initial stirrings of universalism in Greco-Roman Stoicism as well as, of course, eighteenth-century European Enlightenment thinking and its eventual concretization in the American and French revolutions. On the other side is what might be referred to as the "narrow" school of human rights history, represented most prominently by Samuel Moyn in his groundbreaking *The Last Utopia: Human Rights in History* (2010) and its follow-up volumes *Human Rights and the Uses of History* (2014) and *Not Enough: Human Rights in an Unequal World* (2018). Moyn not only rejects any notion of human rights prehistory, asserting that when human rights appeared they constituted something almost entirely new in the world, but he further places the moment of their crystallization much later than the opposing school, specifically in the 1970s.

Despite their many differences, each of the aforementioned studies is alike in that nowhere does the name of Georg Brandes appear; for that matter, the Scandinavians as a whole rarely warrant mention, in spite of the fact that today they are so often held up as exemplary adherents to and advocates of the various international human rights conventions adopted in the postwar era. The elision of Brandes (and to a lesser degree the Nordics in general) from established historical narratives is certainly understandable, and not only because of the general Anglophone and Francophone bias of historical studies, to which human rights history has hardly been the exception.[7] The initial genesis of the idea of universal human rights in the 1940s, as an initiative of the victorious World War II powers, occurred after all almost entirely in English; the same can be said of its global diffusion in the 1970s, albeit with essential contributions from the Soviet sphere and Latin America. It is thus not much of an exaggeration to say that when human rights have spoken, they have historically done so overwhelmingly in English or to a lesser extent in French. Each of the influential national Nordic human rights institutes, accordingly, were founded well *after* the watershed year of 1977, in which US president Jimmy Carter, in his memorable Notre Dame commencement address, formally announced the dawn of the era of human rights: Sweden in 1984, Denmark and Norway in 1987, Iceland in 1994, and Finland in 2012.

It must further be acknowledged that the fundamentally Anglophone and Francophone origin story of human rights has yet to be challenged by Scandinavian historians themselves; indeed, even the not insubstantial history of the Nordic role in the evolution of human rights thinking and law *after* 1948 largely remains unwritten.[8] A critical first step in this direction has been taken by the recent founding of the Nordic Human Rights History Network, which published a special issue of the *Nordic Journal of Human Rights* in October 2018, presenting the results of workshops held across Scandinavia between 2015 and its publication. While the individual essays in the issue carefully document the significant Nordic role in the diffusion and development of universal human rights in the postwar period, that is, the era of human rights *history*, the editors (and the network in general) do not address the separate matter of the *prehistory* of human rights.[9] In this specific sense, the scholars of the Nordic Human Rights History Network effectively affirm the Anglophone-dominated narrative of the history of this noble idea, conceding that historically "the Nordic countries have more often reacted to international trends and processes" than taken the lead in them.[10]

This book, in contrast, argues that the Nordic engagement with human rights, at least in the single case of Brandes, is of a significantly older vintage. As such, it is positioned firmly within the "expansive" school of the subdiscipline along with all those historians who maintain that the initial coinage of the phrase in the 1942 Declaration of the United Nations did *not* in fact emerge ex nihilo, that its genesis was at least to some extent the culmination of earlier developments within European and global thinking. Once more, it must be emphasized here that this book in no manner suggests that Brandes played any role whatsoever in the strictly genealogical conception of human rights history. No evidence that Brandes's early rights activism figured in the thinking and the deliberations of the framers of the 1948 Universal Declaration is likely to emerge, and for good reason—as has been noted, the legacy of Brandes, in politics and literature and alike, had by the 1940s largely been written out of Anglophone and Francophone discourses. Paradoxically enough, this process of erasure was more than anything the result of his earlier activism, particularly his principled and sustained opposition to World War I, reflected in his refusal to endorse the Allied cause, for which the French and British never forgave him.[11] Had the triumphant powers of 1945 looked to Scandinavia for inspiration in the framing of the Universal Declaration, the very last place they would have sought it would have been Brandes, who had so stubbornly served the role of gadfly to their efforts in the first war and even more so in its aftermath, as a critic of the Treaty of Versailles and the newly established League of Nations.[12]

That no reasonable case can be made that the essays and speeches in this volume served any role at all in the genealogy of universal human rights does not, of course, preclude a space for Brandes in the *prehistory* of the idea, as long as we remain within the broader parameters defined by the expansive school of human rights history. What this book suggests, once again, is that historical circumstances in his native Scandinavia permitted Brandes to approach something *approximating* what would later come to be called the doctrine of universal human rights; in his own curious manner, Brandes thus *anticipated* later developments in the major powers. One historical condition of the late Belle Epoque that was indeed categorically distinct from those of the post–World War II era was the nature of the overwhelmingly dominant rights issue of the age, namely that of collective self-determination. We happy few who have been blessed with long traditions of self-rule and autonomy can never be reminded enough that when the guns of August erupted in 1914, fully half of the current European Union member states did not exist, and that nearly three-quarters of current United Nations members remained under colonial rule in 1945. Historians of both the expansive and the narrow schools are in general agreement that human rights emerged in an era in which the most pressing rights issue of the age was state oppression of individuals within the borders of the nation-state itself; they are in this sense a wholly postcolonial phenomenon. What distinguishes the two schools is of course that the former sees earlier rights struggles, including those for self-determination, as part of a much longer historical arc. With respect to the expansive school, no substantial obstacles present themselves to the incorporation of Brandes into preexisting frameworks. Ishay in particular devotes considerable space to the struggle for collective self-determination, although she is rightfully skeptical as to whether national independence movements ought to be considered properly "human" rights struggles.[13] At minimum, this book seeks to carve out a place for Brandes in such historical narratives.

Regarding the narrow school of human rights history, it would seem at first glance that Moyn's categorical denial of the legitimacy of any form of human rights *prehistory* would suggest that the figure of Brandes has little to offer it.

Yet I argue that this is precisely *not* the case, that certain aspects of Moyn's thinking are necessary for acquiring a fuller understanding of how Brandes conceives of the rights of peoples and, even more ambitiously, that Brandes's peculiar form of rights thinking and especially praxis suggests that we may need to reconsider Moyn's narrower historical horizon.

For Moyn, the rights discourses of the late eighteenth century, critically, belong to a tradition distinct from that of specifically "human" rights; the 1789 French Déclaration des droits de l'homme et du citoyen (The Declaration of the Rights of Man and of the Citizen), therefore, should not at all be considered a precursor to 1948, since in fact the very rights granted by the revolutionary declarations were strictly conceived as circumscribed within, a function of, and wholly guaranteed by the emergent nation-state: "the 'rights of man' were about a whole people incorporating itself in a state. . . . Thereafter, they were about the meaning of citizenship . . . the justification for the creation or renovation of a citizenship space, not the protection of 'humanity.'"[14] Human rights differ from the rights of man in that they are in their essence transnational; indeed, human rights claims must seek redress beyond the nation-state because most often, as has been suggested, they concern the abuse of individuals by the nation-state itself. Whereas the rights of man conceived of the sovereign state as the proper home and guarantor of the rights of individual citizens, the much younger idea of human rights views the state as the principal violator of individual rights. Because Brandes focuses almost exclusively on collectivities, on the manner in which imperial state power is employed to deny the rights of national minorities and the colonized, Moyn would presumably place Brandes within the older and distinct tradition of the rights of man and its subsequent outgrowths, revolutionary nationalism and anticolonialism.[15] Thus it would seem incorrect to attribute to Brandes a nascent theory of specifically "human" rights, if only because the historical conditions of the Belle Epoque were not conducive to such thinking.

One further, and equally critical, pillar of Moyn's larger argument, however, significantly complicates this understanding of Brandes. As has been noted, Moyn further dissents from the expansive school of human rights history in his largely dismissive treatment of the 1948 Universal Declaration. Despite the boldness of its language, Moyn reminds us, the Declaration was greeted with generalized indifference around the world; those working toward a more humane and just world in the decades following continued to operate according to older and, importantly, much more ambitious programs. In the "free world" of the West, the rights of man and the old *liberal utopia* remained largely intact, while in the Soviet-dominated East, the Marxist-Leninist *communist utopia*, which had always prioritized social over individual rights, persisted as the aspirational ideal. And in the vast territories of the still colonized South, the *anticolonial utopia* of sovereign postcolonial states remained the governing ideology; in this configuration, understandably enough, the right to collective self-determination was primary, the rights of individuals secondary. The decisive event in the genesis of human rights as a legitimate global phenomenon, according to Moyn, was the general collapse of public confidence in each of these older utopias. The idea of universal human rights, therefore, emerged not in a triumphal annunciation, not as the end result of gradual, progressive historical evolution, but as in its essence an acknowledgment of the *failure* of far grander utopian schemes. Signal events in this process of general disillusionment included the 1968 Soviet suppression of the Prague Spring; the 1973 overthrow of Salvatore Allende in Chile, orchestrated by the United States; and, in the postcolonial sphere, a manifold of discouraging developments demonstrating that all too many of the young states proved to be as adept at denying the rights of individuals (as well as, even more so, those of ethnic and religious minorities) as their former colonial masters had been. It was against the backdrop of the generalized global crisis of the 1970s that the idea of universal human rights began to make its mark on the world, as disaffected idealists executed the "imaginative transformation" manifested in the "move from politics to morality."[16] As such, universal human rights constituted the "last utopia," in which "morality, global in its potential scope, could become the aspiration of humankind."[17]

What the essays and speeches of this book suggest is that historical circumstances unique to Scandinavia permitted Brandes to approximate the "imaginative transformation" toward universal human rights much *earlier* than his counterparts in larger and much more influential countries. Moyn's argument, in its core, asserts that before the decidedly minimalist utopia of human rights could begin to acquire meaning in the larger world, the older, maximalist utopias had first to expend themselves. Another way of conceiving this monumental historical phenomenon is that it amounts to what is here termed the collapse of the idea of a *national destiny of greatness*, defined as a collective faith in the inherent superiority of one's own civilization as well as, even more importantly, a sense that one's particular civilization is called upon to perform a unique world historical mission, specifically that of remaking the globe in its own allegedly superior image. Aside from its (by all means much more decisive) vulgar and purely material concerns, the idea of national destiny served at least to some extent as the animating spirit of British and French neocolonialism as well American Manifest Destiny; it was also of course the central justification of Allied efforts in both the world wars. The general decline in British and French power after World War II, reflected most concretely in the loss of empire, has of course compelled Britain and France to scale back their national ambitions, however clumsily this process of the reinvention of national destiny has been executed. In the United States, as is all too well known, this sense of national greatness has stubbornly persisted into the present in the form of "American Exceptionalism," this in spite of repeated military misadventures in the decades since the United States eclipsed Britain and France. In an important 2017 essay on exceptionalism's specific foreign policy doctrine, that of liberal internationalism, Moyn asserts that the central task for American foreign policy thinkers is the long overdue repudiation of the liberal internationalist project inherited from the British, who "especially in the age of Gladstone" made the fatal error of "assuming that the cause of humanity was served by the geopolitical advancement of a single nation (and empire)."[18] National defeat in Vietnam for a time provided the conditions necessary for at least the initial germination of this process—hence the sudden emergence of human rights in the United States in the mid-1970s—yet again as is all too familiar to the rest of the world, the critical project of the reimagination of American national destiny along more modest lines was almost immediately aborted.

In Scandinavia, the demand for the reimagination of national destiny occurred much earlier. While it would be incorrect to suggest that such small countries ever dreamed of remaking the globe—such grand delusions are after all reserved for larger lands—Denmark and Sweden were in fact once considered to be among Europe's major players, if on the far low end of the scale, and both had been minor colonial powers.[19] The Danes under Christian IV (r. 1588–1648) and the Swedes under Gustavus Adolphus (r. 1611–32) had once terrorized the European continent, yet by the age of Brandes this was all a distant memory. Sweden's relevance as a European power formally ended with defeat in the early eighteenth-century Great Northern War, and while Denmark hung on a little longer, it suffered national humiliations of even greater consequence in the nineteenth century; Norway was stripped from the kingdom in 1814 as punishment for siding with Napoleon, and defeat in the 1864 Dano-Prussian War, even more catastrophically, resulted in a substantial reduction of its traditional homeland, as the roughly 200,000 ethnic Danes of Schleswig came under Prussian rule.[20] Thus Denmark at the turn of the twentieth century found itself in the unusual circumstance of being both colonizer and colonized; the number of Danes under foreign rule, in fact, well exceeded Denmark's overseas colonial subjects. Even more importantly, the very nature of nineteenth-century Danish national identity itself was constructed against the backdrop of national *decline* and *contraction*. In his seminal 1894 address "Om nationalfølelse" ("On National Sentiment"), Brandes makes much of a passing comment in a review of the 1878 Exposition Universelle; after celebrating the admirable Norwegian and Swedish contributions, the reviewer has only this to say of Brandes's native land: *Le Danemark s'efface* (Denmark fades away).[21]

Because Denmark and Sweden had by the mid-nineteenth century been so thoroughly marginalized on the global stage, Danes and Swedes were compelled much earlier to begin the process of reimagining their national destinies, of rethinking their place in the larger world and even more importantly their relations to it; a similar compulsion was imposed on the much younger Norwegian and Finnish states, both of which would soon enough find their hard-won independence threatened by a new round of great power predation. It was under these conditions—inexorable decline and even the perilous threat of national extinction—that Brandes came to international rights advocacy. Despite the proudly internationalist orientation of the essays and speeches that make up this book, it must always be remembered that Brandes's political activities, like his better-remembered comparative literary studies, are always underpinned by an equally significant *national* component. Brandes seems to have believed that because of their unique history and the precipitous fall from minor European power to, for all practical purposes, occupied country, Danes ought naturally to be in sympathy with all the other similarly put-upon nations of the globe. His sincere hope, it seems, was that Denmark would come to serve as a kind of beacon of humane and just values for all the world, a friend to the oppressed and a principled opponent of the oppressors. As Julie Allen has recently uncovered, Brandes makes explicit his ideal imaginary of Denmark in a 1904 address on the Danish isle of Møn.

> More important is to develop within the people a sense of freedom and justice, *not just for their own use*. . . . Thus it was my ideal that it should be known that, despite the small size of our country, men lived here who felt sympathy with all wronged individuals or peoples across the world and who lifted their voices, spoke on their behalf. In a matter such as the case of Mano Negra, the Spaniards ought to turn to Denmark. All Poles and Finns, Ruthenians, Georgians, Armenians, should know that freedom and justice lived in Denmark.[22]

It must by all means be immediately conceded that the Danes have hardly lived up to the rather impossible standard Brandes has set for them; indeed, as would certainly be an immense disappointment to him, Norway and Sweden have historically come much closer. There is no more painfully clear example of this than the recent harassment by Danish state authorities of Syrian refugees simply transiting the country en route to safe harbor in Sweden.[23] Yet the chasm between ideal imaginary and actually existing reality in no manner diminishes the immensity of the leap in Brandes's thinking, for in refashioning the concept of Danish national destiny Brandes has in a certain sense anticipated the "imaginative transformation" from politics to morality that Moyn attributes to the human rights pioneers of the 1970s. The circumstances are by no means the same, yet the general movement in thinking is strikingly similar, from exhaustion with political struggle toward a new sense that specifically moral struggle might be able to overcome a position of abject weakness—in its essence what Václav Havel would later so memorably term "the power of the powerless."[24]

If Brandes's thinking and activity in the first quarter of the twentieth century had amounted to a historical dead end, it is still arguable that he would warrant a place within established narratives of human rights history. Yet importantly this is hardly the case, for his peculiar ideal imaginary of Denmark as an international beacon of "freedom and justice" would eventually begin to manifest itself broadly both in Nordic conceptions of national identity and, even more importantly, in foreign policy discourses. It should be emphasized here that the Nordic countries at the turn of the twentieth century were notable for their general *lack* of engagement with the larger world. As Christine Ingebritsen has noted, after the national defeats of the eighteenth and nineteenth centuries, Scandinavians largely "turned inward, to resolving conflicts between different power centers within these societies," that is, toward the construction of their widely admired (and, by the other side, equally maligned) national welfare states.[25] Returning to Moyn, it should be emphasized that while a certain measure of utopian aspiration has traditionally underpinned the erection of what the Swedes call the *folkhem*—we need only look to the memorable speech of Swedish prime minister Per Albin Hansson in which the term was announced for evidence of this—in no manner or form did it ever really function as a legitimate alternative to the *maximalist* utopias cataloged by Moyn, that is, those programs of global transformation eventually displaced by the *minimalist* utopia of human rights. In this sense the *folkhem* might be considered a form of minimalist utopia itself, in that it is predicated on the acknowledgment of the inherent limits of the nation-state to exert its influence beyond its borders.[26] While the "Middle Way" has long served as an aspirational ideal for countless Leftists across the world (the present editor among them), it must be understood that the *folkhem* was conceived and constructed entirely within the frame of the national state, and little if any effort has historically been exerted to export it abroad—the idea of a "Social Democratic Comintern" remains laughable in and of itself. The only exception worthy of mention here is Gunnar Myrdal's 1960 *Beyond the Welfare State*, in which the

Swedish economist, tragically blind to the coming tide of neoliberal reaction, argued that the next great task of humanity was the extension of the national welfare society to the globe, that is, the construction of a "welfare world."

Few Scandinavians were more acutely aware of their generally inward-looking nature than Brandes, who indeed regularly admonished his countrymen and women for their lack of engagement with the wider world; in the 1900 essay "Armenia," for example, he chastises the Danes for exhibiting "no interest in anything outside of Copenhagen and its suburbs" and the Norwegians for their exclusive concern for their "independence and . . . the reputation the kingdom and its great men enjoy." Much of the specifically national component of the essays and speeches in this book thus amounts to a sustained effort by Brandes to persuade his fellow Scandinavians to reengage with the larger world. Happily he would not have to wait long for his countrymen and women to respond, as the Nordic states, ever-mindful of their marginalization on the global stage, would come to serve as pioneers of what theorists of international relations term "small state status seeking."

> While great power status is attributed on the basis of how central, strong or influential a state is in the running of . . . international society, small states achieve status through making themselves *useful* to greater powers . . . small-power status is about being noticed or seen . . . when a small state seeks status, it masquerades as a great power. In doing so, it is trying not to be mistaken for a *great power*, it is simply seeking to be acknowledged as a *good power*.[27]

In an effort to secure for themselves at least some measure of influence in international relations, the Nordic countries have attempted to adapt Brandes's ideal imaginary into a concrete approach to foreign policy—what is generally referred to in Nordic discourse as "global Good Samaritanism." And as Ingebritsen has demonstrated, in this project they have been remarkably successful; Norway and Sweden especially have come to act as what she terms "norm entrepreneurs" in the areas of environmentalism, global welfare, and after the heavy lifting had been performed elsewhere, universal human rights.[28] The degree to which Scandinavians have come to define themselves as "global good citizens" is attested by two signal catchphrases in Nordic foreign policy discourse. In her 1992 New Year's address, Norwegian prime minister Gro Harlem Brundtland famously noted that with respect to Norway's relations to the outside world, "it is typically Norwegian to be good"; since then this sentiment has hardened into the oft discussed notion of a "regime of goodness."[29] In 1994, within the context of the vote against European Union accession, Norwegian prime minister Thorbjørn Jagland would introduce an equally consequential turn of phrase into the national lexicon, that of his intention to make Norway a "humanitarian superpower." This latter coinage has caught on in Sweden as well, especially since foreign minister Carl Bildt began to employ it extensively in 2013.[30]

It must be conceded that the Nordics have all too often failed to live up to the lofty standards they have set for themselves; it should also be noted that the concepts of the "regime of goodness" and "humanitarian superpowerdom" are widely contested at home, from all sides of the political spectrum. Abroad they understandably tend to provoke exasperation among the world's remaining major powers, that is, all those countries whose seats at the grown-ups' table of international relations are taken as matters of course. Neoconservatives and neoliberals alike, after all, delight in poking holes in what might be termed Scandinavia's own unique form of exceptionalism.[31] Yet these ideas very much retain their potency within Scandinavia as well as, even more importantly, in the larger world outside. With respect to universal human rights, whether rightly or wrongly, the Nordics have most certainly come to be viewed as exemplary; indeed in many ways they have eclipsed the reputation of the countries in which the idea initially emerged. Thus Ingebritsen cites an illuminating 2002 comment from a Sri Lankan activist: "None of us in the human rights community would think of appealing to the U.S. for support for upholding a human rights case—maybe to Canada, to Norway or to Sweden—but not to the U.S."[32]

In a certain sense it can be asserted that the Nordics, Norway and Sweden especially, have historically served as the Peter and the Paul of universal human rights. Once more, it must be emphasized that the doctrine is not, strictly speaking, indigenous to Scandinavia, yet once it had germinated elsewhere, these countries quickly came to serve as perhaps its most consistent upholders and defenders. The Nordic turn toward morality in foreign policy after World War II was rooted in what Christopher Browning terms "internationalist solidarism," which is in its very essence distinct from the animating spirit of largely Anglophone universal human rights.[33] As the editors of the recent *Nordic Human Rights Journal* special issue on Nordic human rights history note, it was only later that this "moral component" became "equated with human rights."[34] Yet the gradual embrace of universal human rights in the Nordic countries has most certainly been intertwined with processes in larger countries. In some ways this explains why the major powers have so often turned to Scandinavians for leadership on sensitive matters of international cooperation and mediation. It was likely no accident that in the period immediately following World War I it was a Norwegian, Fridtjof Nansen, who was selected by the League of Nations to oversee the resettlement of displaced peoples, or that after World War II a Norwegian and a Swede were elected as the first secretaries general of the newly founded United Nations.[35] The appointment of Gunnar Myrdal to oversee a comprehensive study of American race relations in 1938 indicates that major countries have looked to Nordics for leadership even on purely national matters.[36] With respect to human rights history, the pivotal 1975 Conference on Security and Cooperation in Europe (CSCE, also known as the Helsinki Accords) began as a Finnish initiative.[37] And in recognition of Swedish prime minister Olav Palme's leadership in the international movement against apartheid, Nelson Mandela's first trip abroad after his release in 1990 was to Sweden.

Returning to Brandes, it thus emerges that his value for human rights history is twofold. In the national/Scandinavian context, his early activities in the first quarter of the twentieth century effectively lengthen the historical arc of the Nordic engagement with human rights. It is arguable that later concepts such as "global Good Samaritanism" or the "regime of goodness," so central to the story of Scandinavian human rights after 1948, initially crystallize in Brandes's work. As such, the precise nature of the relationship between Brandes as progenitor and later developments in the era of human rights proper must be determined through new historical inquiry. In the broader European and global context, and especially within the domain of the history of ideas, the remarkable degree to which Brandes anticipates the "imaginative transformation" of the postwar era in his thinking and praxis must also be acknowledged and explored. In a certain sense Brandes can be said to bridge the gulf between the expansive and the narrow schools of human rights history. If Moyn is largely correct in asserting that the opposing school has been too careless in attributing a concrete prehistory to universal human rights, then it must also be conceded that the crux of his argument—that before the idea could begin to acquire significance in the world, the older "maximalist" utopias had first to run their course, and that this only occurred in the 1970s—is at the very least complicated by the presence of Brandes, who had already undergone a strikingly similar imaginative transformation at the turn of the twentieth century. Narratives of human rights history without him, therefore, remain profoundly impoverished.

Much of the remainder of this introduction is devoted to teasing out the characteristics of Brandes's rights thinking and praxis, with constant reference to their relation to contemporary human rights doctrine. Before proceeding to this, however, it is first necessary to explore how in fact Brandes did come to advocacy work at the dawn of the new century, since for many of his contemporaries this was a rather surprising turn of events.

Brandes's Path toward Political Journalism

> A Beetle once begged the Eagle to spare a Hare which had run to her for protection.
>
> —Æsop

Georg Brandes was fifty-seven years old when in the summer of 1900, in a gesture familiar to us at least since the days of Hanoi Jane, he began to attempt to leverage his global celebrity in an effort to intervene directly in international affairs of state. It should be noted here that his efforts did not emerge out of a vacuum, for some years earlier, beginning with his memorable 1894 address "On National Sentiment," Brandes had already served as an energetic defender of the rights of peoples within the national sphere, issuing a steady stream of essays and speeches in defense of the rights of his countrymen and women suffering under German rule in North Schleswig, which he continued right up until the resolution of the matter in 1920.[38] What changed in the summer of 1900, the starting point of this book, is that Brandes made the fateful decision to turn his considerable critical abilities outward into the larger world; had Brandes limited his efforts to his fellow Danes, he would warrant no more than a footnote in Benedict Anderson's *Imagined Communities*. Yet despite the "dry run" of Sønderjylland activism, Brandes's emergence as international tribune of oppressed peoples around the turn of the century, given the general drift of his *literary* work in the immediately preceding decade, would hardly have seemed to have been a likely outcome. The peculiar pathway of Brandes toward international rights advocacy is of significant complexity and thus deserves close examination.

Brandes's name has, from the very beginning of his long career, whether rightly or wrongly, always been closely associated with politics. As mentioned, he first made his mark on the world in November 1871, when in his introductory address to the lecture series that would form the basis of the six volumes of his *Main Currents*, he called for a literature of engagement with political and social problems. As Allen has argued, Brandes had from the beginning viewed "literary movements as political events," and Brandes himself affirmed this in 1923, confessing that the organizing principle of *Main Currents* had been political rather than literary.[39] As a work of comparative literary history, *Main Currents* is thoroughly ideological in its approach, tracing the dialectical interplay of eighteenth-century Enlightenment ideals and the reaction following 1789 through the Romantic literatures of France, Germany, and England. Yet within the national and Scandinavian context, the immense project was also conceived as a political event in and of itself. Unlike Europe's most advanced countries, Brandes asserts in the introductory lecture, the Nordics had never executed the dialectical turnabout toward the old revolutionary ideals—in the fourth volume, *Naturalism in England* (1875), Brandes credits the singular figure of Lord Byron with heralding this monumental reversal—and instead they became mired in reaction, some "forty years behind Europe." Brandes's clearly stated intention with *Main Currents* is thus the jumpstarting of a similar Byronic turn in his native land; the recent historical experience of Europe's major countries constituted for young Brandes a model worthy of emulation by the backward Nordics.

Main Currents was nearly two decades in the making. Its sixth and final volume on the poets of Young Germany appeared in 1890, and by the second decade of work on the project clear signs began to appear that Brandes's faith in its central organizing principle had begun to falter. According to the Hegelian frame in which the work was conceived, the individual authors treated in the various volumes are in effect subordinated to the broader "currents" (*strømninger*) of intellectual and cultural history; the poets are for all practical purposes mere vehicles for the expression of progressive Absolute Spirit. As the scholars of the Digital Currents project have demonstrated in their recent reappraisals of *Main Currents*, this began to change in the 1880s, as Brandes increasingly evinced an ever-greater interest in the individual genius of select poets at the expense of Hegelian metaphysics.[40] The signal event in this decisive reorientation of Brandes's thinking was his encounter with Nietzsche in the late 1880s, after which his critical focus shifted almost entirely to exploring the personalities of the individual "great men" of world history and their capacity to create culture. Not only did the nature of his literary production change during his mature years, from comparative literary history that was politically charged and ideological to a long series of relatively apolitical "great men" monographs, among them influential studies of William Shakespeare (1895–96), Henrik Ibsen (1899), Johann Wolfgang von Goethe (1915), Julius Caesar (1918), and Michelangelo (1921); Brandes also substantially reworked later editions of the volumes of *Main Currents*, always with an eye toward the personalities at the expense of the ideas.[41]

If we look exclusively at Brandes's *literary* work, the shift from his early, politically charged "literary radicalism" to his mature, Nietzsche-inflected "aristocratic radicalism" can most certainly be seen as clear evidence of a general *retreat* from political engagement and even disillusion with the very idea of democracy itself. His influential essays on Nietzsche, "Aristocratic Radicalism" (1889) and "The Great Man: The Source of Culture" (1890), are in fact infused with a disturbing measure of contempt for ordinary human beings, the function of whom is here strictly limited to working toward "the bringing forth of the thinker and the artist, of the lover of the truth and of beauty, of the pure and good personality."[42] The emergence of such "great men" now constitutes the very "purpose of history" itself, and the old Hegel-inspired conception of history as the progressive and dialectical unfolding of Enlightenment ideals is now largely abandoned.[43] Everything in his literary work of the 1890s, it would seem, was pointing away from political engagement, and yet as the content of this book demonstrates, Brandes would eventually return to political engagement, and in a manner much more direct and more urgent than that of his early practice of relatively abstracted ideological critique.

Brandes's pathway back to politics has been meticulously traced by the Danish Marxist critics of the 1970s, specifically in the important 1973 study titled *Den politiske Georg Brandes* (*The Political Georg Brandes*). As Olav Harsløf demonstrates, it is in a certain sense incorrect to say that Brandes turned away from politics after Nietzsche; instead, Brandes effectively shifted his political convictions into a new and separate medium; Harsløf describes this as a movement from early, indirect "cultural-political criticism (ideological criticism)" toward mature, direct "political-journalistic criticism (social criticism)."[44] This immense shift in Brandes's thinking and praxis was motivated by a dramatically revised understanding of nineteenth-century European history. As has been indicated, young Brandes had held up the example of Europe's most "civilized countries," France, Britain, and Germany, as the aspirational ideal of backward Denmark. In one of the few instances in which the Danish term *menneskerettigheder* (human rights) appears in this book, Brandes presumes that "the eighteenth century worked out the ideals of rights, asserted human rights, and coined the word 'humanity.'"[45] At least among the major Western powers, everything appeared to be moving in the direction of progress and freedom, and it could still be hoped that the dialectical interplay of history in Denmark might be turned back toward the example of its more advanced neighbors. Some thirty years later, however, in a seminal *Studentersamfund* (Student Union) address titled "Tanker ved aarhundredeskiftet" ("Thoughts at the Turn of the Century"), Brandes would concede that as a young man he had in fact been troubled by two disturbing historical developments, each of which had presaged a general European catastrophe. On the one hand, French revanchist rage at the loss of Alsace and Lorraine, together with the emerging system of alliances, seemed to signal an eventual world war, while on the other, the establishment of the short-lived Paris Commune appeared to suggest the inevitability of social revolution in Europe.[46] That neither of these simmering tensions had yet to erupt into open conflict, Brandes asserted, was due almost entirely to the fact that they had been effectively muted by the expansion of overseas empires, which had served both to curb class conflict at home and to transfer great power rivalries to far-flung regions of the globe. If young Brandes had been seduced by all the glamor and seeming sophistication of Europe's major powers, "Thoughts at the Turn of the Century" amounts to a kind of homecoming for Brandes; here all his sympathies are with the small nations of Eurasia as well as, to a lesser extent, the newly colonized abroad.

> The decisive political event we have experienced at the end of the nineteenth century is this: the great powers divide the world among themselves. They try to do this as peacefully as possible, in that they attempt to avoid a world war. Yet still they act with an injurious recklessness, because for the sake of economic advantage they sacrifice not only those peoples whom they conquer by fire and by sword and in all manner of horrors, but further all the small nations within their immediate orbit, which are either absorbed for the sake of national unity or exchanged as bounty or delivered up to brutality, all in order that the peace be preserved. Thus with the permission of Christian Europe the Sultan has had 300,000 Armenians murdered. We have seen Poland sacrificed and forgotten and the downfall of Finland, and have witnessed the spread of political savagery in Southern Jutland.[47]

If a new round of imperial predation had forestalled world war and revolution, it had come at the expense of the progressive and enlightened values the young Brandes had so celebrated. As they demonstrated their absolute military and material supremacy over the many subject nations of their ever-growing empires, a new sense of racial supremacy, informed by the pseudoscience of Social Darwinism, increasingly took hold among the British, French, and German people; as such, the central premise of *Main Currents*, that of the progressive unfolding of Enlightenment ideals as manifested in the major countries, had effectively been undermined. Even more disturbingly, the fate of Europe's small nations had also worsened, as Europe's old continental empires, those of the Hapsburgs, Romanovs, and Ottomans, sought territorial expansion within their immediate orbits. These declining imperia, locked into intractable conflict with one another and beset by internal unrest, had resorted to increasingly repressive measures against their national minority populations; even the rising young empire of the Hohenzollerns, despite its overseas conquests, employed Germanization policies of its own. France and Britain, whose subject peoples were mostly located outside Europe, remained discouragingly preoccupied with the Great Game abroad, and proved more than willing to barter away the independence of small nations in the interest of territorial concessions and the maintenance of great power peace.[48]

This general darkening of the European political climate effectively engendered a new sense of urgency in Brandes, which accordingly necessitated a rethinking of previous practice. No longer was the method of abstract ideological critique, the charting of the dialectical interplay of progress and reaction in the literary discourses of Europe, sufficient to the immense tasks confronting the progressive public intellectual of the new century. "Thoughts at the Turn of the Century," which contains all the central elements of his coming foray into international rights advocacy, thus functions as the annunciation of his newfound role. As is evidenced fairly frequently in the essays and speeches that make up this volume, Brandes himself is well aware of the long odds of such an enterprise; in his initial essay on Armenia, Brandes openly confesses his considerable doubts that "one can help them through newspaper articles." Yet try he must, and try he will.

~

During his visit to the United States in 1914, Brandes famously said of himself that he is more than a literary critic but less than a philosopher.[49] Unfortunately for present purposes, the same can most certainly be said of his political journalism; indeed, this is even more so the case. While there is far more in this volume than a mere documentary record of the daily indignities suffered by the various oppressed peoples of his era, he produced no comprehensive theoretical treatise on the domination of the weak by the strong, in the manner of a Hannah Arendt, a Frantz Fanon, or an Edward Said; the same is true of his critique of imperialism, in that he produced no work comparable to John Hobson's *Imperialism: A Study* or Vladimir Lenin's *Imperialism: The Highest Stage of Capitalism*. As has been indicated, Brandes's turn to direct political advocacy was motivated by an increased sense of urgency; as such, it was the demands of practicality and expediency that largely governed his political journalism rather than those of internal coherence or theoretical sophistication. Thus inconsistencies, cracks, and fissures are a feature of his rights advocacy when viewed as a whole; a striking example of this is found in his treatment of institutional Christianity, for Brandes was, among many other things, one of the most prominent anticlericalists of his age.[50] His commentary on the Boxer Rebellion was accordingly unsparing in its condemnation of efforts to spread Christianity in the world outside Europe; as his 1901 essay on missionaries makes abundantly clear, Brandes lays the blame for provoking the uprising solely on the China missions. His reflections on partitioned Poland, where historical circumstance had placed the Catholic Church at the very center of the independence movement, are, by contrast, characterized through and through by a warmth and affection for Polish Catholicism.[51]

Despite his decidedly practical orientation and the resultant inconsistencies, there are of course certain general principles that serve to guide his advocacy work throughout the quarter century of his activity as rights tribune. What follows is a survey of these central principles, in the domains of theory and praxis.

The Brandesian Imperative of Disinterestedness

> Persuasion is achieved by the speaker's personal character when the speech is so spoken as to make us think him credible.
>
> —Aristotle

If there is a singular principle running through the entirety of Brandes's political journalism, it is that he always observes a clear distinction between his advocacy work in the national sphere (the Danes of Sønderjylland) and his activity on the international stage. As has been indicated, the idealized conception of his native land does indeed underpin all his international advocacy work, yet in practice he is always careful to maintain a separateness between these two distinct yet intimately related spheres. This is plainly clear in the organization of his collected works, the editing and production of which he himself oversaw; the Danish material is kept separate from his international writings, which generally appear under the specific heading of "Oppressed Peoples."[52] There is in fact far more to this than the dictates of editorial convenience, for Brandes seems to have believed that proper advocacy ought to be *disinterested*, that any hint of advantage on the part of the tribune himself inevitably results in the corruption and the dilution of the effort. As always, theory and praxis are closely intertwined in Brandes; what could be called a Brandesian "imperative of disinterestedness" is thus just as much a practical as theoretical consideration. Yet while Brandes seems to have understood this intuitively, there is likely much more at work than the demands of praxis. His insistence on tribunal disinterestedness thus bears certain similarities to Kant's famous assertion that aesthetic judgment must itself be disinterested; in effect, Brandes transposes this principle from the domain of judgment to that of practical reason.[53] Regardless of its precise origins, he upholds this imperative with a fanaticism bordering that of Lenin, who of course in his own very different struggle always denied any kind of loyalty to his native Russian people in favor of an absolute commitment to internationalist communism.

The stubbornness with which Brandes observed this principle often brought him into conflict with those who could stake a claim to his personal identity as a Dane and a Jew. Despite his tireless efforts on behalf of his countrymen and women in Sønderjylland, the degree to which his relations with his fellow Danes were troubled cannot be overstated. As Brandes ranged ever farther abroad in his engagement with the oppressed peoples of the globe, he earned ever greater opprobrium at home, as Danes increasingly accused him of neglecting matters much nearer to hand. Indeed, in 1905, at the peak of his first burst of tribunal activity, the American critic Albert Shaw noted that Brandes was widely viewed by his countrymen as "a traitor, a cosmopolite, and enemy of the nation."[54] It is only after the outbreak of the Great War that Brandes was at least partially reconciled with the Danes, as his spirited defense of Danish neutrality aligned closely with both official state policy and the opinion of the overwhelming majority of the public.

As prickly as relations with his countrymen and women could be, Brandes's relations with his fellow European Jews were even more difficult. The reader might understandably be surprised that the fact that Brandes was born into the small Danish Jewish community has not already been discussed; one would think, after all, that his membership in a national minority within his native land would have some bearing on his views of national minorities in the larger world. Yet if we can take him at his own word, this was most decidedly not the case. In the deeply embittered 1908 essay "The Jews in Finland," Brandes claims of his Jewish ancestry that if he "had not been unceasingly reminded of it by others," he would certainly "have forgotten it." Given his propensity for such inflammatory comments—the 1908 essay is by no means the only place where he expresses such sentiments—it is not surprising that Brandes has attracted little interest from the discipline of Jewish Studies, even though for a half century he was among the most prominent European intellectuals of Jewish descent. Despite these denials, Brandes could hardly be said to have been uninterested in this aspect of his identity, as is clearly evidenced in his early long-form monographs on Benjamin Disraeli (1878) and on the great German Jewish socialist Ferdinand Lassalle (1881). Nor was he in any manner averse to speaking out against the persecution of Jews; indeed, one of his very first forays into political journalism was a lengthy 1901 essay on the beleaguered Jewish community of Romania for which he was ultimately unable to find a publisher; this would be followed up by a condensed treatment of the subject in 1903, "The Agony of a People and Utopias," which is included in this volume.[55] But these efforts were never enough to satisfy the demands of Europe's Jewish activists, who, in contrast to the Danes, did seem to have legitimate grounds for accusing Brandes of neglect. Brandes's uneven record of speaking out on Jewish affairs is particularly evident in his Polish advocacy work; out of an understandable fear of damaging the Polish cause, for many years he maintained a disturbing silence on the issue of Polish anti-semitism; indeed, his regular public appearances in partitioned Poland were occasionally boycotted by local Jewish communities. It was only after his silence became untenable, when undeniable reports of Polish-initiated pogroms began to appear during the first year of the Great War, that Brandes with broken heart finally took up the pen against his beloved Poles.[56] Yet again there is more than practical consideration at work here, for if Brandes had spoken up earlier and more vigorously (as he most certainly should have), then he would have been at odds with his own self-imposed standards.

The example of the Polish Jews reveals a further problem complicating Brandes's efforts at disinterested activism; his intense loyalty to the peoples whose causes he lent his name, sadly enough, often resulted in considerable conflict with even more oppressed groups within their immediate orbit. This is most clearly illustrated by his long-standing tensions with the Ruthenian minority of Austrian-ruled, Polish-majority Galicia. Far and away the most generously governed sector of partitioned Poland, the Austrian authorities had in fact granted the province its own *sejm* (parliament) in the mid-nineteenth century, inaugurating a new era of electoral politics within the old homeland. In this limited experiment with representative government, the majority Poles had hardly acted in exemplary fashion, for they used every electoral dirty trick, including gerrymandering and voter intimidation, to marginalize the minority Ruthenians. As early as 1898 Brandes had been approached by representatives of Galicia's Ruthenian community, who over the course of the ensuing decade would repeatedly seek his assistance. Out of understandable fear of damaging the Polish cause he had made his own, Brandes always refused; his single essay dedicated to the Ruthenian cause is concerned only with conditions in the Russian empire, where the vast majority of Ruthenians (some twenty-five million) lived a precarious existence under the czar. Denied the support of Europe's most prominent advocate for the rights of oppressed nations, the Ruthenians of Galicia eventually turned to longtime Brandes ally Bjørnstjerne Bjørnson, who at the very end of his life rather improbably emerged as Europe's principal defender of the Ruthenians. Whereas Brandes's rights advocacy is generally measured and calculated, the septuagenarian Nobel Laureate's activity was as much an anti-Polish campaign as pro-Ruthenian; as Brandes notes in his 1915 essay "Conditions in Russian Poland," Bjørnson had even likened the Poles to "the devil nearly like the Middle Ages had imagined him to be."

The Brandesian Conception of Nationhood

> To have nationhood, which is a sign of maturity, is greater than any weapons in the world.
>
> —Ho Chi Minh

As has been indicated, Brandes's overriding concern in these essays and speeches is with the rights of peoples rather than of single individuals. If, as Moyn has argued, universal human rights as they emerged in the 1970s were fundamentally about "the protection of 'humanity'" (that is, the securing of the individual against abusive state power) rather than "the justification for the creation or renovation of a citizenship space" (as in the older doctrine of the rights of man), then it would seem that Brandes's activity would fall exclusively under the category of collective self-determination.[57] Yet the Belle Epoque hardly lacked examples of state persecution of individual dissidents, nor international advocacy campaigns on behalf of them; Brandes himself had been an active participant in many of them, including the affair of Captain Dreyfus, which is important here in that it provided Brandes with a kind of template for his later activism, as well as the Spanish Mano Negra case and the Wrześnian Children's Strike, both of which are well represented in the current volume.[58] For Brandes it seems that the persecution of individuals is distinguished from the broader oppression of entire collectivities in quantity rather than in kind. Historical conditions for such a leap of thought, from a generalized conception of rights encompassing those of the individual and of whole peoples to a strict division between such, were simply not present at the time, as for Brandes there remained far larger fish in the sea of global oppression. In his early essay on Armenia, for example, he chastises Hans Kaarsberg, one of the few Danes to address the plight of the Armenians, for comparing "the situation of the Armenians (or the Romanian Jews) with that of the prisoner on Devil's Island."

Because Brandes's rights advocacy is overwhelmingly preoccupied with the oppression of collectivities, a matter of immense import is of course how precisely Brandes defines a given collectivity as a people, how he construes nationhood and national identity. His particular conception of national identity is of considerable sophistication, yet not without serious problems; it is really in this issue that the fault lines within his rights thinking begin to manifest themselves. In one important sense, Brandes is remarkably attuned to our contemporary understandings of nationhood, specifically in his categorical dismissal of the biological factor of racial descent. For Brandes the very idea of a *folkeslag* (nation) is determined entirely by the factors of language and of culture; there is plainly no role whatsoever for any conception of blood descent. The key texts here are his essays "The Aryan Race" (1905) and "Race Theories" (1912), both of which strike the contemporary reader as rather astoundingly prescient in their anticipation of our contemporary, post-Mendelian understandings of race. In the 1912 essay, for example, he notes that "every person now living has billions upon billions of ancestors," and that "every modern people, like every one of antiquity, is the result of a nearly immeasurable intermixing of tribes." In the 1905 essay, a review of Jean Finot's seminal *Le préjugé des races*, Brandes accordingly lists no less than fifty distinct ethnicities that have contributed to the composition of the modern Frenchman, whose essential "purity" was still very much at the time celebrated by the followers of Arthur de Gobineau.

Brandes's categorical dismissal of the factor of race in the determination of national identity is of further importance in that it reveals that there is ample room in his larger thinking for cultural pluralism. That Brandes's articulation of pluralism is upon close examination rather less than fully developed can most certainly be attributed to the historical circumstances of his age. Throughout these writings, he consistently distinguishes between two separate kinds of minority populations. On the one hand there are what might be termed "national minorities greater," that is to say all those subject peoples numerically large enough to stake a legitimate claim to self-determination; such claims are made all the stronger if the given people is possessed of a history of self-rule. The signal example here is of course the Poles, who in many ways could make a stronger case for independence than the more numerous Ruthenians, since the historical existence of the old Polish-Lithuanian Commonwealth was almost within living memory. On the other hand are what might be referred to as "national minorities lesser," that is, all those numerically smaller peoples whose struggle is conducted within the confines of the majority-dominated nation-state; another way of understanding the very idea of cultural pluralism, indeed, is that it is a solution to the problems generated by the coexistence of two or more peoples who, for all practical purposes, are stuck with another. The historical conditions of the Belle Epoque, and indeed onward until decolonization, understandably demanded that the cause of greater national minorities be prioritized. It was, after all, the collapse of the old continental empires after the first war and the evaporation of overseas colonialism after the second that first brought the fate of lesser national minorities into greater focus. As evident in the Ruthenian case, Brandes was well aware that the universalization of a right to collective self-determination would hardly resolve all the world's internecine conflicts. Partitioned Poland is again the instructive case here, for even before they had won back their freedom, it was plainly evident that the presence of even more oppressed national minorities within their immediate orbit was an entirely separate matter; when the Polish state was reconstituted after the conclusion of World War I, its sovereignty was made conditional upon international guarantees of the rights of Polish Jews.[59] And when the grand process of decolonization began its sweep across the globe after World War II, the fate of many similarly situated national minorities within the new nation-states suddenly became a pressing concern; indeed, a large number of the postcolonial states were not possessed of a uniform language and culture.[60] And just as important, it must also always be recalled that Europe's colonial powers cynically played the national minority card in their efforts to resist decolonization; particularly egregious in this practice were the Belgians, who had themselves, as colonial masters of the Congo and Ruanda-Urundi, largely created the ethnic divisions that would erupt soon after independence.

Brandes's nascent pluralist sensibility is most clearly attested in his writings on Sønderjylland. Until German defeat in World War I, prospects for the return of North Schleswig to Denmark were dim to say the least, and thus Brandes's early writings on the matter amount to a kind of defense of cultural pluralism. His 1904 address "To the Students of Germany," for example, constitutes an appeal to the younger generation to reject the belligerent nationalism of their elders; invoking Germany's own earlier struggle for national unity, in which "Germanness and humanity were nearly synonymous words," Brandes holds out hope that in the future "a powerful German national sentiment can well be reconciled with goodwill toward the small peoples and a lively aversion to their brutal and barbaric oppressors." Brandes is also effective when addressing a matter of immense personal significance for him, namely that so many of the national heroes of Europe, whether in culture, politics, or in military exploits, have in fact been of foreign descent. Much of the essay titled "Race Theories" consists of a long inventory of representative examples: Michel de Montaigne was the son of a Portuguese Jewess, Léon Gambetta and Napoleon Bonaparte were of Italian descent, yet each in himself remains to this day virtually synonymous with Frenchness.

The Brandesian dismissal of the role of blood descent in the construction of national identity, finally, serves to throw further light on his conflicted relationship to his Jewish identity as well as, more generally, the project of Zionism. The formal occasion of the 1912 essay "Race Theories," in fact, was the appearance of an essay by Danish author Jakob Knudsen titled "Georg Brandes og den danske Dannelse" ("Georg Brandes and Danish Culture"). In the most "respectful" terms possible, Knudsen asserts that "intellectually speaking we are conquered, by no means by an enemy, but still by a foreign power, a foreign race. And of this Georg Brandes is nearly the sole cause." Relative to the kinds of antisemitic discourses circulating in Europe at the time, Knudsen's exercise in Jew-baiting is comparatively mild; he even concludes his essay by expressing hope that the two men might remain friendly. Yet Jew-baiting it certainly is, and what is most surprising in Brandes's response is its degree of restraint; in measured and methodical argumentation, he dismisses in detail the general European view, all too prevalent since Richard Wagner's notorious 1850 "Das Judenthum in der Musik," of the damaging effects of the "Gypsy spirit" of the Jews on the proper development of the cultures of the noble Aryan race. His subsequent inventory of essential Jewish contributions to

European high culture is equally compelling, and serves as a rare olive branch to his many critics *within* the European Jewish community.

When Brandes is attacked by representatives of European Jewry, however, the tone and the very nature of his responses change dramatically. At the heart of his conflict with his Jewish critics is an irresolvable disagreement with Hebraic theology and tradition: Brandes simply does not believe that the Jewish people constitute a "race." In effect, Brandes's strikingly modern understanding of racial descent, at least from the qualitatively distinct perspective of the early Zionist movement, is purchased entirely at the expense of the cause of world Jewry. This first comes to a head in 1905, when Danish Jewish physician Louis Frænkel, founder of the Danish Zionist Forbund, published an open letter calling Brandes out because he had allegedly left "the cause of the Jews in the lurch." While Brandes devotes much of his response, the 1905 essay "Zionism," to recounting the considerable advocacy work he had in fact already done on behalf of European Jewry, his real point of contention is with Frænkel's assertion of the "tribal purity" of world Jewry. Here Brandes resorts to the now almost entirely debunked "Khazar Hypothesis" of Jewish origins, which he had largely absorbed from Ernest Renan, in his effort to oppose the idea of Jewish racial purity. As for the Zionist project in general, Brandes's general lack of interest is motivated by several considerations, yet the most decisive factor by far is his categorical objection to the racial component of its ideology.[61] The idea that largely "imaginary" ties of blood and tribe ought to entitle world Jewry to a homeland of its own is plainly too far outside Brandes's understanding of nationhood.

If the essay "Zionism" gives us a glimpse of Brandes's harder edges, then the 1908 screed "The Jews in Finland" shows us Brandes with gloves off. The circumstances of Brandes's May 1908 visit to Helsingfors were exceedingly complex, but for present purposes it is important only to note that the visit was a commemoration of Brandes's previous efforts to mobilize European universities in opposition to extremely harsh Russification measures directed against the Imperial Alexander University in Helsingfors; Brandes was in Finland to be honored as a friend and hero of the Finnish people.[62] During his stay in the capital, he was approached by representatives of the small Finnish Jewish community, who beseeched him to speak out against the onerous Jewish regulations that had been instituted by the Finnish Senate in 1889. The meeting did not go well, as evidenced in Brandes's deeply embittered, even spiteful account, which is here quoted at length.

> It occurred to me that the visiting card with which the deputation approached me was not written in either the Swedish or the Finnish language, but had this

> German text: *Deputation des Central—Comitée für die Befreiungsbewegung der Juden in Finland.* Therefore my first utterance to the deputation . . . was this: "This visiting card is in German. What language do you gentlemen speak with one another?" The answer was: Yiddish. It did not seem as if this spokesperson, aside from this dialect, understood any language other than German. Really it should be said that the first thing one who seeks civil rights in a country ought to do is learn the language of that country, especially if one was born there. It is perhaps too much to ask that the Jews of Finland should feel themselves to be Finns after the treatment they have received. But if they themselves do not consider themselves to be Finnish, then they cannot demand that the authorities in the country should view them that way. They must begin with speaking one of the country's two languages internally among themselves. Otherwise they are and remain foreigners, even they who themselves are in fact native born.

There is so much that is wrong in this, so much that is plainly anti-Brandesian. In his memorable 1905 letter "To the Schoolchildren of Russian Poland," Brandes had boldly asserted that the right "to speak and read one's language" constitutes "the most undeniable of human rights," yet here Yiddish is offhandedly dismissed as mere "dialect." For the first five years of the new century, in fact, Brandes had served as the primary Western European voice in defense of the striking schoolchildren of German and Russian Poland, who had endured years of beatings and isolation for their refusal to consent to the efforts to remove the Polish language from school instruction, yet here Brandes suggests that the Finnish Jews ought to give up their language even in their own homes. The anger and the frustration that is everywhere evident in the 1908 essay, and it should be noted that the article is far and away the angriest and most frustrated in this book, can only really be explained by the fact that the Finnish Jews, as well as the negative press coverage of the meeting that followed in the European Jewish press, have clearly touched a nerve in Brandes. And thus Brandes unloads on his native land.

> If in a deeper sense there is anything I am *not*, then it is this. Denmark and Finland are saturated with Judaism, their God is Jewish, their festivals are Jewish, their religion is a reworked, further developed Judaism with a few mystical additions. . . . Half of Denmark's culture comes from Palestine; half of its literature is inspired from there. Even the names, the authentic Danish names, Petersen, Hansen, Jensen, etcetera, are Jewish names, biblical names. . . . There was a time when I was almost the only person in the country who was not a Jew. And nevertheless practically the only thing people in this country know about me, and the only thing they regularly communicate to foreigners, is that this is what I am.

Beyond the matter of so-called Jewish "racial purity," Brandes further contends that the biological fact of his Jewish birth in no manner or form entitles the Jewish community to stake a claim on him; Brandes in essence reserves the right to establish his identity in sources distinct from Jewishness. This is of course an ancient conflict within Judaism, dating all the way back to the days of Moses and of Ezra, and living on in the current tensions between diasporan and settler. It is of course dangerous to speculate how he might have felt about the eventual founding of the state of Israel, as he was fortunate enough to have lived out his long life before the coming of the Shoah. Perhaps he would have supported it in the end, perhaps not, but it is probably safe to assume that he would have been uncomfortable with the racial component of Israeli nationhood.

The Centrality of Literary Culture

> What the eye is to the lover . . . language . . . is to the patriot.
>
> —Benedict Anderson

If Brandes's conception of national identity is in general rooted in language and culture, then it is particularly so in specifically *literary* culture. Even in the decades since *Imagined Communities* taught us the importance of print culture in the development of national identity, the overwhelming focus on the literary achievements of the many oppressed peoples discussed in this book must surely appear, at least at certain points, rather overblown. As previously indicated, Brandes had in 1905 asserted that the right "to speak and read one's language" must be counted as the very first of human rights. In one of the more lyrical moments in this volume, he lauds the Polish students for understanding that the new language policy was far more than mere bureaucratic meddling; it was in fact the beginning of "the reorganization of all conditions from the ground up." And yet at the risk of unfairly downplaying the courage of the Polish schoolchildren, it must be observed that this was written *after* the bloody suppression of the Lodz Insurrection in June, in which thousands of striking Polish workers had been shot by Russian forces. Likewise with Brandes's Armenian material; in the 1917 essay, published long after the second outbreak of mass killing in Eastern Anatolia, he is still at pains to remind us that "in our time the Armenians have upheld their old reputation as poets and artists."

Much of Brandes's pronounced literary bias may of course be attributed to the fact that he was through and through a man of letters and, in particular, a man of specifically "national" letters. As outlined in his seminal 1899 essay "On World Literature," he conceives of the global literary system as a grand panorama of individual national literatures, literary cultures that are of course, when properly mature, open to ideas and influences from the larger world, yet in their essence bearing "the scent of the Earth."[63] Because of the marginality of his native language, he is painfully aware of the fundamentally unfair conditions of this system, "of how an author of the sixth rank in a widespread language, a world language, can with ease become more known than an author of the second rank in a language spoken by only a few million."[64] The 1899 essay, in its essence, functions as kind of critique of the imperialist nature of the world literary system, in which French, English, and German writers drown out the voices of the periphery; in some sense, then, Brandes's activity as tribune of the political rights of oppressed peoples can be seen as an extension of his larger struggle on behalf of small and marginalized languages in the domain of literature; what offends him most, accordingly, is the efforts of the great powers to suppress the languages of their respective subject peoples.

We must, however, be wary of excessively judging Brandes here, as there is in fact a legitimate practical and strategic component to his literary bias. As Allen has recently demonstrated, Brandes was firm in his belief that while "culture may not be able to prevent military conquest, it is a powerful force for resisting foreign domination."[65] As has been noted, Moyn has persuasively argued that the central event of human rights history is the "imaginative transformation" from political to moral struggle as reflected in Havel's conception of the "power of the powerless." What separates Brandes from Havel, and from contemporary human rights doctrine at large, is his insistence that it is in the domain of *culture* rather than morality that subject peoples can best resist their oppressors; Brandes's seeming move from "politics to culture" is thus properly understood as anticipating the similar and yet distinct move of the famous Czech dissident.[66] Thus his appeals to Europe on behalf of the Armenians, as Allen further notes, were rooted less in sympathy or morality than in culture, "both admiration for the cultural wealth created by Armenians over the past four thousand years and fear of the destructive effect of tacit complicity on European culture."[67] The ultimate efficacy of Brandes's efforts to employ the cultural sophistication of oppressed peoples in their defense is certainly subject to debate, for one need only recall Victor Hugo's notorious "Address to the Germans," in which he had appealed to the invading Prussian forces to spare Paris by virtue of the city's status as the capital of world culture and civilization. Yet if we look at this from the perspective of the imperial powers, it is abundantly evident that the issue of minority languages was in fact no laughing matter. Why else would German authorities attempt to criminalize the languages of their Danish and Polish subjects? And why would the Russians expend so much effort to do the same to their own Polish population, their Ruthenians, their Finns? Even today, Finnish and Estonian efforts to preserve the many Finno-Ugric languages still spoken in the Russian Federation are vigorously resisted by Russian authorities.

One aspect of Brandes's literary bias that is deserving of criticism is the uncertain status it renders to the manifold indigenous subjects of European colonialism across the globe, many of which during the Belle Epoque were of course largely preliterate. It would be entirely unwarranted to surmise from this that Brandes's larger thinking is in some way tainted by the presence of an inherent conception of civilizational hierarchy; nothing in these essays and speeches supports such a contention. And furthermore, the near complete absence of indigenous peoples in this book can in part be attributed to the fact that Brandes simply lacks the tools to defend them. As previously discussed, Brandes is at his most effective when he makes the case that the erasure of a given oppressed people from the global community would constitute an immeasurable loss to world culture; for all those nations yet to register much of an impact on the global cultural canon, his peculiar form of "cultural defense" can hardly be as effective. It is therefore unsurprising that the two non-European peoples with whom he engaged extensively, the Persians and the Chinese, were each possessed of literary traditions far older than those of Northern Europe. Of no less significance is the fact that the efforts of European Orientalists over the centuries had further induced educated Europeans to acknowledge the immense civilizational accomplishments of Persia and China, even if, as is well known, these accomplishments were in the eyes of the Orientalist located in the distant past and not the present. Because Europe at least on some level admired Persian and Chinese culture, Brandes is able to employ the ancient provenance of their cultural traditions as a weapon against European predation. In addition, both peoples were themselves in the early stages of the kind of modernizing project Brandes had a generation earlier called for in his own country. In Persia, as Brandes documents in this volume, this process was largely political; what enrages him most is that British and Russian maneuvering in the "Great Game" was designed to thwart the efforts of progressive Persian elites to establish a modern, representative republic. In this example the naked truth of imperialism is laid bare for all the world to witness, for British and Russian authorities alike, at every step of the way, opposed the attempts of the Persian constitutionalists to fulfill by their own efforts the so-called "civilizing" mission of colonialism.[68] With respect to China, matters are more complex, in that no one may argue that the Boxer rebels represented a similar modernizing impulse; indeed, they were largely fighting for a return to feudal tradition. Yet this by no means prevents Brandes from speaking out vigorously in their defense; given the hysterical outbreak of "Yellow Peril" terror aroused in Europe by the Boxers, it is a profound testament to the universalism of Brandes's conception of the rights of peoples that he is able to say, in effect, that the real barbarians in this conflict are found within the ranks of the Eight-Nation Alliance. And as the new century unfolded, it must also be remembered, a general spirit of modernization would begin to take hold in late imperial and early republican China, and within the domain of literature Brandes and Brandesianism would loom large.[69] Yet despite these efforts to reach beyond Europe, the relative absence of indigenous peoples within the pages of this book remains troubling.

The Universality of Brandes's Conception of the Rights of Peoples

> Vague promises were made concerning human rights and the development of peoples toward self-government and social uplift, but promises only without implementation.
>
> —W. E. B. Du Bois

Human rights historians, theorists, and activists are in all agreement that any conception of specifically "human" rights must be universalist in its essence; this is what make human rights "human" rather than the "rights of man," which are conditioned by membership in a nation-state.[70] As noted, expansive accounts of human rights history generally locate the first stirrings of universalism in Greco-Roman thought, particularly in Stoicism; as Ishay notes, it was the Greek Stoics who first asserted that "reason and the capacity for good judgement," the necessary precondition for individual rights, were "not limited to free citizens but were possessed by everyone . . . including those living beyond the Greek city-states."[71] Yet if this idea has roots in antiquity, its general diffusion in the larger world is a relatively late phenomenon; even in the age of Brandes, no less a quintessential "rights state" than the French Third Republic was perfectly comfortable denying any real form of rights to its millions of colonial subjects. A measure of just how conscious of their hypocrisy the French were is found in the fact that they cynically dangled the prospect of rights to their colonials in exchange for loyal service in World War I; as Brandes himself would remind them after the conclusion of the peace, no change was forthcoming in the status of the hundreds of thousands who had answered the call.

With respect to universalism, Brandes's record is not entirely clean, yet taken against the backdrop of the era, his critique of imperialism is extraordinary in its consistency. As noted, the scope of his engagement with the oppressed peoples of the globe is characterized by steady outward expansion, from the national Sønderjylland Question through the small nations of Europe toward the planetary anticolonial perspective of his final years. Given this gradual evolution, it is not surprising that Brandes seems to observe a further distinction between two separate categories of oppressed peoples. On the one hand are the national minorities of Eurasia, that is, all those subject peoples of Europe's continental empires, the Danes of North Schleswig, the Poles, the Ruthenians, the Armenians, the Georgians, and so on, while on the other are grouped the far more numerous subjects of European overseas colonialism, that is, all those peoples subsumed today under the categories of postcoloniality or the Global South; in some ways Brandes can be said to have roughly anticipated the Cold War distinction of Second and Third Worlds. This distinction is also, importantly, the result of sound understanding, for Brandes is well aware that these two distinct groups of peoples are possessed of very different historical trajectories, and moreover that the manner in which the German dominated the Polish peasant was by all means qualitatively distinct from his treatment of, say, a Herero tribesman. Brandes does, perhaps, open himself to some measure of criticism in that he seems to prioritize the cause of the subject nations of continental rather than overseas empire. This is already evident in "Thoughts at the Turn of the Century," in which he acknowledges the greater misery inflicted by the imperial powers on all those whom "they conquer by fire and by sword and in all manner of horrors"; the specific reference here is to the many victims of European aggressive expansion during the period of neocolonialism. Yet Brandes makes plain that his primary concern, at least at this early stage, is instead with all those "small nations within their immediate orbit," that is, the national minorities of Eurasia. This is further reflected in his 1903 commentary on far-off Transvaal, in which Brandes asserts that "no worse horrors are found elsewhere" in the world, yet his particular inventory of these horrors is limited to the Boers and includes not a single mention of the far greater suffering of the native population of South Africa.

As discussed below, Brandes's monumental 1922 Christiania (since 1925, Oslo) address on imperialism largely redeems him from any charges of a continental bias in his rights advocacy. A much more problematic area, however, is his uneven treatment of his native land's continued colonial presence in the larger world. By the time of his activity as political journalist, much of the old Danish empire was a distant memory. The kingdom's slave trading outposts on the West African coast as well as its foothold on the Indian subcontinent, Tranquebar (now Tharangambadi), had been sold off in the mid-nineteenth century.[72] The Danes had also been masters of a slaveholding colony, the Danish West Indies; while the slave trade was abolished by the crown in 1803 and the remaining slaves emancipated in 1848, the territories remained under Danish rule until their sale to the United States in 1917, which renamed them the US Virgin Islands.[73] Of greater significance in Brandes's era were the kingdom's

North Atlantic possessions, considerable in geographical expanse if not population, including Iceland (independent after 1944), the Faroe Islands, and Greenland (both still in political union with the kingdom). With respect to Greenland, only a single mention of the fate of the Inuit is found in these pages; in the 1905 essay "The Rights and Duties of the Weaker," Brandes concedes that the Danes "have ruled poor Greenland in a way of which we must be ashamed," but only in passing, as a prelude to the larger point that "we have of course not even understood how to rule ourselves." If Brandes disappoints us in neglecting the Greenlanders, his commentary on the burgeoning movement for Icelandic independence is outright shameful. Since his initial engagement with Icelanders in the 1880s, Brandes had been widely admired there; indeed, in 1888 and 1889, the young Icelandic poets Hannes Hafstein and Gestur Pálsson had delivered a series of lectures in Reykjavik calling for a kind of Icelandic Modern Breakthrough on the Brandesian model, and Brandes for decades had regularly chastened his countrymen for their neglect of material conditions on the islands as well as their general lack of interest in the emerging new literary culture. Yet when an Icelandic delegation, led by none other than Hannes Hafstein himself, traveled to Copenhagen in 1906 to propose constitutional reforms, Brandes unexpectedly, indeed unforgivably, sided with the oppressors. And as his biographer Knudsen notes, Brandes would never again return to Iceland in his writings, whether literary or political.[74] Given his carefully constructed image as the very scourge of all great power imperialism, one would expect Brandes to apply the same form of ruthless critique to his own people that he so vigorously directs at the Germans, the Russians, and the British; however, in this single instance he fails entirely.

Before proceeding to the 1922 address on imperialism, it is first necessary to examine Brandes's aforementioned activity as principled opponent of World War I; the war itself was, after all, immensely disruptive to the old world order he had so vigorously critiqued at the tail end of the Belle Epoque. After an initial burst activity, from the summer of 1900 through 1905, Brandes's advocacy work began to taper off, only resuming in earnest during the war.[75] Almost immediately at the outbreak of armed conflict, he embarked on a second process of self-reinvention, quickly establishing himself among the world's foremost anti-war activists. From August 1914 through the conclusion of the war, Brandes would issue forth a torrent of critiques of the origins, the justifications, and the conduct of the great powers in the world war; indeed, Brandes's attacks would continue well after the cessation of hostilities in November 1918, as he was among the earliest and most vehement critics of the Versailles treaty. While his condemnation of the war is universal in its reach, his critique as always is focused on the fate of the neutrals, all those small nations of Europe and beyond, such as Belgium, Poland, and Persia, whose traditional homelands now found themselves the principal battleground of great power conflict.[76] The issue of small nation neutrality is, indeed, central to the larger case that Brandes directs against the war. His essay on Belgium, for instance, is a rather devastating critique of the Anglo-French claim to be prosecuting the war on behalf of "Brave Little Belgium," while his commentary on Persia reveals how great power alliances, in this case the Anglo-Russian Entente of 1907, are often purchased at the expense of the independence of small nations; indeed, in a 1915 essay, he would declare this to be a general principle: "when two modern great powers conclude a properly bilateral and sincere union, whether it be called an alliance or an understanding, the true aim is always to deprive a smaller state of its independence." One of the few relatively salutary consequences of the Great War, paradoxically enough, was that its conclusion effectively resolved many of the national minority issues within the old zone of continental empire, if only for a brief moment before the outbreak of the next conflict. The very idea of empire, at least on the European continent, had endured a profound beating during the war, which had of course claimed no less than four of the old imperial houses among its victims. The Danes of North Schleswig were happily returned to Denmark, the Poles were at long last free again, and the Armenians, while hardly free themselves, were at the very least safe from further Turkish aggression in the newly founded Armenian SSR.

Yet after the war Brandes was by no means prepared to declare even a tactical victory over imperialism, for beyond the issue of the long-term security of the new states in Eastern Europe there remained the larger matter of the persistence of European overseas empire. If Brandes's early record on the colonized peoples of the contemporary Global South is uneven, then his sweeping 1922 address in Christiania on imperialism goes a long way in redeeming him; the fact that the speech was delivered in the Norwegian rather than the Danish capital, indeed, might indicate a tacit acknowledgment of his native country's continuing imperial entanglements. Brandes opens "Imperialism" by revisiting an earlier trip to Norway, in February 1914, in which he had asserted that the world war certain to come would demand, in a distant echo of Nietzsche, that "the old ideals must be replaced with new ones." Yet four years of mechanized bloodletting, the death of some eighteen million soldiers and civilians, had hardly seemed to register an impact in the national consciousness of the victorious powers: "the old ideal, imperialism as the expression of nationalism, is at the moment dominant in all the countries whose attitude means something for the population of the world, the unfortunate mass of humanity." His ensuing survey of the remaining unfortunates is here truly planetary in its scope, and even more importantly, the peculiar form of "cultural defense" he had pioneered in his earlier work on the Persians and the Chinese is entirely absent; thus the inherent equality of all the world's colonized peoples is at least tacitly affirmed.

Because France had been "the most eager power to fight German imperialism," it is here especially singled out as the object of contempt. His commentary on conditions in French North Africa differs in kind from his earlier material, in many ways anticipating the rhetoric of the global anticolonial movement that would soon sweep across the world.

> The natives have no citizenship rights, are subjected to the violence and the arbitrariness of the administration, are worse off than the population was in the czar's Russia. The natives have no representatives in the French parliament. In Tunis the conditions are such that if there is a legal dispute between an Arab and a Frenchman, the case regardless of the law is not referred to a French court but instead decided administratively to the detriment of the Arab.
>
> The Tunisians are forbidden from exporting grain; the government has ordained that all the fruits of the soil shall be sold by the military quartermaster at prices that are fixed by the administration . . .
>
> After nearly a century Algeria is still treated like a conquered country, must to this day pay war indemnities to the victors, has no legal safeguards, no justice, no freedom, yet by contrast has responsibilities enough, among them military service.

Even at the age of eighty, clearly, Brandes is capable of revising his views on the fate of oppressed peoples around the globe, for here his critique is rooted in solidly political and material claims rather than the earlier appeals to cultural sophistication.

If the address on imperialism largely redeems Brandes from accusations that his conception of the rights of peoples is somehow less than planetary in its scope, then it must also be noted that his critique of empire is just as much possessed of a localized, specifically European component. At one important point in the speech, he refers to the imperial impulse as a kind of "poison," in a certain sense referring back to his foundational "Thoughts at the Turn of the Century." In that essay Brandes had asserted that the advent of neocolonialism had served to paper over the far more pressing issues *internal* to European civilization, that "the inner tensions within the great powers had been slackened by tensions external" to the continent.[77] In effect, preoccupation with territorial expansion abroad had blinded the great powers to the far more dangerous threats festering on the home front. The imperial impulse, as well as the belligerent nationalism and racism that powered it, was poisonous to national character in that it inculcated in the oppressor a false sense of superiority and self-regard; Brandes here in some ways anticipated Martin Luther King Jr., who a generation later would say much the same regarding segregation. Imperialism thus functioned much like an anesthetic, blinding the oppressor to all the social and political ills within his immediate surroundings. As such, the impulse to dominate the weaker abroad functioned as the precise inverse of a means of acquiring national greatness, which for Brandes consisted in the willingness to engage in the practice of radical self-critique.

Brandesian Rights Advocacy in Praxis

> Send us to prison and we will live there as in a paradise. Ask us to mount the scaffold and we will do so laughing.
>
> —Mahatma Gandhi

Just as the theoretical frame underpinning Brandes's rights activism sheds light on the history of human rights, so do the practical strategies he employs in defense of oppressed peoples. Brandes does little to push beyond the circumscribing frame of the nation-state in his understanding of the rights of peoples; in this respect he is much more a man of the rights of man than of human rights. Yet in the domain of praxis, his peculiar form of rights activism is in its very essence transnational in character; his many years of advocacy are just as much motivated by a desire to push his fellow Scandinavians toward greater engagement with the world outside Norden than by genuine concern for foreign peoples.

It is therefore abundantly evident in these pages that Brandes at least in this respect is far ahead of the game in anticipating what Moyn describes as the "central event in human rights history," that of "the recasting of rights as entitlements that might contradict the sovereign nation-state from above and outside."[78] It should be conceded that Brandes expresses little faith in the possibilities of what would seem the logical outcome of this thinking, namely the establishment of transnational courts of appeal to which the oppressed might turn for redress. No such institutions, we must remember, were in existence until after the conclusion of the Great War. International guarantees of the rights of national minorities had existed in the nineteenth century, even concerning some of the very same peoples Brandes worked to defend; the 1878 Treaty of Berlin, better remembered for clearing the path for the denial of the rights of untold numbers of African peoples, had for example stipulated an international regime for the monitoring of the conditions of two of Eurasia's most embattled minorities, the Jews of the young Romanian state and the Armenians of the Ottoman Empire. Yet Brandes's 1903 essay "The Agony of a

People and Utopias," prompted by a US diplomatic note urging the Romanian government to uphold the conditions of the treaty, is wholly dismissive of the possibility of the great powers living up to their own treaty obligations; Secretary John Milton Hay's celebrated communique, Brandes contends, was motivated just as much by the US desire "to rid itself of an immigration of helpless, penniless people, to close off for them their last place of refuge" than by any real concern for Romanian Jews. Brandes is even more dismissive of the famous article 61 of the treaty, which had placed the Ottoman Armenians under the "protection" of the great powers, in his 1900 essay "Armenia," written just a few years after the Hamidian massacres: "those who made the promises did not for a moment think of keeping to them; those who received the promises did not for a moment think of upholding them by force of arms." And when the largely toothless League of Nations was established after the war, Brandes was rightfully skeptical of the intentions of the great power diplomats who founded it; commenting on the February 1919 proposal of the League, Brandes belittles it is as nothing more than a reconstitution of the early nineteenth-century Holy Alliance.[79]

Given the absence of legitimate transnational courts of appeal, Brandes had to resort to the only international forum available, that of the European court of public opinion, reachable only through the medium of the European press, despite all its limitations and deficiencies. Throughout these pages Brandes regularly expresses doubts about whether his journalism is in fact producing a meaningful impact on the larger world.[80] His 1903 Berlin address to the Armenian Student Union ("Armenia and Europe"), an effort to mobilize German public opinion against the government's close relations with Turkey, opens with the concession that Brandes is "not inclined to overestimate a simple author's spoken words and know[s] well enough that in questions of grand politics the decision lies with those in power." Brandes's appeal of the following year ("Finland"), for a pan-Scandinavian and ultimately pan-European show of solidarity with the embattled Finnish university in Helsingfors, in sharp contrast, is much more hopeful, and indeed contains all the elements of the kind of coordinated pressure campaign pioneered by the Dreyfusards.

> The student youth of the three Nordic countries, together with their university teachers, ought to express their sympathy with students and teachers at the university in Helsingfors and register their protest against the violence and abuse that is inflicted on them. We dare hope that the movement then spreads further, so that other countries' universities . . . attach themselves to the protest, and that it therefore rolls over the Earth, steadily more polyphonic. . . . It is our purpose to bring the Russian government to perceive itself isolated.

This is the very essence of Brandes as a strategist; he acts to mobilize public opinion in Europe's "civilized countries" against the predations of great power governments in an effort to encourage more just and humane treatment of the oppressed peoples within the imperial orbit. As a practical methodology it must be conceded that its record of success was not impressive. The moral judgment of the enlightened element of the German public had hardly managed to affect state policy, as the German presence in the Ottoman Empire only intensified in the years leading up to the second wave of mass killing. While Brandes might have claimed at least a tactical victory in the cause of the Finnish university, the general easing of Russification in Finland was of course just as much the result of the general chaos engulfing the entirety of the Russian Empire in 1905; when the czarist regime had recovered, they were back at it as before. Yet despite its many demonstrable failures, it remains undeniable that in its essentially transnational character, Brandesian rights advocacy in praxis comes tantalizing close to approximating the later activism of the era of universal human rights proper.

If with respect to human rights history it is precisely in this that Brandes demonstrates his greatest strength, then it is also, paradoxically enough, in the specific nature of his transnationalism that his most significant weakness as a thinker and activist reveals itself. As noted, one of the results of his late 1880s encounter with Nietzsche was in fact the cultivation of a robust mistrust of "the mob" and of mass politics.[81] With respect to his advocacy work, this is most evident in Brandes's understanding of the concept of "public opinion," which in many ways is out of step with contemporary values. As is often evident in this book, the peculiarly Brandesian appeal is targeted less at the masses of Europe than at its elites, the "leading men" (and occasionally, women) who constitute a country's cultural and intellectual aristocracy. The 1904 appeal for Finland thus concludes with the injunction that "Russia's leading men" must be made to feel "that they are set apart from European civilization by Europe's intellectual aristocracy." Because the czarist regime had exiled "Finland's best men," Europe must expel Russia's from its cultural circles. Because Brandes is so deeply skeptical of the promises made by great power governments, and at the same time, as an "aristocratic radical," remains just as ambivalent toward the masses, he places all his faith in his fellow freethinking and progressive elites. That the essential elitism of Brandesian rights advocacy is indicative of his limits as a thinker and strategist was in fact already recognized by the Marxist Brandes scholarship of the 1970s; as Thomas Nordby then observed, Brandes plainly overestimates the capacities of what he once, with apparent seriousness, referred to as the "Intellectual Aristocratic Internationale."[82] Brandes's insistence, says Nordby, that "social conditions can be changed from the outside by reforming consciousness," falls flat in its failure to recognize "the significance of social conditions in the formation of consciousness."[83] And from subsequent developments in postwar Denmark, it is clear that this was very much understood in his own time. The new generation of intellectuals and artists who looked to the aging critic for inspiration, figures like the architect Poul Henningsen, the collective novelist Hans Kirk, and the poet Otto Gelsted, the so-called "cultural radicals," would ground their work on a solidly materialist foundation; as Henningsen would note in 1933, it was his discovery of "the existence of the working class" that made him as artist and thinker.[84]

If Brandes's praxis in political journalism is flawed by his aristocratic proclivities, then his reflections on how oppressed peoples might *themselves* engage in emancipatory struggle strikes us as much more praiseworthy. With no transnational authority to which they might appeal, subject peoples could of course resort to armed resistance against their masters, as they often did in the nineteenth century and well into the twentieth. While Brandes does not oppose violence on principle, and indeed is eager to praise the valor and the heroism of armed insurrectionists, as in his commentary on the Armenian uprising of the early 1890s and the Polish revolts of 1905, he is, as Julie Allen has noted, generally opposed to the idea of violent revolution.[85] The mass murder of 300,000 Armenians in Turkey, the violent reprisals against civilians in China, Macedonia, South Africa, and Russian Poland all seem to have convinced him that armed struggle against imperial domination, in the end, only made matters worse. One of the most terrible ironies of the twentieth century, after all, is that in the end freedom for the world's oppressed nations was purchased largely at the expense of the lives of millions of citizens and soldiers of the great powers; they simply exhausted themselves in the contest for global supremacy, providing the conditions necessary for the unraveling of empire.

All that really remained for the oppressed peoples of the globe, in Brandes's thinking, was nonviolent civil resistance within the existing strictures of the imperial states, supported, of course, by regular expressions of solidarity and sympathy from abroad. In this Brandes is largely attuned to his age, which was very much witnessing the genesis of the form of nonviolent, active resistance to oppression that would soon come to make its mark on the new century. If Brandes is possessed of a kind of theory of civil struggle, it is surely found in the aforementioned 1905 essay "The Rights and Duties of the Weaker." Like the earlier address "To the Students of Germany," this article is concerned only with the national matter of Sønderjylland, yet Brandes also places it within the section on "Oppressed Peoples" in his *Samlede Skrifter*, indicating that he himself was aware of its larger significance. He opens by sadly conceding that his appeal "To the Students of Germany" of the previous year had come to nothing, producing only a single, profoundly dismissive response. The present age, Brandes can only conclude, "is steadily in a more marked attunement with the right of the stronger," for it "views the various peoples as it does the single individual, whose desires are self-assertion with evermore increased power." How might a people resist such belligerent nationalism? Brandes's proposal is revealing.

> What can we set in opposition to this right of the stronger? First and foremost what I will call the right of the weaker, which at the very least is still acknowledged in Europe: the right to be judged and to be treated not according to one's external weakness, but according to one's internal strength, one's value for universal civilization, the example one provides, the cultural heights one has achieved.
>
> Assuredly it is of no real use to insist on a right to consideration or to mercy; however, neither will it do to stop publicly asserting one's right to respect. Publicly there must be discussion of something else, namely that of the responsibility of the weaker.
>
> If we have the right to assert and develop ourselves, then it is still to a greater degree our duty. If we have the right not to lose sight of Danishness in southern Jutland, then it is to a still higher degree our duty to do so. The smaller the country and the weaker the people, the higher the degree to which they must protect their language and their territory. Indifference in such cases is degeneration.

All the emphasis here, importantly, is on the *duties* of the subject people; in this Brandes's thinking is commensurate with the now largely forgotten liberal tradition of duties, represented principally by Giuseppe Mazzini, architect of the Italian Risorgimento, as well as, more importantly, Mahatma Gandhi.[86] In spite of the considerable perils of likening arguably the holiest man of the twentieth century to one of its most vehement atheists, Gandhi is in a certain manner the appropriate reference point here, for Brandes seems to echo certain aspects of the great Indian activist's thinking about the nature of nonviolent, active resistance to oppression. For Gandhi and Brandes alike, the subject people must always take care to reveal the best in itself to the subjugator, must always act to maintain its absolute moral and ethical supremacy. Thus Brandes, again like Gandhi, always speaks to his own people (the Danes and even more so, European Jewry) in a manner qualitatively distinct from addressing the oppressor. By no means does Brandes seek to indulge the subject people's vanity, instead enjoining his countrymen to exceed their masters "in the fear of self-satisfaction, in the openness of our gaze to our weaknesses and our national errors, in that self-critique that is the spur to all self-development." The formal occasion for the 1905 essay, accordingly, was the recent passing of a corporal punishment law by the Danish Folketing (parliament), which had resulted in a flood of anti-Danish press coverage in Germany; Brandes is ruthless in his condemnation of his fellow Danes, even suggesting that "if we act unworthily, then Germany's attitude toward Danishness becomes not only justified but deserved." These are stern words, indeed, and it must be recalled that Brandes is generally more forgiving in his addresses to all those subject nations who could make no claim to his own identity as a Danish Jew, although he is still fully capable of employing the same kind of tough love toward those foreign oppressed peoples whose cause he made his own; see here in particular the 1908 essay "The Jews in Finland," and the 1914 article "Conditions in Russian Poland."

The uniquely Brandesian conception of the rights of peoples, it seems, departs from contemporary human rights thinking in that it is rooted less in some sort of abstract conception of the inherent value of all the world's nations than in the willingness of oppressed peoples to seize what *ought* to be theirs. For Brandes, freedom and human rights, upon close examination, are something to be *earned*, through the practice of relentless radical self-critique and through the continuous demonstration of one's "value for universal civilization." The odds are long, defeats are sure to far outnumber victories, yet freedom for all the world's oppressed peoples is in the end there for the taking.

Notes

1. The six volumes of Brandes's monumental comparative study of French, German, and British Romanticism, *Hovedstrømninger i det 19de. Aarhundredes Litteratur* (*Main Currents in Nineteenth-Century Literature*), based on lectures delivered at the University of Copenhagen, were published between 1872 and 1890. Considered by many to be the foundational document of comparative literature, *Main Currents* was translated into each of the major European languages (an English edition was issued in 1906) as well as Russian, Polish, Yiddish, Spanish, Japanese, and Chinese (some 300,000 Chinese copies circulated). Commenting on Brandes's death in 1927, Thomas Mann famously referred to it as "the bible for young intellectuals thirty years ago." Despite its decidedly internationalist frame, *Main Currents* was also very much possessed of a national component. In the famous inaugural lecture of November 3, 1871, the formal start of the twenty-year series that would become *Main Currents*, Brandes had attacked his native literary culture as persisting in a state fully "forty years behind Europe." As a remedy to the alleged "spiritual deafness" of the Nordic countries, Brandes proposed a literature "that provokes debate"; by addressing social issues in what would come to be called *problemlitteratur*, authors could effectively play catch-up with the mature literary traditions of France, Germany, and Britain. Within a few short years Brandes's call would be answered by numerous young Scandinavian writers, among them Henrik Ibsen and August Strindberg, and by the mid-1880s Scandinavia had established itself as a literary power rivaling the traditional metropoles. The full text of the November 1871 lecture has recently appeared in a new translation by Lynn Wilkinson,

"The 1872 Introduction to *Hovedstrømninger i det 19de. Aarhundredes Litteratur* (*Main Currents in Nineteenth Century Literature*)," *PMLA* 132, no. 3 (May 2017): 696–705. For an excellent summary of Brandes as literary historian and critic, see Svend Erik Larsen, "The Telescope of Comparative Literature," in *The Routledge Companion to World Literature*, ed. Theo d'Haen, David Damrosch, and Djelal Kadir (London: Routledge, 2011), 21–31.

2. Brandes's German-language Kierkegaard monograph inaugurated the long vogue of the Danish philosopher. His 1888 Copenhagen lectures on Nietzsche, quickly disseminated in Berlin through the Danish colony there, were published to much acclaim in the Danish journal *Tilskueren* as "Aristokratisk radicalisme" ("Aristocratic Radicalism"), *Tilskueren* 6 (August 1889): 565–613, and "Det store menneske: Kulturens kilde" ("The Great Man: The Source of Culture"), *Tilskueren* 7 (January 1890): 1–25. Ever since Nietzsche readers have been made aware of Brandes through a single reference in his autobiography: "Ten years: and no one in Germany has felt duty-bound to defend my name against the absurd silence under which it lies buried: it was a foreigner, a Dane, who first had enough fineness of instinct *and* fortitude to do this. . . . At which German university today would lectures on my philosophy be possible such as were held last spring in Copenhagen by Dr. Georg Brandes, thereby proving himself once more a philosopher." Friedrich Nietzsche, *Ecce Homo*, trans. Thomas Wayne (New York: Algora, 2004), 89.

3. James MacFarlane, perhaps the last great historian of literary modernism to have fully understood the essential Nordic role in its early phase, notes that it was Brandes who transformed "the epithet of 'modern'" into "a rallying slogan of quite irresistible drawing power" across the Germanic world. If two generations prior Charles Baudelaire had introduced to France the idea that literature *ought* to be modern, it is Brandes who did so in the German-speaking sphere. See James MacFarlane, "The Name and Nature of Modernism," in *Modernism, 1890–1930*, ed. Malcolm Bradbury and James MacFarlane (New York: Penguin, 1991), 37.

4. Within the young discipline of new world literature studies, English translations of the long-neglected 1899 essay "World Literature" have been featured in both the *Princeton Sourcebook in Comparative Literature* (2009) and the *Routledge World Literature: A Reader* (2011). The aforementioned Larsen essay in the *Routledge Companion to World Literature* and the Wilkinson translation in *PMLA* have further increased Brandes's profile in contemporary literary studies. Julie K. Allen's groundbreaking *Icons of Danish Modernity: Georg Brandes and Asta Nielsen* (Seattle: University of Washington Press) appeared in 2012.

5. The DC, founded in 2016, may be found at www.georgbrandes.dk (last accessed April 29, 2019).

6. Allen, *Icons*, 122.

7. In their introduction to the recent *Nordic Journal of Human Rights* special issue on Nordic human rights history, Hanne Hagtvedt Vik, Steven L. B. Jensen, Linde Lindkvist, and Johan Strang charge that "with a few notable exceptions . . . empirical studies have strongly focused on the Anglophone world, and particularly on the United States" and further acknowledge that "the process of challenging US-centred accounts of human rights history has only just begun." "Histories of Human Rights in the Nordic Countries," *Nordic Journal of Human Rights* 36, no. 3 (October 2018): 191.

8. Thus the founders of the Nordic Human Rights History Network call for empirically based "studies that are written on the basis of wide-ranging work with primary sources," in order to chart the complex and largely unexplored nature of Nordic engagement with human rights since 1948. Ibid., 194.

9. The mission statement of the Nordic Human Rights History Network specifically limits its historical frame to the period "since the international human rights system emerged in the 1940s." Hanne Hagtvedt Vik, Linde Lindkvist, and Johan Strang, "Nordic Human Rights History Network," University of Oslo, last modified November 29, 2017, https://www.hf.uio.no/iakh/english/research/networks/nordic-human-rights-history-network/index.html.

10. Vik et al., "Histories of Human Rights," 190.

11. This refusal so incensed his old friend and ally, Georges Clemenceau, that the French premier would devote a rather disturbing amount of 1915 to a heated press feud with Brandes over the issue of Danish neutrality. The following year, after the publication of Brandes's widely circulated appeal for a general armistice, the process was repeated in Britain, where another close associate, the Scottish translator and scholar William Archer, would take the lead in denouncing the Danish critic. Brandes's wartime writings were published in Danish in two volumes, *Verdenskrigen* (Copenhagen: Gyldendal, 1916) and *Tragediens Anden Del. Fredsslutningen* (Copenhagen: Gyldendal, 1919). The former, which includes Brandes's rebuttals to Clemenceau, was translated by American peace activist Catherine Groth and published in 1916 in New York. Archer's anti-Brandes pamphlet *Colour-Blind Neutrality: An Open Letter to Doctor George Brandes*, had appeared in Britain earlier that year; Groth's volume also includes Brandes's response to it.

12. For Brandes's views on the League, see, in particular, "Den Hellige Alliance" ("The Holy Alliance"), *Tilskueren* 36 (March 1919): 207–25.

13. For her excellent commentary on self-determination struggles in the early twentieth century, see Micheline Ishay, *The History of Human Rights: From Ancient Times to the Globalization Era* (Berkeley: University of California Press, 2008), 181–99. Ishay's work in general is laudable in that she is the most inclusive and comprehensive of the expansivists. Her initial chapter, titled "Early Ethical Contributions," in particular, is truly planetary in its reach, its geography encompassing the Near East, and South and East Asia.

14. Samuel Moyn, *The Last Utopia: Human Rights in History* (Cambridge, MA: Harvard University Press, 2010), 26.

15. For Moyn's commentary on liberal nationalism, see *The Last Utopia*, 29–31, and for his examination of anticolonialism, the chapter "Why Anticolonialism Wasn't a Human Rights Movement," 84–119.

16. Moyn, *The Last Utopia*, 171.

17. Ibid., 213.

18. Samuel Moyn, "Beyond Liberal Internationalism," *Dissent* 64, no. 1 (Winter 2017): 118.

19. Norway, Iceland, and Finland are of course much younger countries. Norway was a part of the Danish kingdom until 1814, when it was ceded to Sweden, with which it remained in union until 1905. Iceland was also formally a Danish possession until independence in 1944. Finland was part of the Swedish kingdom until 1809, after which it was under Russian rule until the October Revolution of 1917. While the last of Sweden's overseas territories was sold to France in 1878, the Danish empire, importantly, persisted into the age of Brandes; indeed, the Faroe Islands and Greenland remain to this day in union with the kingdom. That Denmark was still a colonial power during the period in which Brandes developed his general critique of European imperialism does to a certain degree undermine his otherwise sterling anticolonial credentials; this will be addressed later in the introduction.

20. Germanization efforts toward the Danish minority of North Schleswig function as a direct link between Brandes and the Poles, who were suffering under the same policies in Prussian Poland.

21. *Samlede Skrifter*, 12:191. Julie Allen has long argued that among Brandes's central, lifelong tasks was the effort to resist the virtual erasure, both materially as well as even more so spiritually, of his native land. See in particular her "Kampen mod Le Danemark s'efface," in *Georg Brandes og Europa*, ed. Olaf Harsløf (Copenhagen: Museum Tuscalanum, 2004), 319–27.

22. Georg Brandes, *Samlede Skrifter* (Copenhagen: Gyldendal, 1899–1910), 15:443. I am partially indebted to Julie Allen's previous translation in *Icons*, 101. The italics are mine, rather than Allen's. For more on the Spanish Mano Negra scandal, see the essay of the same name in the present volume.

23. It should be noted here that progress-minded Danes, given the rise of far-right xenophobic parties after 2001 as well as the punitive anti-immigration and anti-refugee policies adopted since that signal year, no longer really see themselves as exemplars of progressive and humane values. During his 2016 US presidential campaign, significantly, Senator Bernie Sanders regularly held up Denmark's domestic policy as a model from which the United States had much to learn, yet he failed to address troublesome developments in foreign policy and the treatment of immigrants.

24. For a superb treatment of Havel, see Moyn, *The Last Utopia*, 161–66. The full English text of Havel's essay "The Power of the Powerless" is available in *The Power of the Powerless: Citizens against the State in Central-Eastern Europe*, ed. John Keane, trans. Steven Lukes (London: Routledge, 2009), 10–59.

25. Christine Ingebritsen, *Scandinavia in World Politics* (Lanham, MD: Rowman and Littlefield, 2006), 8.

26. Swedish social democratic premier Per Albin Hansson (1885–1946) presented the outlines of the Swedish national welfare society, the *folkhem* (people's home), in a January 1928 address.

27. Ivar B. Neumann and Benjamin de Carvalho, "Introduction: Small States and Status," in *Small State Status Seeking*, ed. Benjamin de Carvalho and Ivar B. Neumann (London: Routledge: 2015), 10.

28. See, in particular, Christine Ingebritsen, "Norm Entrepreneurs: Scandinavia's Role in World Politics," in *Small States in International Relations*, ed. Christine Ingebritsen, Ivar Neumann, Sieglinde Gstöhl, and Jessica Beyer (Seattle: University of Washington Press, 2006), 273–91.

29. For a detailed and, importantly, a critical study of this idea, see Nina Witoszek, *The Origins of the "Regime of Goodness": Remapping the Cultural History of Norway* (Oslo: Universitetsforlaget, 2011).

30. Carl Bildt's "Statement of Government Policy in the Parliamentary Debate on Foreign Affairs" of February 13, 2013, proclaims that "Sweden is a humanitarian superpower" and further reasserts that "human rights, democracy and the rule of law are fundamental principles for our actions, as is respect for international law."

31. Indeed, it is even possible in the contemporary Anglophone world to secure for oneself a well-remunerated sinecure simply by consistently throwing shade on the Nordics; of the many commentators who engage in this, the *National Review*'s Andrew Stuttaford deserves special mention for his maniacal obsessiveness. A recent example is the flood of condemnation that followed in the wake of Sweden's decision to impose immigration controls at

the height of the aforementioned Syrian refugee crisis. A 2017 essay by the Gatestone Institute's Judith Bergman is even titled "Sweden, a Failed State?," Gatestone Institute, July 21, 2017, https://www.gatestoneinstitute.org/10605/sweden-failed-state.

32. Ingebritsen, *Scandinavia in World Politics*, 107. The comment, incidentally, originally appeared in an August 4, 2002, *New York Times* editorial by no less a neoliberal luminary than Thomas Friedman.

33. Browning cites as key factors distinguishing "internationalist solidarism" from the foreign policy frameworks of other Western states during the Cold War as on the one hand the effort to "stand between the East-West conflict," and the other hand to "play a role in overcoming the North-South divide by trying to speak on behalf of the world's poorest and most excluded." Central to the latter aspect is "an emphasis on the right of all nations to be free to develop without external (i.e. great power or colonial) interference," as was most significantly reflected in Swedish opposition to the US war in Vietnam. Christopher Browning, "Branding Nordicity: Models, Identity and the Decline of Exceptionalism," *Cooperation and Conflict* 42, no. 1 (March 2007): 27–51.

34. Vik et al., "Histories of Human Rights," 193.

35. Norwegian statesman Trygve Lie served as secretary general from 1946 to 1952; in 1953 he was succeeded by Swedish diplomat Dag Hammarskjöld, who served until his death in 1961. To this day, the Scandinavians remain the most active member states of the United Nations, relative to national population. According to Paul Novosad's and Eric Werker's 2017 analysis, within the UN secretariat, Finland, Sweden, and Norway are the most overrepresented nationalities; Denmark is sixth, behind New Zealand and Ireland. Paul Novosad and Eric Werker, "Who Runs the International System? Nationality and Leadership in the United Nations Secretariat," Dartmouth College, October 2017, http://www.dartmouth.edu/~novosad/novosad-werker-un.pdf.

36. The Carnegie-funded project resulted in Myrdal's *An American Dilemma: The Negro Problem and Modern Democracy* (1944), which would go on to play a prominent role in the lead-up to the *Brown v. Board of Education* ruling ten years later.

37. As Moyn notes, the 1975 CSCE summit, which resulted in the Helsinki Final Act, was a signal event in the human rights explosion of the 1970s. See Moyn, *The Last Utopia*, 149–50.

38. As stipulated by the Versailles Treaty, plebiscites were held in 1920 to determine the postwar border between Germany and Denmark; North Schleswig was returned to Denmark, while German-majority Central Schleswig remained part of Germany. Brandes's pivotal contributions to the debates over the fate of ethnic Danes under German rule include "Danskheden i Sønderjylland" ("Danishness in Southern Jutland," 1899), "Sønderjyllands Betydning for dansk Kultur" ("The Significance of Southern Jutland for Danish Culture," 1901), and "Tale paa Møn" ("Address on Møn," 1904). In anticipation of the coming plebiscite, Brandes republished much of his material on the issue in book form, *Sønderjylland under Prøjsisk Tryk* (*Southern Jutland under Prussian Pressure*) (Copenhagen: Gyldendal, 1919).

39. Allen notes that Brandes first made this statement in the foreword to the second German edition of *Main Currents*, published in 1897. Allen, *Icons*, 63. Brandes biographer Knudsen cites the new foreword to the sixth Danish edition in the fifth volume of his biography, *Georg Brandes*, vol. 5, *Uovervindelig taber: 1914–27* (Copenhagen: Gyldendal, 2004), 2:424.

40. See, for example, Jens Bjerring Hansen, "Romantik, Modernität und Copyright. Georg Brandes auf dem deutschen Buchmarkt," in *Die skandinavische Moderne und Europa:*

Transmission—Exil—Soziologie, edited by Bjerring Hansen (Vienna: Praesens Verlag, 2016), 121–42.

41. For a superb commentary on Brandes's revising process, see ibid.

42. Brandes, "Aristokratisk radikalisme," 575.

43. Ibid., 574.

44. Harsløf, "Fra kulturpolitik til politisk journalistik" ("From Cultural Politics to Political Journalism"), in *Den politiske Georg Brandes*, ed. Hans Hertel and Sven Møller Kristensen (Copenhagen: Hans Reitzel, 1973), 136.

45. See the 1905 essay "The Rights and Duties of the Weaker" in the present volume for the full context of this citation.

46. Brandes, *Samlede Skrifter*, 12:143. Brandes was among the very first to sound the warning bell of a coming world war, for example in his 1881 "Anelse om Verdenskrigen" ("Foreboding of World War"), available in Brandes, *The World at War*, trans. Catherine D. Groth (New York: Macmillan, 1917), 1–3.

47. Ibid., 144–45.

48. See "The Great Nations' Concern for the Small" in the present volume for a particularly powerful indictment of British complicity in this practice.

49. The full text of Brandes's commentary on his life's work is reproduced in Albert Shaw, "Georg Brandes Visits America," *American Review of Reviews* 50, no. 1 (July 1914): 98. The statement is also the starting point of Jules Moritzen's *Georg Brandes in Life and Letters* (Newark, NJ: D. S. Colyer, 1922).

50. Each of Brandes's final three works—*Sagnet om Jesus* (Copenhagen: Gyldendal, 1925), *Petrus* (1926), and *Urkristendom* (1927)—were critical studies of the historicity of Christ and Christianity; thus Arthur Drews concludes his monumental *Die Leugnung der Geschichtlichkeit Jesu in Vergangenheit und Gegenwart* (Karlsruhe: G. Braun, 1926) with a section on Brandes. Were Brandes better remembered in the larger world today, he would likely have been canonized by the representatives of the New Atheist Movement.

51. Brandes's very first intervention on behalf of the Poles was in fact a defense of the schoolchildren of Września, who had refused to follow a German order mandating that all religious instruction be in German. See "Contemporary Civilization" and "The Women of Poland" in the present volume.

52. The selection of texts for the present volume has observed this distinction; of Brandes's copious material on Danish affairs, only two essays are included, the 1904 address "To the Students of Germany" and its 1905 follow-up, "The Rights and Duties of the Weaker." The reason for this is that each sheds considerable light on his larger thinking about the rights of peoples.

53. The very first distinction drawn in the "Analytic of Aesthetic Judgement" is that between a "pure disinterested liking" and a "liking connected with interest." Immanuel Kant, *The Critique of Judgment*, trans. Werner S. Pluhar (Indianapolis, IN: Hackett, 1987), 46.

54. Albert Shaw, "Some Danish Fiction Writers of Today," *American Monthly Review of Reviews* 31 (January 1905): 107.

55. The essay "Jødiske og kristne Rumænere" ("Jewish and Christian Romanians"), along with two afterwords, appear in volume 11 of the *Samlede Skrifter*, 456–86. Because the article was not published in any contemporary journal, I have chosen not to include it in the present volume.

56. See "Conditions in Russian Poland" in the present volume.

57. Moyn, *The Last Utopia*, 26.

58. Brandes became involved with the Dreyfusards largely through his friendship with Georges Clemenceau, who along with the officer Marie Georges Picquart and the scientist Jules Henri Poincaré served as the de facto leaders of the movement.

59. For more on the Polish Minority Treaty of 1919, see Ishay, *The History of Human Rights*, 188–91.

60. Postcolonial giants Nigeria (some 250 distinct ethnic groups) and India (as many as two thousand!) are of course the best examples here.

61. Among the other reasons for Brandes's skepticism of Zionism, deeply personal considerations play a significant role, for Brandes appears to have had nothing but contempt for World Zionist Organization (WZO) cofounder Max Nordau, whose 1892 volume *Entartung* (*Degeneration*), that singular work of criticism that had introduced the "decadent critique" into European literary studies, had counted the radical Danish critic among its principal targets. Of even greater significance are practical considerations, for while Brandes acknowledges the talents of fellow WZO cofounder Theodor Herzl, he views Herzl's efforts to secure a Jewish homeland in Palestine under Ottoman suzerainty as not only misguided but also fundamentally dangerous. This would only place European Jewry in even far greater peril, given the actions of the "Red Sultan" against the Ottoman Armenian population only a decade before; as such, Brandes seems far more open to the possibility of a Jewish homeland in Africa, the now largely forgotten "Uganda Project," first floated in 1903. It is also worth noting that after the British became the new masters of the Levant after World War I, Brandes was much more open to the idea of a new Jewish state in the ancient homeland yet still maintained skepticism regarding its long-term viability; see "Den Hellige Alliance," 216–17.

62. For more on the bizarre circumstances of the 1908 visit, see the translator's commentary for "The Jews in Finland," and for Brandes's campaign on behalf of the soon to be renamed University of Helsinki, see "Finland" in the present volume.

63. "World Literature," trans. William Banks, in *World Literature: A Reader*, ed. Theo d'Haen, César Domínguez, and Mads Rosendahl Thomsen (London: Routledge, 2012), 27.

64. Ibid., 25.

65. Allen, *Icons*, 108.

66. Perhaps the "cultural" orientation of Brandes is not in the end so far from the "moral" grounding of Havel; both men, after all, were first and foremost men of letters.

67. Allen, *Icons*, 110.

68. The US government would do likewise in the early 1950s, with ultimately disastrous consequences for the Iranian people.

69. For more on Brandes's impact on modern Chinese literature, see Knudsen, *Uovervindelig taber*, 2:9–12.

70. Among the human rights historians, Ishay is especially strong here; in many ways, her expansive narrative account is structured by the dialectical relation between universalist and particularist rights doctrines.

71. Ishay, *The History of Human Rights*, 25.

72. It should be noted that general awareness of Denmark's colonial and slave trading history is minimal among ordinary Danes, who largely do not see themselves as a post-imperial nation in the manner of Britain or France; once again, the idea of national contraction is a far greater factor in national identity. It has in fact only been in recent decades, through the salutary efforts of organizations like the Danish Center for Colonial History

and Århus University's Reading Slavery project, that awareness of Denmark's imperial past has begun to register in national self-understanding. While national amnesia and excessive self-regard certainly play a role in this, it must also be noted that the presence of the overseas empire simply did not play as decisive a role in the construction of national identity as it did in the major imperial powers; while evidence of the empire is indeed everywhere in contemporary Danish culture, there is a reason that Denmark never produced a Joseph Conrad, a T. E. Lawrence, a Rudyard Kipling. If Denmark could be said to have produced an "author of empire," it is most certainly Isak Dinesen, who of course lived in an English colony and, even more importantly, wrote her works in English.

73. While no mention of the Danish West Indies is made in this volume, Brandes does briefly raise the issue in "Thoughts at the Turn of the Century," if in a discouragingly offhand manner: "We have ruled the poor West Indian islands in the mode of Frederik VI, developing them so poorly that they still cost us money and that we are ready to wash our hands of them." Brandes, *Samlede Skrifter*, 12:148.

74. For a comprehensive treatment of the events of 1906, see Knudsen, *Uovervindelig taber*, 2:372–77.

75. Brandes would produce only three articles during this interval, the brief 1909 commentary "The Fourth Partition of Poland," which amounted to little more than an addendum to his earlier work, and the deeply embittered essays "The Jews in Finland" and "Race Theories." These latter two pieces, furthermore, differ sharply in character from his work during the early period of activity; rather than proactive efforts to marshal public opinion against great power predation, these essays are in their essence reactive, as Brandes attempts to fend off criticism from both abroad (European Jewry) and at home (Jakob Knudsen). It is only the eruption of the world war that Brandes had seen coming for nearly a half century that motivates him to return to politics in a manner even more forthright and provocative than his earlier work.

76. In order to maintain thematic coherence in this volume, I have selected only those wartime writings that address directly the fate of the small nations consumed by the war. Of the nine articles taken from the volume *Verdenskrigen*, seven originally appeared in English in Catherine Groth's *The World at War*; I present here new, annotated translations of these texts; the last two wartime essays in this book, "Persia" and "The Armenians," appear in English translation for the first time.

77. Brandes, *Samlede Skrifter*, 12:143.

78. Moyn, *The Last Utopia*, 13.

79. For Brandes's views on the League, see, in particular, "Den Hellige Alliance," 207–25.

80. In addition to the many other hats he wore during his long life in letters, Brandes was also an astute media critic. His now almost entirely forgotten 1911 volume *Armand Carrel* (Copenhagen: Gyldendal) is far more than a portrait of the great pioneer of French journalism; it is also a masterful critique of the origins of the modern European media system.

81. Corey Robin has demonstrated that the signal event in the life of Nietzsche was his horror at the Paris Commune; it was the Communards, in fact, who taught the philosopher to hate the mob. See *The Reactionary Mind: Conservatism from Edmund Burke to Donald Trump*, 2nd ed. (Oxford: Oxford University Press, 2018), 135–40.

82. Thomas Nordby, "Georg Brandes og imperialismen," in *Den politiske Georg Brandes*, ed. Hans Hertel and Sven Møller Kristensen (Copenhagen: Reitzel, 1972), 153.

83. Ibid.

84. Poul Henningsen, *Kulturkritik*, ed. Carl Bay and Olav Harsløf (Copenhagen: Rhodos, 1973), 2:22.

85. Allen, *Icons*, 102.

86. For more on the liberal tradition of duties, see Moyn's superb "Reclaiming the History of Duties," in *Human Rights and the Uses of History*, 2nd ed. (New York: Verso, 2017), 151–68. The attentive reader of this volume, furthermore, will surely notice the absence of the very site in which anticolonial thought and activism was most highly developed during the age of Brandes, namely the British Raj. Brandes's lack of engagement with India might in part be explained by the fact that he spent relatively little time in Britain during his European travels; Berlin and Paris played a much larger role in both his travels and his thinking. Yet still the absence of Gandhi is puzzling, given the centrality of the great Indian leader within the work of Brandes's friend and ally Romain Rolland; Catherine Groth, English translator of Brandes's *Verdenskrigen*, would herself translate Rolland's monograph on Gandhi in 1924. Perhaps at least some of Brandes's lack of interest in Gandhi may be explained by his rationalist aversion to all things "mystical" in nature; while Brandes has nothing but admiration for the role of the Catholic Church in the Polish struggle, he seems to have been turned off by the early twentieth-century European vogue for all things Indian. In the 1922 address on imperialism, for example, he chastises European youth for "celebrating well-spoken and vacuous prophets, breathing most freely in the highest stratums of metaphysics and theosophy, worshiping the hardly profound wisdom of Tagore." That neither Rabindranath Tagore nor Mahatma Gandhi were in any way vacuous is beside the point; Brandes is simply reflecting the way in which they were initially received in Europe.

CHAPTER I

The Hun Speech

1900

Kaiser Wilhelm II delivered his notorious "Hunnenrede" in Bremerhaven on July 27, 1900, on the occasion of the embarkation of the German troops for the punitive expedition against what came to be called the Boxer Rebellion (1899–1901). Brandes's response, published the next day in Copenhagen, is likely the very first critical treatment of this infamous address that is still taught in German schools and still remains a point of reference in contemporary geopolitics. After repeated failed attempts to suppress the Boxers and their Imperial Army allies with local forces, the major world powers (Austria-Hungary, the British Empire, France, Germany, Italy, Japan, Russia, the United States) formed the Eight-Nation Alliance, sending military forces to China to restore order and moreover, to punish the perpetrators of the uprising. The kaiser's address is notable for its paradoxical celebration of the German people as both the proper defenders of Christian civilization and, at the same time, the inheritors of a warlike barbarism all their own; this national self-image would figure prominently in German propaganda during the ensuing world wars.

~

Today all the German newspapers are leading with the kaiser's speech of yesterday, delivered in Bremerhaven to the volunteers about to embark for the China campaign. Of all his many addresses, this one can be counted as among the most characteristic of his manner of being and of thinking. While it may seem a bit immature for a man his age, it is however personal in the highest degree.

The speech is marked by the extraordinary indignation it directs against China, and further is conspicuous in that it makes not the slightest distinction between the Chinese government and people. Broadly speaking, China constitutes for the kaiser *the yellow peril*. This recalls the well-known painting he himself inspired some years ago. In it the European powers stand assembled

---

Originally published in *Politiken*, July 28, 1900. Translated from the version republished in *Samlede Skrifter*, vol. 17.

beneath the sign of the cross with swords drawn for a war of defense. The aggressor in this war is characterized by a peaceful Buddha squatting with legs crossed amid the clouds, yet according to the painting the image should be understood as extremely threatening to the "holy blessings" of Christianity. This was before the European great powers had swarmed like birds of prey over China and ripped her to shreds. There was reason to wonder at the painting, given that China in its many thousands of years of existence has never waged a war against them, but on the contrary has been willing to be at peace with and have as little to do with them as possible. In the meantime the war that Europeans waged against China forty years ago actually had nothing of the character of a war of defense, but was carried out, in spite of the stubborn resistance of the Chinese government, in order to enforce the right of France and England to inject as much opium as was possible into the bodies of the wretched Chinese who had developed a taste for that poison. According to universal opinion the Opium War had no religious or moral purpose whatsoever.

The fanaticism and the barbarism by which the Chinese now seek to expel the foreigners, and especially their murder of the German envoy, hardly fully explain the chain of reasoning in the kaiser's speech.[1]

After reminding the troops that the Chinese had dared to subvert the entirety of international law and had mocked the sanctity of diplomatic hospitality, the kaiser proceeds: "Therefore you can see where a culture not built upon a Christian foundation ends up. Every heathen culture, no matter how beautiful and good it may be, perishes when it is faced with great problems."

It is only with great difficulty that Chinese culture could have been built upon Christianity, given that it is itself so much older than Christianity. Nonetheless the kaiser here presents an entirely novel philosophy of history. No one has ever maintained that heathen cultures like the Greek and the Roman revealed themselves to be incapable of solving great problems; it was held that each in its own manner had resolved extraordinary problems in the areas of statecraft, art, thought, science, and the administration of justice. Now an entirely new understanding is suggested, according to which these cultures succumbed as soon as they were tested.

1. Baron Clemens August Freiherr von Ketteler was the German plenipotentiary in Beijing during the early stages of the Boxer Rebellion. His death on the order of the Imperial Army officer En Hai on June 20, 1900, was the pretext for German involvement in the war. While in the German press he was portrayed as the innocent victim of savagery, this was decidedly not the case. For more on Ketteler, see David J. Silbey, *The Boxer Rebellion and the Great Game* (New York: Hill and Wang, 2012), 79–80.

Immediately after asserting that every non-Christian culture inevitably falls apart, the kaiser next offers up this to the troops: "You shall encounter a well-armed force; but you shall also take revenge. . . . If you come before the enemy he will be killed; *quarter will not be given; there will be no prisoners taken; he who falls into your hands is in your hands*." These words succeed in altering earlier conceptions of Christianity, just as the previous statement changes understandings of history.

Previously it has not been maintained that a Christian culture ought to completely eradicate an enemy which, according to an evidently outmoded doctrine, ought instead to be loved. It was seen as inhumane (even more as unchristian) to maintain beforehand that no quarter be given, that no prisoners be taken, et cetera. The imperial pronouncement opens up perspectives into a wholly new, previously unknown version of Christianity. It is fortunate that the elder Kaiser Wilhelm did not preach this new Christian approach before the campaign in France. It would have presented immense practical difficulties to cut the throats of the more than 120,000 Frenchman at Sedan and the 180,000 at Metz who surrendered. Fortunately the Germans in China are few and the Chinese many.

The kaiser continues: "Just as a thousand years ago the Huns under their king Attila made for themselves a name that still traditionally stands for might, *so* shall you make the German name known in China." Once again this reveals a new horizon. No one before the kaiser has compared the bearers of Christian culture to Attila and his Huns. Even in Hungary itself they are remarkable only for having vanished without a trace, and our Magyars of today disavow any kinship with them. Now they again come to glory in war-crazed Germany.

One recalls that when Napoleon was before Vienna he threatened to descend upon the city if they did not submit, just as Attila in his time descended upon Aquileia (which very likely led to Venice's surrender); but it must be remembered that the threat was not seriously meant, and that Napoleon was at that time far from acting as a standard-bearer for Christian culture. At that point he still saw himself only as the revolution in human form.

The kaiser concludes: "Display your courage wherever you come, and God's blessing will raise your banners and grant that *by your hand Christianity will arrive in that land*." These last words suggest that troops who cut down everyone and everything and who never burden themselves with prisoners are not only demonstrating the values and the power of their Christian culture, but also blazing a trail for it in the enemy land, carrying it with them and spreading it there. Here is the missionary enterprise understood as it was by Charlemagne and by Saint Olav. It had been thought that this kind of thing had been given up in our time, or at least that it would never be declared officially. The new century that promises so much will apparently reveal that the old methods of the rulers of a thousand or twelve hundred years ago, used for the glory of God and the benefit of man, are still in full employ.

The kaiser's speech sparkles with novelty and, like columns of light in the desert, testifies as to where we stand at the moment and to where we are heading.

This is characteristic of contemporary Germany; for the Germans have gradually been transformed into a warlike folk, while the French, who always speak of the dagger, have just about become the world's most peace-loving people, thunderously applauding their generals at their endless military parades. When the nationalists in Paris were made aware that the fatherland was in danger and that the Chinese rebellion demanded vengeance, 120 men rallied to the flag. And the officers, for their part, demanded and received increased pay in addition to the already increased wages provided by the colonial war. In Germany 120,000 men have answered the same call for the China campaign, and the officers without the incentive of pay increases compete against each other for the privilege of going along, the only exceptions a few newly married reserve officers who express a small measure of complaint.

But anxiousness prevails among those who remain at home. It is certainly grand for a country to have a man with a temperament in the forefront, and yet . . . it is splendid to witness a man who cuts a fine figure in every uniform, on horse or at sea; yet for all that . . . it is a great pleasure to have one of the century's most verbose speakers as a ruler and yet at the same time a man who is just as great as a general, an admiral, a preacher, a composer, a painter, a hunter, and so on; nevertheless . . .

CHAPTER 2

Armenia

1900

This essay is the first, and by far the most loving, of the writings Brandes would produce on the fate of the Armenian people during the final quarter century of his long life. Only the Poles come close to the Armenians with respect to the amount of energy and passion Brandes lavished upon them; his sincere and thoroughgoing affection for each nation is indeed everywhere evident in the present volume. Still, an important distinction must be observed regarding Brandes's portrayal of the *tormentors* of these unfortunate peoples. In his many essays on partitioned Poland, Brandes is always careful to maintain a relatively evenhanded attitude toward the Germans, the Austrians, and the Russians; when he does go on the offensive, he is always mindful of distinguishing between the actions of the governments of the great continental empires and their respective peoples. As is already apparent in this early essay, this is not at all the case with the Ottoman Turks, for whom Brandes seems to have nourished a powerful, and often disturbing, distaste.

~

I

Armenia is the Switzerland of Asia Minor, a mountainous country like Europe's own peaceful redoubt, but in contrast an enslaved, abused, and martyred land of mass murder. It is the land of Mount Ararat the double-peaked, around which the mountain ranges of Asia Minor, Mesopotamia, and Persia meet.[1] It was atop Mount Ararat, as every child has learned, that Noah's Ark was stranded. The country has an abundance of seas, among which three are immensely large; but especially it is the land of countless springs. Pure and fresh they arise and flow from everywhere.

Originally published in *Politiken*, October 8, 1900. Translated from the version published in *Samlede Skrifter*, vol. 17.

1. It should be noted here that Mount Ararat, despite its significance to Armenian culture and identity, falls on the Turkish side of the present border. It remains a bitter point of contention between the two countries.

And everywhere there are streams and rivers; with every step one sees them; along all rocky sides they stream down. There are wide stretching meadows and rich grain fields, apple and pear trees, grapevines and pomegranates overflowing. And everywhere the nightingales sing, everywhere the pheasants and the peacocks sun themselves; at the edge of the wood stands a youthful gazelle, on the slope of a cliff the wild ibex; but also bears, wolves, hyenas, and jackals circle around the villages.

Here dwells a little people of a few million. Although they live under constant persecution and are frequently in conflict, they were not until the final decade of the last century threatened with eradication, and they managed to achieve a relatively high level of culture. They are one of the world's oldest peoples, possessed of a four-thousand-year-old culture, an Aryan and early Christian people, ruled by observant Muslims, who despise and hate them for the sake of their creed and for their superior civilization.

Eighty out of one hundred Armenians are peasants; but their merchants are widely known for their business acumen, and they have learned individuals, writers, just like Europe's most developed peoples.

At the Congress of Berlin in 1878 the Armenian Christians were, like the Romanian Jews, placed under the protection of the great powers in order that their sufferings might at last be remedied.[2] Naturally Romania and Turkey promised that there would be improvement. It was all a show. Those who made the promises did not for a moment think of keeping to them; those who received the promises did not for a moment think of upholding them by force of arms. The consequences were that the Romanian Jews have since then persisted in a kind of hell compared to which that of Dante is a cool and peaceful place, and that in the last seven years nearly 300,000 Armenians have been slaughtered under a regime of torture to which the Inquisition was previously thought to have had the exclusive right.[3]

Because of its enormity this figure says nothing to the ordinary philistine, writer, or journalist. It provides no lucid picture. Who can imagine several hundred thousand corpses? And who can imagine the horrors of the violated women breathing their last, or the pangs of hunger the chained prisoners in the prisons of Saint Jean d'Acre suffered before they died?[4]

---

2. Better known for setting the stage for the "Scramble for Africa," this notorious congress was in fact possessed of less cynical measures.

3. The figure of 300,000 represents the high end of estimated deaths during what has come to be known as the "Hamidian Massacres" of 1894–96.

4. One of the world's most infamous places of incarceration, Acre Prison was built over the ruins of an ancient Crusader fortress and used to detain enemies of the state throughout the period of Ottoman rule. During the British Mandate, it was largely employed as place of confinement for Jewish insurgents, a group of whom staged a dramatic escape in 1947.

A young Danish author has even seen his chance to be witty on this occasion, finding that the Armenians "could have found the time to have separated themselves from life in a more painless manner than in turning the work over to their executioners." Such humor in the youth of Denmark!

The thing is that in Denmark there is no interest in anything outside of Copenhagen and its suburbs. The Norwegians are interested only in Norway, in its independence and in the reputation the kingdom and its great men enjoy; in the Scandinavian countries it is previously only Dr. Hans Kaarsberg who has mustered any larger interest for the Armenians, but since he is of the opinion that one can help them through newspaper articles, his naïve faith is less surprising than the good humor of the others.

The nineteenth century will of course be regarded in the future as the great century of scientific discovery and invention; it will seem just as worthy of admiration in this respect as the time around 1500 was with respect to pictorial art. But in nearly everything that concerns politics it will stand as a purely barbaric age. This century can hardly be said to be a hair's breadth ahead of the darkest historical eras with respect to the deprivation of freedom, to extortion, to torture, and to mass murder. Nero's bloodlettings are flat out child's play in comparison to those of Abdul Hamid; Nero's cruelty is dilettantism compared to Abdul Hamid's virtuosity in martyring and murder.[5] It must also be recalled that the mass murders of Nero, although they went unpunished, were regarded by the Christians as the very Beast of Revelation, but in our age all of the Christian powers maintain the warmest relations with Abdul Hamid and no one has lifted a finger to oppose him. The Chimborazo heights of contemporary political-religious hypocrisy are further emphasized by the fact that this same Christian Europe, which without protest has witnessed 300,000 Christians tortured and slaughtered in European and Asiatic Turkey, is so sorely concerned for the fate of the miserable and laughable missionary enterprise in China.[6]

When the now-expiring nineteenth century turned itself on its axis in 1848, it was imagined that its second half would be occupied by addressing the thorniest, the most delicate, and the most up-to-date questions, the social, political, and philosophical questions regarding the lifting up of the individual and of all humanity. The old, simplistic, vulgar questions of the right of

5. The "Red Sultan" ruled from 1876 until his overthrow by the Young Turks in 1908. Brandes's hatred of this single figure is unmatched anywhere in the corpus of his writings on late nineteenth- and early twentieth-century atrocities.

6. Brandes here refers to the large-scale mobilization of the Eight-Nation Alliance against the Boxer rebels of China, which was justified with reference to the attacks on European missionaries carried out early in the uprising.

peoples to self-determination and self-rule, of the inviolability of the nations and the individual, of the freedom of the press and the market, of religious freedom and freedom of thought, of the right to free speech and assembly and so forth would be viewed as questions that had now been answered once and for all, and on which no one any longer ought to waste words.

And now more than a half century later there are in Russia 130 million people enslaved and deprived of rights, and as a consequence they constitute a grave danger to their very surroundings. They dare not read a book or a newspaper, much less produce one that has not already been deemed by the authorities to be of no danger to them. If only the other half of Europe would become utterly demoralized by the fact that more than 100 million of the continent's inhabitants suffer such a fate. All around the nationalities are still oppressed, all around the old conflicts of creed and tribe are taken up, conflicts that should have ended and about which it is impossible to say a new or intelligible word. Yet still the thoughts of the "best among us" awaken enthusiasm, bring forth heroes and traitors, occasion great deeds that would have been called for a century ago and that bring about misfortune and atrocity that should have passed with the Middle Ages. The lives and the thinking of the current generation are wasted on purely obsolete matters, on questions already settled. Every individual has only this one life, and half of it is taken up by the delay and still more delay of human progress.

Because for a long time I have been occupied with the fate of the Armenians, because I have known a few of their best men and women, because I have been witness to the suffering they have endured, the sacrifices they have made, the courage they have displayed, and the manner in which after years of struggle everything has ended in total defeat, it might seem remarkable or heartless that the single word that comes to mind is this: delay.

But since it is impossible that everything can be chaos, seeing that the achievements of science, the intellect, and industry continue to mount and to spread outward and to mutually reinforce each other, since in spite of everything, in spite of the oppression of peoples and of social classes and religious persecution and the tormenting of every independent or eminent individual, yes, in spite of the mass murder of hundreds of thousands among an unlucky people, there necessarily and unavoidably is to be found a kind of forward progress. Thus it is that this setback leaves the impression of a terrible waste of time, of the immense world-historical delay brought about by an unenlightened religious despot, whether from the Red Murderer in the South or the White Czar in the North or from kings upon little bitty thrones or from manikins on still smaller stools.

II

Doctor Hans Kaarsberg is a warm, bold, and frank freethinking man, and it is desirable that there be more like him.[7] Life in the Nordic countries would then be a little less flaccid. Those who see things less rosily can, however, not but conclude that he overestimates the significance of the press to a very high degree. He believes that something he calls the free, independent European power of the press is an actual force with which to be reckoned. It is hardly likely that he has encountered this force at journalist congresses. The sum total of newspapers in Europe that could be said to wield such a force is about the same as the sum total of maritime journals in Switzerland.

Dr. Kaarsberg cites the power wielded by the press in the Dreyfus Affair. But one can by no means compare the situation of the Armenians (or the Romanian Jews) with that of the prisoner on Devil's Island. There the question has to do with a single man accused of crime for which the most meager evidence had not been provided. Because the accused was from a family of means and of influence and because his brother was an intrepid soul who would shun no sacrifice, there soon came to light such an overwhelming number of lies, falsifications, acts of fraud and of conspiracy between the enemies of the accused, his accusers, and his judges, that a few brave men in France, among them a hero, Colonel Picquart, and three great writers, Zola, France, and Clemenceau, were able to make the case difficult for the powers that be by setting in motion the energy of all of Europe.[8] The thinking people of Europe were soon convinced of his innocence, the whole of the diplomatic world got the message, Esterhazy's letters remain preserved in the bunker of the War Ministry in Berlin, and while a few Danish and Russian papers demurred, the European press was by and large clear about the situation and spoke its mind. Four years later Dreyfus is nonetheless not a rehabilitated free man but instead has been twice convicted of treason and pardoned only for the sake of the shamefulness of it all. Zola has lost an immense number of his readers and is one of France's least popular personalities. Picquart has been sentenced to prison and kicked out of the army. To this day he has still not been reappointed

7. Hans Sophus Kaarsberg (1854–1929) was a Danish physician and author of popular travel books and novels. He traveled widely in both the Ottoman Empire and in Western Russia.

8. In spite of the evident bitterness here, Brandes had proved himself an enthusiastic Dreyfusard during the long struggle. Marie Georges Picquart (1854–1914), while serving as head of French army intelligence, exposed the framing of Captain Dreyfus. The novelists Émile Zola (1840–1902) and Anatole France (1844–1924) and the journalist/politician Georges Clemenceau (1841–1929) led the press campaign to exonerate the Captain.

to his post as lieutenant colonel, he who had been in line for France's commander in chief. There is not a single regiment in which officers will serve with him.

That is the power of the press when it takes up a good cause in one of Europe's most sophisticated countries.

If we would not revert to childhood then we ought to speak a little more cautiously about the power of the press. When it is concerned with something other than advertisements or scandals or slander it is extremely limited in its impact.

By publishing such trivialities a newspaper can sign up a thousand new subscribers for every ten an article on Armenia will bring in. Stories of the murders in Asiatic Turkey are not at all circulating around Europe, even when written by a well-known author. They interest neither the editors nor the readers. It is of no use to pretend we do not know what a servile mind is, or that such minds number in the millions.

It is however curious that the unlucky peoples, who in their agony grasp after every straw, attribute extraordinary meaning to every word written about them. Today this is evident among the Finns and the Poles, and there is hardly any European writer (presuming he is not known to be in the service of power) who has not been overwhelmed with requests to employ his pen in the cause of the Romanian Jews. When for my part I write a few words about the Armenians it is truthfully not because I imagine that these might have the most meager meaning or influence, but only to honor promises previously given.

I know an Armenian women who sailed from Piraeus to Egypt in 1895 in order to travel from there to Asia Minor.[9] She was borne up alone by faith in her ideal, for she could still hear the voices of her little children, of her little girl who had said at her departure "mother, don't forgot to bring a doll back!" and of her little boy who had said "and pictures, too, mother!" But she would go along the stone road to places filled with horrors, she would struggle with unconquerable difficulties, carry out plans that were so daring that they seemed crazy, inserting herself into dangers that hung literally over her head. And while she thought of the little ones whom she had left behind sick, she pained herself with the thought they were perhaps sicker now. Every kind of angst

9. Mariam "Maro" Nazarbekian (1864–1941, née Vardanian) was a Georgia-born Armenian activist and journalist. Together with her husband, Avetis Nazarbekian, she cofounded the Social Democratic Hunchakian Party (SDHP) while in exile in Geneva in 1887. The Hunchakians were instrumental in the 1890s reform movement within the Ottoman Empire and served as leaders of the uprisings that were ultimately put down in what came to be known as the Hamidian Massacres. Brandes met the Nazarbekians during an 1896 trip to London, shortly after Mariam's return from her journey to the motherland.

seized her; she saw her children's faces before her and her husband's despair at being left behind in Greece, necessarily idle because as a known revolutionary he would immediately be jailed for setting foot on Turkish soil.

She almost cannot understand how she was able to abandon her little ones with such enthusiasm, perhaps even forever, and that for the sake of people she had never seen, whom she neither knew nor who knew her. Never could these people begin to sense what sacrifices she had made for them. It could very well happen that she would be greeted with ingratitude. And still she continued her journey to be a part of creating a new life of freedom on earth, the promised land of the emancipated human being. She believed in this amid all her sorrow, knowing full well that the day in which her ideal neared its realization was to her a handful of dust. She sat by the expanse of the Nile and listened to the metallic clamor of the mosquito drone; and this noise, which blended itself with the manifold of the noises of sunset, was to her a barbaric hymn that rose up against heaven and the secret-filled stars. In the end it was as if she heard in all of this the distant sighs, despairing screams, heartbreaking sobs of a wholly unlucky and immiserated people who cried out over the earth for aid, beseeched the heavens for liberation, suffered and struggled for the cause of freedom. She heard in the twilight drone the call of these voices. And in this way it happened that she acted as if in a rapture, and yet as confidently as a sleepwalker. She reached Jean d'Acre, obtained by virtue of a wild pretext and an enormous bribe access to the dreaded prisons, managed to get a few prisoners set free, consoled others like the good angel she is, spoke the secret language of the Freemasons before the eyes of the guards. From there she went to Cilicia and energetically contributed to organizing the uprising there. Then the glorious uprising broke out in Zeitun in the fall of 1895, the uprising that for months managed to defeat Turkish troops and Kurdish gangs.[10] Armenian regiments there and in other Cilician areas took on her name. These daredevils and freedom dreamers gave her those honors rebels are able to provide. A typical European traveler who has enjoyed hospitality in her house is unfortunately unable to offer her more than his own humble words of praise.

Avetis Nazarbek, the author of a lively and by all accounts accurate description of life in Armenia, is a young man, a warrior and a poet unusually handsome with coal black hair and beard, who has long published the Armenian Revolutionary Party's journal *Huntchak* (*The Bell*).[11]

---

10. One of the rare Armenian victories, the Zeitun Rebellion of winter 1895 resulted in a negotiated peace settlement, according to which the Hunchakian leaders (Mariam Nazarbekian among them) were permitted to go into exile.

11. Avetis "Nazarbek" Nazarbekian (1866–1939) was a Georgia-born Armenian poet, journalist, and activist, the cofounder of the Social Democratic Hunchakian Party (see note 9).

His work *Through the Storm* is not a novel, although the names of those involved in it who were still alive when it appeared in 1899 have been changed. Were he to issue a new edition now he would presumably be able to use real names. A series of descriptions freely woven together provide a comprehensive portrait of life in Armenia before the outbreak of the rebellion, with only the main characters recurring. There can be no talk of real literary artistry here. Although he was living in London and was well at home in the English language, he could not be induced to write in English, instead writing it down in French that it would then be translated into English. Therefore it is only in the lively descriptions and in the natural flow of the conversations that he has been able to bring art to light. Yet the high points of his work are surely to be found in the personal characterizations, in the portrayal of the contrasts between the ruling and the oppressed races, and in particular, with respect to the latter group, the contrasts between the submissive and "loyalist" faction and those who find it impossible to endure any more. While his heart bleeds at the thought of the fate of his countrymen he does not spare them. All kinds of Armenians appear in his work: the unfeeling and cowardly financiers, the tycoons who included among them one so extreme that he gave up his own son as a rebel so as not to damage his reputation in high places; the deadbeat and insipid journalist from Constantinople who mixes French words into his speech and recommends submission to the sultan; the old peasant who, although forced to emigrate, derided his sons for being rebels during the misery of the journey, in that their actions could make everything doubly unfortunate; the young girl, Arusdak, who abandons her lover because she does not have the courage to cross her parents and instead marries a cowardly and harmless person. And like almost always in life it is the philistines, the moneylenders, the decrepit, the half-hearted journalist, and the characterless young girl who are proven right; their betters are ignominiously destroyed.

There are also many noble and determined men in the book, dockworkers and learned men, warriors and schoolteachers, who demonstrate their mettle as soldiers again and again. There are delightful, humorous sketches of the ignorant, brutal, and corrupt Turkish officials; there are dreadful portraits of the torturers who are employed by the Kurdish tax collectors or when the Turks at the police station interrogate Armenians. And yet Turks as well as Kurds are presented without hate, rather in the tone of superior compassion against their rawness and ignorance, and with an accusatory attitude only toward the government that has turned this semi-savagery loose on a highly gifted little people.

His 1899 *Through the Storm* occupies a central place in the canon of Armenian genocide literature.

There are battle scenes that Carit Etlar would delight in, as well as weighty, thoughtful dialogues that consider all the essential questions that such events and fates force the thinking person in our time to ask.[12]

But nothing of all the worthy and fine things the Armenians have written has been able to slow down the progressive wiping out of their people. Dr. Kaarsberg thinks that the figure of the murdered I have given is too low; I said 300,000, he believes it is as much as a million. That seems to me unreasonable, especially because Pierre Quillard, who still delivers bulletins on the murders each week, does not go far over the figure of 300,000.[13] But even when the figure is set at its lowest, and I for my part intentionally set it as low as possible so as not to be accused of exaggeration, even then this outpouring of blood cries out with such gravity to heaven, that only a Europe such as that of our time has been able to overlook it.

12. Carl Brosbøll (1816–1900), under the pseudonym Carit Etlar, was a Danish author of beloved adventure novels.

13. A prominent Symbolist poet, Pierre Quillard (1864–1912) was an active Dreyfusard as well as the foremost French advocate of the Armenian people.

CHAPTER 3

Missionaries

1901

Each June, until the outbreak of the Great War that would forever set them at odds, Brandes accompanied his close friend Georges Clemenceau (1841–1929)—politician, journalist, future wartime premier of France—to the famous spa at Carlsbad, now known as Karlovy Vary. In the summer of 1901 the resort was host to a rather exotic guest, the unfortunately unnamed "Oriental Prince" described at length in the following essay, perhaps the most intriguing of the present volume.

~

I

In order to learn something new at a popular European spa, one must encounter people who think and who know something. In this respect one cannot be more advantageously positioned than to be staying with a famous friend from France who is sought out by most of those who know his name.

For some time in Carlsbad we had noticed an Oriental fellow, very tall and thin with a thoughtful mien. He would show himself on the promenade dressed in a floor-length violet costume of very heavy silk, with a gold-embroidered scarf around his neck, a turban on his head, and over the silk a long, black caftan.[1] The other day he sought out my French associate. It was revealed that

Originally published in two parts in *Politiken*, August 12 and 15, 1901. Translated from the version published in *Samlede Skrifter*, vol. 17.

1. That Brandes does not identify the prince by name is, at least with respect to posterity, unfortunate, yet it is nonetheless understandable, given the nature of power relations at the peak of the Great Game—it is a testament to his character that Brandes understood the need to protect the identity of his source. According to the *Karlsbader Kurliste*, that remarkable record of every visitor dating back to the seventeenth century, there were four individuals of Eastern descent at the spa in June 1901. Three of these, Ottoman officials from Cairo, do not at all fit the physical description provided by Brandes. The fourth, one Sardar Singh (1880–1911), maharaja of Jodhpur, is likely the person described here. Thanks to Jan Nedvêd of the Karlovy Vary Museum for his meticulous research in the *Kurliste*.

he was an Asian prince, Muslim of religion.[2] He beseeched my friend to express publicly the thoughts that he was occupied with and that he desired to become known in Europe. To our surprise he expressed himself in fluent French, albeit with a strong foreign accent.

The object of his embitterment and his disgust was the European missionary presence in Asia and Africa. He pleaded for my friend to begin a press campaign against the missionaries, speaking as one who knew about this theme inside and out.

He began by asserting that as a rule the Europeans remain in profound ignorance of the attitude of the Muslims toward them.[3] With quite exaggerated self-regard the Europeans suspect that the Muslims secretly admire them. They suspect this not for the simple reason that they believe in one god and only one god. The fact that the Christians believe in a trinity, one god in three or three in one, seems to them a blasphemy, a kind of feigned polytheism. They do not believe in the seriousness of the Christian conflation of the three sides of God together; the notion of God as "bridegroom," as father, as son, the depictions of God as a lamb, as a dove, and so forth are to them a nightmare and an abhorrence. It is the true Muslim's responsibility to root out idolaters, and they do not take action against them only because Islam at the moment is so weak.

Surely you can understand, he said, how we Muslims look upon the Christian missionaries.[4] And (directed at the Frenchman) after all you of course know this intimately in France. Why else has France instituted the strictest ban on missionary activity of any kind in its African territories, be it Jesuit or Dominican, Lazarist or Marist. Nowadays it is eminently understandable that they are forbidden the practice of their calling in Algeria, but surely enough that is only pure necessity at work there. It is all too well known that when they were, the whole of French Africa arose in rebellion.[5] He who teaches that divinity

2. It is highly likely that Brandes has misidentified the prince as a Muslim. Later that summer, Clemenceau published an essay titled "Ce Que Pensent Nos Marocains" in which he describes a meeting, in Paris, with almost certainly the same figure. According to Clemenceau's account, the prince here describes himself as one who "knows Islamic belief too well," strongly suggesting that in the past in his role as prince he has clashed with Muslims.

3. If we may presume that the speaker is indeed Sardar Singh, his remarks on the manner in which Muslims view the West are potentially of great value. As the ruler of the Princely State of Jodhpur, one of his principal duties would have been the management of relations with the local Muslim minority.

4. The change to the first-person plural here is likely in error. It must be recalled that Brandes, a non-native French speaker, is in effect overhearing a conversation between Clemenceau and still another non-native French speaker.

5. The prince is likely referring here to the Kabylie Rebellion, which broke out in Algeria in 1871. It is important to note that the prince, or at least Brandes's representation

in such mysterious forms may be enjoyed as a right is in our view a servant of death.

The stranger thing is that France supports with iron and with fire the missionaries in China, the same missionaries it does not tolerate in its own provinces.[6]

I am well aware that the great majority of the Christians in Europe and America view these missionaries with sympathy, and some even look on them with admiration. They deserve neither the one nor the other.

European public opinion regarding the missionaries is quite misled. Even stranger is that European diplomats imagine the missionaries are doing something useful, paving the way for the political and economic interests of their respective countries.[7] As for political influence, this is not the case for the simple reason that the Chinese almost never understand which country the missionaries represent, since in order to do their business they are required to take on Chinese dress and Chinese habits as well as speak the Chinese language. They know whether they are Catholics or Protestants, but not at all whether they are German or French or Italian. As far as the economic interests of the state go, these have been forwarded so little by the missionaries that it is safe to say that no one has damaged European trade with China more than they have.

They have conducted business for their own benefit and by their methods have brought European business practice into the worst disrepute. The Christians have secured for themselves immunity to Chinese law through violence and warfare. They have thoroughly abused this privilege in order to enrich themselves by fraud. Everyone in China is convinced that the word of a

---

of him, significantly overstates the role of the missionaries in provoking the uprising, which was equally if not more so a result of political and economic factors.

6. It is also notable that the French government never did issue an outright ban on missionary activity in its North African territories; the activities of the Missionnaires d'Afrique (better known, however insensitively, as the Pères Blancs) thus continue to this day. Still, the China missions were in general much more enthusiastically supported by the French state than those in North Africa.

7. This statement reveals an extraordinary degree of knowledge of the politics of the Third Republic, and may be further evidence of Brandes embellishing the words of the prince. Among the thornier contradictions of French Great Game politics was the fact that while anticlericalism was in general the rule at home, it was not at all the case in the empire, where the church was seen as the essential component of the "civilizing" mission of colonialism; as Gambetta infamously proclaimed, "anticlericalism is not an article of exportation." For more on this, see James Patrick Tedesco, "Missionaries and French Imperialism: The Role of Catholic Missionaries in French Colonial Expansion, 1880–1905" (PhD diss., University of Connecticut, 1980).

European cannot be trusted, and that in a country in which reliance on the given word has made signatures superfluous; a spoken commitment replaces that.

Setting aside the claims of Christian doctrine to be regarded as the truth, it is absurd to believe that the missionaries have actually spread Christianity in China. Those Chinese who have converted came thereby under European justice, and the missionaries have sought to make it so that in every legal dispute between a convert and a heathen, the convert is favored. European justice in China has had no other task than to secure for criminals freedom from punishment. Can it be a surprise that the converts, who are wholly seen as traitors against land and people, who have sold themselves to avoid the death penalty for murder or to be able to hold onto purloined booty without punishment, are just as much hated as the foreigners who protect them at the expense of good, native-born citizens?

The European belief that the missionaries have spread enlightenment in China is foolish. A half-century ago they taught reading and writing to the same people who later launched the nefarious Taiping Rebellion.[8] In our time public education in China is so far ahead of that in Europe that the missionaries who think they are bringing enlightenment are only laughable.

The European view of the missionaries as men of peace, even more so, is utterly preposterous. It is the missionaries and the missionaries alone who are guilty in the bloodletting of China.[9] Their activities have in the past and will still more in the future become the goad twisted in the open wound. They drive the people into a rage, and when China like Japan has instituted a modern military system, this rage will become bloody and will make short work of them.

The only good the missionaries have done in China, and this is undeniable, constitutes a danger for Europe that cannot be overestimated. They have made the Chinese aware of Europe's technology. That is to say that while in France

---

8. The Taiping Rebellion (1850–64) is distinct from the later Boxer conflict in a number of important respects. In the first place, the insurgency was sparked not by anti-Western sentiment but instead by an indigenous understanding, however misguided, of Christianity. In the second, the Taiping Heavenly Kingdom Movement was opposed and ultimately suppressed by the forces of the Qing dynasty, with relatively minimal assistance by the French and British.

9. As is to be expected, this understanding of the causes of the war remains contentious. It should be noted, however, that the uprising did in fact begin with an outbreak of violence against missionaries, and that the missionaries themselves undeniably were a factor in the ensuing punitive campaign. For a balanced discussion of the issues, see Silbey, *The Boxer Rebellion*, 40–47, or Diana Preston, *The Boxer Rebellion: The Dramatic Story of China's War on Foreigners That Shook the World in the Summer of 1900* (New York: Berkley, 2000), 25–30.

and in other places around Europe it is imagined that the missionaries have opened up China as a market for the overproduction of European industry, which needed and needs an outlet, they have in reality, long before it was necessary, opened the eyes of the Chinese to the advantages provided by the European model of production. The consequence of this is that before long the Chinese will have established factories that will produce all the European industrial goods at far lower prices than Europe's, so that on the contrary Europe will be the market for Chinese overproduction.[10] How this will turn out goes without saying.

Yet that is a perspective on the future. The point now is the absolute necessity that European missionaries leave China in peace just as completely as they have in our time been forced to leave Algeria. And if the European states, which of course are all under the thumb of the church and will not dare be otherwise because of the prejudices of their subjects, refuse to listen to reason and to admit that they do wrong by sending missionaries to Asia, when none of them will stand for Asian missionaries in their own countries, then there is one further measure that is absolutely necessary. The missionaries and the converts must be subject to Chinese justice. That official envoys have immunity is a separate matter applicable in all countries and is nowhere abused, but this right dare no longer be extended to that ghastly mob that converts to the European religions only in order to claim it.

When the prince had spoken his mind, he stood up with a polite smile and asked for forgiveness for his outspokenness. But the matter weighed on his heart, and he hoped that a highly gifted man such as my friend would be able to enlighten the public opinion in Europe. His face had acquired an unusual liveliness, his brown cheeks burned. He went over to one of the windows that had a view over the low-lying city, sprawling like a horn surrounded by the mountains. How lovely it is here, he said with the peaceful dignity and that thoughtful glance that greeted passersby on the street. I made this long journey here to win back my health.[11] But even though I did not succeed in this, I may have not journeyed in vain, if only my words have fallen on fertile ground.

II

The strategy of the European missionaries in China is to establish congregations, that is to say small footholds led by priests, which seek to usurp as much

10. The prophetic nature of the prince's words here hardly need be noted, given the meteoric rise of the Chinese economy since 1978.

11. That the prince has traveled to Carlsbad for medical treatment offers further support for his identification as Sardar Singh, who like Clemenceau suffered from a lifelong nervous condition.

authority as possible on foreign ground under the protection of one or another European nationality, all of which constantly threaten the Chinese government with encroachment. In my book on Berlin (1885) I have already reproduced a conversation with the Chinese envoy there who complained vehemently about this.[12] The Chinese people are incensed by witnessing foreigners establishing themselves on Chinese ground and evading Chinese law, the same law to which they themselves are subject, simply because these foreigners worship a god about which they themselves are not even in agreement, since the Protestants and Catholics mutually disparage one another, indeed even try to poach each other's "converts." Because the missionaries claim the right of extraterritoriality, the Chinese, who as good patriots would see China independent, must constantly deal with the annoying charade in which Chinese Christians, under the protection of the missionaries, evade the legitimate authority of the mandarins and take advantage therefrom. In legal disputes before Chinese courts the missionaries demand that these renegades get their way. "Otherwise I will write to my minister," the missionary says, and the mandarin yields under compulsion.

The Christians recruit among the least honest people in China. The traveler Giquel uses this expression: "the newly converted are found only among people of the lowest classes."[13] As Paul Boell writes in Charles Guieysses's *Pages Libres*, the Chinese officials have assured him that bands of thieves have converted to Catholicism in toto simply to avoid the punishment of the law: "almost always, he says, it is purely external advantage (sinister court cases, loans, etc.) that leads to conversion. Sometimes entire villages become Catholics against their will, because they are unable to pay back a loan they have received from the missionaries, so that they must choose between misery and baptism."[14] But the main cause of disagreement between the mandarin and the missionary as mandarin is the extension of extraterritorial rights to the newly converted, by which a state within a state is created. In *Revue Blanche*

12. Brandes refers to *Berlin som Tysk Rigshovedstad* (Copenhagen: P.G. Phillipsen, 1885).

13. Prosper Marie Giquel (1835–86) was a French naval officer and diplomat who assisted in the suppression of the Taiping Rebellion, and later served the Qing government in varying capacities. Brandes cites from his *La Politique Française en Chine: Depuis les Traités de 1858 et de 1860* (Paris: Libraire de Guillaumin, 1872), 29.

14. Paul Victor Boell (1858–1909), the author of *Le protectorat des missions catholiques en Chine et la politique de la France en extrême-orient* (1899), was a French diplomat who testified on the causes of the Boxer Rebellion at the Paris Universal Peace Conference. Sandi E. Cooper, *Patriotic Pacifism: Waging War on War in Europe, 1815–1914* (Oxford: Oxford University Press, 1991), 174.

Alexander Ular recently reported at great length the story of a Chinese man's indignation at an American, who "had rudely robbed him and even though he was not a missionary escaped punishment and kept his booty."[15]

That is one of the reasons explaining the Chinese revulsion for missionaries. For China is a country where religious intolerance does not thrive. *Echo de la Chine*, the Catholic missionaries' organ in Shanghai, testified to this on October 24, 1900: "In China there is no religious fanaticism. The almost universal religious indifference goes so far that it permits every creed to be preached unpunished, and allows every form of public worship."

It is surely therefore not because the missionaries have a different religion that those in China maintain a mortal hatred for them. It is among other things because the worship of the dead, the innocent and indeed touching cult of ancestor worship, which is the principal religious obligation for the Chinese, is opposed with passion by the missionaries, Protestant as well as Catholic.

Lord Curzon, the present viceroy of India, writes about this in his book *Problems of the Far East.*

> The Chinese who are fully content with their own religion and only wish to be left in peace see themselves as attacked by propaganda whose first move is to disparage what is most precious to them. . . . Expected of them is a conversion irreconcilable with their character as citizens in the country; they are asked to deny that which for them is the secure foundation of all morality. . . . If preachers who taught a new faith, people of a race who look down on us, came ashore in England and began their agitation by attacking the Bible and anathematizing the faith of the apostles, what reception would they get?[16]

15. One of the more bizarre Orientalists of the Belle Epoque, Alexander Ular (1878–1919) was a German-born Sinologist, Russologist, and journalist who largely published in French. A translator of Laozi, Ular believed in the inherent superiority of Chinese civilization, so much so that in his *Un Empire Russo-Chinois* (1903, published in English as *A Russian Chinese Empire*, 1904) he makes the case that Europe's only hope of long-term survival lay in Russia, which as a half-Oriental civilization itself alone was capable of understanding the Chinese and acting as mediator between West and East. His publication in French in 1901 of a series of Chinese letters describing in detail the purported atrocities of the Eight-Nation Alliance created a storm in the European press. Brandes is here referring to these French translations, some of which he would publish later in the year in Danish translation—see "A Chinese Letter about the War" and "Chinese Letters" in this volume.

16. One of the most decorated of British colonial hands, George Nathaniel Curzon (1859–1925) was viewed at the time as a reliable authority on all matters Eastern.

Pierre Leroy-Beaulieu writes in *Revue des Deux-Mondes*: "The renunciation of ancestor worship in the eyes of the Chinese is a detestable sacrilege, an assassination of morality and law."[17]

The spiritual influence of the missionaries is necessarily nil; the European superstition they import is lost on every cultivated Chinese nature and can only awaken contempt. A prominent Chinese official has expressed as much, namely Gu Hongming, second-in-command under the viceroy of Huguang.[18] He writes in July 1891 in the *North China Herald, Shanghai* about the Protestant missionaries.

> The missionary says to his disciples that it is foolish of the mandarins to take action because of a lunar eclipse. But the same missionary an hour later says to them that the sun and the moon were stopped on the command of a Hebrew general, Joshua, and that the book in which that true story is recorded is a holy book that came into being by dictation from the almighty creator of the universe. Can anything be more hostile to science than this intellectual conjuring trick, not to use a more severe expression? Truly it is laughable, for everyone who knows anything at all about the struggle for the progress of ideas in Europe, to see the people of these religions, who in Europe have burned and persecuted men of science, come here to China and present themselves as the champions of science and of intellectual progress. . . . When an educated Chinese encounters these missionaries' impudent and aggressive attitude and sees such a doctrine supported by the terror of the foreign gunboats, he thus feels for the foreigners a hatred that they cannot understand, which only they who have seen the most precious heritage of their people subjected to the danger of corruption and dissipation can understand.

This Chinese fellow has it right. The entire missionary enterprise is nothing other than a disgrace to the culture of Europe.

From the outset it would be a surprise if the missionaries, especially the Catholics, were not engaging in business and industry in China, since these same men have done so to such an extraordinary degree in their homelands. During the recent negotiations in France regarding the various orders of monks

17. A prominent liberal economist of the Third Republic, Pierre Paul Leroy-Beaulieu (1843–1916) was the author of *La Renovation de L'Asie: Siberie, Chine, Japon* (1900; published in English as *The Awakening of the East*, 1900).

18. Gu Hongming (1857–1928) was an author, diplomat, and academic in late imperial and early republican China. Educated in Europe but steeped in traditional Confucian values, he was an invaluable mediator between East and West, translating European works into Chinese and vice versa.

and of nuns, it was revealed (in the thick book that was distributed to the members of the chamber by the finance minister) that the number of religious institutions running businesses was 2,500. There were 604 orders running tailor shops, 238 monasteries selling plant extracts, 42 monasteries running laundries, 95 running pharmacies. As far as the alcohol business goes, 5 orders sold wine in bulk, 2 only pure alcohol, 7 monasteries liqueur in bulk, 4 in detail, 7 had taverns, 14 had hotels, 15 hotel garni, et cetera.

And now all these holy men and women should be expected to give up business just because they have been placed in China?

Everyone who at all keeps up with the news has followed the shameful revelations regarding the manner in which the sisters at Bon Pasteur in Nancy have made use of orphaned children.[19] Even a bishop denounced their activities. All the way back in 1875 the missionary Father Aubrey, who supervised Shanghai and the surrounding area, found a similar institution for orphans in Lokawei; here "there are numerous workshops: carpentry and shoemaking shops, fabrication of materials and pictures, printing, et cetera. All of these provide useful things, *which sell well.*"

The missionary Father Robert sits on the board of a large American industrial concern. Although a Catholic monk he does not fear contact with Protestant money.

In Hankou the Lazarists run a cigarette factory that does very good business. In Shanghai where the Jesuits own a plot that makes up two-thirds of the French concession, they earn well with the renting of houses. Yet that is negligible in comparison with the following:

On February 24, 1901, Georges Clemenceau asked in his paper *Le Bloc* the following question of the French foreign minister: "Is Mr. Théophile Delcassé aware that there are several brothels among the houses owned by the good fathers of Shanghai, and that the procurer for the order—that is this pious bureaucrat's title—each month comes and collects the Church's income from these houses?"[20]

---

19. In the notorious L'Affaire du Bon Pasteur of 1900, a major boon to the anticlerical movement, the Catholic Church was found guilty of ruthlessly exploiting the labor of the orphans and "fallen women" under its charge in Nancy.

20. While Brandes's sources regarding church involvement in the sex trade cannot of course be confirmed here, it is in fact the case that prostitutes were officially licensed in the French Concession, and that the French authorities resisted all the efforts of reformers, both Chinese and Western, to ban prostitution up until the closure of the settlement in 1943. See Yusheng Yao, "Shanghai," in *The Encyclopedia of Prostitution and Sex Work*, ed. Melissa Hope Ditmore (Santa Barbara, CA: Greenwood, 2006), 338–41.

As soon as this enquiry was publicized, Mr. Delcassé telegraphed an official in Shanghai, whose name I have promised to be silent about, confirming that this rumor was indeed true.

In March Alexandre Zévaès brought up this matter in the French chamber. It was found to be undeniable that the procurer for the Jesuits, a certain L. Tournade, had while in Paris on March 8, 1901, written a denial of these charges. When this untruthful document was distributed in the chamber, Eugène Fournièr, much to the laughter and applause from the Left, responded that a holy father had with all sincerity reassured a friend of his that the Jesuits were covered, since the house was not in their name. The French consul in Shanghai, Mr. Georges Bezaure, like the chairman of the town council, had no desire to fall out with the holy fathers by offering testimony in the affair. But a prominent official in Shanghai, whose name I know but cannot name, wrote in *Le Bloc* on March 17, 1901: "Of *ten* independent witnesses *ten* will verify that the Chinese brothel is installed in the order's buildings."

The missionaries are regarded here in Europe as the self-sacrificing apostles of peace. Yet during the European occupation of China they have been moved only by desire for revenge and for blood. Paul Boell, an eyewitness, writes in the abovementioned place: "At the last executions in Peking I saw missionaries in the first row, gratifying themselves with the gruesome spectacle. It is they who have organized the plunder as well as the murder."[21] In the newspaper *Le Savoyard* on February 21, a French officer tells of how General Maurice Bailloud, who had met some resistance, sent a column in the direction of Tianjin, accompanied by the Jesuit Ducrey [*sic*], who said to the soldiers: "Burn that village; it has not paid taxes to us. Spare that one there, it has submitted."[22]

In the more than one hundred letters from French soldiers that have been published in *L'Aurore*, which are supplemented by the "Hun letters" from the German soldiers in *Vorwärts*, it is invariably the missionaries who give instructions as to where to murder and burn. Since the soldiers relate this quite naïvely, without the most meager disapproval, their testimony is certain enough.[23]

21. See note 14 for more on Boell. It should be noted that Boell's accounts of atrocities committed by the allied forces, as well as the allegations of missionary involvement in them, were vehemently contested by many among the accused.

22. General Maurice Camille Bailloud (1847–1921) commanded the French 2nd Infantry Brigade during the Boxer conflict. Paul Perret du Cray (1856–1909) was a Jesuit official in Tianjin during and after the rebellion. It should be emphasized here that reports of missionary-led atrocities during the punitive campaign, which were (rather startlingly) freely offered up by returning soldiers, were vehemently denied by church authorities and were never wholly substantiated.

23. Clemenceau's *L'Aurore* had previously published letters from French soldiers serving in China describing, in the most casual and unthinking terms, unspeakable atrocities against

And it is said such murders have not occurred under the supervision of the missionaries! One reads what *Le Temps*'s reporter G. Donnet some time ago wrote about the march to the imperial graves. The article begins: "We have killed three hundred boxers, who were perhaps not boxers." These are typical words:

> One grabbed them by the hair, by the skin of the abdomen, or took them by the legs, pulled them, pushed them; their bodies hit the flagstones, their skulls pushed against the stones. The children howled, the women howled. Some of these ripped their clothes apart and in despair offered themselves naked to the troops. When they were spared they remained standing and gazed in horror. The men stretched out their arms, bared their breasts, and the bayonets began their task. Then they wavered and died, the one on top of the other, with face to the earth.

We have read about the manner in which the plundering was carried out in French officer Stephane Lausanne's account in *L'Illustration*. He describes the plundering fury that seized everyone: "high officials, members of the legations, *indeed the missionaries themselves*."

This telegram from Peking is reprinted In the *New York Herald*: "The family of Lu-Sen, the Chinese official who was executed for having approved of the anti-foreign movement, have submitted to the international government in Peking a complaint against Bishop Favier for having a day after the liberation appropriated all of the silver and all of the treasures that are kept in his house, a value that amounts to a million tael."[24]

The missionaries are surely no less a stranger to the noble art of plunder than they are to murder.

---

the Chinese. In Germany, Socialist Party leader August Bebel read from similar German letters in the Reichstag. The ensuing fallout, which included the publication of the letters, which would come to be known as the *Hunnenbriefe*, caused considerable embarrassment for the kaiser and his government.

24. The reference here is to a February 10, 1901, *New York Times* article, which would set off an international controversy involving not only Bishop Alphonse Favier but also his Protestant equivalent, William Scott Ament, who would evoke the ire of Mark Twain. Both men were accused of directing the general looting of Beijing after its liberation, although each would deny the charges, arguing that any expropriations of Chinese wealth were always carried out with the intention of providing for now-indigent Chinese Christians.

CHAPTER 4

A Chinese Letter about the War

1901

The following is an English translation of Brandes's Danish version (from the French translation of the original Chinese) of a letter purportedly describing the observations of Chinese eyewitness to the atrocities committed during the punitive campaign against the Boxers. As indicated, the letter was obtained by German Sinologist and journalist Alexander Ular, who translated and published it (along with a few others discussed in the next chapter of the present volume) in France. It should be noted that the authenticity of the "Chinese Letters" was questioned rather ferociously in the French press as well as, after its publication in Danish, in Denmark. Indeed, in a letter dated August 11, 1901, Brandes's brother Edvard, the editor of the radical newspaper *Politiken* and the principal Danish publisher of his writings on human rights, expressed serious reservations about them, even confessing fear of reprisal from the local German envoy.

~

The letter below, whose authenticity is undeniable, is the property of Mr. Alexander Ular, one of the first contemporaries to have learned the Chinese language and studied conditions there. He has published it in *Revue Blanche* and in *Le Bloc*, whose editor Georges Clemenceau has had the original in his hand.

—

Private letter, sent from Tchang-Tzia-Gu-Ting (250 kilometers from Peking) on December 10, 1900, to Mr. U-Se-Gong, representative of the trading house of Bao-Tchuang-Chang at the Mai-Mai-Tcheng in Urga (the capital of Mongolia).[1]

Originally published in *Politiken*, August 19, 1901. Translated from the version published in *Samlede Skrifter*, vol. 17.

1. Tchang-Tzia-Gu-Ting is traditionally known to Europeans as Kalgan, now known as Zhangjiakou. Mai-Mai-Tcheng is an imperial trading post located near the Russian border in

Honorable father-in-law! For half a year all postal traffic through the Gobi Desert that divides us has been impossible, since as you know the barbarians of the West have launched a military invasion in the center of the kingdom. They have forced the emperor to abandon the royal residence and they have overthrown the government; in this way none of the administration's officials have been able to fulfill their functions. Thus they have flooded over the defenseless land with murder and plunder. These criminals from hell declare that they are in peace negotiations with the emperor, but at the same time they continue torturing the people in an unheard-of manner, with dreadful cruelty and devilish glee. In comparison with these greedy hordes of raging dogs one might almost call those missionary foxes humane, they who have caused all this misfortune, because their rotten business concerns went so poorly.

These are not soldiers like the Russian Tatars; they are bandits, plunderers, thieves, scoundrels, murderers, executioners, who slaughter the elderly and children, rape the wives and girls, lie and torture slaves—in short, they are Christian devils.

I wanted to say this to you, before I dare to provide you with the dreadful information I now must write down, for rage is better than despair.

This city and our house have not been spared any of the horror. And I have long been in doubt whether it would not be best if I willingly put an end to my life. . . . Honorable father-in-law, heaven protect you and preserve your life and your strength! I am the only one left of my whole family. Your splendid daughter, my wife, has almost before my eyes been raped by the beastly gangs and then murdered, as her belly was cut open. Your luminous grandson, my poor son, has been killed by a revolver shot, because he cried too loudly. And the little child whose birth I reported to you in my last letter and who lay trembling from cold while I was bound hand and foot, died shortly thereafter from exposure. Your other splendid daughter, my sister-in-law, was also raped in the house, but avoided death as did her child. Her husband is in danger, because he has been dragged to Peking by the barbarians and is being held there as a driver of the carts on which they have loaded the booty. I myself have been cruelly abused, because for a moment I defended our silk shop against plunder—I had already delivered nearly all I had of money to the prefect—and I do not know precisely why I have escaped death when so many others have been murdered.

Just as many have lost their properties as those who have lost their lives. The plundering went like this:

Manchuria. See Kenneth N. Owens, *Empire Maker: Aleksandr Baranov and Russian Colonial Expansion into Alaska and Northern California* (Seattle: University of Washington Press, 2015), 29. Urga is now known as Ulaanbaatar.

Refugees from Hsiuen-hoa came with the news that the barbarians were advancing with murder and plunder.[2] All shops were closed, some went to the prefect, others went home. Soon the barbarians arrived. Those who knew Peking said they were "Pu" [Germans]. The prefect made no kind of resistance. The commander of the barbarians, a man who was much too young for that position and whose faced gleamed with arrogance and mocking cruelty (Count York [*sic*] of Wartenburg, later killed), had himself shown up at the prefect's house and went in without announcing himself.[3] The soldiers spread themselves in groups on the streets and went into the houses that seemed to be well-off. Anyone who offered resistance was killed by revolver or by saber. Nowhere did they respect the threshold to the inner chambers. All servants, all the employees of the shops and all others who could took to flight; often the soldiers called after them, and when they did not turn around they were shot down.

Our quarter was the last they broke into, but one could not leave the city without falling into their hands. The leader had demanded 20,000 ounces of silver [63,000 kroner] from the prefect. The treasury was empty. Thus he as well as all other wealthy men were threatened with death and total plunder. In mortal angst everyone gave what he had. I gave 250 of the 350 ounces I had in the till. Soon the prefect had more than 20,000; but the leader of the barbarians took it all. Now we were more at ease: we believed that we had freed ourselves with this silver. It was a sorry delusion.

We had not reckoned that the thousands of soldiers had yet to get theirs. They found the stores and plundered them. They went into the houses. They forced everyone to indicate where there were goods or treasures, if he would not be abused in the most frightful manner. A large number of people who gave resistance to the plundering were murdered in their own houses. All objects of value were carried out to the street. All men were hog-tied.

Your daughter's husband, my sister-in-law's husband, would forbid these devils access to the interior of the house. They beat him with rifle butts and tied him to a stake. Four of these dogs then went in. The servant girls tried to flee, but were run down by eight other bandits, who took them by force while laughing. Your daughter, who was horrified, seems to have quickly lost consciousness; she was later found passed out, apparently as a consequence of the most disgraceful, most ignominious treatment. In my house it went still worse. They came in, knocked me to the earth, bound me with rope. Everything

2. Hsiuen-hoa is a prefecture on the road between Peking and Kalgan.

3. Colonel Maximillian Graf Yorck von Wartenburg (1850–1900), a scion of one of Germany's most distinguished military families, died of accidental causes during the campaign.

was plundered. I was in a rage, for I had after all given money. "I have paid; I have paid," I screamed in English. "You have no right to take that."

One of them understood me and said something to me with a frightful grin. I grasped, it should be said, that they had orders from their emperor to murder everyone and steal all possible.[4] Five went into the interior rooms. I heard the women scream and terrible laughter. In despair I called out to my wife. She answered me with a cry for help. And I could not get loose. A shot was fired. My wife let out a fearful scream. I bellowed like a madman. I received a violent kick in the belly and lost consciousness.

When I awoke it was dark. I cried for help. Mr. Y heard me and came with a lamp. He untied my bonds. The murderers were gone. But such horror! In the inmost room lay my wife, dead, with belly slit open, after having withstood outrageous violence. There lay my son with crushed skull, and the two servant girls killed with saber, both raped. I could not cry. I was insane with rage. I cried out for revenge. Never before have innocent people been tortured in this way.

Mr. Y took me and hid me in his now-empty warehouse. There I got sick. But I made a promise to torture and to kill slowly as many of these barbarians as I was capable.

In other respects everything I owned is lost. The bandits loaded 230 carts with all the goods they had stolen, and even forced the victims of this theft to drive these carts to Peking. Also my brother-in-law was led away in this manner. More than a thousand murders have been committed here in the city. Why do the heavens allow such?

As far as your honorable son goes, I do not know where he is or whether he is still alive. After he had beaten up the moneylender of a missionary in Paoting, as he had vowed, he has fled. Last summer he was in Taiyuan. Now that the Emperor has traveled to Taiyuan and then to Sian, I have no more reports from him.

Tsien Lao Gong

4. See "The Hun Speech" in the present volume for the background here.

CHAPTER 5

Chinese Letters

1901

This article appeared shortly after Brandes had previously published a complete Danish translation of one of the "Chinese Letters" collected and published in France by German Sinologist and journalist Alexander Ular. Here Brandes offers his own reflections on the explosive content of the controversial collection, with a special emphasis on the role of the German forces. It must be kept in mind here that Ular was hardly a dispassionate observer of events in China. As described in note 15 of the essay "Missionaries," Ular actively encouraged imperial Russia to act as mediator between Europe and the West. His 1904 *A Russo-Chinese Empire*, in which many of the "Chinese Letters" are reproduced in full, constitutes a sustained argument for such an arrangement. However, little documentary evidence exists to support his contention that the behavior of Russian soldiers during the war was in fact of a qualitatively more humane character than that of the other allied forces.

~

When one has for some time been absorbed by the letters from Chinese to Chinese that Mr. Alexander Ular has brought back to Europe and published in French translation, one obtains a glimpse into the modern Chinese mindset, which is instructive enough. For after all they do not say much regarding the horrors of the war that the hundreds of letters from French soldiers in China published in *L'Aurore* have not already reported.[1] Mr. Ular knows personally the addressees of the letters, of whom one whose daughter was murdered became so destroyed by grief that an illness from which he suffered took a dangerous turn and took him away.

In these letters there is naturally constant mention of the organization that in Europe is called the Boxers and that the Chinese call the Great Society or the Great Fists, or the Fists of Righteous Harmony. It is of course always spoken

Originally published in *Politiken*, August 26, 1901. Translated from the version published in *Samlede Skrifter*, vol. 17.

1. See "Missionaries," note 23.

of with sympathy. One sees young men seek to join up out of indignation over the Europeans' open theft of land and the missionaries' impudence, and the organization is praised in that it has finally come round to "the punishment of the overseas criminals." Yet it is asserted that the organization prefers the liberation of the country without the shedding of blood. In this way the Buddhist monastery in Liang-hsien is spoken of in one place: "The monastery became the temple of the good cause in the area. The monks, as was proper, would not defile themselves with murder. They would drive out the moneylenders (the missionaries) just with threats."[2] It then continues:

> Their goodness became poison for them. The overseas armies came. The rage of the people increased and the missionaries departed. But before they left they paid a visit to the honorable prior of the monastery and thanked him because he had calmed the population, and in exchange they promised to protect the monastery when later the Western army came to punish the Great Society; but they added that they needed 10,000 ounces of silver for the bribery of their country's generals. The prior gave them the money. The same day the others came, the Catholics, and repeated the same; they said that they were from another country and must have the same sum. The prior, who knew that the tidal wave from the West was irresistible, gave.

This describes how those in the city thereafter considered themselves to be safe. They became calm and no one hid his property. The monastery, where there lived eighty-seven monks, was especially known for its magnificent library. But when the "barbarians" had conquered Peking, they came also to Liang-hsien, and the missionaries accompanied them as interpreters. The barbarians murdered all the people, plundered the houses, and set fire to them. The prior quickly had the gates closed. The foreign troops broke through them and the unarmed monks were all shot except one who was believed dead; the monastery was burned and naturally the money that monks had for their upkeep vanished. According to the letters, the missionaries seem to have identified the monastery to the troops as a Boxer stronghold, after first having allowed themselves to be paid off by the monks to secure themselves against the European armies.

In this letter the dishonesty of the missionaries is especially emphasized. Another, a business letter, concerns the arts of blackmail.[3]

2. Liang-hsien, now known as Liangziang, is a district located southwest of Beijing. The full text of this letter is reproduced in Alexander Ular, *A Russo-Chinese Empire*, trans. uncredited (Westminster: Archibald Constable, 1904), 136–38.

3. The full text of this letter is reproduced in Ular, *A Russo-Chinese Empire*, 129–35.

We see here a young banker who has escaped from Peking, dismissed from everywhere he has sought employment because he is a member of the Great Fists; since the banks have business relations with the missionaries they dare not give him a place for fear that those who want to wipe out the Great Fists would then set loose "the overseas barbarian's bloodthirsty armies" upon them. He goes from city to city until the town of Khuang-yang; he is taken on as a partner in a business for which he has a letter of recommendation, into which he invests the 12,000 ounces of silver he has been able to save.[4] But since all business activity in China is at a standstill, the otherwise solid firm finds itself in a precarious position. Under these circumstances it is brought to the edge of bankruptcy, not just because a missionary extorts from it a check on the bank Baocheng, amounting to 5,000 ounces of the 6,000 they have therein, but because the missionaries from the area who abandoned it when the troubles came have continued to pay for all of the goods they bought and that they had sent down to the coast with checks on that bank, even after the sum they had deposited in the bank had long run out. In this way the bank was assailed all at once by the missionaries' debt collectors, and the writer of the letter now sought in his need a loan from a distant relative.

Depictions of private misfortunes and abuses naturally take up a large place in the letters. In one is related the fate of a young man who comes on a visit to Peking and whose horse and wagon were robbed of him by foreign troops, after which they seized his person. In this letter as in the others the passionate hatred with which the Germans are spoken of is striking and in strong contrast to the goodwill, indeed even gratitude that is felt toward the Russians. Every moment there appear phrases such as this: "The U alone resemble humans, the Pu behave themselves as odiously as the Tatars, who are described in the yearbooks from the days of the Qin and Yuan dynasties."[5] One sees from this letter how the foreign army as a matter of course treats Chinese it has taken into its service; they are given nothing to eat and are beaten. The writer of the letter says of his young brother-in-law: "The barbarians, true flesh-eating beasts who do not understand how to eat in a proper manner, used him as a slave, treated him in a way that a Chinese gentleman has never treated his servant. They did not even permit him to relieve himself, and when he became ill in the night the soldiers who guarded the prisoners smeared his impurity in his face while laughing. Some of his fellow prisoners attempted to escape; they were shot down. In Peking the silk clothing he owned was sold to the highest

4. Khuang-yang is now known as Guangyang.

5. The Chinese refer to the Russian soldiers as the "U," the Germans as the "Pu." The full text of this letter is reproduced in Ular, *A Russo-Chinese Empire*, 248–52.

bidder in such a way that pieces that cost 23 ounces (90 kroner) were bought by a priest for a flask of liquor. Of the Germans the letter relates that they go on the hunt two or three times a day after the Chinese, whom they take to belong to the Boxers. When they have captured two or three hundred they assemble them along the river Hunho, fall upon them with their bayonets, skewer them or push them into the water.[6] As in all wars also here there are reported dreadful and naïve rumors about the enemy general: "The barbarians' general Ua da-sze (Waldersee), an executioner from hell, has commanded his bloodthirsty Pu to seize all Chinese and shoot them as rebels. He is cruel to the degree that the U are shocked by it."[7] And in this letter as in the others hope of Russian protection is expressed. One follows clearly how the Russian officers describe the German troops as cruel to the Chinese, how the Russians themselves are kindly disposed, and how the hope of the Chinese more and more clings to the hope of the arrival of a great Cossack army, which the emperor of the U will send across the Gobi Desert to protect the children of the heavenly kingdom.[8]

While the conduct of the European armies in the opinion of individual letter writers recalls that of the medieval Tatars, others are reminded of the Mongols, about which the yearbooks of the Ming dynasty speak.[9] And the shocking thing emphasized is that while the Mongols at the very least behaved openly as enemies, these Europeans come by their own accounts as friends and yet have hardly landed before they have committed the worst breaches of international law. In one place a young man tells of how as an ardent follower of Buddha he had allowed himself to be admitted into the Great Society of the Fists, had taken an oath on the six syllables and thereafter had been forced to flee, when the overseas armies everywhere tortured and killed the Great Fists.[10] He counts himself lucky that his marriage to Miss Tchu with the golden lily still has not taken place, since he has been subjected to such great dangers. Clearly enough he feels himself quite like the German youth who in

6. The Hunho is now known as the Hunhe.

7. Alfred Ludwig Heinrich Karl Graf von Waldersee (1832–1904) served as commander in chief of all allied forces in China from October 1900 onward; having arrived after the conclusion of major combat operations, he was largely responsible for the punitive campaigns that followed.

8. While there may have be some measure of truth in the assertion that certain Chinese placed their hopes in a Russian rescue, there is nothing in the historical record to suggest that this was ever a possibility. Indeed, it was the czar himself who had proposed the hated Waldersee as commander in chief.

9. The full text of this letter is reproduced in Ular, *A Russo-Chinese Empire*, 252–55.

10. Ibid.

the age of Napoleon joined Schill's Freikorps or Lützow's wild hunt during the war of liberation, and it is quite significant that the same people who in Germany admire the Freikorps and in France *les francs-tireurs* only have contempt and disgust for the Boxers.[11]

Very curious is the description in one of the letters of the arrival of the French in the city of Tching-ting.[12] (The Chinese name for the French is the Fats). "The overseas army reached the city one evening. It was those who call themselves Fat and who are recognized by banners that consists of three horizontal stripes of different colors." Their general sent the prefect his visiting card and added calming reassurances. In short, the order to open the gates of the city was given. The Frenchmen hoist their banners up everywhere, demand food and drink, do no harm. Three days later came the Germans, whose emperor "also commanded the French and whose goal is to wipe out the Han people" (the Chinese). Then the prefect proclaimed that all those who for one reason or another fear the Germans, but especially the Great Fists, must leave the city in all haste. A general flight takes place, and upon that follows plunder and burning. The letter writer hopes that the Cossacks will be saviors. The czar is China's friend and protector.

The immediate consequences of the war have evidently been to call forth in China fear of Germany, contempt for France and England, and trust for the Russians, who—regardless of whatever they have done in Manchuria—as half-Eastern neighbors understand the inhabitants of the East, and as men who do not come over the sea, but over land, seem much less strange and therefore wisely have understood to present themselves as those who deeply protest the injustice that China suffers from the people of the West.

The next century's judgment of the China War that has opened it will hardly be mild. More than all of the horrors one will surely feel struck by the unbelievable foolishness with which the powers have proceeded.

If one looks back over the nineteenth century and for example investigates the origins and the conduct of a particular war, what strikes one most is namely not the errors committed in the war but the mistakes from which it sprang. For those who have been occupied with the Crimean War, who, for example, have read a number of English parliamentary speeches regarding it, the awfulness of it now a half century later is not so much the murder as the

11. Ferdinand Baptista von Schill (1776–1809) and Ludwig Adolf Wilhelm von Lützow (1782–1834) each led revolts against French occupation during the Napoleonic Wars. The Francs-tireurs were an irregular force that opposed the Prussians in the war of 1870–71.

12. Tching-ting is now Zhengding. Brandes here continues to cite the letter referred to in notes 9 and 10.

foundational stupidity that lay behind the whole thing.[13] Has there ever been a crazier, less useful war? Millions were squandered, hundreds of thousands of people injured or killed without the most meagerly evident advantage for France, England, Turkey, or Sardinia, who fought the war against Russia without being able to accomplish more than taking down a fortress in the outskirts of the country after years of effort and immense pains.[14] One has been able to imagine that the war in the least was to the benefit of little Sardinia.[15] But of course Italy would have united had Cavour not supplied his little force. How the pathos was lacking in the discussions of the political wisdom that expressed itself in the Crimean War.

Will the future find the wisdom from which the China campaign sprang greater?

13. The Crimean conflict of 1853–56 is widely considered to be among the most pointless of European wars; arguably it had a more lasting impact on literature (Alfred Tennyson, Leo Tolstoy, etc.) than on geopolitics.

14. Brandes is referring to Sevastopol.

15. However improbably, tiny Sardinia did in fact send an expeditionary force to the peninsula, in an effort to curry favor with France and England toward the larger goal of Italian independence.

CHAPTER 6

Contemporary Civilization

1901

As the new century dawned, the Polish people remained oppressed by the terms of the Third Partition of Poland, which in 1795 had divided the lands of the former Polish-Lithuanian Commonwealth between Austria, Prussia, and Russia. Brandes first encountered Polish nationalists during his lengthy travels abroad in 1885, immediately developing a lifelong affection for the Polish people, their literature, and culture, and most of all, their cause of independence. This is the first of his many essays on the Polish question, occasioned by the outbreak of the Wrześnian Children's Strike in 1901, a mass protest against compulsory Germanization that would eventually find support as far afield as the Polish emigrant community in North America.

~

All Polish-speaking populations in Germany, Austria, and Russia find themselves at the moment in a state of intense national agitation because of events that have taken place in the Prussian province of Posen.

Instructive are two cases of a political nature; the one against a group of Polish schoolboys in Thorn, the other against Polish students in the city of Posen, both of whom are said to be guilty of high treason—words that ring oddly when they are applied to half-grown schoolboys and students.[1] In both cases the authorities found no other resolution than to punish these youths for "participation in a secret organization" whose only purpose was this innocent thing: the maintenance and strengthening of Polish national sentiment through reading and discussions.

To be able to condemn the schoolchildren to prison time the law had to be twisted in such a way that the authorities ascribed to their teachers the status

Originally published in *Politiken*, December 16, 1901. Translated from the version published in *Samlede Skrifter*, vol. 17.

1. For a concise contemporary account of the court cases discussed in this essay, see "Germany's Grave Problems," *The World's Work* 3, no. 4 (February 1902): 1700–1701. Thorn and Posen are now of course known by their Polish names, Toruń and Poznań.

of officialdom. Those sentenced to imprisonment were therefore dismissed and thereby prevented from developing their knowledge; indeed, those among them who were entitled to do only a single year's military service were denied this right "because of a lack of moral maturity."

The students in Posen could also be punished for having conducted their meetings in secrecy. To the question of why they had done so, they answered: because the authorities had forbidden the founding of every official organization and because they felt the desire for greater togetherness; their nationality was oppressed with violence and scorn; Polish subjects had themselves been compelled to contribute to the fund of 200 million marks set aside for the purchase of Polish land for German settlement. They were condemned to prison time.

The stir that these two cases created was, however, paltry in comparison with that which a third trial has occasioned in all of Europe as well as outside of it.

Until April 1, 1901, religious instruction in Prussian Poland (as well as in the Russian sector) in the schools had been given in the Polish language.[2] Suddenly an order determined that in the future it should be given in German. Everywhere the children refused, at the prompting of their parents, to answer the questions of the catechism or recite prayers in German. In order to break this resistance as quickly as possible, everywhere the schools employed the copious use of the teacher's cane. Blows rained down on the obstinate children. In the city of Inowroclaw a little boy was beaten completely to a pulp, in another place several teachers held down a boy while a teacher thoroughly beat him with a stick. As expected this behavior did not seem to trouble the school directorate, and neither did the many widespread incidents come to the attention of the greater public.

Then the authorities in the little town of Września decided to make an example through mass punishment. It was decided that on the twentieth of May instruction should be supported by a universal bastinade with the cooperation of the whole region's teaching personnel.[3] They had fourteen small Polish children of both sexes line up in a row and then led them one by one into a side room where the punishment took place. Although the first child came back with bloody fingers, none of the others gave in and remained

2. The language order of April 1901, which extended not only to secular but also to religious education, foreshadowed the infamous Polish Decrees of World War II.

3. The employment of "collective punishment" as a means of social control had long been official Prussian policy, and would achieve world infamy in the opening stages of World War I.

standing, allowing themselves to be beaten by these school tormentors so as not to admit guilt.

But the screams were heard outside the school, and the parents now rushed to protect their children. The mothers were the most eager, because they were the most indignant over the mass beatings. It had in fact been so thorough that the children afterward could not bend their fingers. One child had to stay home for four days. One boy's nerves were affected so badly that he began to stutter and has not gotten back his natural voice again. One of the beaten got appendicitis and died a few days later.

When the mothers entered the school they broke out in indignant and embittered complaint and accusation, but they did not lay a hand on anyone. Their entire offense consisted of a few invectives and seemed so meager and trivial that the local council in Września did not at all think of bringing a case. Only after inflammatory articles began to appear in the Prussian press did the public prosecutor intervene. Six of the mothers and a few fathers were arrested and summoned before the judge in Gnesen.[4] In order that none of the accused should be able to get off, the crimes they were alleged to have participated in were piled up: disturbance of the public order, threats toward public officials as they functioned in their capacity (as stick swingers), incitement to murder, attack on a public building, and so on and so on. The defense had requested that the widow Wiasetzka, who was the mother to seven children, should be released from prison, since she was suffering from serious illness. The doctor backed up the defense's account. The prosecutor demanded that the request be dismissed and the court gave in to him. The widow thus answered the court: "What we want is only that our children should learn religion in Polish, because otherwise we cannot pray together with them." Sick as she was, she was sentenced to two and half years of "harsh incarceration." The others accused were sentenced to similar punishments. One man, who had permitted himself to make a joke about one of the heavy-handed teachers, received two years' imprisonment.

When these judgments became public just the other day, a storm went through the Polish spirit in all three parts of the state. In the first instance the students in both Warsaw and Lemberg tried to storm the imperial German consulate; windows were broken and the consular sign broken—in other words, the kind of unwise and less than useful manifestation of disposition that only brings down misfortune on the aggrieved.[5] Yet at the same time indignant meetings were also held in Prussia's neighboring land, at which vehement

4. Gnesen is known in Polish as Gniezno.

5. Lemberg is now known by its Polish name, Lviv.

speeches of retort were given; it has been much remarked upon that one of the ministers of the Kingdom of Hungary has taken part in such a meeting in Piatek.

Henryk Sienkiewicz, who as Poland's most admired and eldest author is its obvious spokesman across Europe, has begun a collection in support of those condemned at Gnesen and has opened it with a well-spoken proclamation.[6] It is too long to reproduce here, but it begins in this way:

> We are confronted with an astonishing verdict. No hand has been lifted against the torturers of the little schoolchildren, no assault has been made on them; yet the parents of these little children, who are the victims of Prussia's school torturers, were sentenced to long years of imprisonment. Why? Because in a fit of agitation and sympathy they have all too loudly expressed their indignation at such a school and such teachers. Everywhere in which degenerate civilization has not been transformed into a barbaric state, even among the Germans, who would preferably play another role than that of the Prussian police, this judgment will awaken a feeling of horror and contempt.

Sienkiewicz himself gave a hundred kroner; the city of Lemberg a thousand; Count Stanislaw Badeni, the grand marshal of Galicia, gave his contribution at the top of the list. The Poles in Austria, who during their recent passionate national struggle in the kingdom had sided with the Germans there, have been violently thrown back toward the Poles in the other states, and hardly ever has everyone whose language is Polish felt themselves to this degree to be one people. They say to themselves as their consolation that just as Flanders successfully cast off Spain's yoke, that just as the Russians shook off the Tatar overlord after 260 years of slavery, so can their own time come one day.

There can surely be no doubt that the Prussian attempt at Germanization has gone wrong and has had a quite different effect than was foreseen. But from the universal human standpoint this is secondary. The decisive thing is that this is as far as European civilization has progressed in the year 1901. We have come no further.

Very instructive in this respect is Count Bülow's answer to Prince Radziwill's enquiry into this case.[7] Count Bülow was not in the least aware that it

---

6. Henryk Sienkiewicz (1846–1916), one of the major figures of nineteenth-century Polish letters, was awarded the Nobel Prize for Literature in 1905. Brandes was a lifelong champion of his work.

7. Bernhard Heinrich Karl Martin von Bülow (1849–1929) was German Chancellor from 1900 to 1909. Ferdynand Fryderyk Radziwiłł (1834–1926) served in the Reichstag from

might have damaged the German Reich's standing in neighboring lands; on the contrary, the foreign ministers of Russia and Austria had made apologies for the attacks on the German consulates, indeed at their own expense had had the signs repaired. He is astonished that anyone could believe that Germany's internal politics or the attitude of the leading minister could in the smallest measure be affected by foreign attitudes, trends, or expressions of opinion. And he concludes: "For me nothing matters other than this country's national interest and my responsibility to Germanness"—inferior words, the sum of our age's concept of statecraft, greeted with shouts of applause.[8]

One well notices these words! The only thing that is taken into consideration is the national interest and the interest of Germanness. Without a hint of shamelessness obsolete concepts such as human decency and justice are left out.

And the situation is everywhere the same. When France, indifferent to the question of Dreyfus's guilt or innocence, asserted that her national interest demanded his staying on the island, the whole of Europe stood against it and raised an outcry, none more eagerly than England and Germany. The crime was after all precisely to elevate the national interest over the demand for justice. France dismissed with bitterness the intervention of foreign nations.

When Chamberlain recently was asked about England's strategy against the Boers and about the infamous concentration camps, he claimed for his side as a matter of course the national interest, dismissed the foreign meddling in England's affairs, and also bespoke the cause of national pride to resounding applause.[9]

No one is more indignant over England's strategy than the Germans. Everywhere in the German press contempt foams over regarding the ruthlessness of the strong against a minority that would assert its nationality in defiance of the immense superior force. Not for a moment do the Germans in the meantime alter their position in Schleswig, Alsace, or Posen for that reason.[10]

The Poles are now up in arms over the school directorate in Września. They have no state, and therefore have no national interest. But where they themselves have the power, namely in Galicia, and where they have dominance

---

1874 to 1919, during which he was a dedicated defender of the Polish minority under German rule.

8. The chancellor here anticipates Hitler's infamous motto: "Right is what is good for the German people."

9. Joseph Chamberlain (1836–1914) was colonial secretary during the Second Boer War (1899–1902). See "Transvaal" in the present volume for Brandes's views on that conflict.

10. Similar programs of Germanization were underway among the Danes of Schleswig, acquired in 1864, and the French of Alsace, annexed in 1871.

over another nationality, the Ruthenians, the country's two languages are by no means as equal as, for example, the three national languages in Switzerland. And the right to own land, which in Galicia is legally secured for Jews as well as Catholics, is in practice denied the Jews.[11] All the same an approach such as the Prussian method is naturally unthinkable from the side of the Poles.

The Danes are after all a little folk, but that the Danish dominion, when national interest is at stake, would not be more mild toward the foreigners, is suggested by the fact that a group of Danes quite recently treated a much larger group of foreigners much like a conquered people, with suspension of the constitution, illegal raising of gendarme corps, cases of crimes against the crown, jailing of political leaders, and an eagerness to act from the side of the courts, which without exaggeration can be called a European or perhaps more closely, a Prussian phenomenon.[12]

It is so very much alike everywhere.

---

11. Brandes is always mindful of the mistreatment suffered by Ruthenians and Polish Jews at the hands of the ethnic Polish majority; see "Ruthenians" in the present volume for more on this. Nevertheless, his closeness to the Polish people would often earn him the opprobrium of the other main ethnic groups of Greater Poland.

12. Brandes here refers to the mistreatment of the ethnic German population in Schleswig and Holstein, before the provinces were lost to Prussia in the war of 1864.

CHAPTER 7

The Women of Poland

1901

By late 1901 the fate of the Września schoolchildren was well on the way to becoming an international cause célèbre. The occasion for the present essay, Brandes's second on the subject, was the issuance of a statement of support from a Polish women's committee led by the poet and activist Maria Konopnicka (1842–1910), which would eventually appear in newspapers across Europe and North America. The appeal was brought to Brandes's attention through his friendship with the Polish modernist poet Maryla Wolska (1872–1930); the second half of the article thus contains his Danish translation. Before this, however, Brandes briefly addresses a related issue of particular sensitivity, namely the mistreatment of the minority Ruthenian population of Austrian-ruled Galicia, mistreatment not by the Hapsburg overlords but by the majority Poles themselves (see the section "The Brandesian Imperative of Disinterestedness" in this volume's introduction for more on this issue). At the behest of another Polish associate, Józefa Klemensiewiczowa (1862–1938), a prominent Polish translator of Scandinavian literature, Brandes offers his first commentary on Polish-Ruthenian relations. His article "The Ruthenians" of three years later, it should be recalled, effectively dodges the issue, focusing entirely on the Ruthenian population under imperial Russian rule.

~

A Polish lady, Mrs. Józefa Klemensiewiczowa, who by virtue of her language knowledge follows along with what is published in the Nordic languages, has given me more intimate information on the relation between the Poles and Ruthenians, which goes like this:

Galicia has 7,350,000 inhabitants, of which four million are Poles. These people have 2,084 village schools; the Ruthenians have no less than 2,144

Originally published in *Politiken,* December 30, 1901. Translated from the version published in *Samlede Skrifter,* vol. 17.

villages in which their language is spoken.[1] The Ruthenians have four Latin schools, but prefer the Polish, since they lack textbooks. The universities in Austria are independent of the government. In Lemberg the Poles have long fought to establish a Polish university and got it first in 1872; till then the university had been German. The Ruthenians must surely also seek to get a university for themselves; the Poles have nothing against that. Now the Ruthenian students take many of their lessons in theology, law, and philosophy in their own language, only not in medicine, since very few of them study that field (this year there have been ten).

The letter writer adds that, as is well known, the Poles feel infringed upon by the Ruthenians' hostile attitude toward them. The Lithuanians, who earlier were united with the Polish state, have of course fused together with the Poles.[2] She does not speak about the right to vote for the provincial diet and how it is discharged; in that area she would not be able to deny that the Ruthenians have grounds for complaint. But even though the invalidity of every accusation leveled against the Poles by their enemies has not been demonstrated, one can with full sympathy dwell on the fate that has become Poland's, which by virtue of a tragic situation has now lasted into a second century. And the school barbarity in Września (German: Wreschen) once more has revealed that the horror and the resentment has spread like a ground fire through all Poles, and in fact has spread itself across the entire Slavic world, so that even the Russians and the Czechs have taken the side of the Poles with passion.[3] The great Russian newspapers have been given permission to bring out articles that are very much a sign of the times, since they reveal in part that the old Russian national hatred of the Poles is tempered or forgotten, and in part that the Russian government has bestowed upon them a greater leniency, when it otherwise could not reproach the Prussians for what it had previously viewed as necessary.[4] According to (still as yet to be reliably confirmed) reports, there have also been expressions of disapproval outside the German consulate in

1. Galicia is the historic border region between modern Poland and Ukraine. While the meaning of the ethnic term "Ruthenian" has changed over time and remains somewhat ambiguous, Brandes employs it to refer to Ukrainians.

2. After the final dissolution of the Polish-Lithuanian Commonwealth in 1795, the Lithuanian people came under Russian rule. Brandes is, significantly, in error here, for the Lithuanian nationalist movement in the nineteenth and twentieth centuries was every bit as vigorous as that of the Poles.

3. For more on Brandes's views on the Wrześnian Children's Strike, see "Contemporary Civilization" in the present volume.

4. Brandes here refers to the growing sentiment of Pan-Slavism, which would have such disastrous consequences in the late summer of 1914.

Moscow. A large mass of people is said to have torn down the consulate sign and dragged it through the dirt.

No doubt in the meantime it is the case that in Prague, where up to now—heaven knows!—they were not favorable toward the Poles, but viewed them as lucky and cunning rivals, the Czechs have violently made their Slavic disposition known in order to show the Poles their sympathy. A member of the Austrian council, Klofáč, gave a speech in Prague on the Prussian terror regime in the schools in Posen, after which the Czech youth in Prague hastened to the German consulate and made threats.[5] When questioned the detained expressed specifically that their anger was not directed at the universally well-regarded German consul in Prague, but at the Prussian authorities in Września and Gnesen.

Not only in Galicia but among the Poles in America (such as in Buffalo) there have been resolutions not to buy German goods, resolutions that however can hardly engender more than a passing significance.

Women's committees have also taken form all over Poland, and in the name of these (specifically in the name of all Polish women) one of Galicia's foremost ladies, Mrs. Maryla Wolska, has turned to me with a request to publish the following piece, which I hereby permit myself to recommend to the Nordic press:

Appeal to the Women of Europe

For the second time now, in the seven centuries of the Polish nation's struggle against the Teutons, a female voice swells up for a persecuted people against German injustice. It happened the first time when Queen Hedvig threatened the Teutonic Order's grand master with divine wrath, and a short time thereafter the Order suffered the decisive defeat at Grünwald.[6]

Now once again all Polish women, all Polish mothers, appeal their case against German barbarity and against the unjust punishment that has been delivered to their children—Who knows whether the shadows of the future conceal a new Grünwald?

It is not just in the name of our national struggle, but in the name of all humanity that we turn to all peoples, to all women who have a mother's heart.

In their national arrogance the Prussians take upon themselves the right to civilize; they concede not at all that a people under their yoke have other desires,

5. Václav Jaroslav Klofáč (1868–1942) was a Czech nationalist politician, elected to the Austrian Reichsrat in 1901.

6. Queen Jadwiga (1373–99) ruled the Kingdom of Poland from 1384 until her death. Her principal adversary, Grand Master Ulrich von Jungingen, met his death at the Battle of Grünwald in 1410.

other hopes than theirs; they violate the holiest feelings even in the hearts of little children.

We ask in this unheard-of case that fills our hearts with indignation for the judgment of all the peoples who have struggled for their rights and freedom.

In the Catholic school in the little village of Września in the Grand Duchy of Posen, a Polish province under the Prussian yoke, they commanded the Polish children to pray and to learn the catechism in German. The children, who from their earliest years are accustomed to praying in their mother tongue, cannot obey the teacher's order. They locked them up in the school, they whipped them until they bled. A teacher tore the lip of a little girl in order to get her to say the prayer in German. The screams from the martyred children brought a host of people to gather under the windows of the school. The parents and guardians of the children broke out in complaint. But the screams of complaint of the mothers brought the Prussian authorities near; they viewed them as rebels and brought the unfortunate women as well as all who had been willing to take action for the victims before the courts. In spite of the testimony of the parents and of other witnesses, which confirmed that the children were injured in such a way that they could not hold a book in their hands, the twenty accused before the court were sentenced late in November to be put behind bars for a period ranging from six to eighteen months.

What remains unknown is this singular aspect: the state prosecutor had recommended only a small punishment, but the judge did not bother with that, even sentencing a terminally ill mother of seven children to the strictest punishment.

What heart is not seized at the thought of the sufferings and the torture doled out to these unfortunate mothers, whose only crime was that of being mothers . . . and women of Poland?

We who are the sisters of these unfortunates, we rise up as a living statue of grief toward all other people and utter the cry: justice!

Would that our cry find resonance in all hearts and brand our torturers with the stamp of dishonor.

The Women of Poland

This proclamation was sent to all the big cities of Europe and America. It would be bold to assume that, given Europe's level of education, it will make some deeper impression, as long as the various peoples themselves are as a rule guilty of what they most vehemently condemn in others, and as long as there is such a great distance between public opinion in the nations and the behavior of their governments. But it ought not leave any heart unmoved.

After it was accomplished—albeit with no small number of difficulties—that the free thinkers of the various nations were convinced that their political participation should not stop at the borders, that there was indeed a world outside the fatherland, the opposite extreme prevailed for a time, such that these same people became completely indifferent to national questions, which then again had as a consequence that the reactionaries appropriated them and like nationalists, chauvinists, and jingoists, draped all kinds of dark activities in the national flags. The freethinkers then became quite indifferent to the value of the national. We experienced this the other day when we saw Georges Clemenceau accused of nationalism by Jaurès.[7] But in a time like ours in which the less powerful peoples like the Boers or the Armenians are wiped out with fire and sword, and where no heroism, however much this surprises Europe, seems able to save them, while oppressed nationalities like the Poles, Finns, or Southern Jutlanders live in an uninterrupted, albeit passive resistance against oppression, we have reached a point at which nowhere on Earth can the freethinkers be in doubt that the cause of the oppressed peoples and that of freedom are one.

7. Once compatriots in the Dreyfusard cause, Brandes's friend and ally Clemenceau would in the first decade of the new century increasingly clash with French socialist politician Jean Jaurès (1859–1914).

CHAPTER 8

Macedonia

1902

As the Armenian-Turkish conflict simmered in the eastern edges of the Ottoman empire, the Macedonian people suffered similar torment in its far western reaches. While a large majority of ethnic Bulgarians, under Russian tutelage, had acquired independence in 1878, their close relatives the Macedonian Slavs remained under the sultan. With extensive assistance from Bulgarian sympathizers, much of it without official state sanction, a nascent Macedonian independence movement began to emerge in the 1890s, culminating in the outbreak of irregular hostilities in 1902, followed by the more organized Ilinden Uprising of the following year. Hoping in vain for military support from the young Bulgarian regime, the insurrection was savagely crushed by Turkish forces. While Brandes is correct here to identify the disturbing similarities between the fate of the Macedonians and that of the Armenians, he is understandably unable to foresee a further layer of obstacles between the Macedonians and their independence, namely the aggressive intent of the young Balkan states of Serbia, Greece, and even Bulgaria itself. After Ottoman defeat in the Balkan Wars of 1912–13, Macedonia would be carved up among these three minor powers. Full independence (from Yugoslavia) would not be achieved until 1991.

~

The class struggle as a struggle for bread rages in the most civilized lands of Europe and America; immense strikes result in the intervention of troops against the hungry, as soon as it can be deemed necessary. At the same time in Europe's less civilized nations at the beginning of the twentieth century there exist conditions that one is in the habit of calling medieval: religious fanaticism as the law of the fist with daily extortion and killing, with murder by fire, rape, and every form of torture. The Turkish horrors in Macedonia and the Romanian disgraces against the Jewish population become more shocking every day,

Originally published in *Politiken*, October 27, 1902. Translated from the version published in *Samlede Skrifter*, vol. 17.

while simultaneously it seems that Europe, which with steady equanimity is witness to the extermination of the Armenians, daily becomes more indifferent to what is happening in Macedonia and Romania before the eyes of all.[1]

That the North American free states have sent to Romania a very sharp diplomatic note regarding its persecution of the Romanian Israelites has as of yet had no other effect than that Romania has barbarically stopped the flow of a whole slew of emigrants who, having already been supplied with traveling papers, had sold everything they owned, and who now on Romanian soil are forced to eat up the little sum that had been earmarked for passage and settlement in a foreign land, so as not to be destroyed ignominiously.

In Macedonia Europe has yet to make its influence felt, although to do so could not be more pressing.

In the spring the Macedonian intelligentsia, for the instruction of the reading public whose interests are not confined to the land or city in which it lives, began to issue the French biweekly *Le mouvement macédonien*, which (in the same manner as the Armenian-published *Pro Armenia* and the Young Turk organ *Medcheret*) has illuminated the actions of the horrific Turkish government from week to week. Many times the paper has added illustrations to the text, such as in July the picture of the hanged Macedonian leader Slavi Merdjanov, a young man of rare ability and rarer strength of character, who had previously been taken prisoner by the Turks with three wounds, or in August the picture of the Turkish military police, leaning on their sabers, who had allowed themselves to be photographed in Manastir with four severed heads of captured rebels laying before them on a little oblong table.[2]

In the organs of the European press, which in part are willingly servile and in part paid by the Turkish legations, the acts of violence committed by regular and irregular Turkish troops against the Christians are generally described as payback for the criminal attacks of certain rebels. The self-defense of the oppressed is presented as provocation. In reality, Macedonia's Bulgarian population is being martyred. The Greeks, who lay claim to the land, often unfortunately support the Turks. The rebellious flock that has sprung up across

1. Brandes would address Romania's Jewish persecution in the following year; see "The Agony of a People and Utopias" in the present volume.

2. Slavi Merdjanov (1876–1901) was an anarchist activist and member of the terrorist organization known as the Boatmen of Salonika. In 1901, after a lengthy firefight with Turkish forces, he and his comrades were apprehended and later hanged in Adrianople. The Turkish practice of posing for photographs with the severed heads of insurgents was widespread in both Macedonia and, more infamously, Armenia. Manastir (now known by its Macedonia name of Bitola) was at the center of the organized Ilinden Uprising against Ottoman rule in 1903.

Macedonia has not formed itself on the command of a revolutionary committee. They have arisen of themselves in the simplest manner. One or another peasant whose wife has been raped before his eyes, while he was bound from behind, or whose children have been subjected to torture for hours so that that they would scream things they do not know or will not say, or who himself has received bastinado until death was near, form up a band of fellow sufferers to go out and take revenge. One or another shepherd, whose herd has been carried off by the Bashi-bazouks and who owns nothing other than his rifle, which he has buried at a place in the woods for safety, gathers a little host of other desperate men around him.[3] More frequently still it is a young teacher or doctor, who is being sought after by the Turkish police and who flees up into the mountains, because he prefers death over the torture that surely awaits him in prison. Around him gather a half score or so who are persecuted or threatened like him, young men who have been chained or whipped to blood like all the suspected who have fallen into the hands of the Turks. Who can wonder that they become savage when they have escaped torture! Five peasants in the village of Ekshi Su and the teacher Natsev in Zelemitshe, in order to force confessions from them, were after bastinado subjected to that form of torture that consists of the skull being pressed together with tongs until it groans. Thereafter they were buried to their necks in filth, remained in this condition for three days, and then hung up with heads pointed downward. Two of them died from that; the four others were led to Manastir and escaped.

Such events take place literally every day of the year across the whole land of Macedonia.

That the newspaper *The Macedonian Struggle* has not come out in the last few weeks must surely be explained by the fact that the country is now in flames.

Through the Austrian newspaper *Die Zeit* we have been informed of the most important events in the Macedonian issue in recent times.

Major-General Ivan Tsonchev of the Bulgarian general staff has recently sought his dismissal as general in order to take the lead of the Macedonian rebellion into his own hands.[4] He had fought with distinction in the Serbian-Bulgarian War. The government, which was forced by diplomacy to do its part to limit the spread of the rebellion, made him stay put in Drenovo, the city of his birth. And when he attempted to flee clad as a peasant, he was recognized in Sofia, picked up, and again confined to Drenovo. Now he has again fled

3. Bashi-bazouks were irregular troops of the Ottoman Empire, widely known for cruelty and plunder.

4. General Ivan Tsonchev (1858–1910), in defiance of his own cautious government, would eventually make it to Macedonia, where he was a commander in the Ilinden Uprising.

from there to Macedonia and has explained his actions in a letter to *Die Zeit* of the eighth of October. His letter begins: "The festival days in Schipka Pass are now over. There and in Sofia everything has been said that could be said and much more at that."

And he scoffs at the patriots who wait for the roasted dove to fly into their mouths.

> Now the moment has come in which the Bulgarian people and the Bulgarian government, even against their will, must turn their gaze to the south, where daily hundreds are sacrificed in the name of freedom and humanity. These men, who have pledged themselves to certain death, are animated neither by the long-buried San Stefano peace stipulations nor by the ideal, a Greater Bulgaria. They have only the single thought of shaking off the ignominious tyranny and winning for themselves the human rights that were "secured" for them a quarter century ago (at the Congress of Berlin in 1878).[5] . . . The Bulgarian government and the subordinate Bulgarian press can distort the facts as they will, but it is incontestable that now the Macedonian slaves have arisen with weapons in hand. The end of this bloody drama one can already now predict with certainty; it will be the complete destruction of the Christians in Macedonia and in the *vilayet* of Adrianople.[6] But out of the bones of the victims there will arise an avenger. . . . Public opinion and public conscience will inspire courage in this unequal struggle.

Thus speaks a man who heroically has placed himself at the head of all the scattered rebellious bands.

It is instructive to compare his language with that of the official proclamation issued from Constantinople a week later:

> According to telegraphic messages from Ibrahim Pasha, from the commander of the 9th division in Serres, the commander of the 3rd corps, and from the Vali in Salonika, Bulgarian bands from Razlog and Djuma Bala entered Macedonia and forced the Bulgarian population to side with them. The inhabitants of other villages fled from fear up into the mountains. Thereafter Ibrahim Pasha with a sufficient number of troops received permission to pursue the bandits, which

5. The 1878 Treaty of San Stefano between Russia and the Ottoman Empire established the autonomous principality of Bulgaria, but it was nullified by the Treaty of Berlin later that year, which returned Macedonia to Ottoman rule. It is also important to note that not all the Macedonian rebels sought a "Greater Bulgaria," but some instead sought an independent Macedonian state.

6. The Ottoman Empire was divided into numerous vilayets (provinces).

> was energetically carried out according to plan. The bandits were partly destroyed and partly captured or broken up. The majority of the refugee population is now beginning to turn back and to surrender their weapons. Those who for fear of punishment do not dare to return are to be made to understand by the local authorities and clergy that all who request pardon shall receive it.

How this pardon will turn out becomes obvious when one reads the article titled "The Revolt of 17 October" by Stoyan Mikhailovsky, chairman of the Macedonian-Adrianople Committee.[7] It begins: "The period of bloody acts of violence has begun again in Turkey. In the districts of Dshuma, Maleshevo, Melnik, and others, women and children are being shot down by Bashi-bazouks and the regular troops."

The first thing the Turkish troops do when they arrive in a Macedonian village is to demand that all weapons be surrendered. If one is fearful enough to surrender them, the soldiers begin to plunder. However, the arrival of the rebel bands in a village is also a misfortune for it. For support of them is avenged by the Turkish troops, and the rebels cut down without mercy every fellow Christian in whom they see or suspect a spy. Thus lives an unfortunate population under a true horror regime.

And the battle between the soldiers and the guerilla bands itself is conducted with a passion and a contempt for death uncommon in the history of war. In Kadino near Perlepe a little flock of rebels was surprised by the Turks in an old tower. They defended themselves there a whole day and part of the night, and when they had used up their supply of powder and bullets they killed themselves with potassium cyanide. When the Turks entered the tower at daybreak they found seven corpses. The group's chieftain was Metody Patchev, a young teacher in Okrida, full of life, energetic, highly talented, who was known for his views of Turkish hegemony, and who had been sentenced to three years of imprisonment for committing murder, even though he had proved his alibi.[8] When he came out of prison, where he had gotten to know other men who were incarcerated just as unjustly as he himself, he had only the single desire of avenging himself upon their torturers. He met his death in the effort. I wonder if it will go that way for all the other leaders?

I wonder if we will come to see the Macedonians share the fate of the Armenians?

---

7. Stoyan Mikhailovsky (1856–1927) was a Bulgarian poet and leader of the Supreme Macedonia-Adrianople Committee, founded in 1895.

8. Metody Patchev (1875–1902) was prominent in the Internal Macedonian-Adrianople Revolutionary Committee, founded in 1893.

CHAPTER 9

The Agony of a People and Utopias

1903

This rather sprawling essay, occasioned by the appearance of Theodor Herzl's utopian novel *Altneuland* in 1902, represents Brandes's first critical engagement with the young Zionist movement then gathering momentum across Europe. As indicated elsewhere, Brandes always exercises a surprising measure of restraint in his advocacy on behalf of Europe's Jews, largely as a means of forestalling his many critics from attributing any kind of ulterior motive to his human rights work. It is thus likely a conscious decision on his part to refrain from providing the kind of excruciating detail that is elsewhere such a prominent feature of his work regarding the unhappy fate of the Jews of Romania, then along with Russia the very center of antisemitic oppression. Of particular significance here is Brandes's remarkably acute identification of the hidden intent of the famous Hay letter of 1902, which anticipates the contemporary efforts of European governments to stem the tide of Syrian refugees. Brandes's rather conflicted views on the Zionist project, presented in sketch form here, are further elaborated in the essay "Zionism" in the present volume.

~

Young Americans, who are full of the North American Free States' great mission of the future, gladly assert as a sign of the times the diplomatic communiqué that Secretary of State Hay sent last August 11 to the United States' representatives to the powers who signed the treaty in Berlin in 1878, which sets out the reasons that have moved the Free States to address the Romanian government.[1] North America urgently beseeches the Romanians to no longer deny citizenship and therefore human rights to native-born Jews living in the kingdom. The North American government portrays for the major powers

Originally published in *Politiken*, January 26, 1903. Translated from the version published in *Samlede Skrifter*, vol. 17.

1. John Milton Hay (1838–1905), US Secretary of State from 1898 until his death, was a fairly reliable ally of American and European Jewry. His 1902 letter to the Romanian government and his ensuing diplomatic communique to the European powers was followed a year later by vigorous protest against Russian state complicity in the Kishinev Pogrom.

the undeserved and hopeless misery into which those who have fled from Romania have sunk upon their arrival in the Free States, and reports that this misery has made it impossible for America to receive these immigrants in the future, no matter how great the Free States' forbearance had been until now.

This letter to Romania and the note to the powers that explains it has, however, apparently two sides, one side theoretical—North America appeared as the spokesperson for tolerance and humanity—and one side practical—North America sought to rid itself of an influx of helpless, penniless people, to close off for them their last place of refuge. In this way the majority of events in grand politics have a double countenance.

In the meantime the misery in Romania grows from week to week; the new tradesman law has brought the Jewish population to despair, and once again they think only of getting over the border at any cost, from which as a rule they are again and again driven back.[2]

Since conditions in the Russian kingdom, where probably about three-quarters of all existing Jews are living, are not particularly better, it is no wonder that the harassed East European Jews cling to the idea of Zionism. It is hardly an exaggeration to say that in Russia, as in Galicia and Romania, the hope of founding a new, free, happy society on Palestinian land enchants the masses of the highest born and most romantically inclined among the younger generation. Everyone who has come into contact with these youths while traveling will have experienced this enthusiasm. In all probability Palestine will in fact in the course of the twentieth century be cultivated and populated with the goal in view of providing a place of refuge for the despairing and the exiled, a people's *stronghold.* The society that has formed itself under the name of the Jewish Company had already by the end of 1900 a sum of twelve million pounds sterling collected for this purpose.[3]

In our age oppressed peoples come to speak of such plans as a physical necessity. While the Armenian revolutionaries in London at the beginning of the 1890s, young and indignant as they were, overlooked the dangers, imagining the possibility of improving their countrymen's position with efforts at rebellion, there were at that time Armenians of another mind, who dreamed of the establishment of a national fund that would be used to purchase the uncultivated stretches of the Mohammedan properties that had come up for

2. The Romanian government passed the Law of the Guilds, which banned Jewish tradesmen from practicing their crafts, in May 1902. See I. C. Butnaru, *The Silent Holocaust: Romania and Its Jews* (New York: Greenwood, 1992), 23.

3. The concept of the Jewish Company was envisioned by Zionist activist Theodor Herzl (1860–1904) in his *Der Judenstaat* (1896); it would come to fruition in the founding of the Jewish National Fund in 1901.

sale around the Armenian belt in Cilicia. In this way the Armenian people would little by little find themselves in a strategic position resembling that of Montenegro. They would then have a firm foothold in the Mohammedan lands, and from the base in Zeitun and Hadjin, the tide of the Armenian settlement would perhaps little by little overflow in the direction of Adana, Mersina, and the gulf by Alexandrette. They hoped that the Armenians would then gradually become the majority there, and when they first got access to a port they would of course be in continual connection to Europe. The terrible mass murders from 1894 to 1896 made these plans into nothing.[4]

Jewish plans of a similar kind have had better success. The large colonization bank for Palestine has been established, and not a few settlements have been founded and are thriving; there are Zionist gatherings held every year in Basel.[5] Recently the attention of the public has once again been strongly drawn to the undertaking, since the originator of Zionism, Dr. Theodor Herzl, has published the novel *The Old New Land*, which in poetic form—evidently to more easily gain a foothold for the ideas—details the Zionist program as if it had been realized.

The outline of the story is quite simple. Friedrich Löwenberg, a young Jewish law student in Vienna who sees all roads closed to him and whose beloved has just expressed a preference for an insipid rich suitor whom she knows not at all, is about to give up when he reads this announcement in a newspaper: "Seeking an educated, desperate young man who is prepared to take one last chance at life."

A rich man weary of Europe seeks a companion for a stay on an unpopulated island in the South Seas. After taking the time to help a Jewish family living in the most wretched poverty out of its agony, he then departs with his new benefactor. On the way they call at Jaffa and visit Palestine, which they find devastated, neglected, and impassable. But when after a twenty-year sojourn outside of civilization they turn back and come to Haifa, everything is changed. The anchorage between Akka and the foot of Mt. Carmel is full of huge ships, and the coast is covered with splendid villas. The mountain is crowned by gleaming buildings, and the soil seems a single garden.

Immediately upon landing they are by a fortunate coincidence received by the very same Jewish boy whom Löwenberg had helped before leaving Vienna, and who has now grown into an unusually capable and influential man. Through him we get to know in entirety the new Palestine.

4. See "Armenia" and "Armenia and Europe" in the present volume for Brandes's commentary on the Hamidian Massacres.

5. The First Zionist Congress, initiated by Herzl, took place in 1897.

It has become the model land among the world's countries, the midpoint for all trade between Europe and Asia, a country that has appropriated all the discoveries and lessons of the nineteenth century. Without the troubling ballast of the past, it has emerged anew as an independent and entirely prejudice-free civil society without a state, where all progress is carried out, all the beautiful dreams of the future are realized, and utopia has become the daily bread. All religious faiths thrive here gently, side by side with each other; society peacefully rules itself, freely chooses its spokespeople, all the way up to the highest, but is saddled with no state apparatus and only pays the Turkish government a yearly tribute.

The novel describes how bit by bit, step by step, the new state of affairs has developed out of the old. Businessmen and practical types familiar with Eastern conditions must judge how much of what is presented here could actually be achieved, not in just twenty years, as it happens in the novel, but in a hundred years, for in so great a matter the question of time is after all not the most important. Dr. Herzl placed on his title page the words: "If you will it, it is no dream," and only the well-informed have the right to call him a fantast or a prophet. It is, however, at any rate remarkable that in his book the Turkish government, indeed even the Turkish suzerainty, has made itself invisible, is conspicuous in its absence. It has in this utopia gently pulled back so as not to disturb; likewise with Christian Europe. The Turkish government has in reality done no such thing; it has refused to sell Palestine to the Jews.

Yet the significance does not lay in the numerous obstacles in the way of the Zionists' plans, but in the fact that millions of hungry and intelligent people have been brought to feel themselves a nation. It will go with Zionism as with socialism; the movement will reveal itself to be more significant than the goal. Even though the socialist future state fades more and more out of view, the movement has been able to organize a class, and although the Zionist future state will not be realized, the movement has given the masses courage and substance. There is, however, always a possibility that a kind of Jewish culture could still some day develop inside this narrow strip of land, and at that a modern culture.

For the time being the various peoples, tribes, and creeds are occupied with making life miserable for one another. While the Turkish method employs torture and murder with greater frankness, the German method in accordance with their higher level of culture proceeds almost exclusively through language suppression, and it must be said that therein the highest virtuosity and the most extreme consequences are achieved. Last week all Polish language instruction was forbidden by Berlin. All Polish children's schools were already banned three years ago, and now a ban has followed for all instruction in the Polish language for adults.[6] The provincial teaching staff who had been delegated the decision by the president of the police, and who have been informed that "young people under twenty years" have ventured to seek instruction in language teaching and continuing education, have allowed the last educational institute to close.

That is of course nothing in comparison to what is happening in Sasun or in Jassy. But it is something nonetheless.[7]

6. See "Contemporary Civilization" and "The Women of Poland" in the present volume for Brandes's commentary on the Germanization program in German Poland.

7. Brandes here refers to the 1894 Turkish suppression of the Armenian uprising in Sasun (modern Sason) and to Romanian antisemitic persecution in its second-largest city (Iași in Romanian).

CHAPTER 10

Armenia and Europe

1903

The publication of his 1900 essay "Armenia" at the behest of the activists Avetis and Mariam Nazarbekian established Brandes among the small group of European activist intellectuals speaking out on behalf of the Armenian people. The following Berlin speech of 1903 differs from the earlier essay in a number of important respects. In the first place, Brandes has considerably focused his critique, here zeroing in on the essential role of the German Reich in preventing any kind of meaningful intervention on the part of the major powers. While Brandes hardly excuses France and England for the relative ineffectiveness of their efforts at isolating the Turks, the increasingly close relations between the kaiser and the sultan are singled out for special scrutiny; it was in fact in 1903 that construction on the Berlin-Baghdad railway would begin. In the second place, the speech of 1903 is evidently marked by a relative sense of measured optimism regarding the potential effectiveness of agitation within the public sphere to bring about substantive change. Largely absent is the resignation and pessimism of the earlier essay, for now Brandes clearly sees a viable pathway toward real reform, namely the mobilization of German public opinion against the state's enabling of the Turks. Finally, the Berlin speech differs from the earlier essay with respect to the degree of indignation and outrage evident in many of its passages. It is clear that Brandes now believes that the stakes have been raised in Eastern Anatolia, an observation that sadly would prove itself prophetic some twelve years later.

~

Speech Delivered in Berlin on February 2, 1903

The fact that I am among the European writers who have earliest lifted their voices for Armenia, earliest have attempted to draw attention to the most terrible and most shocking national tragedy in recent times, explains why I

Speech delivered on February 2, 1903. Originally published in *Tilskueren* (1903). Translated from the version published in *Samlede Skrifter*, vol. 17.

have the honor of being asked to speak here tonight by the Armenian Student Union in Europe.

I am not inclined to overestimate a simple author's spoken words and know well enough that in questions of grand politics the decision lies with those in power. But even those in power are in our days compelled to consider a strong and unanimously expressed public opinion, and it is therefore a matter of crying out until such a public opinion awakens in all countries.

This is especially the case in the German Reich.

All of you know that Turkish Armenia in the last ten years has been the scene for such horrors that documented world history hardly speaks of anything comparable even from the roughest of ages. Nobody had believed, before we had experienced it, that it was possible that a whole population could in this way become the object of extortion, torture, and mass murder. The blood of hundreds of thousands cries out to the heavens.

I know that Turkey is united with Germany as a friendly power. Precisely this has given the Turkish government free reign. I will not devote a syllable to discussing the personality of the sultan.[1] But the friendship that is his good fortune cannot prevent a spokesman for humanity from coming before the German public.

Hungary is by virtue of mutual heritage and tradition stretching back over centuries united in friendship with Turkey. No less a brave advocate of Armenia's cause than Pierre Quillard created a stir in Budapest when he recently, in the middle of December, laid out the facts of Armenia's recent history for the Hungarians.[2]

The German people stand much farther from Turkey than the Magyars, and they are as a whole much mightier. An awakening of public opinion in Germany for the Armenian cause would perhaps now have some decisive meaning.

Since the Armenians have little more for themselves than their misfortune, it has been impossible to deny them sympathy. They have suffered, almost unspeakably so, let alone in a manner that may be described, because the listener would turn away his ear. It is said that 300,000 lives have been extinguished, in part because of acts of violence, in part because of hunger and cold; this only makes a meager impression, for it does not set the power of the imagination in motion.

1. As previously mentioned (see "Armenia," note 5), Brandes nourished a special hatred for Abdul Hamid II.

2. Quillard, as noted in "Armenia," note 13, was the preeminent advocate for Armenia in France at the time.

Of what use is it, for example, to announce that in August 1894 in the villages around Muş the site of a mass murder was found that had lasted three weeks; that men, women, and children were cut down indiscriminately; that everywhere there was violence against women before they died, that at first more than two hundred, then three hundred women at a time were violated by the soldiers before they were murdered with bayonets and sabers.[3]

Of what use is it to report what a German traveler witnessed while in Kendránz: the Kurds had told each other to rape every female being from a five-year-old child on up![4] Or to say: at another place upward of 300 women and girls were locked in a little church, delivered to the soldiers and finally murdered by them! A stream of blood ran out under the door of the church.

If one would make an unforgettable impression one must go into the domain of the individual. That a hundred thousand have been murdered makes less of an impression than describing how a single individual was killed. A woman fell on her knees and beseeched the soldiers to spare her life; in reality, two lives. "Is it a boy or a girl?" shouted the soldiers, "Let us see!" And they split open her abdomen. The person who tells this story can provide all the circumstances and name the names of witnesses. At another place the Kurds have bet on whether they could with a single blow cut off the heads of four small children, and have done so before the eyes of the mother.

On the first day of the bloodbath in Trebizond an Armenian came out of a bakery where he had bought bread for his sick wife and his children.[5] He was surprised by a rampaging gang. He begged for mercy. They made a show not to do him any harm. He believed it and thanked them sincerely. But they were only having fun with him. They bound his feet together. They cut off his hand and hit him in the face with it. Then they cut the other hand off. They then asked him to make the sign of the cross, while others requested that he scream louder, so that his God could hear him. One cut off his ears, stuck

3. One of the early Hamidian massacres, the mass killings outside the city of Muş were a part of a campaign of reprisal against the Sasun Rebellion. During the catastrophe of 1915 the entire Armenian population of the region would be liquidated.

4. Brandes here cites Paul Rohrbach, *Vom Kaukasus zum Mittelmeer* (Leipzig: B. G. Teubner, 1903), 74, as his source, although it should be noted that Rohrbach, for all his (by no means consistent) support of the Armenians, represents views diametrically opposed to those of Brandes. Rohrbach is better remembered today as the principal theorist of German colonialism, who maintained the right of Europeans to displace and even exterminate African peoples. For more on Rohrbach's racial views, see Karl A. Yambert's entry in *Modern Genocide: The Definitive Resource and Document Collection*, ed. Paul R. Bartrop and Steven Leonard Jacobs (Santa Barbara, CA: ABC-CLIO, 2015), 1:1074–75.

5. The mass killings in Trebizond (now Trabzond) in the fall of 1895 were unusual in the fact that no local "pretext" whatsoever was available to attempt to justify the atrocities.

them first in his mouth and then threw them in his face. Another yelled: the Effendi's mouth must be punished because it has refused such a delicacy. And they cut out his tongue. Now he can longer engage in blasphemous speech. With the tip of a dagger one popped his eye out of the socket. His dreadfully twisted face, the spasms of his wretched body made these fanatics still wilder; they also popped out the other eye and chopped the feet off him before they gave him the mercy thrust with a dagger to the throat.

(Many women cry; others stand up; not a few leave the hall.)

In a report from the English consulate in Erzurum a scene from the village of Semál is described, somewhat before the bloodbath.[6] The Armenian Azó had refused to inform against some of the locale's best men. The judge Talib Effendi and two Turkish captains therefore allowed him to be tortured the whole night through. First he got the bastinado. Then they bound him naked with arms outstretched on two beams and the whipping began. The unfortunate man could not move a limb; the convulsions in his face revealed his sufferings. The more he screamed, the more they struck. He beseeched his torturers to kill him. He tried to smash his skull to pieces against the beams. That was stopped. When he would still not give witness against his own, would not besmirch himself with innocent blood, Talib first had the hair of his beard ripped out with tongs, then had his body prodded with glowing irons, burned him on the hands, in the face, on the feet, and on still other parts of his body. With a glowing tong they burned his tongue. Three times he fainted, but he remained steadfast. In the neighborhood his wife and his children, hearing his cries of pain, were stiffened with horror.

And now to the conditions in the prisons, for example in Bitlis, where the prisoners, who were crammed together in the hundreds and at times could neither lay down nor sit in the dreadful filth, were additionally subjected to hunger and torture.[7]

I am aware of and have felt it: you have been listening to me unwillingly. You have had to force yourself to refrain from screaming at me: enough! enough!

I have also noticed that many ladies have left the hall. It has been shocking for them to listen to this. I ask them to multiply the horrors I have reported to them by many hundreds of thousands and to keep this in mind:

What Berlin ladies have been unable to stand to hear, the Armenians have endured a hundred-thousand-fold.

---

6. The massacre in Erzurum occurred some three weeks after the initial outbreak of violence in Eastern Anatolia in Trebizond.

7. Conditions in Bitlis Prison rivaled those of Acre in infamy.

It has happened in our times, in the last decade, about four or five days' journey from here—and we have allowed it to happen, have not done anything to prevent it.

For a long time Europe was warned. The preparations for the murder in Sasun were carried out so openly that the English consul in Erzurum requested protection for the Armenian population in a long report.[8] England would "not involve itself in a friendly power's internal affairs." That is always the response.

None of these pleas were heard. After Europe was no longer in ignorance, the horrible state continued still longer. The Armenians were still constantly denied their freedom, plundered, abused, cut down one by one or in groups.

I could provide examples in the hundreds. I name one: on the third of July 1900, five hundred Kurds surrounded the village of Spaghank. With bullets, sabers, and bayonets they went at it. Women and children ran to meet the soldiers beseechingly. The small children who were still alive were lifted up in the air, screaming, on the tips of bayonets; the women were undressed, violated, murdered. Both sides of the mouth of the eighty-year-old village priest were slowly split and his jaws ripped out. The belly of a pregnant woman, Timene, who was married to the parish supervisor, was cut open; the child was cut to pieces and the woman was killed with fifty cuts of the knife.[9]

We have always known that our culture is not without its atrocities, those of the single individual or the predatory lust and blood deeds of the criminal gang. As awful as that can be, it does not seem to us evidence against our belief in the heights to which our culture has climbed.

We have likewise always known that our culture, even in our most civilized countries, is not without social misfortune, poverty, and neglect of the poor. But even the misery of the most wretched does not speak against the elevation of our contemporary culture.

We have always known what war brings out in us, how it inflames the passions, what horrors it engenders. But we do not conduct wars today as they were conducted in earlier times. The leaders of armies only reluctantly do harm to the peaceful population; women and children are involved only in certain conditions of war, for example when cities are bombarded. Neither does war speak against our certainty that we have reached a very high level of civilization.

Even though we therefore must admit to frequent crimes, social injustice and cruelty, racial hatred and religious hatred, the horror of war, so there are

---

8. Such pleas for intervention were sent to the European capitals from diplomats and private citizens all over the Ottoman Empire.

9. Brandes here cites Quillard's *Pour l'Arménie* (Paris: Cahiers, 1902), 4, as his source.

always misdeeds left over, which in our day seem to us unthinkable and which are stamped as belonging to antiquity or the Middle Ages.

We must stop this. After Europe has failed to hinder the horrors that were set in motion in Armenia and now today also in Macedonia, it is impossible to assert that our age may claim any meaningful superiority over history's darkest eras.[10]

But the Armenians are one of the world's oldest civilized nations with nearly 4,000 years of history, and have at that done civilization itself a great service in their own country and still more outside of it.

Like the Poles, the Armenians are divided between three great powers.[11] They are under the thumb of Russia, Persia, and Turkey, whose three languages the educated among the people not rarely master in addition to their own, while they often furthermore understand and speak a European language.

This is one of the peoples of the East that has most acquired European humaneness; it has, as one if its best sons, Arshag Chobanian, has said, been "the vanguard of European civilization in Asia."[12]

Although this country, which is located on the road of Asia's conqueror peoples, has time and again been inundated with and subjugated by foreigners (all the way back in antiquity from Assyrians to Medes to Arabs), it has exhibited a quite unusual spirit of resistance, and almost as great a spirit to assimilate the foreigner in its midst. The Parthian kings, who ruled Armenia from the second century before Christ, had become Armenians. It seems as if the remarkable kings of the house of Bagratruni who followed them were in part Armenian Jews, although the matter is not clear since in that time it was seen as an honor to descend from the House of David.

From the earliest time the Armenians have reconciled themselves to foreign peoples, providing them with great men. In the Byzantine Empire the Armenians were prominent warriors, stimulating thinkers, and more than a half score of the emperors were of Armenian descent. In the Turkish Empire they maintained their position as a dynamic element; they excelled at commerce and distinguished themselves as artists, businessmen, and statesmen. Nubar Pasha, who long governed Egypt, was an Armenian, as was the Russian statesman and general Loris-Melikov.[13]

---

10. See the essay on Macedonia from the previous year in the present volume.

11. The fate of partitioned Poland was a cause equally as dear to Brandes; see his many essays and speeches in the present volume.

12. Arshag Chobanian (1872–1954) was one of the principal figures of modern Armenian literature, as well as a dedicated activist on behalf of his people.

13. Both Nubar Nubarian Pasha (1825–99) and Count Mikhail Tarielovich Loris-Melikov (1826–88) were indeed of Armenian descent.

When the Armenian people became the first to adopt Christianity, their old heathen poetry was largely lost.[14] Not just the ancient temples, but also the poetry that exalted gods and heroes was destroyed. We have only fragments left that bear witness to their lyrical talents, and yet these are sufficient enough to revive the pantheon of Armenian gods. They have neither the Asiatic gods' warrior attitude nor the Greek gods' beauty; they are, like the people who begat them, industrious, sober, and good.

Also in the country's rich old architecture is found a mix of Assyrian and Persian forms with a Hellenic style.

Christianity became for the Armenians a new cultural element, and a national one. When the Armenians lost their political independence, the church became the emblem and the guardian of the national tradition, much as it later would be in Poland.

Literature now became in part historical, in part strongly ecclesiastical, consisting of religiously colored chronicles and mystical poems, but it retained a dark and singular poetry. Golden hymns came to light. A significant place in the canon was occupied by Movses Khorenatsi's poetic and ardent historical writing; he had studied in Greece and knew the *Iliad*.[15] He praises the courage of the heroes. And he loves his land. He has glorified the marvelous beauty of the area round Van, which was chosen by Semiramis as her summer residence: "In a land," she said, "where the climate is so mild and the air so pure, we must build a city and a royal castle so as to dwell in all that splendor."

Another famous historian from ancient times, Yeghishe, who has told of the Armenians' war against the Persians, in a famous excerpt praises Armenian women, who have always displayed a rare courage—most recently some years ago in Sasun, when fifty young women threw themselves into a chasm so as not to fall into the hands of the Turks, and in Palu, where thirty for the same reason leapt into the Euphrates while singing a hymn.[16] Yeghishe has described the gravity and the renunciation of the widows during the hard times of war.

A chronicle authored by Aristakes Lastivertsi tells of the invasion of the Tatars and the Persians and describes Armenia, already 900 years ago, as "naked,

---

14. Armenian contact with Christianity began in the first century CE; it was adopted as the state religion in 301.

15. Movses Khorenatsi (fifth century CE), the "Armenian Herodotus," was the author of the first historical chronicle of the Armenian kings.

16. Yeghishe Vardapet (410–75 CE) was an important source of inspiration for Armenian resistance into the twentieth century. Stories of martyred Armenian women are found all over the literature and the folklore of the genocide.

lying by the edge of the road, tread under foot by all peoples, hounded out of home, like prisoners and slave women."[17]

From the fifteenth through the nineteenth centuries the spirit of the Armenian people was completely oppressed and destroyed. Only the church stood upright. In the monasteries the old manuscripts slumbered.

A monk by the name of Mekhitar, who saw that a fertile ground for Armenian intellectual life could not be allowed to develop in Turkey, brought the worthiest manuscripts to Venice, where he founded the monastery of San Lazzaro, which served as a kind of Armenian university and in which Lord Byron began to learn the Armenian language.[18]

This monastery's inhabitants performed an immense labor as translators and in this way made their countrymen familiar with all of Europe's new and old literary treasures, from Homer through Jean Racine and Vittorio Alfieri to Friedrich Schiller.

Now modern instead of ancient Armenian began to be employed in literature, the consequence of which was the great flowering of Armenian intellectual life in the nineteenth century. Young men who returned home from Europe brought with them the fruits of European Romanticism, founding a national theater in Constantinople. Poets such as Gabriel Sundukian and later Avetis Nazarbekian have in their plays attacked philistinism and prejudice among their countrymen with wit and passion.[19]

The spirit of 1848 was planted in the mountains of Armenia. The Armenian national soul became steadily more Europeanized. From the influence of the Russian novel and the German social democratic movement a second Armenian literature emerged, awakening the people to rebellion against Turkish injustice. Nalbandian gave the Armenian people their song of freedom.[20]

The talented Raffi wrote his novel *Jalaledin*, which was translated into French and German and which describes conditions in Armenia in the year 1877, providing a gripping picture of the people's martyrdom at that time (and now).[21]

---

17. Aristakès Lastivertsi (1002–80) was the author of *History Regarding the Sufferings Occasioned by Foreign Peoples Living around Us* (ca. 1072–79), trans. Robert Bedrosian (New York: n.p., 1985), https://archive.org/details/AristakesLastivertsisHistory.

18. Mkhitar Sebastatsi (1676–1749), the most important figure in the preservation of Armenian antiquity, was founder of the Mekhitarist Order, and was beatified in 1914.

19. Gabriel Sundukian (1825–1912) was the founder of modern Armenian theater. For more on Nazarbekian, see "Armenia" in the present volume.

20. "Mer Hayrenik," the national anthem of Armenia, is based on a poem by Mikael Nalbandian (1829–66).

21. Hakob Melik Hakobian (1835–88, popularly known as Raffi) was a major figure in nineteenth-century Armenian literature.

That which we have recently experienced of horrors, attacks, and acts of violence, all of the figures of misery, those who have been impaled on stakes, those who have been martyred in glowing iron—all this is already found here.

The novel seems almost like a letter that has been written from the scenes of catastrophe from 1894–96.

Nazarbek's *Through the Storm*, published in English, handles in novel form the Armenian Uprising, which brought forth horrors and became the occasion for new horrors.

During their long period of intellectual slumber, the folk song always remained fresh, and no people has modern folk songs like the Armenians, the exile's song of complaint, the beloved's passionate verse.

A generation grew up that was at the same time well familiar with ancient Armenia and that, modern minded, registered protest against the injustice of the government and the cruelties of the Kurds.[22]

In this way the Patriarch Nerses could send men with written authority on behalf of the Armenians to the Congress of Berlin.[23] And he found success, obtaining article 61, which seemed to secure the Armenians' future. To this day every friend of Armenia must cling to the unfulfilled promises of that article.

Europe seemed to have taken an oppressed people under its protection.

Unfortunately the participation of the powers was not serious. And the mere fact that the Armenians had dared to approach Europe sharpened the Turkish government's bitterness against them to the utmost.

The Armenian theater in Constantinople was closed, instruction in Armenia's history, gatherings, parties, speeches, and so on banned. The press was subjected to the severest censorship. Imprisonments and persecutions began to occur more frequently than before. The Kurds were organized against the Armenians as cavalry regiments under the name Hamidiye.[24] The sultan gave these irregular troops his name and set them loose on their unfortunate neighbors to plunder them and cut them down.

When the Armenians began to offer resistance at many points, permission was granted for the mass torture and murder of this infidel Christian population.

---

22. Brandes here cites Archag Tchobanian, *L'Arménie, son Historie, sa Littérature, son role en Orient—Poëms Arméniens, traduits par A. Tchobanian* (Paris: Cinquième, 1897).

23. Article 61 provided reassurances from the Turkish state regarding the Armenian minority, as well as similar promises from Romania regarding its Jewish population.

24. Conceived as a border guard against Russia and modeled on the Cossacks, the Hamidiye after their founding in 1891 were employed largely to harass and oppress the Armenian population.

At the Congress of Berlin the Ottoman government had pledged to introduce the necessary reforms, ensure the safety of the Armenians against the Circassians and the Kurds, and from time to time give an account to the powers thereabout. The undersigning governments were granted the right to watch over the Turkish precautions.

For fifteen years Turkey put off the powers with empty words.

Emboldened by allied indifference, Turkey failed to introduce reforms, continuing to answer the earnest diplomatic inquiries from the English, Russian, and French legations while simultaneously arranging for a mass bloodbath. All of this was facilitated by the Germans, for even so enthusiastic a friend of the German fatherland as the well-informed traveler Paul Rohrbach confesses that the actions of the Turkish government were made possible by its "remarkable relationship to Germany."[25]

Turkey would have had to concede if all the major powers had presented a united front. It had been blockaded from all sides. But the friendly relationship with Germany gave it breathing room. The blockade to which it had been subjected was not effective.

It slipped through and could without vexation bring the Armenians to silence with bayonets and lances, with sharp sabers and glowing iron, with rape and conflagration.

No one will deny that individual Germans, women as well as men, have revealed themselves to be helpful in the aftermath of the most horrific events. German generosity has taken care of the orphaned children and let them be brought up. Everyone also is familiar with Eduard Bernstein's speech, and everyone knows that a man like Lepsius, who typically enough lost his priestly office over his efforts, has devoted himself to exposing to his countrymen the truth regarding Armenian conditions.[26]

---

25. Here again Brandes cites Rohrbach, *Vom Kaukasus*, 160, albeit this time with considerably more reserve.

26. Eduard Bernstein (1850–1932), a German Jewish social democratic politician and theorist, convened a meeting on Germany and Armenia in Berlin in 1902. He was among the first to recognize the alarming manner in which anti-Armenianism in his country borrowed heavily from antisemitic tropes. Like Brandes, he was among the earliest to sense in the Hamidian Massacres not the exception but the rule. For more on Bernstein, see Stefan Ihrig, *Justifying Genocide: Germany and the Armenians from Bismarck to Hitler* (Cambridge, MA: Harvard University Press, 2016), 79–80. Johannes Lepsius (1858–1926), a German Protestant missionary, was a tireless advocate of the Armenian people; Franz Werfel (1890–1945), the author of the 1933 Armenian Genocide novel *Die vierzig Tage des Musa Dagh*, would later refer to him as Armenia's "guardian angel." Lepsius's *Bericht über die Lage des armenischen Volkes in der Türkei* (1916) is considered to be among the most authoritative accounts of the catastrophe of 1915.

Nevertheless the last century's grossest political crimes would have been an impossibility without the warm relations between the German Reich and the Turkish cabinet. Therefore the important thing is to call forth public sentiment for the Armenian people, most of all in Germany.

In the famous old Icelandic saga a woman throws the completely blood-soaked cloak of her murdered husband around a relative, who is rather unprepared to be party to her cause, so as to move him to act as the avenger of the dead.[27] No one thinks of revenge here. But if it was possible to throw the cloak of the slain Armenian victims, quite stiff from blood, around the shoulders of the German people so as to move the German government to demand security and freedom for the survivors of the ancient, honorable, Armenian tribe, that would be a useful act.

27. Brandes is referring to *Njáls Saga*.

CHAPTER 11

Mano Negra

1903

The qualified success of the campaign to free Captain Dreyfus in the 1890s had awakened European public intellectuals to the power of the press in counteracting state-orchestrated miscarriages of justice. Some years later, in 1902 and 1903, many of the same old Dreyfusards, among them of course Brandes and Clemenceau, turned their attention to Spain, where twenty years previously the Andalusian authorities had executed one of history's more successful "false flag" operations against peasant day laborers attempting to organize a rural labor union. Employing the fictional pretext of the existence of an organized criminal gang—La Mano Negra—Spanish courts used capital punishment and life imprisonment en masse across the province. Some two decades later, the efforts of Spanish activist Soledad Gustavo alerted the European press to the fate of the eight alleged conspirators still suffering imprisonment and torture in Spanish prisons. As in the Dreyfus Affair, the campaign to free the falsely accused achieved a limited success, as eventually the Spanish government would commute the sentences of the La Mano Negra Eight from life in prison to exile. The essay is of particular interest because it is the sole example of Brandes engaging with what is in its essence state repression of *class* struggle rather than his usual preoccupation with national minorities and colonized peoples.

~

For a little more than a year now, the Spanish Worker's party has been aware of a breach of justice that has gradually come to the attention of the enlightened and progressive men of Europe, so that public meetings on the affair were conducted in Paris and twice in London in the month of February alone. From Spain the movement for the convicted innocents has reached France, from France Italy, and since then English, Belgian, and Dutch organs, Swiss newspapers, and a single German one, *Frankfurter Zeitung*, have lifted their

Originally published in *Politiken*, February 16, 1903. Translated from the version published in *Samlede Skrifter*, vol. 17.

voices in the cause, while at the same time those who work for the release of these unfortunates have turned to the men in Europe whom they think have an influence on public opinion, and have beseeched them to contribute to raising awareness of this event.

The honor of having first raised the issue belongs to a courageous and persevering Spanish woman, *Soledad Gustavo.*[1] But the movement has only become European since some of the foremost Frenchmen have taken it into their hands.[2]

Twenty years ago the Spanish press reported that a widespread criminal organization by the name of *Mano Negra* (*The Black Hand*) had been discovered.[3] It was accused of engaging in murder, thievery, and arson and it was argued that it could only be curtailed through mass imprisonment, including numerous capital and life sentences.

The recent conscientious research into the nature of the trials, which has relied heavily on the not insignificant number of letters that those involved in the affair yet still living have succeeded in smuggling out of their prisons, has revealed that La Mano Negra appears never to have existed. It owes its artificial life only to a ploy by the police and has played no other role than to provide a pretext for the oppression of the worker's organization and for the leading men among the workers, who because they appear most independent and therefore most dangerous to the local authorities are sentenced to either civil death or outright execution.

The country in which these events are taking place is Andalusia, celebrated by numerous romantic poets, a country that is in itself fertile, but whose land belongs to a landowning class that is idle and few in number. Thus a whole population of agricultural workers, which with difficulty sustain themselves on a paltry wage, are in danger of hunger again and again and therefore have fallen into despair, which has compelled them to organize themselves into unions to look after their interests.[4] These unions were like a thorn in the side of the ruling class that they would pluck out at any price. While the *International*

1. Teresa Mañé Miravet (1865–1939), who wrote under the pseudonym Soledad Gustavo, was a Catalonian feminist and anarchist activist.

2. Due to Gustavo's efforts, statements in support of the accused Mano Negro conspirators appeared across the French press in 1902 and 1903; many of these are collected in the 1903 illustrated pamphlet titled *La Mano Negra*, initiated by Georges Clemenceau and published by *Les Temps Nouveaux.*

3. Not to be confused with the better-remembered Serbian organization of the same name, reports of La Mano Negra activity began to appear in late 1882.

4. The Federación de Trabajadores de la Región Española, founded in Barcelona in 1881, inspired the day laborers of Andalusia to organize the following year.

was banned, the local unions were not, but still the commandant of the Guardia Civil in *Jerez de la Frontera* decided to crush them. This man, one Don *Tomás Pérez Monforte*, has driven a multitude of people into misfortune on the pretext of a few random killings and a few attacks and acts of arson, which happen at all times but especially in areas in which the population is agitated by hunger.[5]

Monforte's manner of action is best revealed by the testimony a simple yet educated worker named *Manuel Sanchez Alvarez* has sent to the Spanish newspaper *Tierra y Libertad*. He relates how one day when he was working in a vineyard he was summoned by a gendarme to the commandant in Jerez. After showing him courtesy, the don asked him to sit and offered him a cigar, before promising him four or five times the daily wage of the normal worker if he would give up the names and addresses of the politically most prominent workers, so that the police would know whom to persuade to set fire to a cornfield or to cut down the vines in one or another plantation. Monforte sent Alvarez home with a request to think his answer over carefully. The commandant had many ingratiating phrases: "We can speak together as a son speaks with his father, but just don't forget that I am the father!" Yet the next time, when Alvarez came to deliver his refusal, the commandant reminded him that he had the means to compel him. And thus a few months later began a trial for the setting fire of a cornfield and the cutting down of vines with thirty to forty accused, in which Alvarez was held twenty months on remand.

And so it was that *Mano Negra* went into action. None of those accused of belonging to it have ever revealed of what it consisted. The only certainty is that one day in Villamartin, one of the parishes in which the so-called "revolutionary" movement among agricultural workers was strongest, a black hand was seen two or three times imprinted on a wall—which in and of itself should not be seen as proving anything more than that somebody or other had dipped his fingers in a paint bucket. But Monforte asserted that this black hand was a symbol of the peasants' "secret justice," the goal of which was arson and the murder of the propertied class. This conjecture was confirmed when he himself and his captain, Oliver, "found under a stone the secret society's by-laws with a confession of all the crimes for which the members claimed responsibility; thievery, arson, and murder."[6] That such an exclusive society should hide its laws under a stone in a field was already a completely childish idea, but

5. Don Monforte concocted his plan in November 1882 and received extensive support from Madrid.

6. Don Monforte and Guardia Civil captain José Oliver y Vidal "found" the alleged cache of documents during the mass arrests at the end of 1882.

that it should set down a confession of its crimes was a whimsy that seems to rely on the public's credulity to much too high a degree. And yet it was believed. And from that moment the authorities had the means to tie all the labor unions in Andalusia to the sham criminal organization *Mano Negra*.

In reality the "liberal" governor in Cadiz issued an 1882 order in which, in violation of the constitution, he declared that all property damage and fires that are not demonstrably the result of accidents shall be seen as the work of the local people or lacking that *the local leadership of the so-called labor union*.

There followed three big court cases, the *Parilla* trial, the *Arcos* trial and the trial of *The Four Roads Public House*, all of which served the goal of destroying the worker's movement under the pretext of punishing a convicted murder.[7]

The Parilla trial was the one that garnered the most attention. A worker by the name of Bartolomeo Campos was beaten to death in December 1882 during a fight with his cousin Manuel Gago; both had been members of the local labor union, but Campos had been dismissed since there was displeasure with his relationship to another member's wife. This murder case surely had a purely private character. Although Gago had only one companion, no less than *one hundred* workers were jailed on the occasion, and the public prosecutor, Don *Manuel Azcutia*, demanded a sum total of *fifteen* death sentences. It is worthwhile to study his speech before the judge sentence by sentence.[8] One could search for a long time for a more disgusting exercise in official eloquence. For a critic this document is one of the most instructive of its kind. It ought to be published in a book that serves as rhetorical instruction as proof against all the errors a speaker ought to avoid. There is rarely an adjective that does not appear in the superlative, never a noun without a train of adjectives. Not a single subscription library cliché is spurned, no cheap effect is rejected. The style is this: "it concerns here the most hideous, the most dreadful, the most inhuman and most ungodly murder that has ever been recorded in the annals of crime, a murder which, carried out with most refined consideration, the cruelest treachery" and so on and so on.

The public prosecutor's whole effort went into proving that the local labor union and *Mano Negra* were one and the same criminal organization, a terror and a horror for the whole area. One of the accused, who in a now-publicized letter has testified to his innocence, went insane under torture and only after some time had passed regained his reason. Six were sentenced to a lifetime in

---

7. For more detailed information on these cases, see Clemenceau's essay (which serves as Brandes's principal source here), published in the pamphlet referenced in note 2.

8. Brandes cites from a report by Marcel Collière: "La Mano Negra," *La Revue Blanche* 30 (1903): 168–69.

chains. Seven were *garroted*, that is to say executed according to the method used in Spain, in which the victim is placed on a chair with back to a crossbar from which an iron shackle projects and which from behind is screwed around his neck.

The now-publicized letters from Antonio Valero, Jose Ortega, and Salvador Moreno, written respectively from the prisons in Gomora, Puerto de Santa Maria, and Alhucemas, are flat-out appalling documentations of this human injustice and history of brutality.

The two other trials were quite the same as the first, and the result is that still to this day eight of those left alive remain in Spanish prisons, some in Puerto de Santa Maria, some in Ceuta. These eight men have been punished for participation in the criminal conspiracy of *The Black Hand*—a conspiracy that never existed.

At the meeting in support of the innocent that was held on January 29 in Paris, Jaurès, with his customary eloquence, drew attention to how the Dreyfus Affair had opened contemporary eyes to the possibilities that the administration of justice contains.[9] With a reference to the double shackle in which the prisoner on Devil's Island was placed, he cried out, "How can we wonder that torture has been employed in the land of the Inquisition, when it has thus recently been employed in the land of the revolution! . . . This crime, which among us was carried out by the rulers, has radiated a magnificent clarity, the avenging truth, and will far across the world illumine both the victim's and the perpetrator's countenance."

In London the meetings for the innocent were held on February 7 in Athenaeum Hall and on February 14 in Liberty Hall (East End); furthermore there is contemplated a general popular meeting in Trafalgar Square.

In France Pierre Quillard and Georges Clemenceau wrote for the cause, in London Kropotkin spoke for it.[10]

The names of the eight, who for twenty years have innocently been shut up in chains, are these: Jose Ortega, Augustin Martinez, Antonio Valero, Salvador Moreno, Cristobal Gil, Diego Morales, Francisco Prieto, Jose Doblado.

---

9. A founding figure of the French Left, Jean Jaurès (1859–1914) was also an active Dreyfusard.

10. Symbolist poet Pierre Quillard (1864–1912) was already familiar to Brandes from his work on the Armenian question, while Clemenceau was a longtime friend and collaborator. Anarchist philosopher Petr Alekseevich Kropotkin (1842–1921), from his base in Geneva, had in fact spoken in favor of the accused while criminal proceedings against them were still underway in 1883.

CHAPTER 12

The Georgian People

1903

Of all the subject peoples of the Russian empire who began to assert themselves at the conclusion of the nineteenth century, Brandes was particularly impressed by the efforts of the Georgians, like the Armenians an ancient people with a long tradition of independence. Unlike his beloved Poles, whose alleged rashness in the face of intractable foreign domination he always criticized, the Georgian demands for autonomy were relatively modest and practical, as described below. The chaos in the Russian Empire that Brandes predicted would erupt only two years later, but the Georgians would have to wait until October 1917 for a brief foray into independence, which sadly lasted only a few years before Soviet reconquest. Lasting independence would finally come in 1991, but as the events of 2008 remind us, the status of independent Georgia remains contested to this day.

~

A human lifetime ago it could have seemed as if the class struggle would in the future replace the struggle of the nationalities. The class struggle rages everywhere in steadily expanding scope, but at the same time the tension between oppressor and oppressed peoples has in our day reached a pitch that in earlier times was hardly known.

Continuously new nationalities step forward before the European forum with their complaints. New not in the sense that these peoples represent some new nationality, for they belong to the Earth's oldest historical peoples, but in that they have suffered in silence for centuries. After the Poles come the Bulgarians, after the Bulgarians the Armenians, after the Armenians the Finns, after the Finns the Macedonians.

All of these peoples and numerous others strive through the publication of writings in the world languages to draw the attention of the European conscience. All of them have their regularly appearing organs, most often in French

Originally published in *Politiken*, June 29, 1903. Translated from the version published in *Samlede Skrifter*, vol. 17.

but also in English or German. The organ of the Russian refugees is in English; the Jewish Zionists publish in French and German; Poles, Armenians, Finns, and Macedonians each employ French.

Quite recently one of the small peoples, who like the Armenians and Jews look back on a history many thousands of years long, has gotten itself an organ in Paris and now strives to interest an indifferent Europe in its misfortune and its national endeavor.

These are the Georgian people.

Until the Russian government a hundred years ago, by virtue of a breach of faith and promises, declared Georgia to be a Russian province, the Georgian nation had from the most distant antiquity asserted its independence.[1] The first native-born Georgian king, Pharnavaz, reigned in the third century before our reckoning of time, and with the exception that the Georgians were overwhelmed by the Arab caliphs between the seventh and tenth centuries and by Mongol hordes in the thirteenth and fourteenth, this brave and gifted people, who by last count in 1897 numbered 2.5 million, have maintained themselves independently all the way to the year 1801.[2]

Georgia is the land that stretches south from the Caucasus between the Black and the Caspian Seas, a mountainous country with numerous rivers, a mild climate that permits the cultivation of wine, cotton, rice, tobacco, and tea and a wealth of minerals such as naphtha, coal, silver, and copper. The capital is Tiflis, in the language of the native-born Tbilisi, so called because of its warm springs, from the Georgian word *tbili* (warm). The land, roughly 26,000 square miles inside, makes up the two Russian *gouvernements* of Tiflis and Kutaisi. In the Georgian language the land is called Sakartvelo and the inhabitants the Kartveli. The language itself is so peculiar that it is seen by some of the learned as Aryan and by others as Turanian.[3]

This is the land that the ancient Greeks called Colchis, and when it was named the legend of Jason and Medea about the Golden Fleece and the Argonauts came to mind among a people who remembered the whole of the Hellenic mythological world. It also recalls the myth of Prometheus, who was stretched

1. Czar Paul I issued a formal order of annexation in 1800.

2. Pharnavaz I ruled the Kingdom of Kartli (known to the ancient Greeks as Iberia) from 299 to 234 BCE. After centuries of struggle to remain independent, the Persians formally abolished the monarchy in 580 CE, governing the country as a province until the Arab conquests began in the seventh century. Georgia was finally reunited under a single crown in 1008, after which it flourished until the arrival of the Mongols.

3. The term "Turanian" is now obsolete in historical linguistics; in the eighteenth and nineteenth centuries it referred to an umbrella category uniting the Uralic and (now discredited) Altaic families.

over the Caucasian mountains. But as a rule that is everything that the name of Georgia recalls in the modern European's reckoning. And it is a long way from Prometheus, Jason, and Medea to our day's Georgian men and women.

In the year 312 the land became Christian and established its own church; in the following centuries it sought courage from Byzantium's counterbalance against its Persian neighbors' efforts to introduce Mohammedanism.[4] In 1088 Tiflis was conquered by the Turks, but immediately thereafter Georgia entered into its period of greatness (around the same time as Denmark). The Georgian king David the Restorer (1089–1125) drove out the Turks and secured his dominion between the two seas.[5] His daughter Tamar, whose legendary name is glorified in numerous folk songs, did not just preserve the inheritance from her father, but repeatedly threw back Mohammedan armies and extended her conquests out to Trebizond.[6] Under her rule Georgian literature, which had been influenced by three civilizations, the Arabic, the Persian, and the Byzantine, reached its greatest heights, and great poets, among whom Rustaveli has become most famous through translation, brought the Georgian language to classical perfection.[7]

The Mongols overwhelmed the land in the thirteenth century; Tamerlane razed it around the year 1400. After Constantinople's seizure by the Turks there began a steady series of wars between Turkey and Georgia. From the fifteenth century the kingdom came into contact with Russia, which now began to compete with Turkey and Persia for influence in the conflict-ridden land, which at that time was divided among many Georgian kings and thus possessed a lesser ability to resist.

Nevertheless in the year 1761 one of these kings, Heraclius II, who united two of Georgia's three crowns on his head, subjugated a part of Persia, which

4. Brandes's precise dating of the conversion cannot be verified. While Christianity was present as early as the first century CE—indeed, Georgian tradition holds that it was introduced by Saint Andrew himself—its formal adoption as the state religion occurred sometime in the early fourth century under King Mirian III. See Christopher Haas, "The Caucasus," in *Early Christianity in Contexts: An Exploration across Cultures and Continents*, ed. William Tabbernee (Grand Rapids, MI: Baker Academic: 2014), 116–33.

5. David IV (b. 1073), more commonly known in English as David the Builder, was the principal figure of the Georgian Reconquista.

6. Brandes appears to have merged two distinct figures. Princess Tamar, daughter of David IV, lived much of her life in Constantinople before returning to Georgia and taking the habit. Tamar the Great (1160–1213), the great-granddaughter of David IV, reigned from 1184 until her death.

7. Shota Rustaveli (1160–ca. 1220) was the preeminent poet of the Georgian Golden Age and author of the national epic poem *The Man in the Panther's Skin*.

at that time was ripe for plunder because of internal struggle. And in 1783 he made an agreement with Russia, according to which Heraclius promised to give the Russian troops free passage through his land during the war with Turkey and Persia, while Catherine II in exchange pledged to protect and defend Georgia against these powers.[8]

The treaty was honorably intended from Heraclius's side, but not from Catherine's. Russia eventually wanted to tear Georgia away from Turkey and Persia, but first it would abandon it to Turkish and Persian deprivations so that it would be all the easier for Russia to conquer Georgia after it had been weakened in its unequal struggle against the Turks and Persians. Immediately before a battle against the Turks the Russian general Totleben pulled back with his army, and although Heraclius alone won the battle of Aspindza, he could not persuade the Russians to resist the 50,000 Persians who in 1795 occupied, plundered, and burned Tiflis.[9] Only after this did Catherine declare war on Persia, but when she died Paul I called the army back.

In 1798 Georgi XIII inherited the ravaged kingdom from his father, and the year after was compelled due to his weakness to seek support in a new agreement with Russia, according to which Russian suzerainty was acknowledged, but full self-rule for Georgia as well as the protection of the ruling house was solemnly ensured.[10]

But Georgi died even before the treaty was signed, and out of the blue Czar Paul issued a new proclamation, according to which he faithlessly announced Georgia's unconditional affiliation with Russia. In vain the crown prince David objected in Saint Petersburg, and when Alexander I ascended the throne upon Paul's murder, political conditions forced him, against his will, to occupy the country and destroy the independence it had claimed for twenty-one hundred years.

For a century Georgia's political life had to cease. But now, as a general breath of liberation blows over the enormous Russian kingdom, the Georgians come forward anew, and it is evident that their intelligentsia is a wholly modern youth movement, just as practical as it is freethinking.

---

8. Heraclius II (1720/21–98), who ruled from 1762 until his death, believed that cooperation with Russia was Georgia's only means of survival against Turkish and Persian aggression.

9. Gottlieb Heinrich Totleben's (1715–83) betrayal at Aspindza in 1770 was the first of many Russian betrayals of Georgia. The forces of the Iranian Qajars defeated Georgia at the Battle of Krtsanisi in September of 1795, after which they razed the capital.

10. Giorgi XIII (1746–1800) was the final monarch of the thousand-year Bagrationi dynasty.

In no way do they entertain a desire for the reinstatement of the national royal house; they have no medieval ideals. They do not desire any kind of full independence for the old Georgian state, which after all would not be possible unless Russia gives up the Caucasus, a condition that of course will never come to pass.

What they demand is this one thing: Georgia's national self-rule.

In the first place they demand to stand on equal footing with the provinces in Russia's center. They have after all not even a minimum of their rights: they have no provincial assemblies (*zemstvos*) and no juridical rights. Furthermore, their mother tongue is unconditionally banned from all schools in the country, and as a recently intercepted communication from Pobedonoststev to Georgia's highest clergymen openly declares, the intention of schooling in Georgia is not that they should provide children with instruction, but that they should work for the spread of the Russian language, which the children to this date understand so imperfectly that a priest, whom Pobedonoststev would have punished, has declared the instruction to be "counterproductive to upbringing, unjust, and shameful."[11] In reality the schools are so few and so poor that not a quarter of the children can read and write.

But in the next place they demand, in affiliation with the entirety of the Russian opposition party that has now lifted its head, not just a constitutional agreement for the state, but a constitution with decentralized centers of state power under which all of the previously oppressed nationalities can breathe again. And they outline how they think of themselves in the particular, such that Georgia's constitution shall guarantee that none of the immigrant peoples in the country, Armenians, Russians, or Tatars, shall come to suffer injustice. They complain about the fact that their sons in the army do not, as was promised in 1801, remain in the Caucasus, but are sent to Siberia's most distant regions.

Georgia's present behavior is especially instructive because it is among numerous testimonials that suggest that the autocracy in Russia is heading for a fall in our time. It can be said that it cannot last but a few years longer.

One after another the oppressed peoples and societies come forward with their demands. One class after another rises up to defend itself. The various peoples, previously so divided, come to find each other. No cleavage can be larger than that which just ten years ago divided the Finns from the Russian opposition party; the Finns, the czar's most faithful subjects. Now there is not a finger's breadth between them. No cleavage could be deeper than the one

11. Konstantin Petrovich Pobedonostsev (1827–1907), a lion of Russian reaction, served three czars in varying capacities for a half century.

that only twenty years ago divided the Russian intelligentsia from Russia's working class and peasants. Now the students and workers are intellectually as one, and the peasantry in a threatening fermentation.

For the single individual it might appear that the coming uprising is all too far off, and the older among us may perhaps not experience it. But that its coming can be foreseen is as certain as that spring follows midwinter.

CHAPTER 13

Transvaal

1903

By 1903 Brandes's initial human rights advocacy had garnered enough notoriety that he had begun to receive requests from all over the globe, as evidenced by this essay describing for the Danish reading public the conditions under which the war-ravaged Boer population of South Africa suffered in the aftermath of the Second Anglo-Boer War (1899–1902). That particular conflict had resulted in the introduction of a pair of widely reviled concepts into British military practice, those of the "scorched earth policy" most recently employed by General William Tecumseh Sherman in the American Civil War and the "concentration camp," first instituted by the Spanish in 1897 during the Cuban uprising against colonial rule. These two practices had largely laid waste to the Transvaal Republic, the largest of the Boer republics. Sadly for the contemporary reader, although in keeping with conventions of the age, the native population of the region, which also suffered immensely, does not merit mention here.

~

Again and again I have received requests to awaken the compassion of the Danish people in order to motivate them to help the unfortunate who are dying of hunger down in Transvaal. Nevertheless I have remained silent for two months, the reason being that Danish charities have been occupied with problems that are much closer to Denmark. My correspondents furthermore appear unable to see how little Denmark is. They know that a significant sum has been collected for the impoverished and mistreated Armenians, and conclude thereby that Danish charity reaches far and wide. Since in spite of all they might perhaps be right, the Danish public ought at least to be informed of how things look in Transvaal these days.

Yet who outside of Holland now thinks of the Transvaal? The war down there belongs to the past, and just now as the horrors in Macedonia surpass everything Europe has seen in the last ninety years, and when one cannot open a Western

---

Originally published in *Politiken*, October 26, 1903. Translated from the version published in *Samlede Skrifter*, vol. 17.

European newspaper without encountering the Bulgarian-Macedonian Committee's *Appeal to the Civilized World*, it might seem a poorly chosen moment to want to remind us of what vestiges the war has left on the South African fields.[1] Yet in the first years of the new century no worse horrors are found elsewhere than those in Transvaal.

The information on the contemporary conditions in Transvaal are owed to a courageous young lady, Miss *Emily Hobhouse*, who while the war still raged reported to England what the so-called concentration camps were in reality.[2] In the last six months she has crisscrossed Transvaal, the most out-of-the-way areas as well as the more familiar, finding the whole of the country destroyed in entirety. The misery is everywhere appalling; bread, clothing, shelter, agricultural implements are lacking everywhere. In the newspaper *South African News* she has described the state of affairs. Still stronger in impact are the letters that have not been chosen for publication, but that were written to her relatives in England and that her aunt Lady Hobhouse has had published in the *Manchester Guardian* and the *Daily News*. I have a series of them before me that contains her diary from a journey through the Orange River Colony, which is the area that is in the best shape, from which she intended to travel to steadily worse places of suffering, where all is misery and ruin.

The first point she makes is that the compensation that had been promised to the injured inhabitants by the English government has revealed itself to be an illusion.

She comes to a burned-out farm; one half of the once prosperous family lives in the rearmost, roofless room, which has been covered over somewhat with rush, while the other half dwells in the wagon shed, in which the ground is covered with sacks and a few goatskins. The family has received rations for two months that it has had to collect from three to four miles away, as well as an offer of oxen for plowing, once another family has used them first. But they kept the oxen so long that the offer only brought disappointment. Otherwise no compensation or help has been forthcoming. Meal times consist of coffee, bread, and some jam they ate with the bread; that was it. When she asked the head of the house whether he expected the promised compensation, she received from him as everywhere an unbelieving smile. The wife could speak English and had supported herself with needlework for twenty-three months while in the Bloemfontein camp.

1. See "Macedonia" in the present volume for Brandes's commentary on the Turkish atrocities in Macedonia.

2. Emily Hobhouse (1860–1926), born into a family of prominent peace and social welfare activists, would later join Brandes in infamy for her opposition to World War I.

At another farm the same thing. The claim for compensation had been submitted, but not a penny had come. The people here also live in a hastily pasted-together space; they had no oxen with which to plow and for that reason had to miss plowing time twice.

At the next farmer's house they have no coffee to offer the charitable guest, "and for Boers it is terrible not to be able to offer coffee." When this family left the camp they received rations for ten days; that was all. The people there had no cows. They had a few hens, but these did not lay eggs for want of nutrition. The people lived off goats' milk and off hares and birds, when they could catch them. They could not shoot them, since they did not have rifles. The Boers have of course been deprived of their rifles. At rare intervals they nevertheless shot antelopes, which otherwise made up the main part of their nourishment. That was when the English gendarmes came by on their rounds. Then the Boer says to the gendarme, "Loan me your rifle and five or six cartridges. Then I will show you how one shoots antelopes and will give you one." The antelopes have come back after the war, and since everything else is slaughtered, it is good to see the veldt populated with something living again. But it is sorrowful for the farmers, who are hungry, to see the savannah covered with food for them and be unable to take possession of it.

Everywhere the Boer families show themselves to be so hospitable that they turn over their only habitable room to Miss Hobhouse and themselves sleep under the open sky; everywhere they are extremely religious; they pray and sing during the mornings, pray at their so poorly provisioned tables, pray and sing before they give her something to eat, so that in the meantime she nearly swooned from hunger.

At the next farm the house and outbuildings had been burned down, twenty-eight horses killed and between 4,000 and 5,000 sheep slaughtered. The pale bones and skulls lay there, as everywhere, in heaps or spread along the roads. The family had not even been able to borrow a wagon from the English council to transport building materials out there. The health of the children had been completely destroyed since their stint in the concentration camp.

The men who gave themselves up after Lord Roberts's proclamation are called *Hands Uppers*.[3] They have been given the promise of full compensation. One had had a loss of 250 pounds sterling and received in compensation a

3. The scourge of colonized peoples across the empire for nearly half a century, Frederick Sleigh Roberts (1832–1914) offered amnesty to all Boer militants willing to lay down arms on March 15, 1900. Those who accepted were largely viewed as traitors and referred to in Afrikaans as *henoppersor* (Hands Uppers). See Martin Marix Evans, *Encyclopedia of the Boer War* (Santa Barbara, CA: ABC-CLIO, 2000), 109.

check for fifteen pounds, but since he had earlier received rations for a month, this sum was deducted and he thus received only eight pounds five shillings. The Boers have now learned that of the distribution of the three million pounds that was promised them at the peace agreement as good as nothing will come to their benefit. The second planting time after the peace agreement has passed, and nothing has been able to be sown.

Of the rations themselves Miss Hobhouse says that they are still worse than those that were provided in the concentration camps; they consist only of flour and raw beef in tin cans, but there is provided neither coffee, sugar, nor milk. Many surely live for months at a time on these two things.

The troops at the time issued receipts for the goods they had requisitioned from the populace. The receipts were submitted after the peace, but nothing was made good. Then when Chamberlain gave his big speech and claimed that full compensation would be made for every military receipt, they were sent in from everywhere.[4] Miss Hobhouse has in the meantime never heard talk of any man who has gotten payment for such a receipt, but has heard of a few cases where small sums have been given.

A schoolteacher in Bultfontein had been taken to the concentration camp in Brandfort and since then had been living in Paardeberg. His claim was submitted. Since his earlier home had been in Bultfontein he was told that he must appear in Hoopstad. It was a seventeen-hour trek by mule wagon. It cost him twelve pounds to travel and more than ten pounds to feed the mules. He waited three days and then received the message that his check was sent to Bultfontein. He traveled there and learned that his check had now been sent to Paardeberg; he turned back home again and found a check for one shilling nine pence. They could have paid him a few eggs instead, but the sum he did receive had cost him over fourteen pounds for the journey alone. He did not cash the check, but kept it for the memory.

Still worse off than the landowners are the tenant farmers, who have no land to use as collateral and who remain to this day without a penny. The lowest class, the agricultural laborers, the so-called *bijwoner*, die of hunger without rescue.[5]

Ready money is hardly able to be procured in the country; that collateral one can put up does not satisfy. A previously prosperous farmer went eight Danish miles on foot to Hoopstad to see if he could buy a few cattle. Since he

4. Joseph Chamberlain (1836–1914) served as British colonial secretary from 1895 to 1903, as such he was the effective leader of the British war and reconstruction efforts.

5. In semi-feudal Dutch South Africa, the *bijwoner* class lived in a state almost indistinguishable from serfdom.

had no money he could not get overnight lodging, thus sleeping on the open field in the winter cold and turning back the next day without having achieved anything.

A *bijwoner* related to the de Wets had accommodation with his family in a stable without windows, where he lay sick with rheumatic fever.[6] The stable, in which neither air nor sun had entry, was so damp and cold that Miss Hobhouse could not bear to stand there where the family lived day and night. Two of the family's children had died in the concentration camp, the oldest daughter's health had been altogether destroyed there, and now those left over huddled there and were consumed by hunger.

Around the area even healthy children were emaciated from lack of full nourishment. This misfortune sometimes made the head of the house inventive and resourceful. One farmer, who earlier had been rich and owned immense flocks of sheep, had now procured for himself a half score of sheep, which he had gotten cheaply because they had mange, and had thereafter cared for them so well that they were healthy. He had seven small mouths to feed, and had in vain planted potatoes but the drought killed them.

While the population is without roof overhead, Miss Hobhouse saw by the nearest camp piles of tents lying on the ground, rotting and unused, but one does not take them unless they are paid for, which the destitute of course cannot afford.

Thus are conditions in the area of the Transvaal that has suffered the least. One can surely deduce how it looks in the other areas. But even in the former, conditions are characteristic of a people who have been at war with the Englishmen, who are of course among the world's most highly regarded peoples. One can surely further infer how it is in a country like Armenia or Macedonia, where the villages have been burned down and the population has been according to ability wiped out by Turkish troops, Kurds, and Albanians.

---

6. The de Wets were among the more prominent burgher families of Dutch South Africa; Christian Rudolf de Wet (1854–1922) was a highly successful general in the Second Boer War.

CHAPTER 14

The Ruthenians

1904

As indicated in his ample writings on the Poles, Brandes's relations with their Ruthenian neighbors were never particularly warm. In Austrian-ruled Galicia, in which the Polish majority enjoyed considerable autonomy, tensions with the Ruthenian minority were particularly intense, due in large part to Polish gerrymandering. In fact, Brandes notes in his 1914 essay "Conditions in Russian Poland" that he had already clashed with Ruthenian leadership in 1898, before he had even embarked on his long career as a human rights activist. Yet in spite of this his 1901 article "The Women of Poland" opens with a summary of Polish-Ruthenian relations in the province, provided for him by the Polish activist and translator Józefa Klemensiewiczowa, who is clearly at pains to defend the actions of her countrymen. The conflict would again erupt into Brandes's professional life in 1906, when an aging Bjørnstjerne Bjørnson, having anointed himself as the defender of the Ruthenian people, included Brandes in his relentless attacks on Polish abuses of power. Regardless of this complicated history, Brandes does here see fit to address the Ruthenian question directly, although his discussion is strictly limited to Russian rather than Polish offenses.

~

As is well known, among the many peoples that make up the Russian Empire there are those that feel less than fortunate under the czardom and who observe the war between Russia and Japan, in which they are forced to participate, with mixed feelings. Everyone will mention the Poles, Finns, Jews, Georgians, and Armenians. Curiously enough Western Europe has previously almost completely overlooked how a much larger people under the Russian scepter views this crisis. After all, there are testimonials about this available.

That people is the Ruthenians, Europe's sixth largest population, of which twenty-five million are under Russian rule, three million under Austrian, and a half million under Hungarian. One is in the habit of calling them Little

Originally published in *Politiken*, March 14, 1904. Translated from the version published in *Samlede Skrifter*, vol. 17.

Russians, an appellation they themselves reject, so much more since they rightfully assert that they are the actual original *Russians*, while the Muscovites, who are of another tribe, have much Tatar blood in their veins. Sometimes one sees them called *Rusyns*, sometimes simply *South Russians*. They are a people with an independent language who inhabit a plain that is more than double the size of Austria's. Their mother country is *Ukraine*. Their old capital is Kiev.

One who reads attentively the *Ruthenian* (later *Ukrainian*) *Revue*, a journal that the Ruthenian intelligentsia began to publish in the German language in May 1903 so as to come into contact with Europe, will gather that the Ruthenians view the threat of Pan-Mongolianism—the Yellow Peril—as quite imaginary and to them an indifference. It is almighty Russia that is the chief threat and source of misfortune for a people repressed by the czardom. And the Ruthenians assert that as far as they know no *ukaz* like that which in 1876 gave their own intellectual life such a blow has ever been issued against any Mongol state.

With a stroke, the Russian *ukaz* forbade twenty-five million people from reading and hearing their own language.[1] It goes like this:

The Czar is pleased most graciously to command:

1. It is forbidden—without special permission of the censor—to issue within the boundaries of the kingdom any kind of publication in the Ruthenian language that may be published outside the kingdom.
2. Within the monarchy the printing and publication of original works in and translations into this language are forbidden, with the exceptions of (a) historical documents and (b) belletristic works, which however should be noted are permitted only if Russian orthography is employed in them. Therefore permission for the publication of Ruthenian books can only be given after the censor's examination of the manuscript.
3. Likewise theater productions of any kind, public lectures, and the publication of Ruthenian texts for music are forbidden.

From then on the Ruthenian language was as good as dead in Russia. Once in a while a larger collection of tales or verse is permitted (provided that the word "Ruthenian" does not appear therein), but individual short stories and individual poems that might have a large circulation were and are forbidden. Last year the last Ruthenian journal (*The Scientific Literary Revue*) was

1. The Ems Ukaz was signed by Alexander II while on holiday at the German spa Bad Ems.

banned. Not a single Ruthenian newspaper may be published in Russia, not a single organ measures up to the threshold. In this immense kingdom, in which, in spite of the censorship, at the very least officially sanitized journals and newspapers in the Russian, German, French, Polish, Lithuanian, Hebrew, Finnish, Swedish, Armenian, and Georgian languages appear, no one dares publish a newspaper or give a speech in Ruthenian. Is it any wonder that now in the twentieth century there are signs of fermentation among the twenty-five million over whom the imperial *ukaz* sits like a glacier under which nothing living can grow?

Dr. Puluj, professor at the technical college in Prague, published the New Testament in Ruthenian in Vienna in 1881, and in 1902 the Old Testament.[2] When in 1881 he sought permission to distribute the New Testament in the land of the Ruthenians, *Ukraine*, he received an unconditional refusal.

Now he has renewed his application, supported by the fact that the New Testament is for sale in Russia in thirty-six languages, even in the language of the Mohammedans, so that the Tatars might dare read it in their own tongue. A renewed ban will surely make for bad blood. It is crazy enough already that distinguished Ruthenian translations of Shakespeare and Byron are forbidden.

In *Impressions from Russia* I described the agonies of the greatest Ruthenian poet in recent times, Taras Shevchenko (1814–61), after whom the most significant Ruthenian institution, the scientific Shevchenko Society in Lemberg, is named.[3] He was born as a serf and only had his freedom purchased by benefactors after he had demonstrated his artistic gifts. In 1847 he was condemned to knouting for his poem "Caucasus" and then knouted again in 1848 for his poems of freedom; he was then on the express command of Nicholas I sent as an ordinary soldier on a punitive campaign to the Kirghiz steppe and only returned in 1858; his health was by then ruined and he died three years later. His memory is now idolized wherever the Ruthenian language is spoken.

Officially, of course, no one dares to speak the language on Russian soil. This ban was placed in a bizarre light during the great national festival that was celebrated recently in Ukraine, the festival in Poltava on the twelfth and thirteenth of September 1903. At the festival, a memorial was unveiled for the founder of modern Ruthenian literature, the poet Ivan Kotlyarevsky, who laid the groundwork for a modern literature in Ukraine (albeit through a curious work with respect to the founding of a national literature, a parody of *The*

2. Physicist Ivan Puluj (1845–1918), an X-ray pioneer, was also a lifelong advocate for the Ukrainian language.

3. Brandes's *Indtryk Fra Rusland* appeared in 1888.

Aeneid, the Ruthenian *Peer Paars*).[4] On such an occasion the Ruthenian speakers from Galicia and Hungary could not be forbidden to use their own language; however, it was strongly presumed that the Ukrainian Ruthenians would do the same. And after all it was not without meaning that the Ruthenians, amid representatives from all the Slavic tribes, celebrated their national festival in precisely that city in which Peter the Great broke the power of their national hero Mazepa when he allied with Charles XII.[5] The national rebirth was celebrated where the nation's leader fell.

The speeches went on for a long time in Russian, first by the authorities and then by Ukrainian Ruthenians. But when the author Mrs. Koszaczewa offered a sentence in Ruthenian there arose a cry of joy, and when the Austrian cabinet member Julian Romanchuk began his speech in Ruthenian, the masses of people roared with absolutely tempestuous enthusiasm.[6] The Ruthenian language had not been heard in an official capacity in a human lifetime.

From then on the Ruthenians seized every opportunity to proclaim their national character. The authorities cannot suppress it these days. The manner in which the national composer *Mykola Lysenko*'s thirty-fifth jubilee has been celebrated in city after city, first in Galicia, then in Bukovina, and finally in Ukraine itself, evinces the spirit of independence that has spread among the people of Gogol and Shevchenko.[7]

Lysenko (born 1842) is an especially popular musician because he has artistically harmonized hundreds of Ukrainian folk songs and has pledged his entire life to the cultivation of the national music of the Ruthenians. He has,

4. Ivan Kotliarevs'ky (1769–1838) published the first literary works in the Ruthenian language, among them his mock epic *Eneïda* (1798). Ludvig Holberg's (1684–1754) *Peder Paars* (1719–20) also parodies Virgil.

5. Ivan Mazepa (1639–1709) was hetman of Zaporizhian Host from 1687 to 1708, in effect a kind of regional governor over much of modern-day Ukraine. Mazepa had long resisted the efforts of Peter I to centralize political and military power under the czardom, which ultimately resulted in his defection in 1708. In the decisive Battle of Poltava of 1709, Mazepa and his followers fought alongside Charles XII's invading Swedish forces, which were soundly defeated in the pivotal engagement of the Great Northern War.

6. "Fru Koszaczew" unclear. Perhaps Hyrtsko Hryohenko, pen name of Oleksandra Kosach, wife of Mikhaylo Kosach. Julian Romanchuk (1842–1932) served in the Reichsrat from 1891 to 1897 and 1901 to 1918.

7. The thirty-fifth jubilee celebrations of Mykola Vitaliiovych Lysenko (1842–1912) in the fall of 1903, like the dedication of the Kotliarevs'ky monument earlier in the summer, were major events in the Ukrainian cultural reawakening. See Maxim Tarnawsky, *The All-Encompassing Eye of Ukraine: Ivan Nechui-Levyts'kyi's Realist Prose* (Toronto: University of Toronto Press, 2015), 66. While he wrote in Russian, Nikolai Vasil'evich Gogol' (1809–52) was in fact of Ruthenian descent; his father, Vasilii Gogol-Ianovskii (1777–1825), wrote a number of his own works in the language.

among other works, written melodies to Shevchenko's songs and composed three operas. His significance to Ruthenians is comparable to that of Grieg for Norway.[8]

He was honored in Podwoloczyska, in Tarnopol, and in Lemberg, the capital of Galicia, for three days in succession. In Lemberg alone he received forty-two laurel wreaths and untold panegyrics. Three concerts of his music exclusively were performed, each concluding with the national song he has composed. Then he was still more honored in Galicia in the three cities of Stanislav, Kolomyia, and Czernowitz. But the culmination took place in Ukraine's capital, Kiev, in December 1903. Among other things Lysenko was presented with a villa.

The panegyrics and festival speeches were never-ending. The general tenor of these addresses was so aggressive, so irresistibly contrarian, that the old *ukaz* of 1876 was quietly suspended. All the speakers expressed themselves in Ruthenian and the authorities dared not reply.

Under these circumstances it is of some significance that the leading article in the latest number of the *Ruthenian Review* concludes with these words: "We believe that victory for the Japanese in this war will be fortunate for the people of Russia, for the Russian authorities, their Asiatic instincts affronted, will be forced to treat their peoples more as Europeans and must for a time at least allow its Asiatic plans to lie fallow."

8. Edvard Grieg (1843–1907), Norway's most prominent composer, is of course best known for composing the incidental music for Ibsen's *Peer Gynt*.

CHAPTER 15

Finland

1904

The transfer of Finland from Swedish to czarist rule in 1809 had, in a twist of fate largely without parallel in the long history of Russian expansionism, resulted in a profound increase of local autonomy as well as, equally importantly, a general flowering of language and culture. While Alexander I's remarkably benevolent policies toward the new Grand Duchy of Finland may in some small measure be attributed to his own high-mindedness, the overriding concern of the regime was the retrenchment of the cultural dominance the Swedes had exercised over the Finns since the Middle Ages. Under Alexander political and cultural power was gradually shifted eastward, and the czar himself functioned as a patron of the Finnish language and its literature; central to this project was the establishment of the Imperial Alexander University (after 1917 the University of Helsinki), transferred from its previous location in Swedish-dominated Turku to the new capital in 1827. Relatively warm relations between Finns and Russians would persist until the conclusion of the nineteenth century, when Nicholas II's notorious February Manifesto of 1899 announced that the policy of Russification then in practice in other sectors of the empire would be introduced in Finland. Particularly galling to Finns was the advent of the Conscription Law in 1901, under which young Finns were drafted directly into the Russian Army; many young men, including many students at the university, would refuse the call in the ensuing years. As Brandes indicates in the appeal presented here, the university had largely been exempted from the worst aspects of the new policy, mostly thanks to its historical ties to the person of the czar. Yet still its students were subject to conscription, and the academic council felt confident enough in its position to issue an appeal to the university's Russian authorities on their behalf in 1903. The ensuing "Letter to the Chancellor's Office at the Imperial Alexander University" provoked a response as severe as it was swift, and the leading figures of the council were in fact sent into exile. In Brandes's subsequent appeal, he employs a new tactic in his rights advocacy,

---

Originally published in *Politiken*, August 1, 1904. Translated from the version published in *Samlede Skrifter*, vol. 17.

attempting to tap into a solidarity emanating not from shared ethnicity or religion or common humanity, but the fellow feeling of scholars and intellectuals engaged in the pursuit of truth and knowledge.

~

As a rule, great political violations of rights and acts of violence carried out against whole tribes occur unchallenged in our time as in the past. The states do not involve themselves in each other's internal affairs; the voice of the individual is meaningless if he is not either a Voltaire or a Tolstoy. We have seen how the numerous voices from the most varied civilized nations that have spoken up for Finland can be ignored by those whom they address, even if they are otherwise heard everywhere.

Daily this view has become more widespread, namely that nothing is less useful than a protest that has no means of power behind it.

The many futile speeches give rise to the sense that mere speech is as such not effective among those who would see matters clearly and thus cannot view them optimistically. If injustice cannot be warded off then it is more valuable to be silent than to scream or scold, and even this indignant insight surely seems superfluous.

If this understanding takes hold in even greater measure it would be a true satisfaction to all powerful men of violence, for they would get permission to commit every violation of rights in profound peace. Those against whom these acts are committed are after all muzzled, and all the so-called interlopers would be content to look on in cautious silence.

If this understanding becomes ever-more widespread, then the lot of the put upon will become doubly as hard. Everyone who has suffered a loss knows that even that sympathy quite unable to assuage the loss does bring relief from the pain to the weak, a little glimmer of joy called consolation. And for those who are abused the agony is enlarged terribly by the fact that those around them do not look upon them sympathetically.

For these reasons Scandinavians as well as non-Scandinavians ought never tire of speaking in favor of Finland. It ought to be made known in Russia that we follow attentively the ever-increasing oppression perpetrated on Finnish soil, and that we feel in solidarity with those against whom ever-more violent violations of rights are committed.

It will not do that the fate that has recently befallen the university in Helsingfors has been received in Europe with a silence that resembles consent. All of Europe's universities ought to feel injured by the blow that has injured one of their own, and from them all manner of protest ought to resound, so that public opinion could have no doubt that those who according to their own self-conception constitute the essence of free, truth-loving scholarship, the highest striving for knowledge and insight, also feel themselves to be the guardians, advancers, and spokespeople for the conception of justice.

Certainly the injustice exercised in Finland upon the men outside the university, who without law or conviction have been exiled or sent as prisoners to inner Russia, is no less than that which has been exhibited against university teachers like Baron Wrede, Professor Homén, and Dr. Estlander, but here is a specific recorded instance of a violation of the Finnish university that exceeds all the others.[1]

The pretext for the Russian government's violent intervention is here more doubtful than in any other. And this pretext is furthermore a testament to the honor of those university teachers who have been driven into exile because of their actions.

The measure of their honor may only be judged by those who have read their unanimously agreed upon "Letter to the Chancellor's Office at the Imperial Alexander University," that document that is the pretext for the acts of violence.

This statement, which is composed with considerable moderation in expression but with manly firmness in argumentation, has the following content:

It asserts that since the military order of 1901 a significant number of students have not gone before the draft medical board and that others will fail to do so in 1904. This is due not to youthful arrogance or defiance; here there is no talk of the whims of the single individual being at odds with the concept of justice prevailing in the country. No, the students have been motivated by the entirety of the Finnish people's concepts of justice and duty, which the representatives of those people have expressed unequivocally. The academic council must therefore express its conviction that the behavior of the student youth, by whatever political measuring stick employed, does not contain anything worthy of punishment in a moral sense.

These youth, who are only now beginning life, are confronted by the authorities with the demand that they behave differently from what their understanding of justice and duty is, and that if they obey their inbuilt faith in the holiness of the legal system, they will not only be barred from official activity in the service of the fatherland and prevented from entering into marriage, but will also be compelled to face the choice of either fleeing the country

1. Law professors Rabbe Axel Wrede (1851–1938) and Ernst Henrik Estlander (1870–1949), as well as physicist Viktor Theodor Homén (1858–1923), were exiled from Finland in 1904. All were recalled the following year, although whether or not Brandes's appeal played a role in this is debatable.

or being pursued and rounded up like criminals and thereafter imprisoned for sentences shorter or longer, and finally shipped off into one or another penal battalion among the Russian troops stationed outside Finland.

The academic council does not indicate what conditions in such a penal battalion would be like, but in fact it is nearly identical with the death penalty, nay even worse than a swiftly executed capital sentence.

But the academic council disavows its right to conceal from the university's highest leadership its fear of how these conditions threaten the mission of the university. In part it invokes in the student body a state of unease, which is highly unfavorable for studies and intellectual training; in part it has made it difficult for the university to awaken and to fortify the love of truth and justice among the youth, who witness their own faithful acts of conscience punished like severe crimes.

The academic council permits itself to request that the chancellor's office bring its grave concerns, shared by all its members, to the attention of His Majesty the Czar, trusting that he who has so often shown the university goodwill and interest will grant its statement attention.

It is to this letter that Plehve as minister of the interior has responded by violently carrying off to inner Russia a number of university teachers, selected from among the most influential representatives in the council.[2]

This step goes farther than any other previously taken against Finland, in that the university in Helsingfors and its teachers were expressly excepted in the dictatorial order that gave the governor-general (Bobrikov) permission in all other respects to deal with matters in Finland at his own discretion.[3]

In two orders, the one that introduced the dictatorship and the one that more closely defined its parameters, the university was unequivocally exempted—perhaps out of a certain respect for the country's highest educational establishment, though no doubt mostly because its bylaws, which have the incontestability of constitutional provisions, originate from the Russian czar himself.

Now the government has overstepped even the boundaries it itself had reluctantly drawn for the arbitrariness of the dictatorship.

It must not be allowed to believe that Europe observes its behavior with indifference.

---

2. Viacheslav Konstantinovich fon Pleve (1846–1904) was assassinated later in the year by Russian Socialist Revolutionary Party activists.

3. Nikolai Ivanovich Bobrikov (1839–1904), the hated implementer of Russification in Finland, was assassinated soon after by Finnish nationalist Eugen Schauman (1875–1904). This incident, which took place on Bloomsday, is mentioned in James Joyce's *Ulysses*.

Perhaps those who protest expose themselves to the misunderstanding that they harbor ill will toward Russia or the Russian people. After all, hardly any other people, when its men and women are taken individually, capture and awaken sympathy like the Russians. And the more one gets to know individual Russians, the more one will as a rule feel drawn to them, the more highly one will regard them. Lively affection for the Russian people can very well be reconciled with sorrow and indignation at the behavior of their government in Finland. In any case the possibility of a misunderstanding, intentional or not, must not preclude action.

What should happen is this:

The student youth of the three Nordic countries, together with their university teachers, ought to express their sympathy with students and teachers at the university in Helsingfors and register their protest against the violence and abuse that is inflicted on them. We dare hope that the movement then spreads further, so that other countries' universities, first and foremost England's and Germany's, perhaps also France's, surely Italy's, attach themselves to the protest, and that it therefore rolls over the Earth, steadily more polyphonic. Plehve should be made to understand that he cannot take lightly such a pronouncement from Europe's most enlightened class of men. He himself has clearly demonstrated as much by taking up the pen to oppose Stead on the Finnish question, and it is further attested by the Russian government's care to secure through certain French newspapers a protective order regarding European public opinion.[4]

It is our purpose to bring the Russian government to perceive itself isolated, an isolation it more steadily begins to feel.

The French parliament is near to inviting delegations from all European representative bodies in the interest of arbitration. This began with English PMs, and now it is Norden's turn. But there is one country to which no invitation can be extended, because it has no parliament, and that is Russia, France's only alliance partner—that country itself from which the proposal for the establishment of a court of arbitration was issued.

A similar sense of isolation ought to be instilled among Russia's leading men, the sense that they are set apart from European civilization by Europe's intellectual aristocracy. This government has expelled Finland's best men from their fatherland. In return Europe must expel Russia from its culture.

4. William Thomas Stead (1849–1912) was a pioneering British investigative journalist and a longtime friend of Finland.

CHAPTER 16

To the Students of Germany

1904

As has been indicated, Brandes always appears to observe a distinction between the "disinterested" segments of human rights advocacy and those aspects that could be said to involve a personal interest on his own part, namely the fate of his fellow European Jews as well as that of his Danish countrymen suffering under German rule in North Schleswig, which had been annexed by Prussia after Denmark's defeat in the 1864 Dano-Prussian War. Ever-mindful of his many critics among the European nationalist Right, Brandes seems to exercise relative restraint in speaking out on behalf of his "own" people, or at the very least this is how these peoples perceived it. In spite of his efforts to remain impartial, Brandes does, as evidenced by the present volume, produce a considerable body of work on Jewish and Danish affairs, even if it is never enough to satisfy his detractors. With respect to the latter, Brandes is motivated to speak out by the appointment of Ernst von Köller (1841–1928) as *oberpräsident* of Schleswig-Holstein, under whom Germanization efforts were dramatically accelerated, often approaching the kind of severity witnessed in German Poland. Between 1899 and 1905, Brandes published a series of essays on the Danes of Sønderjylland that would be collected and republished in book form in 1919 in anticipation of the Schleswig plebiscites scheduled for the following year. Brandes selected two of these articles for publication in his *Samlede Skrifter*, the address "To the Students of Germany" and a follow-up from the following year titled "The Rights and Duties of the Weaker," both of which appear here for the first time in English translation. In the essay below, Brandes uses the platform of a German student journal to urge German youth to take the lead in persuading their government to ease its oppression of its Danish subjects.

~

Originally published in German in *Freier Almanach deutscher Studenten: Deutschland, Oesterreich, Schweiz*, October 1904. Translated from the Danish version published in *Samlede Skrifter*, vol. 17.

The request from the editors of the *German Students' Free Almanac*, which provides me the opportunity to address the students of Germany for the first time, gives me an unexpected pleasure; I have something precise on my mind that I gladly would bring before them in plain speech.[1]

Although the three Nordic kingdoms do not constitute a political whole, and although all attempts to make them such must be viewed as misguided, their intellectual life is, however, closely related. A large number of pan-Scandinavian organizations, societies, and associations are in full swing; the literatures are close to one another; the artists are personally such good friends that when abroad they see each other as countrymen.

There is especially intellectual communication between the universities of Scandinavian Norden and of Finland. The one university's teachers visit the neighboring land's universities as guest lecturers, the learned men of the primary and secondary schools convene meetings in the capital cities; colleagues are often as closely connected as is otherwise only the case within national borders.

In earlier times pan-Scandinavian student meetings were frequent in the various university towns. After the Dano-German War of 1864 they became rarer, because the sometimes openly expressed, sometimes silently agreed-upon precondition for the meetings was that the three countries would also militarily stand united against the Germanness that threatened Denmark.[2] When this precondition did not hold up the pan-Scandinvaian attitude was lacking and since then such meetings have only taken place with longer intervals between. Nevertheless the reciprocal feelings in the academic world are quite hearty and are often on display.

The limitations of language make similar gatherings between Danish students and those from countries outside of Norden quite difficult. During the last few years English guests have arrived here during the summer, and there have been lectures for them in English by university teachers. French journalists and artists have at various times visited Copenhagen as a group and have been received here with great distinction. Every year here there are French lectures, and more often than that French theater productions have found numerous spectators.

---

1. The *Freier Almanach deutscher Studenten: Deutschland, Oesterreich, Schweiz* was a Munich-based pan-German youth journal.

2. The Norwegian "betrayal" of Denmark in 1864 famously infuriated a young Henrik Ibsen. As for Brandes, Danish defeat in 1864 for a time led him surprisingly close to the kind of provincial nationalism he would later so vehemently reject. See Sune Berthelsen and Ditte Marie Egebjerg, "Europa i Danmark, Danmark i Europa: Georg Brandes som national kosmopolit," in *Det stadig moderne Gennembrud*, ed. Hans Hertel (Copenhagen: Gyldendal, 2004), 99–122.

Only German lectures are never held in Copenhagen and would never attract an audience; only German painters and sculptors have never exhibited in Copenhagen and would hardly sell here; only German students have never been the guests of Danish students and would never be welcome.

And yet there is no foreign language that is as well understood and as passably spoken in Denmark as German; trading connections with Germany are extremely lively, and without doubt scientific books from Germany have greater sales than those from any other country.

The reason for this continuing coldness is known to you. With the peace agreement of 1864 a Danish population came under Prussian hegemony, and although the little population has never thought of rebellion, and although Denmark is much too weak to be able to think of reconquest, the Prussian government cannot bring itself to a just, let alone high-minded treatment of the North Schleswig population.

An undeniable war is conducted against the Danish language; everywhere it is driven out of the church and the school. Expulsions, harassment, imprisonment, and continuous spying makes the lives of the North Schleswig farmers difficult and yet cannot break their resistance. In the last five years efforts at Germanization have been carried out with ever-greater ruthlessness. The German kaiser's visit to the Danish court last year, about which certain individuals harbored great expectations, has not brought any change. Certainly the kaiser just after his return telegraphed to the Danish king that in the future he viewed himself as a son of the house of Denmark; but immediately the persecutions in North Schleswig began again.[3]

This kind of politics is of course only a part of larger Prussian practice in conquered border provinces with other languages. Any non-German language is fought with violent measures and, if possible, the land itself brought into German ownership. They make life hard for those who in their hearts cling to their language and their national memories; they neglect no means of humiliating them, of suppressing that which is holiest to them, and portray the feeling that they nourish in their innermost selves as criminal.

It is a sign of the imperialist spirit that has gotten the upper hand in Germany and that views and treats the non-German peoples as second rank. In other words, this is not done by the German government against the will and the desires of the German people; no, this kind of politics is sanctioned

3. Parts of Wilhelm II's 1903 state visit were filmed by Danish film pioneer Peter Elfelt (1866–1931). Unlike his British (George V) and Russian (Nicholas II) counterparts, the kaiser was not a descendant of Danish king Christian IX.

by the large majority of the nation, especially—it must be feared—by the academically educated classes.

In earlier times student circles in all countries held the ideals of humanity; nowadays in not a few countries, especially in Germany, these are driven out by national ideals, and in spite of all the inventions and means of communication that should unite peoples there persists a gulf that divides even peoples of common origin, a gulf not traversed by any bridge, no, a gulf growing steadily deeper and wider.[4]

An inordinate amount of time will pass before the ruling classes in Germany change their basic view; before, for example, good relations with a little country like Denmark become so important to them that they themselves are zealous for a treatment of the Danish-speaking population of Schleswig that resembles the treatment Switzerland provides its Italian speakers. But much would be gained if the German students, their national pride unabridged, here take the lead in shaping public opinion.

Then the day would be near when the students of Copenhagen would receive the students from the German universities as brotherly comrades, and also in which the youth from all the other Nordic universities would realize and feel that the old bad feelings were overcome.

That the honorable editors of the almanac have at this time turned to a man like me I take as a good sign.

The occasion recalls, as you know, the appeal I made some time ago to the universities of Europe. I sought to urge students and university teachers to write a letter to the university in Helsingfors, which the Russian government has been abusing so nastily with the banishment and imprisonment of innocent professors and students.[5]

The Finnish students responded to the appeal at the beginning of the academic year, and the student union in Copenhagen has heeded my call and sent an address to the students in Helsingfors. Although the French students and professors have been compelled to account for their sympathies toward Russia and the Russian alliance, private and public declarations from student and faculty circles in France have come to me that leave no doubt that Frenchmen are willing to protest ardently against Russian injustice.

In Germany everyone has been silent up to now. The only messages I have received from German cities before the receipt of their appeal were those that

4. Brandes here invokes the spirit of "progressive nationalism" that had animated German youth in the early nineteenth-century German Wars of Liberation and in the Young Germany movement that he had chronicled in the final volume of *Main Currents*.

5. See "Finland," published earlier in 1904, in the present volume.

advised me to take into account the freethinking of the German students. For example a correspondent wrote this to me:

> In the summer of 1901 a report spread through Europe that defenseless demonstrating Russian students had been cut down by clubs. The burgeoning indignation of civilized Europe—especially the academic youth—expressed itself in enthused expressions of solidarity with the victims of the czardom. It happened even in politically backward countries like Austria.
>
> Only in Germany was there silence.
>
> It moved me and I published a call: where were the German student youth? The consequence was, apart from laughable chicanery against me, that the student youth stole away, denying me the courtesy of a refutation in its newspaper, and the rest was silence. One said to me that nothing comes of declarations of sympathy—how realistically the Germans can think! Right?—There were threats of dissolving the organization and suppressing the newspaper.—It was the stone in the bog about which Goethe spoke.[6]

The Russian envoys to the small Nordic states at present exert everywhere a strong pressure on the governments, at the very least through a friendly request not to create any difficulties for Russia in the universities and the newspapers. It is already difficult for Finns to find a paper in which they are permitted to have the floor. Germany stands as an equal power to Russia. Russian envoys will not be able to behave imperiously there. German newspapers like German universities can, if they want, maintain their independence. German students can do so best and most easily.

Scandinavian culture is attacked from two sides, in Schleswig from the south, in Finland from the north.

My wish for the German students is this: that they would consider that at one time Germanness and humanity were nearly synonymous words, and that a powerful German national sentiment can well be reconciled with goodwill toward the small peoples and a lively aversion to their brutal and barbaric oppressors.

---

6. The reference here is actually to Arthur Schopenhauer, who wrote in an 1818 letter to Goethe that the unenthusiastic reaction to his *On Vision and Colors* was like "throwing a stone into a bog—no ripples." See David E. Cartwright, *Schopenhauer: A Biography* (Cambridge: Cambridge University Press, 2010), 336.

CHAPTER 17

The Rights and Duties of the Weaker

1905

Brandes's appeal to German youth on behalf of the Danish subjects of the Reich (see "To the Students of Germany" in the present volume) not only failed but in fact produced a significant backlash, as is detailed in the follow-up below. This essay is characterized by an unusually strong measure of acerbic humor, directed at the rather grotesque spectacle of representatives of one of Europe's most severe and repressive states attacking Denmark for its own historical failings; particularly rich is the invocation of no less a military disciplinarian than Helmuth von Moltke the Elder condemning the Danish army for its mistreatment of its soldiers. It is also of particular interest in that here Brandes, whose rights advocacy is almost always narrowly focused on practical and immediate matters, appears to offer at least a measure of theoretical reflection on the relation of dominated and dominator, namely his nascent theory of a "duty of the weaker," according to which a particular oppressed people is possessed not only of a right to fair and dignified treatment by the dominant people, but also the *duty* always to act in such a manner that the weaker people proves worthy of such consideration. Brandes here anticipates certain aspects of Gandhi's principle of satyagraha, although without the religious element, in that the oppressed subject is called upon to practice ruthless self-examination and self-critique in the interest of establishing a clear moral authority over the oppressor.

~

I

In the fall of 1904 it happened that the publishers of the *German Students Free Almanac: Germany, Austria, Switzerland,* in light of the proclamation I had issued to Europe's universities in support for the university in Helsinki, asked

---

Originally published in two parts in *Politiken,* May 16 and 17, 1905. Translated from the version published in *Samlede Skrifter,* vol. 17.

me to send them a letter of a similarly freethinking bent to the students of the German Reich.[1]

A unique opportunity to engage Germany's students was presented to me. There could be no doubt about what I had to say to them; I viewed it as a responsibility to make use of the occasion.

I wrote that it would be a very long time before the ruling classes of Germany came to accept that good relations with a powerless country like Denmark was of importance to them. Yet at the same time I suggested that there was much to gain if these same students would prepare a public statement on the issue.

My proclamation was an experiment. Assuredly I did not expect much from it. But I considered the possibility that among the various responses some would be characterized by a kindliness, an obligingness, a youthfulness.

Altogether there came only one response (in *Kölnische Zeitung*), vehemently nationalist; but it was reprinted all over Germany from town to town, paper to paper, as if echoing from millions of throats, and later only new terms of abuse and more personal attacks were added to this first response: it was inconceivable that in the German universities there should be agitation against the country's own government for the advantage of Danish interests.

The German socialists include in their program, whether written or unwritten, the equal rights of the nationalities, although of course they are still in the opposition. For the ruling classes only the rights of the stronger apply. We all know what the right of the stronger means. The expression is quite paradoxical in that it entails something that has nothing to do with the state of rights, but instead the very upper hand that the greater strength provides.[2]

Our age is steadily in a more marked attunement with the right of the stronger. The time is long past when one contemptuously referred to it as the right of the fist. A modern understanding views the various peoples as it does the single individual, whose desires are self-assertion with ever-more increased power. The eighteenth century worked out the ideals of rights, asserted human rights, and coined the word "humanity." In the nineteenth century the principal of nationality arose, which functioned in part to unite and in part to break apart the states and introduced entirely new conceptions of rights. On toward the conclusion of the century imperialism appeared, which has altogether washed away the contradiction between power and right. In its particular German form it involves denying the subjugated Poles, French, and Danes their language and their national identity. Of these peoples two are

1. See "Finland" and "To the Students of Germany" in the present volume.

2. Brandes's thinking here in some ways anticipates the general tenor of Carl Schmitt's later reflections on the exercise of sovereign power.

numerous enough: there are twenty million Poles, twenty-four million French.[3] We Danes alone are few.

What can we set in opposition to this right of the stronger? First and foremost what I will call the right of the weaker, which at the very least is still acknowledged in Europe: the right to be judged and to be treated not according to one's external weakness, but according to one's internal strength, one's value for universal civilization, the example one provides, the cultural heights one has achieved.

Assuredly it is of no real use to insist on a right to consideration or to mercy; however, neither will it do to stop publicly asserting one's right to respect. Publicly there must be discussion of something else, namely that of the responsibility of the weaker.

If we have the right to assert and develop ourselves, then it is still to a greater degree our duty. If we have the right not to lose sight of Danishness in southern Jutland, then it is to a still higher degree our duty to do so. The smaller the country and the weaker the people, the higher the degree to which they must protect their language and their territory. Indifference in such cases is degeneration.

We Danes have not manifested the ability to rule non-Danes. When Norway was united with us, we did not understand the necessity of either making our union desirable to the Norwegians or simply granting the Norwegians their independence. When the upheaval came they separated from us without pain.[4] When we had Schleswig and Holstein under the Danish crown, we did not understand to preserve Schleswig as Danish or later to preserve the goodwill of the southern Schleswigers.[5] For centuries we have misruled Iceland, using it only to procure ample profits for certain Danish firms, and only now has the island gotten its reasonable demands fulfilled.[6] To this very day we have ruled poor Greenland in a way of which we must be ashamed.[7]

3. With respect to the latter, Brandes of course refers to German oppression of the French-speaking population of Alsace-Lorraine.

4. The Kingdom of Denmark-Norway was dissolved in 1814 after Danish defeat in the Napoleonic Wars, after which Norway entered in to a much less oppressive union with Sweden, before full independence was achieved in 1905.

5. The German-speaking majorities of Holstein and southern Schleswig revolted against Danish rule in 1848 but were defeated at the Battle of Isted. After Danish defeat in the 1864 Dano-Prussian War, all of Schleswig and Holstein, including the Danish majority of north Schleswig, were incorporated into Prussia. The Danish population would remain under the rule of the German Reich until the Schleswig plebiscites of 1920.

6. Iceland would achieve full independence in 1944.

7. Greenland remains in political union with Denmark to this day.

For a long time we have of course not even understood how to rule ourselves. All through the conclusion of the previous century the ruling party persisted only by limiting or dismissing the freedoms of the press and of association as well as the right to administer the federal budget and by suppressing the people with an illegally established gendarme corps.[8]

In all of this we have counteracted the responsibility of the weaker. For the weak, who constantly must appeal to the sense of right and humanity against brutality, have far more than the strong the responsibility never, on those occasions when they are in power, to reveal themselves to be power-mad or brutal.

We must remember that we are not alone in the world, and that precisely our efforts at self-assertion toward Germany sharpen Germany's critique of us. If we act unworthily, then Germany's attitude toward Danishness becomes not only justified but deserved.

II

We believe that with impunity we can permit ourselves something like the corporal punishment law, that we can with impunity expose ourselves to the contempt of the civilized world.[9] In the Italian newspapers the news is conveyed under the headline of "A Return to the Middle Ages." In the German paper *Der Tag* there was this:

> The Danes have after all always been beaten. On the Danish isles the rural population (although by the seventeenth century they were already literate) was adscripted in a manner not seen even in Mecklenburg. Until 1848 there were barbaric beatings in the Danish army. Even in the cadet academy there were beatings; Moltke always complained of its rawness.[10] The children in Denmark are punished for petty thievery with flogging by the police.
>
> Because of the remarkable aesthetic and literary overrefinement of the Danes they have often believed themselves justified in looking down on our German vulgarity. Now is revealed what all this education really means.
>
> As is well known, in Russia since the time of Peter higher society has unharnessed the team and galloped away, while the cart containing the whole population remains stuck in the dirt. Politically Denmark has long been a branch of

---

8. Denmark became a limited constitutional monarchy in 1849, but many of the stipulations of the constitution were revoked during the period 1885–94, known to Danes as Provisorietiden.

9. The Folketing adopted its notorious Prygleloven in April 1905. Much maligned at home and even more so abroad, it was repealed in 1911.

10. Helmuth Karl Bernhard Graf von Moltke (1800–1891) led the Prussian forces to victory in the 1864 Dano-Prussian War.

Russia. But also with respect to cultural politics the smallest Scandinavian state has once more proved itself the equal of the massive Russian kingdom.

In a letter I received from a sailor circumnavigating the world, dated San Francisco, March 9, there is this, word for word:

> For four months I have not been able to be informed of conditions in Denmark. When we acknowledge our own insignificance in the universe, we express our belief that we are providing an example of the modesty that is the result of wisdom. But alas! It hardly comes as a surprise when traveling around the Earth to experience how little Denmark is. One reads the newspapers of the world—of immense size—every day, but never sees his fatherland named. I have come across only a single note about Denmark, a telegram indicating that the Danish government had presented its parliament with a proposal for the introduction of knouting. It was in Honolulu that the editor of the paper inquired of me whether, as he had it, the 70,000 Japanese of the Hawaiian Islands ought not to believe that Denmark belonged to Russia. But when I gave an honest answer to his enquiry, he omitted reporting the conversation. He simply did not understand that a state bound by laws could have instigators of unrest that could not be tamed by those laws, and he would not bring the white race into further ill repute with the yellow.

If national character is anywhere lacking in us, the Germans are ready with a demonstration of how indeed we have distinguished ourselves, gladly acknowledging that the Danishness on which we insist is in fact not very original.

A German by the name of Alfred Lichtwark has recently praised Denmark's culture in a book titled *A Summer Voyage on the Yacht Hamburg*, which incidentally is not on the market.[11] He especially lauds our sense of aesthetics, strongly at the expense of the German. In the March 8 number of *Hamburger Nachrichten*, in which his work was reviewed and an attempt at rebuttal was made, he was accused of viewing Denmark with *Brandesian* eyes. While seeing something with such eyes in Denmark means to look down on the native born, in other places it means the very opposite, the overestimation of the Danish.

Now the little pamphlet *Danishness in Southern Jutland* that I published in 1899 is attacked in the German press, six years after the fact.[12] Everything

11. Art historian Alfred Lichtwark's (1832–1914) *Eine Sommerfart auf der Yacht Hamburg* appeared in 1904.

12. In protest of the severe policies of Schleswig-Holstein *oberpräsident* Ernst von Köller, Brandes issued *Danskheden i Sønderjylland*, which after several failed attempts finally

I had referred to as "proof of a Danish *urkultur*" [original culture] was in fact of German origin. I had among other things said that in the German-speaking world it would not be possible to distinguish a group of two million people that possessed all the organs of an independent culture, from agriculture and seafaring and lively political interest to painting and poetic arts of rank. I had written that "there is furthermore no place in Germany where one can run a dairy or paint a piece of porcelain or bind a book as we do in Denmark."

As for Danish seafaring, it is demonstrated by a Mr. K. J. Clement, who has conducted a penetrating analysis of Danish sailors' language, that its actual origins are German, or more properly Frisian.[13] As for dairy processing, the impulse to that actually emanated from the Germans of Schleswig-Holstein; a Mr. J. G. Kohl had in a book from 1846 called *Travels in Denmark* reported that everywhere he encountered dairymen from Holstein who had brought the art of marling to Denmark, and that the Danish landowners all around acknowledged the Holsteiners as more capable growers than the Danish farmers.[14]

Another responds:

> With respect to Danish painters and poets, their German colleagues can perhaps venture into a contest with them, and as highly as Copenhagen porcelain and bookbinding (of which the porcelain is influenced by Japan, the binding by England) are esteemed, this can however not be viewed as determinative for a culture. How deeply the Danes love alcohol is evident in that a brewer by virtue of this love has been able to emerge as a patron of the arts.[15]

The well informed will reasonably be able to refute what has been said about our sailors' language, which seems more Dutch than Frisian, and certain foreign

appeared in German in the journal *Die Zukunft*. For a comprehensive treatment of the Danish-German border conflict, see Troels Marstrand Trier Fink, *Båndene bandt: Forbindelsen over Kongeåen, 1864–1914*, 2 vols. (Copenhagen: Institut for Grænseregionsforskning, 1999).

13. Knut Jungbohn Clement (1803–73), born under Danish rule on the ethnically Frisian island of Amrun off the Schleswig-Holstein coast, was a German linguist and a rather fanatical advocate for the racial superiority of North Germans, of whom he did not consider the Danes to be a part. His many mid-nineteenth-century studies of Dano-German relations were widely cited in the 1905 attacks on Brandes.

14. Johann Georg Kohl (1808–78), a German travel writer and the author of *Reise durch Dänemark und die Herzogthümer Schleswig und Holstein*, was also cited frequently in the 1905 debates.

15. Jacob Christian Jacobsen (1811–87), the founder of the Carlsberg brewery, established the Carlsberg Fund in 1876. His son and successor, Carl Jacobsen (1842–1914), was a prominent art collector and the founder of the Ny Carlsberg Glyptotek, a Copenhagen art museum established in 1897.

words did not hinder us from being superior to the Germans at sea until 1864, that year included. It is also rather unimportant whether Holstein dairymen were better than ours in 1846, as in any event ours are now superior. That our porcelain painting is influenced by Japan is true. But Japan's is once more dependent on China's. That our bookbinders have learned from England is doubtful, but what of it when they now stand at the heights of the age! In fact, I never spoke of a "*Danish urkultur*" in the first place, nor have I ever believed in such a thing.

As for the painters and the poets, a comparison between two million people and sixty million is not fair. Regardless of who deserves the laurels, it is at the very least doubtful that the two million are more artistically inclined.

In one respect we ought preferably to be superior to the Germans: in the fear of self-satisfaction, in the openness of our gaze to our weaknesses and our national errors, in that self-critique that is the spur to all self-development.

The upcoming generation must be imbued with a sense of how strongly our weakness as a state society requires our government and representation to maintain a dignified attitude in our internal politics, and how strongly it commits every single one of us to make the most out of our abilities and in all external relations feel ourselves mutually responsible for Denmark.

CHAPTER 18

The Aryan Race

1905

In all his writings on oppressed peoples, never once does Brandes invoke the concept of race, as for him the identity of a given people is entirely determined by language and culture. In some ways this strikingly progressive view is a biographical necessity, since Brandes is of course himself of Jewish ancestry, a fact that he insisted throughout his life played no role whatsoever in his thinking and writing; indeed, the avowed atheist and secularist critic would maintain that his particular ancestry would never have even entered into his own understanding of himself, were it not for the occasional efforts of the Danish Right to undermine his status as public intellectual by pointing to his alleged foreign blood—see the essay "Race Theories" in the present volume for a vigorous rebuttal of just such an attempt. The article below, occasioned by the appearance of Jean Finot's *Le préjugé des races*, while a tightly argued and eminently reasonable dismissal of the pseudoscientific foundations of Aryanist racial theory, in many ways reveals a tragic blind spot within Brandes's larger thinking, namely the powerful popular appeal of the demonstrably nonsensical doctrines articulated by figures like Houston Stewart Chamberlain, Arthur de Gobineau, and eventually, of course, Adolf Hitler himself.[1] Just as they are today, advocates of racial supremacy were in the early twentieth century all too effortlessly dismissed by intellectuals like Brandes and Finot, who ultimately failed to see in the savage internal consistency of their worldview and in the all too irresistible emotional impact of their appeals a primal force more than potent enough to overcome their logical and historical deficiencies.

~

Were I fortunate enough to have a prize to give out at my discretion, I would certainly give it to *Jean Finot*, not because of his meticulous helming of the well-informed and multifaceted journal *La Revue*, but because he has written

Originally published in *Politiken*, June 25, 1905. Translated from the version published in *Samlede Skrifter*, vol. 18.

1. Finot's *Le préjugé des races* (Paris: Félix Alcan) was first published in the spring of 1905.

the striking and joyful book *Race Prejudices*. It is as if the trumpets of Jericho resound through this book. The walls of stupidity, whole mountains of pseudo-scientific nonsense, collapse before one's eyes while one reads it. Would that it be read by many!

Yet certainly that will hardly happen here in Norden. Like a kind of curse, those barren and false books, those that contain a web of baseless and self-important claims, and that abroad have only found circulation because they have strengthened national conceit and tribal arrogance, have caught on in Norway and here, and one sees their teachings everywhere repeated in the Nordic journals and papers, just as they earlier appeared in the German and French press. Nearly as loathsome as the doctrine in these books is the tastelessness with which it is proclaimed. We have, it seems, reached the point at which tastelessness no longer injures.

Has the Nordic public ever had taste? Once it was said to have possessed discernment. In the very least its taste is at present quite in question. Books as thick as Bibles, books whose actual content might fill twenty thousand pages, books that contain a single paltry and tired thought, half trivial and half nonsense, are read with rapt attention. The shocking works of Mr. Chamberlain and Otto Weininger stand as examples.[2] (When any kind of opposition, however humble, is registered against Weininger in Denmark, the offender is accused of obstinacy).

In contrast to such German pearls of wisdom, Finot's book arrives as a liberator.

He dares to speak the simple truth about Gobineau, who with his *Essay on the Inequality of the Races* introduced the first thread from which so much of the modern web of phantasm has been spun.[3] It was truly no injustice that during his lifetime he was overlooked as a thinker in France. That fame he now enjoys is owed to the enthusiastic support of Richard Wagner, although the worship of the Wagnerians will eventually reveal itself to be quite a passing

2. Houston Stewart Chamberlain (1855–1927) was a British-born racial theorist of the late nineteenth and early twentieth centuries, although his work made much more of an impact in Germany and Austria than in Britain, as he wrote in German and spent most of his life on the continent; in the 1920s he would become an associate and supporter of Adolf Hitler. He is also remembered as a rather fanatical Wagnerian, having married the composer's daughter Eva von Bülow in 1908. The legacy of Austrian philosopher Otto Weininger (1880–1903) is significantly more complex; while aspects of his *Geschlecht und Charakter: Eine prinzipielle Untersuchung* (1903) were eventually embraced by the Nazis, he was also an important influence on Ludwig Wittgenstein and August Strindberg. Perhaps not coincidentally, Weininger was also an admirer of Richard Wagner.

3. French racial theorist Arthur de Gobineau's (1816–82) magnum opus *Essai sur l'inégalité des races humaines* (1853–55) articulated the concept of a master "Aryan" race.

phenomenon. As a poet he is admired in France by few other than critics influenced by Wagner, such as Schuré, and as an ethnologist he is arbitrariness itself.[4] At present his good qualities as well as his bad have in equal respect been portrayed in a positive light in the first exhaustive work about him, Robert Dreyfus's *Count Gobineau's Life and Prophecies*.[5]

If there is something that especially deserves notice in Finot's extensive work, I would first note that he has dealt a powerful blow to the faith of the global reading public in the existence of the Aryans as an *urvolk* from which Europe's main peoples descend. Regarding actual scientists, there has been no need to instruct them, for already K. Hartmann has expressed that "the so-called Aryans have never existed in the form of a primitive people, but only as a discovery by bookish people."[6] And Virchow has already asserted "that the Aryans, as a place-specific entity, have never been discovered."[7]

Finot pokes fun at the popular belief that the French are an Aryan people, descended from a race in distant times settled in India and Persia, for we know that people were living in ancient Gaul all the way from the quaternary period. The discoveries in the rock caves of northwestern France as well as on the banks of the Seine and the Somme prove that humans have lived there alongside two large elephant species for over 200,000 years, that is, numerous centuries before the immigrants from Asia, the most eager adherents of the Aryanism allege, are said to have arrived.

Yet the question of where exactly these supposed forefathers of the European peoples originated, science has learned, is a matter of sheer skepticism and contradiction. According to Fr. Schlegel's account they came from India and settled in Europe; Link believes they came from Georgia; Adolphe Pictet that they came from Bactria.[8] The famous Belgian geologist Omalius d'Halloy

---

4. Éduard Schuré (1841–1929) was one of the few French intellectuals to remain a fervent admirer of German literature and culture in the decades following the Franco-Prussian War, largely due to his enthusiasm for Wagner.

5. Robert Dreyfus (1873–1939) is better remembered as lifelong friend and confidant of Marcel Proust. His *La vie et les prophéties du comte de Gobineau* appeared in 1905.

6. German ethnographer Karl Eduard Robert Hartmann (1832–93), whose research focused on Africa, regularly ran up against the racist tenets of his discipline as it existed in the nineteenth century.

7. German physician and anthropologist Rudolf Ludwig Carl Virchow (1821–1902) debunked much of racialist craniometric pseudoscience in the 1880s.

8. Friedrich Schlegel (1772–1829) staked his claim for Indian origins in *Über die Sprache und Weisheit der Indier* (1808). Heinrich Friedrich Link (1767–1851) was primarily a botanist, but his views on the Aryans appear in his *Die Urwelt und das Alterthum, erläutert durch die Naturkunde* (1820–22). Swiss linguist Adolphe Pictet (1799–1875) published his massive *Les origines indo-européennes ou les Aryas primitifs* between 1859 and 1863.

demonstrates with ingenious arguments that the Asiatic Aryans were simply Europeans; it is, he asserts, Europe that has sent these conquerors to Asia.[9] Archaeological discoveries like Schliemann's have furthermore established that when the West came into contact with the East for the first time, Western civilization was already old.[10] The working of bronze originated in Europe and then passed to Asia.[11] Clémence Royer maintains that the famous Aryan language was originally spoken in Europe and reached Asia through the Caucasus.[12] Benfey thinks that the land by the mouth of the Danube is the actual cradle of the Aryan civilization.[13]

It has also been demonstrated that the Greek language does not have Sanskrit as its forerunner, as has long been believed, and that the Indian script descends in a direct line from the Greek and Aramaic alphabet.[14] The age of the Avesta and the Vedas has been pushed back a dozen centuries by the earliest zealots.

Not only have the various doctrines placed the Aryans in different locations; they also describe them differently. For Huxley they are long-skulled, for Tylor they are short-skulled, for Gobineau tall and blond, for Sergi small and brown.[15] In the end it is evident that faith in the idea that the Aryans are the

9. In spite of his rather comical racial theories, Jean Baptiste Julien d'Omalius d'Halloy (1783–1875) was acknowledged by Darwin himself as an important forerunner of evolutionary theory.

10. Heinrich Schliemann (1822–90) is best remembered for his efforts to demonstrate the historicity of the Homeric epics.

11. Brandes himself here falls victim to the kind of overly expansive understandings of "Europe" and the "West" characteristic of his era.

12. Clémence Royer (1830–1902), the first French translator of Darwin, holds the dubious distinction of being the only woman in this rather sorry cast of characters.

13. German philologist Theodor Benfey (1809–81), a pioneer of Sanskrit studies, is the only figure of Jewish descent discussed by Finot.

14. The former claim is correct; while Greek and Sanskrit share a common ancestor, it is not the case that the one derived from the other. The second claim regarding scripts is unsupported by any evidence.

15. Thomas Henry Huxley (1825–95), "Darwin's Bulldog," weighed in on the issue in his 1890 essay "On the Aryan Question." Edward Burnett Tylor (1832–1917) is considered the founder of cultural anthropology. While his reflections on race in his seminal *Primitive Culture: Researches into the Development of Mythology, Philosophy, Religion, Art, and Custom* (1871) are shot through with common nineteenth-century prejudices, his methodological and disciplinary innovations should be credited with laying the groundwork for their eventual undermining. Italian anthropologist Giuseppe Sergi (1841–1936), the lone southern European discussed by Finot, was in fact opposed to Nordicism, arguing that the first Europeans, the "Mediterranean race," were in fact of African descent.

tribal ancestors of the Celts and other Europeans rests on a misunderstanding, on certain observed similarities between the language they call Aryan and the European languages.

There was a need for a scientific explanation of the relationship between a series of languages, and then along comes a novel about a secretive people, the Aryans, who during their wanderings across the Earth begat the different European nations. Modern linguistics itself is now the first to denounce the talk of an Aryan race. What we know is that there is a family of Aryan languages. But race and language cannot be conflated. The Latin language took possession of Gaul, but the Gauls did not therefore become Romans. Max Müller has aptly said that "he who speaks of the Aryan race, Aryan blood, Aryan eyes and hair, makes the same mistake as he who would speak of a long-skulled dictionary or a short-skulled grammar."[16]

After exorcising the old ghost of the "Aryan race," Finot deserves credit for making light of the modern Frenchman's belief in the pure Gallic blood coursing through his veins.

With ease he confirms that among the peoples who have contributed to modern French blood, there have in the least been the following: Aquitani, Iberians, Basques, Silures, Salians, Libui, Suanetes, Vulgentes, Sordones, Pictones, Cambolectri, Agesineses, Turones, Andegades, Carnutes, Veneti, Curiousolitae, Redones, Osismii, Abricantuens, Lexovii, Aulerci, Veliocasses, Caletes, Parisii, Lingones, Helvetii, Ædui, Leuci, Alans, Vandals, Teifales Agathyrsi, Ruthenians, Poles, Veneti, Belgians, Galates, Cimbri, Visigoths, Burgundians, Franks, Saxons, Allemanni, Suevi, Phoenicians, Saracens, Jews, Etruscans, Pelasgians, Sabines, Mongolian and African peoples, Romani, et cetera.

Finot shares the opinion of Arbois de Jubainville, who has argued in his work *The Celts* that there is probably more Gallic blood in Germany than in France, a view that has more than a little to recommend it.[17]

Other aspects of Finot's big book are less well thought out. He expresses admiration for authors who deserve no admiration because they have opinions that suit his book, and he stumbles in areas that his knowledge of language does not reach. What he says about the Normans is in this way quite poor. He knows all the main European languages other than the Slavic, but of the

16. German-born Oxford professor Max Müller (1823–1900), a founding figure in the study of comparative religion, stands out among nineteenth-century Orientalists for his vehement opposition to any form of racial supremacism.

17. Marie Henri d'Arbois de Jubainville (1827–1910) was the principal nineteenth-century French expert on the peoples of ancient Gaul and the Celtic language.

Nordic tongues he naturally knows nothing. Nevertheless, as I have said before, he has done a good deed in writing this book. When compared to Gobineau's dreadful chatter about the inevitable descent of the French as a Latin (!) people and the inevitable world domination of the Germans as pure Germans, or Weininger's still more dreadful nonsense about the infinite superiority of the Aryan race over the Semitic, it is refreshing once again to listen to the sober talk of a reasonable person . . .

CHAPTER 19

To the Schoolchildren of Russian Poland

1905

Russian defeat in the Russo-Japanese War of 1904–5 and the consequent revolt against czarist rule would eventually result in similar unrest in greater Poland, a period of resistance sometimes referred to as the revolution in the Kingdom of Poland of 1905–7. Initially a general strike, the workers were soon joined by the students of Russian Poland at all levels, who in February walked out in protest of Russification policies much as their brethren had previously done in the Prussian sector. The events of 1905, as evidenced by the breathless tone of this essay, indicate that Brandes's hopes for Poland have peaked.

~

Dear children!

I know that among your parents and guardians there are a few who hope that the effort to break your resistance and get you to go back into the Russian schools once again will succeed. I know that such significant personalities as the head of the reconciliation party, Count Adam Krasinski, and Archbishop Popiel, have attempted, both with admonitions and with means more effective than admonitions, to force you to give up your decision.[1]

But be assured that most of your parents and superiors, and all the best among them, are with you in all their hearts, would with sadness see your will broken, as the will of the adults has all too often been broken in Poland as well as Russia.

Among the Polish men who follow you with the best of wishes there are some who have turned to me, a foreigner, whose name is however known to you, to ask me to say an encouraging word to you, implore you not to have

First published in Danish in *Politiken*, August 14, 1905. Translated from the version published in *Samlede Skrifter*, vol. 17.

1. One of the most prominent aristocratic families of Poland, the Krasińskis after 1795 historically vacillated between support of Polish nationalists and their foreign overlords. Vincent Teofilo Popiel (1815–1912), a scion of another of Poland's leading families, was archbishop of Warsaw from 1883 to his death.

second thoughts about your undertaking, and more than anything to hold out. Without such a request from the Polish side my letter to you could look like an uncalled-for interference in affairs that only concern your countrymen and women. Now no one will view it as such except those whose judgment carries weight for neither you nor me.

You must not believe that the civilized world, which for forty years has been idle regarding the fate of your fatherland, is in our age an indifferent witness to the scattered and desperate efforts at liberation that are found in the Kingdom of Poland.[2]

Believe me that the intellectual nobility in all the free countries follows with excitement the progress of events, and the young souls, girls as well as boys, who have first and most courageously held up the Russian government's coercive dominance of the Polish school system, will not be forgotten in either Europe or America. You have sunk the ax into the great root of evil. You children have put to shame the adults by providing an example. The civilized people who admire your talent for action and the steadfastness you have long shown will not lose sight of you, and they wish you success and victory with hundreds of thousands of voices.

You know that you have made a strong impression on the schoolchildren in the free states. The beautiful albeit childlike letters you have received from Switzerland have assured you of this. But grown men and women have no less sympathy with your bold manner of action than the children, who still only faintly grasp what life is.

You yourselves are young in years, but the misfortunes of your fatherland have matured you faster than other children of your age, and when you saw tyranny totter, you were willing to give odiousness the first push down into the abyss with your tender hands. All honor to you for that!

You have acted out of your best and surest natural instincts; out of enthusiasm for the most undeniable of human rights, that to speak and read one's language; out of enthusiasm for that language itself, in which immortal works are written; out of enthusiastic love of your people, your country, and its history, but especially its future.

In a word, you have acted from enthusiasm without regard for either the nearer or more distant consequences of your actions, for the punishment that threatens and awaits you. Too cold-blooded and still more too hostile observers took your behavior as a sign of madness, and sensible calculation was certainly

2. Brandes here refers to the last great outbreak of Polish resistance toward Russia, the January Uprising of 1863, put down the following year.

not found in it; but there is a heroic madness that is more valuable and more effective than reason, when reason is cowardly.

Friends of your cause and your people have been reminded by your action of the children's crusade of the Middle Ages. It is, however, only the childlike enthusiasm that calls forth the point of comparison. Otherwise it is the differences that stand out. Those children were led by a monk. You yourselves have the archbishop against you. The actions of those children were not useful and their goals were fantastic. Your action is useful, in that it is a tribute to justice, a response to oppression. It is the spear hurled into the camp of the enemy, which the adults must help you to get back. It is a shining banner with the white eagle hoisted high over Poland, visible in all countries. Your countrymen cannot at all allow that banner to fall again by surrendering. And since your action is useful, in this way your goal is a reality: Polish language resounding from all lips in Russian Poland, Mickiewicz's language, set down like a queen on her throne at the university in Warsaw as in all schools, and thereby the highest spiritual good, freedom for all ages and social classes, is established and secured.[3]

For the many who have followed from a distance the Russian kingdom's crises in East Asia and in Europe, powerful impressions of wide-ranging events have clashed with one another: the battles on land and at sea, many defeats, sieges, fortress battles, outpost clashes, huge battles in open fields, generals who fell or surrendered, admirals who went down or were taken captive. And then in the kingdom itself: the killing of princes, ministers, governors, policemen high and low, immense strikes, the murders in Petersburg, in Tomsk, in Kursk, in Zhytomyr, in Baku, in Lodz, in Warsaw, in Odessa, in Nizhny Novgorod; peasant uprisings and worker revolts, mutiny in the navy and unrest in the army, a bloody anarchy in fits and starts of progress and abominable reversals to the old state of affairs, all that has now for a second year so stunned, dazzled, and confused the reading masses that they have lost the measuring stick for what in these actions and horrors is essential and what is, albeit horrifying enough, only of passing significance.

This much is certain, that the Polish schoolchildren's revolt against the Russian schoolmasters is of lasting significance.

I know all the objections leveled against you: that resentment of school instruction, which was originally a sign of enthusiasm, maintains itself because of laziness and a desire for idleness. That Russian instruction is better than no instruction at all. And finally that you now act precisely accordingly to the

3. Adam Bernard Mickiewicz (1798–1855) is Poland's national poet.

will of the Russian government, for what else does the government desire than a Polish youth made incompetent by ignorance.

But these objections make no impression on me. Naturally there are those among you for whom the break from school provides a pretext for idleness and its vices. But these will and must be exceptions. You others must seek knowledge to the best of your abilities, albeit along secret paths and by hiding your books. By no means was anything worse than an ignorant and because of its ignorance powerless Polish youth. Knowledge is not just in general power, but it is for you yourselves your superiority over your enemies, the sharpest weapon, the utmost guardian, the source of intellectual and economic riches. Your efforts therefore also involve your securing that all the necessary knowledge is imparted in the mother tongue. And now you have acquired, in the eyes of all Poland's adult men and women, the great point of honor not to have halted before they have won for you the first of the great universal human goods, the use of the language, which will have political freedom as its consequence.

In general it is a sound political rule that one does not send children into the breach. Yet it is you yourselves who have put yourselves into the breach, and that is immense. In Poland it has been shown that the most recently born, those who look back on the longest historical experience, despite how short their personal experience still is—that these youngest are in reality the oldest. A breath of the courage of bygone heroes and heroines has passed over your heads and has carried you away.

A people whose children are as advanced as you are necessarily has a future before it. A language that is loved as highly as the Polish language necessarily has a tremendous power of expansion through you. It is surely also evident that in spite of the efforts of two great powers to suppress it, its usage increases from day to day with rapid speed.

You have felt that the holiest right is that to use one's mother tongue, to be instructed in one's mother tongue, to get to know the past and the present of one's fatherland in the mother tongue. You have grasped the criminality of a government that treats as an offense among you what it praises as a virtue among its own, the love of the fatherland and its language. You have seen that the school's linguistic reorganization was the reorganization of all conditions from the ground up. And so you have allowed your insight to determine your will and have unequivocally brought your will to light. The Russians have not been able to break your will. If only lesser Poles were capable of such! Tell your elders who are faltering: our sense of justice is stronger and finer than yours!

According to its nature the child is weak and soft. If it is stubborn, then as a rule its resistance lasts only a short time, and when it is defiant, it is often out of an evil will, because it will not give up on one or another harmful or amusing enjoyment for which it has a desire. Never before in world history has it been seen that children have stood up to their teachers, indeed against the authorities, on the strength of an idea, at once a moral and a political idea.

A political idea. For the Polish schoolchildren have not just demonstrated national sentiment and a sense of justice; they have also demonstrated political savvy. They have understood that now the moment has arrived, now or never! They have seen that if Russian Poland cannot liberate itself now, when the defeats have rained down on the czardom and when its status in Europe is shaken just as it has been destroyed in Asia, then Poland can once again for a century cloak itself in sorrow and scatter ashes on its head.

But that will not happen.

Now, precisely now the great moment has come. Now all the cocks crow. Soon all the larks sing. Now all hearts blaze, where there was only a spark of the holy fire of the love of freedom. The sun of freedom itself still stands only blood red on the horizon. But soon it will rise, luminous and golden, over all the oppressed peoples in the immense Russian land.

You, Poland's youth, have believed in it. Your faith like your will gives you honor. Long live the Poland that is reborn in you! Long live the freedom you would see established! And would the enthusiasm that you in your earliest youth have felt be preserved pure and unadulterated in your hearts that you may transmit it to the coming generation.

CHAPTER 20

The Future of Russian Poland

1905

This essay marks the cessation of Brandes's initial flurry of activity on behalf of the Poles, and further represents the peak of his optimism regarding the fate of that people whom he loved so dearly. Conditions in partitioned Poland did indeed seem encouraging at the conclusion of 1905, particularly in the Russian sector, in which Polish nationalists were finding increasing common ground with liberal activists in Russia proper. The notorious threat issued by Skalon, discussed at length below, represented a clash between the old imperial principle (codified in the agreement of 1795) and the rising tide of national liberalism. Sadly, of course, Brandes's hopes, and even more so those of freethinking Poles and Russians, would be resoundingly dashed in the coming years, as the czarist regime proved to be much more resilient than expected. The Poles would in the end have to wait until the catastrophe of the Great War and the total collapse of the Russian Empire before their dreams of independence would be fulfilled.

~

A significant and promising development for the future of Russian Poland involves an episode that occurred during the negotiations at the meeting of the representatives of the cities and the zemstvos in Moscow, which the newspapers of the various countries have reported without being properly informed of its importance.[1] Since I am personally acquainted with all of those whose names have on this occasion come to the attention of the greater public, I would gladly dwell on the issue for a moment.

A Polish priest, *Chelmicki*, appeared before Skalon, the governor-general of Warsaw, as the spokesperson for a deputation that demanded the repeal of the

---

Originally published in *Politiken*, December 5, 1905. Translated from the version published in *Samlede Skrifter*, vol. 18.

1. The zemstvos were local governing councils initially set up during the relatively liberal reign of Czar Alexander II in the mid-nineteenth century.

military dictatorship in Russian Poland.[2] According to Chelmicki's statement, Skalon responded that if the Poles continued to insist on their right to self-rule then they would soon be in a bad way. What would they say if Kaiser Wilhelm sent one or two army corps over the border?

The German newspapers, such as the December 2 edition of *Der Tag*, considered it impossible that a highly placed official could have used "such a meaningless phrase," thereby attempting to undermine any Slavic embitterment over the matter.

But Chelmicki is not a man who traffics in idle talk. For twenty years he has been one of the most influential clergymen in Warsaw. He belongs to Sienkiewicz's innermost circle and is one of the few priests to whom their superiors have early on given the full freedom to participate in worldly life; he has been able to go about in society, to the theaters, participate in every amusement as in every patriotic effort.[3] He is wise, adroit, and firm. There is no doubt that he has reported Skalon's utterance accurately.

Last year in November Polish and Russian envoys met as friends in Paris for the first time and together made plans. Since then there has been continuous communication between the friends of freedom in Russian Poland and those in Russia proper.

Russian prince Pyotr Dolgorukov, who brought up Skalon's answer in the Russian parliament, was present last summer at a meeting between leading Russians and patriotic Poles in Carlsbad, and there for the first time they came together in friendship and agreement at a place where previously they had avoided one another.[4]

It is in the home of Prince Pyotr Dolgorukov that the parliamentary gatherings in Moscow are held; in his palace he has a hall that is large enough to accommodate five to six hundred persons comfortably. He is a millionaire many times over, but belongs heart and soul to the freethinking movement in Russia, and has from the very beginning called for universal, direct, and secret voting for the coming national assembly. It was he who uttered the strongest words about Skalon, that if he had really used the aforementioned phrase, then he had branded himself with indelible shame and ought to be at the

2. Georgi Skalon (1847–1914) had introduced martial law earlier in 1905 in response to Polish uprisings. Canon Zygmunt Chełmicki (1851–1922) was a prominent Polish activist in Warsaw circles, one of the very few clergymen for whom Brandes expressed a lasting admiration.

3. For more on Sienkiewicz, see note 6 to "Contemporary Civilization" in the present volume.

4. Prince Petr Dmitrievich Dolgorukov (1866–1951) was a leading liberal politician and activist.

mercy of public contempt. Dolgorukov was for Polish self-rule without hesitation. For him as for Maksim Kovalevsky and for others among Russia's most significant men, the goal is a great Russian confederation with independent provincial diets for the non-Russian peoples.[5]

On this point the next speaker, *Guchkov*, whom the freethinkers demand be appointed as governor of Moscow, was not in agreement; he desired no provincial diet for Poland.[6] But he felt nonetheless no small measure of fear that the Poles should rise up against the Russian people or think about seceding.

And on the last point he is right; Sienkiewicz has recently issued a solemn declaration on behalf of the Poles stating that they do not aim at any succession from Russia or rising against Russia, but only desire the same freedoms as the Russians themselves enjoy, and further promises that as a consequence of that, order and harmony will prevail in Russian Poland.

Guchkov took Sienkiewicz at his word, but interjected: from this we must not conclude that the Polish people absolutely will not rise up. They will rise as one, when the bell tolls for the fateful struggle against our common enemy, whom all the Slavs hate, who persecutes Slavs in Poznan and Silesia, who takes joy in every sorrow that afflicts us, and entices us toward a conduct such as that which is now carried out in Russian Poland.

After further speakers had affirmed that the Russian officials in Poland acted according to the advice of anti-Polish newspapers, *E. de Roberty*, the earlier leader of the Russian high school in Paris, concluded the negotiations with the statement that he did not consider the czar to be ready for the treachery that calling the German troops would be; that could only be done by the impudent camarilla "that surrounds the czar and deceives him."[7] E. de Roberty is a man of violent temperament; it was he who at the first assembly of the parliament had objected to the police entering the chamber to record the names of all of the members present: "Sign all of Russia up!" He belongs to those radicals of the intelligentsia with the firmest convictions.

As the current flows and the waves rise in Russia, men like Dolgorukov and Roberty will soon be accounted as the most moderate of those whose voices are heard, for public opinion becomes ever-more revolutionary. Peter Struve has already lost his influence.[8] Had Prince Trubetskoy, who died in Petersburg,

5. Maksim Maksimovich Kovalevskii (1851–1916) was the most prominent social scientist of the late Russian Empire.

6. Aleksandr Ivanovich Guchkov (1862–1936) was a conservative politician of considerable liberal tendencies, who advocated a kind of "constitutional czardom."

7. Eugène de Roberty de la Cerda (1843–1915) was a sociologist of the late imperial era.

8. The economist Petr Berngardovich Struve (1870–1944) was one of the principal agitators of the 1905 revolution in Russia.

lived a month longer, he would surely have been shoved to the side as all too moderate.[9] The affronts he suffered on account of his servile attitude to the czar in the end contributed to his death. He was a fundamentally honest man, a pupil of the remarkably endowed thinker and humanitarian Solovyov; but he believed all too much in the goodwill of the ruling party.[10] The present leaders are all to the Left of him and even almost ready to be the Girondists of the revolution.

The national hatred that burned between Poles and Russians has gone out. The important thing is to prevent the class that is still ruling, which supports every reactionary government, from once again breathing life into it.

9. Prince Sergei Nikolaevich Trubetskoi (1862–1905) was a philosopher and theologian who largely abandoned his early liberal views at the end of his life.

10. Vladimir Sergeevich Solov'ev (1853–1900), a significant influence on both Tolstoy and Fedor Dostoevskii, also drifted away from freethinking in his final years.

CHAPTER 21

Zionism

1905

As is abundantly clear in the essay below, Brandes had come to see his seemingly never-ending advocacy work as an undue burden by the conclusion of 1905; indeed, the coming years would see only a handful of advocacy writings, before he returned to the subject in earnest at the outbreak of the Great War. Yet exhaustion alone cannot be blamed for the fact that the Zionist movement would end up as the object on which Brandes would vent his frustrations. Due credit must also be given to the substantial history of cold relations between Brandes and the initial Zionist leaders, Theodor Herzl and Max Nordau, the latter of whom for years had regularly attacked the father of the Modern Breakthrough on purely aesthetic grounds. Brandes's dismissive attitude toward the Zionist project must furthermore be attributed to the movement's efforts to appeal to Ottoman sultan Abdul Hamid, for whom Brandes nourished a lifelong (and understandable) hatred. Perhaps even more so, finally, the Zionist insistence that European Jewry constituted a race with a subsequent right to a homeland clashed inevitably with his own very different views on what constitutes a given people, as evidenced in his essays "The Aryan Race" and "Race Theories."

~

The many inquiries, requests, and invitations I receive on a daily basis have consumed three months of my working life this year. The manuscripts and books I shall read, the letters I shall answer, the reviews I am requested to write, the introductions I am asked to give, the speeches I am invited to deliver have gradually reached a fantastic number. Add to this the fact that in Europe and America I am viewed as if I were a one man (gratis) clearing house for information regarding the Scandinavian countries. A request from Athens urges me to report on what has been written on Macedonia by northerners, one from New York asks me to produce a "philosophy of literature" and to provide Strindberg's

Originally published in *Politiken*, December 12, 1905. Translated from the version published in *Samlede Skrifter*, vol. 18.

address, and one from Vienna humbly beseeches me to send a bouquet of flowers from Hamlet's grave, since the author's lover is mad about Hamlet.

For every private and personal request I receive, there are those from people who have an issue that is dear to them and who point out that it is my duty to make myself a spokesperson for it, while at the same time they readily express their surprise that I have not spoken up. They know so little of me that even this assumption of theirs is as a rule incorrect. But in every instance they find that I ought to intrude myself into every issue for which they have use of me or my name.

For example, some time ago a splendid lady, who occupies a leading position in the peace movement, asked me to issue a manifesto that could be read at a peace congress in Rome, and in which I declared myself to be a friend of world peace. When I bade her rather to direct this request to Kaiser Wilhelm she resented my answer exceedingly and our correspondence of many years ceased.

While the conflict between Norway and Sweden and later the internal conflict among Norwegians was going on, I was passionately urged by Norwegians to take up the cause of the Norwegian republic, and by Sweden to speak out for Sweden's just cause in Europe.[1]

Every time the Nobel Prize is to be awarded, the Italians and Italianesses beseech me to get the prize for Carducci and the Poles to intervene for Sienkiewicz, without the slightest regard for the fact that the Swedish Academy has not even asked for my opinion and that the secretary and most influential man has written several hundred articles denouncing me.[2]

For a number of years now German clerical newspapers and French antisemitic books have featured a standing complaint against me: I cut down the noblest and best Christians such as Luther or Joseph de Maistre, only instead to glorify and praise the Jews.

But at the same time in contemporary Hebrew literature my name is rarely or never mentioned except for complaints of how sad (or disgraceful) it is that I have completely left the cause of the Jews by the wayside. When I was in Prague last week I was beseeched by Bohemian Jews and Jewesses to speak out about the bloodbath in Russia.[3] In Berlin I was asked to hold a public meeting

1. After centuries of Danish and later Swedish rule, Norway acquired its full independence in October 1905.

2. Henryk Adam Aleksander Pius Sienkiewicz (1846–1916) was in fact awarded the prize for the year 1905, Giosuè Alessandro Giuseppe Carducci (1835–1907) for the year following. Carl David af Wirsén (1842–1912), Swedish Academy permanent secretary from 1884 until his death, also regularly denounced Strindberg and Ibsen.

3. This is likely a reference to the Kishinev Pogrom of 1903, which had briefly reignited in October 1905.

in support of the Russian Jews, and when I declined I was asked at the very least to excuse myself in writing, since they were—as strange as it sounds—convinced that my voice would contribute to putting an end to the persecution and murder.

There is something touching in the ignorance of real conditions that is displayed by this.

However, I confess that I do not find anything touching in Dr. Fraenkel's *Open Letter* to me.[4]

It is crazy enough that a writer is continuously held accountable for every single word he has written every time the first and the best among the reading public determine he has erred.

But it is worse that a writer is called to account for what he has not said, and is further expected to indicate the reasons for his silence.

Worst of all is when without further ado the accuser assures the public that the writer in question "has not made a stroke with his pen," thereby ignoring the entire corpus of said writer.

If Dr. Fraenkel had only read what is clearly found in the eleventh volume of my *Collected Writings*, pp. 456–86, or if he was familiar with the no small number of articles on the issue, for example, "The Agony of a People and Utopias," then he could have spared us this public inquisition.[5]

Not to justify myself, but to enlighten the general public, there is this to keep in mind:

There is a great deal of ignorance in the assumption that writing for one or another cause is synonymous with its advancement. Naturally the written word has rarely had any effect. But just getting the writing distributed is sometimes difficult enough. To write in Danish is of course the same as writing in water. It's a matter then of getting the writing out in one of the world languages that it might be noticed. Do you believe that happens on its own?

In the year 1901, in response to urgent and repeated requests from Romania, I wrote a longer article titled "Jewish and Christian Romanians," a plea for the persecuted and abused Romanian Israelites. It was first to be published in French; Alliance Israélite would see to its publication and distribution. I asked not a single øre for the writing, but required for the translation an honorarium similar to the one that I myself am in the habit of giving, in this case one

4. Danish Jewish physician Louis Herman Nikolai Fraenkel (1868–1935) was the first chair of the Danish Zionist Forbund, founded in 1903.

5. Brandes here refers to his 1901 essay "Jødiske og kristne Rumænere" ("Jewish and Christian Romanians"), which as described below was ultimately nixed by French and Austrian publishers and only later appeared in his *Samlede Skrifter*, 11:456–86. "The Agony of a People and Utopias," translated for the present volume, first appeared in 1903.

hundred or one hundred fifty francs; I do not remember the precise sum. When Alliance Israélite found this honorarium too high (!) and denied paying it, publication did not take place.

In German its publication was to be in a world-class Viennese newspaper under Jewish leadership and financed by Jewish capital. The article was accepted, but remained unpublished for one month, two months, three months, in spite of repeated requests from my side. Lack of column space and similar editorial evasions were blamed. At last I learned that the paper feared putting itself on the outs with the Romanian government, with which it had financial ties, and the article was never published. It is consequently not as easy to work for the oppressed Jews at all times and in all places as Dr. Fraenkel imagines it; one meets among others non-oppressed Jews along the way.

Neither does Dr. Fraenkel impress me with his assertion that the Jews are a "tribally pure" people. About this I can only restate what I said in the year 1901:[6]

> Renan explained in his book *Judaism* that Judaism is a religion, but does not constitute a race; he showed how many nonsemitic elements have entered into the tribe, how West European Jews are partly descended from Frenchmen and East Europeans from Khazars, who thousands of years ago adopted the Jewish religion, and he explains the typecasting of Jews as a result of the influence of the ghettos. In our time learned and discerning scholars like Goldstein, who writes in French, have demonstrated the immense intermixing of blood out of which the Hebrew tribe emerged in antiquity, and in latter times scholars are not at all inclined to take the Jews for Semites. Thus the purity of the race is in any case a phantom.
>
> But more and more now Zionism has come to a head on the assertion that the Jews are to this day a nation and must demand their state—an assertion that ignores what has occurred over the last two thousand years. Especially when certain boisterous mediocrities like Max Nordau act as its spokesman it takes on outright repulsive forms, and unfortunately it seems as if he has founded a

6. Brandes cites from his essay "Jødiske og kristne Rumænere," 486. Philosopher and historian Joseph Ernest Renan (1823–92), an important influence on young Brandes, first offered his insights on Jewish racial identity in an 1883 lecture titled Le judaisme comme race et comme religion. His "Khazar Hypothesis" of Jewish racial origins has few modern adherents. Brandes's many essays on Renan are collected in his *Samlede Skrifter*, 7:3–52. Anthropologist Édouard Goldstein published a series of studies in French on Jewish ancestry in the 1880s; by no means should he be confused with the German journalist Moritz Goldstein, who argued precisely the opposite—see the author's commentary to "Race Theories" for more on the latter.

> school among the Zionists: an eternal insistence on Jewish nationality, continuous contemptuous attacks on the Israelites who have identified with the peoples who have received them among themselves, loud assurances that antisemitism will never subside and that the Jew who calls himself a Frenchman or an Englishman is a despicable person who denies his brothers.[7] It is only natural that the great Jewish financial dynasties withhold support from a movement that is so illogical and inept, and that literally proposes expulsion as the only answer.

When in 1894 Theodor Herzl initiated Zionism with the publication of his book *The Jewish State*, he was, as one who earlier had eagerly combated the view of Jewry as a nation, still so unclear over the issue that he did not know whether *Argentina* or *Palestine* ought to be preferred as the destination of the emigration.[8] At that time he right away sought a connection with me, took offense at my somewhat reserved attitude (and thereafter as *Neue freie Presses* feuilleton editor showed me an immensely severe ill will for ten years).

Herzl was an outstanding, unselfish, quite ambitious man, yet in no respect up to the task of leading the immense enterprise he set in motion. A portion of Eastern Europe's believing Jews even see him as a true messiah who would lead them back to the promised land. During Kaiser Wilhelm's visit to Jerusalem he sought the protection of the German monarch; he obtained audiences with Abdul Hamid, received a Turkish decoration, and was childish enough to rely on the vague promises of the crowned murderer.[9]

Quite apart from the poverty and infertility of Palestine, which makes it incapable of supporting seven to eight million impoverished new inhabitants, a new obstacle has emerged in that the sultan will neither give up the land nor provide the Jews the security they demand. Any child can therefore grasp that if they do succeed in reaching prosperity on Turkish ground, the Mohammedans would treat them like the Kurds treated the Armenians in the land of Ararat.

---

7. Hungarian-born critic and Zionist activist Max Simon Nordau (1849–1923, b. Simon Maximilian Südfeld) was cofounder, with Herzl, of the World Zionist Organization. His hatred of Brandes in fact predates his embrace of the Zionist cause, as is evidenced in his appropriately titled *Entartung* (1892, published in English as *Degeneration*), a sweeping indictment of all things "modern" in literature.

8. Hungarian-born Theodor Herzl's (1860–1904) *Der Judenstaat* in fact appeared in 1896, although it does indeed consider the possibility of an Argentine homeland. His reporting on the Dreyfus Affair as Paris correspondent for *Neue freie Presse* was essential in raising awareness of the case in Austria-Hungary.

9. Herzl's entreaties to Abdul Hamid began in 1896; he first visited Jerusalem in 1898 during the kaiser's state visit but would not gain an audience with the sultan until 1901.

The whole plan with Palestine has in reality been given up by the leading men of the movement, and the magnanimous offer that the British government has made to the Zionists for the transfer of rich and fertile land in *Uganda* ought therefore to be seized with both hands.[10] But it has already been revealed how much damage the senseless agitation for Palestine has done. The great majority of Jews have still not been able to hear talk of Uganda as a transitional land. Herzl had been weak enough to associate himself with the most narrow and bigoted elements among Eastern Europe's Orthodox Jewish rabbis, as the deceased Bernard Lazare has derided him for vigorously, and he was not able to conjure up the patriotism he himself had awakened in the people.[11] Then he died (at the right moment for him), and since last year Max Nordau, best known for the vulgarity of his polemics and the wretchedness of his critique, has been Zionism's regrettable leader, a leader who has no power over his "people" whatsoever.

Therefore when I am asked why I do not contribute to dangling a "homeland" in Palestine as an asylum before the unfortunate Russian Jews—an asylum in the midst of Abdul Hamid's violence—the reason is that in Palestine, as I fear, there awaits them nothing other than hunger and, over the course of time, murder.

A close associate of mine had an audience with Plehwe a few months before his death to request his support for Jewish emigration.[12] Plehwe expressed on this occasion that the Jews, who were the actual bearers and leaders of the Russian Revolution, should never be shown the least mercy. He proceeded to claim that he had the fate of Russia in his hand, like I have this pencil, and that if the Jews wanted to go their way, he would prefer that. My associate then had to make him aware of the impossibility of exporting more than at the very most 80,000 in a given year, and this is precisely the number that those left behind would reproduce annually. The total number would thereby not be diminished.

Fortunately Jewish youth in Russia in our time have, instead of romantically dreaming of a new home in Palestine, pledged their lives to conquering

10. The "Uganda Project" was first floated in 1903.

11. French Jewish Dreyfusard Bernard Lazare (1865–1903) initially clashed with Herzl over the Armenian question. See Yair Auron, *The Banality of Indifference: Zionism and the Armenian Genocide* (London: Routledge, 2017), 102–21. The conflict between the two men was also the subject of Hannah Arendt's 1942 essay "Herzl and Lazare."

12. Viacheslav Konstantinovich fon Pleve (1846–1904) was Russian minister of the interior from 1902 until his death at the hands of the Socialist Revolutionary Combat Organization; as such he was responsible for containing the subversive forces that would be unleashed in the 1905 Russian Revolution.

their old home and to establishing decent conditions there. They have felt and known that not flight but revolution with weapon in hand is the way forward, and they have exhibited a courage that is rarely demonstrated in any country at any time. At the barricades in Lodz alone there have fallen more young Jews than those who perished in the great French Revolution.[13]

The time is hopefully not too distant when it will be seen that the blood of these heroes has not been shed in vain. In a matter of years, as the municipal Duma in Moscow has already demanded, Russia's Jewish inhabitants will enjoy the same rights and the same freedoms as all the other peoples of the Russian kingdom.

---

13. The Lodz Insurrection in Russian Poland broke out on June 21, 1905, and was eventually crushed by Russian forces on June 25.

CHAPTER 22

The Jews in Finland

1908

The increasingly frustrated tone of Brandes's political journalism of late 1905 makes it clear that he had reached a point of general exhaustion with his advocacy work; indeed, Brandes would take on no new causes until the outbreak of the Great War. Between 1906 and 1914 he would issue only the present article and a 1909 commentary on the Polish question, both of which may be designated as follow-up work based on his prior activities, as well as 1912's "Race Theories," itself a necessary response to a provocation in the Danish press. In many ways the essay below should also be counted as a response to a provocation, namely an editorial that had appeared in a Hamburg Jewish newspaper attacking Brandes for the allegedly cold reception he had given a Finnish Jewish delegation that had attempted to reach out to him during his May 1908 visit to Helsinki. That particular visit, in large part an effort to laud Brandes for his 1904 efforts on behalf of the university in Helsinki, had brought about a minor controversy, given that as a foreigner of Jewish descent, Brandes was at least in theory subject to the onerous Jewish regulations instituted by the Finnish Senate in a decree of 1889. Here were the makings of an embarrassing scandal; an adopted national hero would, according to the letter of the law, face deportation, since his stay would extend past the mandated three-day limit for foreign Jews visiting the grand duchy. In the end the authorities would not interfere in the great critic's plans, due at least in part to a press campaign launched in his defense by progressive Finns, in which, as Brandes notes, the Swedish-speaking minority played a leading role. His apparently dismissive response to the approach of the Jewish delegation echoes similar episodes from his earlier Polish advocacy work, in which he was regularly accosted by angry Jewish (as well as Ruthenian) representatives who were upset by his general refusal to criticize the Poles for their own repressive treatment of minority groups within partitioned Poland; as indicated here, Brandes maintained that it was a matter of personal honor not to speak ill of a given people when acting as their spokesperson. It is therefore only with the

---

Originally published in *Politiken*, June 14, 1908. Translated from the version published in *Samlede Skrifter*, vol. 18.

greatest reluctance that he takes up the cause of the Finnish Jews in the present essay; the same reticence is present in the 1914 essay "Conditions in Russian Poland," in which Brandes would at long last address the issue of Polish antisemitism. The essay below is significant in two particular respects. In the first place, Brandes provides the clearest and most definitive statement of his attitude toward his own Jewish heritage found anywhere in these writings, asserting that it has only figured in his self-conception because his fellow Europeans of "Christian descent" have constantly made reference to it; in fact, he goes so far as to suggest that his Christian countrymen and women are in every way far more Jewish than he himself. In the second place, his rather belligerent chastisement of the Jewish representatives for their inability to speak Finnish speaks volumes about his general views on immigration and assimilation, which surely must strike the contemporary reader as somewhat reactionary, perhaps even inconsistent with his vigorous defense of the right of the Poles and Ruthenians not only to speak their own language at home but also to be educated in it. This apparent fissure in his thinking may only be reconciled by conceding that Brandes views European Jewry as essentially distinct from other oppressed peoples. The Poles and the Ruthenians, in effect, constitute occupied populations and ought in an ideal world to have their sovereign states; the Jews, in contrast, do not seem to warrant the same consideration in his thinking—see his essay on Zionism in particular on this matter.

~

I

The latest issue of a newspaper previously unknown to me, *Israelitisches Familienblatt*, has been sent to me from Hamburg with this note attached: "This paper contains an article concerning you."[1]

It turned out to be an attack on me sent into the paper by the spokesperson of a deputation that some months ago sought me out in Helsinki. This attack is just as unseemly as it is foolish. The author complains that I did not immediately receive the deputation. (I had a visitor and was further expected at a place in the city a few minutes after our conversation.) He objects to the "ice cold" reception I am said to have given the gentlemen. (I had in particular asked them, without further introduction, what in fact they wanted from me.) I had listened to them "cold-bloodedly" instead of warm-bloodedly. On and on and on. And all of this in spite of the fact that I am their "co-religionist." (They seem altogether too serious actually to consider me a co-religionist.)

1. *Israelitisches Familienblatt* was published in Hamburg from 1898 until 1935, after which it moved to Berlin before it fell victim to Nazi censorship in 1938. That Brandes was unfamiliar with the paper is unsurprising, given its decidedly petit-bourgeois orientation.

In conclusion the author expresses the hope that in return I shall fulfill their request all the more energetically.

The gentleman author, who as spokesperson made an exceedingly unfavorable impression on me, has acted shamelessly in providing a quite distorted image of what was said in my hotel room. If I had not been good-natured enough to give in to him and to send away the friend who was with me—and who now had to wait an hour outside the door—then I would have had a witness who could correct this incorrect and incomplete summary, in which only one thing is accurately reported, namely my openly expressed disinclination to write anything that would be unfavorable to the Finns after the hearty reception I had received in Finland. Because I allowed myself to be bothered by receiving this gentleman, I was compelled to reveal myself inattentive to other men with whom I had made an appointment elsewhere; but this insistent man is not satisfied with that. He begins with a public attack initiated by a quite private conversation. If the Finnish Jews would acquire something of an advantage in their cause, they must surely secure themselves more diplomatic spokespeople.

It occurred to me that the visiting card with which the deputation approached me was not written in either the Swedish or the Finnish language, but had this German text: *Deputation des Central—Comitée für die Befreiungsbewegung der Juden in Finland*. Therefore my first utterance to the deputation, which was not reported in the summary, was this: "This visiting card is in German. What language do you gentlemen speak with one another?" The answer was: Yiddish. It did not seem as if this spokesperson, aside from this dialect, understood any language other than German. Really it should be said that the first thing one who seeks civil rights in a country ought to do is learn the language of that country, especially if one was born there. It is perhaps too much to ask that the Jews of Finland should feel themselves to be Finns after the treatment they have received. But if they themselves do not consider themselves to be Finnish, then they cannot demand that the authorities in the country should view them that way. They must begin with speaking one of the country's two languages internally among themselves. Otherwise they are and remain foreigners, even they who themselves are in fact native born.

II

During my May visit to Finland there was no small amount written about me in the newspapers, many times such kind and lovely things that I could not express my gratitude enough. Generally my Jewish birth was touched on there, mostly in a joking tone.

A parenthetical: there is no danger of my forgetting the congregation into which I was born.

I confess that if I had not been unceasingly reminded of it by others throughout my life, I would have forgotten it, so little meaning has it had for me myself.

Here I can only recall Börne's words: "It is a wonder. A thousand times I have experienced it, and yet it is still new to me. A mob of people reproach me for being a Jew. Another forgives it. A third praises me for it. But all of them think about it. It is like once they are lured into the magical Jewish circle, no one can come out of it."[2]

As soon as somebody puts pen to paper to write something about me, for or against, invariably the first thing said is that I am a Jew.

How funny this is! If in a deeper sense there is anything I am *not*, then it is this. Denmark and Finland are saturated with Judaism, their God is Jewish, their festivals are Jewish, their religion is a reworked, further developed Judaism with a few mystical additions. The Old Testament is there as here a holy book, and the New, which is still more holy, was like the Old written by Jews. Half of Denmark's culture comes from Palestine; half of its literature is inspired from there. Even the names, the authentic Danish names, Petersen, Hansen, Jensen, etcetera, are Jewish names, biblical names. If an individual young man manages to liberate himself from this reigning Judaism for a brief time, then he soon after falls back on it wholeheartedly, like so many Danes turn back to one of Jerusalem's many representatives, to the pope or to Grundtvig or (like Strindberg) to Swedenborg. There was a time when I was almost the only person in the country who was not a Jew. And nevertheless practically the only thing people in this country know about me, and the only thing they regularly communicate to foreigners, is that this is what I am.

They all live and breathe the atmosphere of Jerusalem. The churches are full of it. It was not long ago that it was the same in the university.

And it was precisely me among the Danes who earliest and most eagerly and aggressively sought a return to Athens in intellectual life. Yet they never tire, whether dismissively or with feigned acknowledgment, of leading me back to that Jerusalem they themselves can never get beyond.

III

In Finland the conditions are such that no one who is born of Jewish parents has the right to more than three days' stay in the country.[3]

---

2. Karl Ludvig Börne (1786–1837, b. Loeb Baruch) was a German satirist and Lutheran convert associated with the Young Germany movement. Brandes had profiled him in the sixth volume of *Main Currents*.

3. Restrictions on Jewish settlement in Finland dated back to the era of Swedish rule, which permitted Jews to live in only select areas, none of which were in Finland. The first Jewish settlers thus only arrived in the nineteenth century, mostly Russian soldiers who had

As suggested, there was much joking about this in the press on the occasion of my coming.

A feuilletonist in the May 17 *Hufvudstadsbladet* declared that he would highlight a side of my character on which none of them who had spoken of me favorably had dwelled, namely my courage:

> He has dared to come up here and give a speech and he has risked staying here for four days—one day longer than he has the right. He has subjected himself to being sent home in prison transport or in a similar manner. The poor devil, if we had treated him according to the letter of the law!
>
> In the first place he has given a speech. He had no right to do that. He has the right to sit on the university steps and sell shoelaces or matches or oranges or postcards, but by no means to lecture in the university's ceremonial hall. The law permits him to sell a cast-off overcoat or a pair of old boots, but the law does not permit him to present the results of his research.
>
> The law naturally makes no distinction between individuals. At least in theory. In practice the matter works out differently. But what the hell does the law have to do with religion? Why should a Christian pickpocket who is a foreigner have the right to stay in this country as long as he wants, while Brandes may not stay here more than three days? Yes, say it! I cannot deny that it would have been funny if yesterday evening at nine o'clock, when the three days had passed, the law had interrupted perhaps the greatest intellectual of our time (the expression must be taken as the opinion of the author) and had sent him away on the first departing boat. I suppose that Europe would have had a hearty laugh at the expense of one of its pioneering peoples. And I would not have begrudged Europe this little enjoyment.[4]

These jocular words reveal the difficulties faced by a foreigner of Jewish descent in Finland, and that not by virtue of one or another provision laid

---

completed their terms of service in the grand duchy and due to pressure from the Russian military were permitted to stay. Even then these small numbers were closely monitored by the autonomous Finnish authorities, hence the "three-day rule" still at least nominally in effect during Brandes's 1908 visit. The new independent Finnish state would grant full citizenship to its Jewish residents on December 22, 1917; decades later this would result in Finnish Jewish soldiers fighting alongside their German allies against the Soviets, three of whom would even earn the Iron Cross. See Rachel Bayvel, "The Jews Who Fought alongside the Germans," *Jewish Quarterly* 202 (Summer 2006): 25–28.

4. Brandes cites from the editorial column titled "Småbetraktelser" ("Brief Observations") in number 134 of Finland's largest Swedish-language newspaper. Jews in Finland largely made a living through trading in second-hand goods, one of the few professions permitted by the state.

down by the Russian authorities but by virtue of a decision by the Finnish Senate, a decision no older than 1889.[5]

IV

Foreigners can however get around it. It is worse for the Jews who were born in Finland. By no means are they the equals of the other citizens of the country.

One recalls the immense effort with which the Finns liberated themselves from Bobrikov's *ukaz*, according to which they were required to perform their military service in the Russian army on Russian soil.[6] Mass emigration and a general work stoppage insured that this condition was lifted. But when the Finns liberated themselves in this way, the Jews living in Finland, some one thousand in all, were exempted from the right not to be a Russian soldier. These young men were turned over to the Russian army, and although this sounds unbelievable, it was confirmed for me by a young student who himself was next on the list to serve in Russia. After their service they were forbidden to return to their Finnish homes.

If it goes this way for Jews born in Finland who have been in the Russian army, then it is understandable that the Russian soldiers born outside Finland who wish to stay in the country have difficulties themselves. Before me is a document from the chancellery of Nyland province (in which Helsinki is located), dated February 18, 1907. In a dreadful, bureaucratic style, adapted by me, is found the following:

> Since it is ordained by the senatorial letter of March 29, 1889, that every Israelite who has previously obtained permission from the governor to live in the district must apply for a residence card or trade license every six months, it is hereby permitted that soldier A. K., with wife and children, is allowed to live in Helsinki for six months, valid from today forward. Their children may stay no longer than they remain in the home of the parents, therefore not if they marry or enter into military service; in that case they are required to leave the country without right to live here at a later time.

5. The "three-day rule" was instituted by the autonomous Finnish authorities in a decree of 1889.

6. Nikolai Ivanovich Bobrikov (1839–1904) was appointed governor-general of Finland, inaugurating the period of Russification known to the Finns as *sortovuodet*; he was assassinated by the Finland Swedish patriot Eugen Schauman in 1904. Bobrikov's infamous *ukaz* eliminated the Finnish army and made all young Finns subject to conscription; this was lifted in 1905 due to intense Finnish resistance.

> It is permitted for the soldier A. K., after registering with the magistrate, to sell the following goods: works of art or other goods he himself has fabricated, bread and other baked goods, berries, fruits, cigars, cigarettes, matches, old clothing and shoes, to trade in simple kitchen utensils and table linens, caps and other hats of lesser value, all this toward payment of the taxes levied on him according to appraisal, together with the responsibility to deliver his residence card or trade license to the city police after the six-month time limit is expired, at which time a new license can be procured, if the political authorities deem it correct. Furthermore it is strictly prohibited for A. K. and his family to visit markets outside of Helsinki or to travel around the country to do business or carry on a trade; likewise it is strictly forbidden for him to travel to other places within the borders of the country, for example to Vyborg. Should this prohibition be breached, or should A. K. or his family become involved in begging or other unseemly behavior, and should there be any registered complaint against his conduct, then he and his family shall be conveyed by police measure to their place of origin.

A meeting has been called in Helsinki on the twenty-eighth of May at the Nyland Nation House on behalf of more Jewish families who have lived in the country for many years and who have received the order to emigrate from the Senate. On this occasion the Helsinki journal *Fyren*, which is otherwise assuredly a humor newspaper, contained on May 23 a seriously intentioned article titled "Some Thoughtful Words for our Jew-Bawlers" (that is to say those who cry for the Jews), which contained an excerpt from Bishop Martensen's well-known thoughts on the absurdity of granting the Jews civil rights in his *Christian Ethics*.[7] It makes a strange impression to see the words of this man, who a lifetime ago stood for the most extreme reaction in Denmark, now employed by young, Swedish-speaking men in independence-seeking Finland.

V

These gentlemen seem to be quite unaware of the answer to this attack provided by another bishop, namely D. G. Monrad, in his book *Liberalism's Reply to Bishop Martensen's Social Ethics*.[8]

---

7. *Fyren*, a conservative and antisemitic satirical journal, was published in Swedish from 1898 to 1922. Hans Lassen Martensen (1808–84), remembered today as the great foil of Kierkegaard, published his multivolume *Den christelige Ethik* in the 1870s.

8. Bishop and National Liberal politician Ditlev Gothard Monrad (1811–87) is best remembered as the head of state who led Denmark into the disastrous Dano-Prussian War of 1864. His *Politiske Breve, Nr. 14–18: Liberalismens Gjenmæle til Biskop Martensens sociale Ethik* inaugurated a furious debate that would draw in Danish intellectuals from across the spectrum, the secular Brandes of course not included.

Among other things Martensen had asserted that during great historical crises decisive for the fate of the nation modern Jews had been observed running their businesses undisturbed as well as indulging in speculation on the rise and fall of government bonds. Monrad asks whether Christian bureaucrats during such crises decline to draw their salaries, whether farmers cease plowing and sowing, whether those who have money in savings banks forget to rush to have it withdrawn, thus reminding us of the great crisis in the spring of 1848.[9] He asserts that it is in the interest of the state that the citizens continue their business as undisturbed as possible during great moments of decision.

Bishop Martensen had dismissed the Jews for harboring "a feeling of their own superiority, whether or not this is acknowledged by anyone other than themselves." Monrad answers:

> Martensen draws attention to the fact that the Jews view their nationality as the royal nationality to which all other nationalities should stand in a kind of vassal relation. I concur with this Jewish understanding, although in part for other reasons than the Jews.

And with that admixture of sound human understanding and a bishop's orthodoxy that defines Monrad, he continues:

> The Jewish people are not just remarkable, they are altogether unique. The Jews in our midst, not by their creed but by their existence, stand as witness to the truth of the revelation. It has been said to me that Jewish blood is stronger than all other blood, that in mixed marriages the Jewish character is transmitted much more powerfully than any other. When one considers the small numbers of the Jewish people and then considers how many have raised themselves up to significance in society, one cannot but acknowledge the superiority of the Jewish nationality. Think if Denmark was ruined, if the Danish people were sold away into slavery and spread across the world. How many years would we last before every trace of Danish nationality vanished? What is said here about Denmark and the Danish people applies to every other country and people. But it is now more than 1,800 years since Jerusalem was taken, the Jewish state destroyed, and the Jews spread across the world, and to this day the Jewish nationality persists. Is that not remarkable? When we see it, do we not see a miracle with our own eyes?

9. The spring of 1848 in Denmark saw the beginning of the end of absolutism (a constitutional monarchy would be established the following year) as well as the outbreak of the First Schleswig War.

Monrad is so struck by this that he is not satisfied with a scientific explanation. He continues like the orthodox Christian he is:

> How did this come about? Because the Jews were God's chosen people. When God's only begotten son took on human form, he also took on a nationality. Which nationality? The Jewish. Therefore I regard the Jewish nationality so highly that it is correct they are called royal. Christ sits at the right of the Almighty Father and governs the world, not only as God's but also man's son, not alone with the divine aspect but also with human nature. If it is now such that human nature, no matter how pure it is, bears a national mark, *then the Jewish nationality really participates in the governance of the world*, and thus all other nationalities stand in a vassal relation to it.

VI

Let us less orthodox types think for a moment that Jesus had been born to a Finnish mother or to a Norwegian or a Jutlander. Can anyone imagine the heights to which Finns, Norwegians, or Jutlanders would have climbed? None of them have even come close! The savior of the world a Jutlander? If the adherents of the Jutlandic movement are even now undaunted, how much more so would this be were this the case?

And it is not said that the Jewish nationality has lost its part in the governance of Sirius, Orion, and the Milky Way by virtue of the fact that it crucified its most famous son. Is there anyone who doubts that the other nations have behaved similarly? Did the Greeks not give Socrates poison? Did the French not burn Joan of Arc alive? Or think of the Italians or the Bohemians: to what end came Giordano Bruno or Jan Hus? None other than death on the pyre!

But Monrad also has an answer for this objection. He writes: "One could perhaps admit that the Jews had been God's chosen people, but then ask whether they had not by crucifying the savior forfeited their glory and have become the children of perdition and of God's wrath. Let the Apostle Paul answer this question. He writes in his letter to the Romans: "For I would not, brethren, yet ye shall be ignorant of this mystery, lest ye should be wise in your own conceits; that blindness in part has happened to Israel; until the fullness of the gentiles be come in. *And so all Israel shall be saved.* As concerning the gospel, they are enemies for your sakes: but as touching the election, *they are beloved for the father's sakes. For the gifts and calling of God are without repentance.*"[10]

10. Romans 11:25–26, 28–29 (King James version).

The publishers of the journal *Fyren* will learn from this that during Bishop Martensen's time there was another and greater bishop in Denmark, whose manner of thinking was quite different from his and in better agreement with actual conditions as well as true Christianity.

VII

It occurs to me, however, that the men of Jewish birth who by allowing the biblical mythology to go unchallenged would have secured for their tribe a part in the governance of the world, deserve merit for having done their part to undermine faith in the Jews as God's chosen people. It is and remains uncertain whether in the instance of the Almighty having allowed himself to be born in Finland, Norway, or Jutland, he would have appeared as a Finn, Norwegian, or Jutlander in order to deprive his nationality of the royal designation and thus an ample part in the mastery of the universe.

A man of Jewish ancestry who speaks out against the doctrine of the Jews as God's particular people, or who speaks out for the Finns' right to political independence and civil freedom, can at least in none of these cases be mistaken for looking out for his own.

This supposition is akin to the fact that it was for confessional reasons that modern Finland placed the Jews living in the country outside the law. The Finns are after all by and large an orthodox people, in which spirituality has preserved no small influence.

It is however asserted to me from all sides that confessional reasons do not mean anything in this instance. Jewish competition is feared because of their capacity for business, which would come into play if they were given permission to vie with Finnish businessmen on equal terms. This of course results in their being punished for their alleged competence.

Or it is alleged that if Jewish access to Finland was permitted there would be fear of a mass immigration from Russia of the poor, oppressed, and abused who live there? This fear ought to be groundless. The immigrants would soon work themselves up out of poverty, and they would perhaps in the second or third generation provide Finland with a contingent of remarkably useful persons.

Yet that is not the question right now. The question before us at present is this: why do the Finnish people, who themselves have suffered under harsh treatment, who still continually protest against oppression, and who as a whole are a freedom-loving people, not provide humane treatment to the only little flock of people over whose well-being they are almost the masters? It is not unknown to me that the Russian monarch has placed obstacles in the way of the friends of freedom. Neither is it unknown to me that the Swedish party's most outstanding men, men like Mechelin, like J. W. Runeberg, like C. G. Estlander, A. Kumlin, J. Grotenfeldt, and finally Axel Lille have since 1872 again and again sought change in the direction of freethinking.[11] But the efforts are still stalled by the resistance of the Finnish-speaking population, to which now is added that of the Russian monarch.

The Finnish people ought to do unto others as they would have others do to them.

11. Leopold Henrik Stanislaus Mechelin (1839–1914), among many other things a cofounder of Nokia, led the Finnish resistance to Russification. Under his leadership the Finnish Senate introduced universal suffrage in 1906. Physician Johan Wilhelm Runeberg (1843–1918), the son of Finland's national poet, represented the oft-besieged university in Helsinki as ombudsman from 1882 onward. Carl Gustaf Estlander (1834–1910) was professor of aesthetics at the university in Helsinki; his nephew Ernst Estlander (1870–1949) was one of three university professors briefly exiled in the 1904 academic purge—see "Finland" in the present volume. Alexander August Kumlin (1844–1912) and Berndt Julius Grotenfeldt (1859–1929) were prominent members of the Finnish Senate in the final years of Russian rule. Axel Johan Lille (1848–1921) was the founder of the Swedish People's Party of Finland.

CHAPTER 23

The Fourth Partition of Poland

1909

As the chaos of 1905 came increasingly under its control, a resurgent Russian absolutist state would begin to take measures to redress the concessions made during the revolutionary period, both at home and in its foreign possessions. Prime Minister Stolypin's 1909 proposal to incorporate a considerable portion of eastern Poland into Russia proper here motivates Brandes once again to take up his pen in defense of Polish sovereignty, albeit on this occasion with considerably more reserve. In particular, Brandes's concern with Polish mistreatment of the Ruthenians, and with a perceived myopia on the part of Polish nationalists in general, is palpable.

~

The Polish-speaking world has as a whole and for a long time been in great excitement because of the plan for the dismemberment of Russian Poland that Stolypin has either conceived or merely endorsed, and which in May was introduced to the Duma for passage, where a majority think it is assured.[1]

The plan is symptomatic of the short-sighted, narrow-minded statesmanship that has for the last half century defined the Russian government's attitude toward the Kingdom of Poland. In a way it comes as a surprise, as even a few years ago, in the time of the first Duma, it was still possible to believe in a coming reconciliation and understanding between Russians and Poles.[2] In reality the leading men of both of these most significant Slavic peoples were making preparations for this during the brief, bright interlude when one expected that Russia would seriously join the club of constitutional states, and

Originally published in *Politiken*, August 18, 1909. Translated from the version published in *Samlede Skrifter*, vol. 18.

1. Petr Arkad'evich Stolypin (1862–1911) was a conservative politician who served as Russian prime minister from 1906 to 1911.

2. The First Duma convened briefly in 1906. See "The Future of Russian Poland" in the present volume for Brandes's commentary on this much more hopeful period.

that the czar's famous October Manifesto portended a reality.[3] One imagined then that the Poles, aside from gaining a measure of representation in the Russian parliament that corresponded to their numbers, would acquire extensive self-rule in all local affairs through a provincial diet in Warsaw. From then on the inhabitants of Russian Poland would have as little to complain about as the inhabitants of Austrian Poland, and it would gradually become difficult for Prussia to maintain forced dominion over Posen.

It has been revealed that all of that was a dream. Reality came to look quite different. The Russian reaction for the time being triumphed over everything. The constitution was rescinded and a sham constitution adopted as a gift of grace, after which a manifold of uprisings in the vast kingdom were suffocated in blood.

Anyone who wants to understand the Russian regime at present and in its essence needs only to read the piece titled *The Terror in Russia*, which has been sold (at only two pence) in an untold number of copies, and in which Prince Kropotkin, on the basis of incontrovertible and generally official documents, has given an account of the horrors—worse than the worst of the Middle Ages—that now every day take place in the spacious hell that geographically is called Russia.[4] In numerous European countries, this piece has led to protests against the czar's visit by the representatives of the masses, who are treated as industrial fodder in peacetime and cannon fodder in war, and who feel for the hundreds of thousands of political martyrs in Russia.[5] (In February 1909 there were 181,137 prisoners in the prisons, while there is actually only room enough for 107,000).

In contemporary official Russia the triumphs of the reaction are celebrated, and in this way also the inclination of the Orthodox Church to reduce and to humiliate the Roman Catholic Kingdom of Poland is once again active, as in the time of Pobedonostsev.[6]

---

3. Nicholas II's manifesto of October 1905, which promised constitutional government for all the empire, is now considered by historians to have been a disingenuous ploy for time to reassert absolutism.

4. The anarchist philosopher and activist Petr Alekseevich Kropotkin (1842–1921) was a close friend of Brandes, who agitated for his release during his long imprisonment in France.

5. After the 1907 Anglo-Russian pact, Russia formally joined Britain and France as members of what would eventually become known as the Triple Entente. Brandes is here referring to the complex diplomatic maneuvering of Britain or France to restore respectability to its new ally after the disasters of 1904–6; these measures at reconciliation with an absolutist regime provoked furious protest at home and across Europe, reaching a peak during Nicholas II's state visit to Britain in the summer of 1909.

6. Konstantin Petrovich Pobedonostsev (1827–1907) was principal advisor to the throne during the reactionary reign of Alexander III (1881–94).

Stolypin's bill removes from the Kingdom of Poland the governorships of Siedlce and Lublin and forms from them a new governorship, Chelm, into which furthermore a certain number of districts are incorporated.[7] The new governorship, which includes a population somewhat over 758,000, is incorporated into Russia.

The status of the inhabitants is thereby subjected to a series of essential changes. While earlier, like in all of Russian Poland, they were under the Napoleonic Code, they now come under Russian justice. Their credit terms, their insurance firms, their banking system, and their rural districts had previously been arranged on a basis that is now often forbidden, and in every case these are quite different from conditions outside Poland. While they previously had used the Gregorian calendar, they are now forced backed to the Julian. It is now forbidden for them to close their offices and schools on the Catholic holidays as they did previously. Instruction in the Polish language, which previously was allowed in the schools, as well as the use of the Polish language in the courts and for certain judicial acts, is now forbidden. Theater performances in any language other than Russian can no longer occur without special permission from the governor-general, which not coincidentally is always denied. Poles can no longer acquire any property that is in Russian hands and it is just as impossible to lease any land that belongs to the state.

The principal motive for the new ordinance is, however, ecclesiastical. The party of "the true Russian men" seeks to wipe out the consequences of the ukaz on tolerance of April 1905, which had been greeted so jubilantly by the population.[8] Those consequences were that the earlier Uniates (the Greek Orthodox churches united with the Roman Catholic) openly declared themselves to be Catholics.[9] Now that these congregants are coming directly under Russian dominion, the Orthodox authorities can by force "convert" them once again to Greek Orthodoxy by virtue of the Exception Law that applies to Russia proper. And in the eyes of "the true Russian men" this is a victory and triumph.

Under pressure from this menacing danger—a new dismemberment of the already thrice-dismembered country—the Poles appeal to the sympathy of the civilized world and implore the mighty of the Earth to register protest. This time they especially place their hope in France, in that they try to prove to the

7. Siedlce, Lublin, and Chelm are located in contemporary eastern Poland, near the Belarusian-Ukrainian border.

8. Nicholas II's April 17, 1905, *ukaz* titled "Regarding Confirmation of the Rule of Tolerance of Religion" guaranteed religious freedom to all subjects of the empire. It was vehemently opposed by the extreme rightist Union of the Russian People (URP).

9. The Uniate churches of Eastern Europe and the Middle East are in communion with Rome but maintain much of the traditional Eastern liturgy and structure.

Frenchmen (who once more will expound this to their ally, the Russians) that none other than the German kingdom will benefit from new hatred and new division between Slavic peoples. The basis for Poland's existing configuration was previously, they say, the borders from 1815. If Russia can now unilaterally alter these, then why cannot Germany also do the same? The Poles go so far as to imagine that German influence stands behind the plan to establish the governorship of Chelm, but that appears to be a rather unlikely hypothesis. However, it is hardly doubtful that if there is any power to whom the Russian government could be thought to be willing to lend an ear in this matter, which incidentally is not particularly important to the interests of the state, then it is *France*. Setting the public opinion of Europe in motion—which they hope to achieve through the French press—ought to be of comparatively little weight, and indeed it could easily lead to the result opposite that desired, making Russian "patriotism" still more defiant and obstinate.

It is of so little use to have "enlightened opinion" on one's side. The Poles have in recent days received proof of this. On the occasion of the now-instituted Expropriation Law in Prussian Posen they issued, with their most famous man Henryk Sienkiewicz in the lead, a call for notable men in all states to speak out against the proposed bill in the Prussian provincial diet.[10] More than 250 men have answered the call, some at length and with political or moral observations, and the results show that with the exception of the statements of two or three German professors the condemnation of the bill is unanimous. Everywhere outside of Germany it has been found to be indefensible, indeed outrageous to expropriate a man's property because of the language he speaks, to wrest away a people's inherited land because of that people's nationality. Nevertheless the bill has smoothly passed, and the great work *Prusse et Pologne* has been just as ineffective as instructive.[11]

It seems that the Ruthenians, who should not be confused with the Russians, have in the planned governorship of Chelm taken on the Polish language and thereby brought down the government upon themselves (see, for example, *Revue pour les Français* of July 25). If that is correct, then the case ought to be unique. Otherwise as is known the Ruthenians are quite far from nurturing kind feelings toward the Poles, and nothing has surely done more harm to the sympathy the Poles have everywhere received than the twenty-five-year-long

10. The 1908 Expropriation Act permitted the Prussian Settlement Commission, active in purchasing Polish land for German settlement since 1886, to confiscate Polish property without consent.

11. Sienkiewicz's *Prusse et Pologne* was a book-length critique of the Expropriation Act, published in 1909.

persistent Ruthenian agitation against them over the attitude they have taken toward the Ruthenian population in Galicia. The hunger strike of the Ruthenian students after the riots in Lemberg, the murder of the governor of Galicia, Count Potocki, and other related events have kept the memory of this relationship fresh.[12] Here in Norden, as is remembered, Bjørnstjerne Bjørnson has with vehemence made the Ruthenian standpoint his own, not sparing the strongest words of contempt for the Poles, and has surely been opposed with passion from their side.[13]

It is not within the purview of an outsider to suggest to an entire people what it ought to do in its own best interest. But it can generally be said that the matter of the Poles would stand in a clearer light in the eyes of enlightened Europe, if a reconciliation between Poles and Ruthenians took place in Galicia, as it did in the days of the first Duma between the best men of Russia and the Kingdom of Poland.

At this moment, however, Poland presents to the observer the same schism, further deepened, that is found all around between the upper and lower classes. The Polish party in the German Reichstag, which recently contributed to the toppling of Prince Bülow, the Polish Duma members in the first Duma as well as in later iterations who asserted the unconditional inviolability of property rights to such freethinking and high-minded men as Prince Peter Dolgorukov and Maxim Kovalevsky, convey to Europe the impression that the Poles, when they participate in a law-giving body, constitute a dogmatic, conservative-clerical party whose interest in freedom and progress is limited to their own interest.[14] Conversely, the Polish proletariat in Lodz and in Warsaw has revealed itself to be recklessly revolutionary during the Russian Revolution. It went to extremes not just politically, but also risked life and limb with rash temerity, and in the end crossed the boundary between political violence and common criminality. On the streets and the squares the Polish underclass

12. Brandes refers to the conflict over the language of instruction at Lemberg University, which had been a point of contention between Poles and Ruthenians since it was ceded by the Austrians in 1870. In 1907 in protest of new Polish restrictions, Ruthenian students had rioted; many later staged a hunger strike while incarcerated. Count Andrzej Potocki (1861–1908), long suspected of interfering with elections to ensure strong Polish majorities in the provincial diet, was assassinated by the Ruthenian student Myroslav Sichynsky.

13. The Polish-Ruthenian conflict reveals how easily the oppressed could become the oppressor in the late Belle Epoque. Brandes and Bjørnson were lifelong friends and allies—indeed the latter had been included among the former's *Men of the Modern Breakthrough* (1883)—yet in this specific case they often found themselves at odds.

14. Bernhard Heinrich Karl Martin von Bülow (1849–1929) was ousted as German chancellor in July 1909. For more on Dolgorukov and Kovalevskii, see "The Future of Russian Poland" in the present volume.

behaves as a socialist-anarchist party that brings about a general instability that frightens the peaceful population no less than the Russian police.[15]

The better-off of Russian Poland have made an immense effort to help and to lift up the poor and ignorant layers of society, and this has been conducted under the thousands of difficulties the government has placed in the way. Nevertheless the schism, as has been said, is quite deep between the upper and lower classes, or as one perhaps could express it, between those who have national interests and those who have mostly social interests, sometimes *only* social. In Poland in the meantime the national interest is woven together with the interest of the church, and it is at once the Polish language and the Catholic Church that Orthodox Russia now will affect with the establishment of the governorship of Chelm.

This much is certain, that the Poles will spare no pains, no means, no funds in order to avoid the *fourth* partition that threatens their unfortunate country.

15. The Lodz Insurrection of June 1905 did indeed raise alarm among bourgeois Polish nationalists.

CHAPTER 24

Race Theories

1912

After the evisceration of racialist theory that was his 1905 essay "The Aryan Race," Brandes is not again motivated to address the rising appeal of racialist theory in Europe until seven years later, although this time around he is motivated by a deliberate provocation, namely the February 18 appearance of an article titled "Georg Brandes and Danish Culture," a rather execrable effort on the part of author and Grundtvigian priest Jakob Knudsen to portray Brandes's allegedly outsized impact on Danish belles lettres as a kind of "foreign occupation" detrimental to the proper unfolding of the national character. Given the nature of Knudsen's argument and the fact that his essay was timed to coincide with celebrations of Brandes's seventieth birthday, the relatively restrained tone of Brandes's response the very next day must surely strike the contemporary reader as curious, at least in comparison to the *Kunstwarte* debate that same year in Germany, which in many ways proceeded along precisely inverse lines. That much more volatile feud had in fact been initiated by a German Jew, the journalist and Zionist Moritz Goldstein, who in an infamous March essay in the journal *Kunstwarte* titled "Deutsch Judischer Parnass" ("The German-Jewish Parnassus") had echoed many of the claims made by Knudsen, principally that the leadership of German culture had long ago been taken over by German Jews. In absolute contrast to Knudsen, however, Goldstein had made the case that the principal victim in this had been Jewish identity, which had never been properly allowed to develop because of the strictures of its German framing; the Germans themselves, in Goldstein's view, had functioned as the unappreciative recipients of Jewish genius.

~

In an article titled "Georg Brandes and Danish Culture" by the distinguished and universally acknowledged author Jakob Knudsen is found the following:

Originally published as a letter to the editor in *Politiken*, February 19, 1912. Translated from the version published in *Fugleperspektiv*.

> Georg Brandes is of course of Jewish descent. I know that he has on many occasions brushed aside this observation as something irrelevant, but when the conversation concerns him, it is not. I know of hardly anything more complimentary to say about a man than that he was born a Jew, but there is nothing more dangerous for the non-Jewish people he lives among, mind you, than if he becomes that people's *intellectual leader*. In a mediocre man the national does not mean much, it does not define him further; but in a great man the national is a mighty force, it defines every fiber of his being; regardless of whether he knows it or not, it is in his blood, in his soul. It determines his own relation to the foreign people he lives among.
>
> Intellectually speaking we are conquered, by no means by an enemy, but still by a foreign power, a foreign race. And of this Georg Brandes is nearly the sole cause.

Knudsen further explains that thereby, "especially the literary world, but in part the artistic world as a whole" has gotten something of the Gypsy spirit into it.[1]

The article is in other respects marked by a strong measure of goodwill, and from a purely personal point of view I could not possibly desire a stronger acknowledgment than that which it contains. Therefore it allows the good personal relationship I am pleased to have with the highly gifted author to remain altogether undisturbed.

His fundamental point of view, which is found everywhere in our age and thus is not new to me, does not therefore strike me as any less misleading; but since I have more than once explained why right-thinking opponents like Mr. Knudsen have paid such poor attention to my words, I must be excused for repeating myself here.

As worthy of acknowledgment as the talents of the modern race theorists occasionally prove to be, their ignorance is quite certainly just as extraordinary.

First two purely ordinary observations:

1. Jakob Christian Lindberg Knudsen's (1858–1917) essay "Georg Brandes og den danske Dannelse" appeared in *Politiken* on February 18, 1912, two weeks to the day after Brandes's seventieth birthday. Relations between Knudsen and Brandes were exceedingly complex; in spite of what appears to the contemporary reader as the hostile and even disturbing attitude of the quoted text, somehow the two men seem to have avoided engaging in a heated public feud. For a superb unpacking of their relationship, see Johan Christian Nord, "Nordens grundtvigske Nietzsche og fritænkeriets førstemand: En historie om Jakob Knudsens morallære og møde med Georg Brandes," in *Den gode den onde: Om grundtvigianister og branditter*, ed. Katrine Frøkjær Baunvig and Michael Schelde (Copenhagen: Eksistensen, 2017), 73–98.

Every person now living has billions upon billions of ancestors. It takes a great deal of simple-mindedness to maintain that all were of one tribe.

In every so-called family, the real father of the children has at various points in time been different from the official father.

Richard Wagner, for example, has become the national demigod of the German nationalists. He signifies the utmost artistic culmination of the German tribe. In a famous article he has expressed his disdain for the "Jewish presence in music" and has set the old Germanic mythology to music.[2] Yet it is possible, perhaps even certain, that his real father was the Jewish actor Geyer, with whom his mother had relations while Wagner's father was insane and whom she married immediately after his death.[3] If that is the case then there goes the whole of nationalism, in that all the certainty that pedigree bestows collapses.

In the next place: every modern people, like every one of antiquity, is the result of a nearly immeasurable intermixing of tribes. Finot has demonstrated that far more than fifty races have merged into the modern Frenchman; Goldstein has demonstrated the same for the Israelites of antiquity.[4] The rubbish about the "Aryan" and "Semitic" races, long ago abandoned by the learned, is of course constantly and faithfully repeated by the ignorant, yet it can hardly make much of an impression these days. There was a need for a scientific explanation of the relationship between a series of languages, and thus a fantasy was forged about a secretive people, the Aryans, who during their wanderings across the Earth begat the different European nations. But race and language cannot be confused; when the Latin language took possession of Gaul, the Gauls did not become Romans.

In my article "Nationalism" (*Collected Works XV*) I have drawn attention to how instructive it is that in the two great national unifications that took place in Europe in the nineteenth century, those of Italy and of Germany, it was the smallest Italian province, Piedmont, and the originally smallest German kingdom, Prussia, that took the lead. This corresponds to the fact that the Russians are the leaders of the Slavic peoples, and they are halfway Mongolian.

Bound up with that is the fact that national heroes quite frequently are of foreign descent. Austria's national hero, Prince Eugene, was a Savoyard; Bavaria's national hero, General Tilly, was Flemish; Hungary's national hero, General

2. Wagner's "Das Judenthum in der Musik" originally appeared pseudonymously in 1850; it was reissued in an expanded edition under the composer's own name in 1869.

3. For a comprehensive discussion of Wagner's paternity, see volume 1 of Ernest Newman's *The Life of Richard Wagner* (Cambridge: Cambridge University Press, 1976), 3–18.

4. See "The Aryan Race" in the present volume for Brandes's review of Finot's *Le préjugé des races* (1905). For more on anthropologist Édouard Goldstein, see note 6 in "Zionism."

Bem; was a Pole and therefore of an entirely different race; France's Moritz of Saxony was a German, its Napoleon Bonaparte an Italian; and Denmark's Tordenskjold a Norwegian.[5]

Just consider a single large country like France, which in recent times has developed xenophobia and ill will toward foreign blood. A very large number of its most outstanding men have been of foreign descent. Montaigne's mother was a Portuguese Jewess, yet who typifies the French mind as does Montaigne?[6] The cardinal of Retz, the marshals and the dukes of Broglie, Gambetta, Émile Zola descend from Italy; André Chénier, Jean Moréas, Henry Houssaye from Greece.[7] Jean-Jacques Rousseau, Benjamin Constant, Madame Staël were Swiss. Mirabeau had Italian, Sainte-Beuve English blood in their veins.[8] And just as there was negro blood in Russia's national poet Pushkin, so was there negro blood in the elder and the younger Alexandre Dumas.[9]

---

5. Prince Eugene of Savoy (1663–1736) served three Holy Roman emperors as a soldier and statesman. Count Johann Tserclaes (1559–1632) commanded Catholic League forces in the Thirty Years' War. Polish patriot Józef Zachariasz Bem (1794–1850) earned the love of the Hungarian people as a commander in the 1848 Hungarian Revolution. Moritz (known to the French as Maurice), elector of Saxony (1521–53), sided with the French king Henry II against Holy Roman Emperor Charles V in the mid-sixteenth-century religious wars. Napoleon Bonaparte was of course of Corsican descent. Peter Jansen Wessel Tordenskiold (1690–1720) served as vice-admiral in the Dano-Norwegian navy during the Great Northern War.

6. Michel Eyquem de Montaigne (1533–92) was the principal pioneer of the essay form.

7. Jean François Paul de Gondi, cardinal de Retz (1613–79), was a scion of the Gondi banking dynasty of Florence. The Piedmontese House of Broglie settled in France in 1643. Léon Gambetta (1838–82) was minister of the interior during the Franco-Prussian War and later prime minister of the Third Republic. Émile Édouard Charles Antoine Zola (1840–1902) was the founder of literary naturalism as well as a prominent Dreyfusard; his father emigrated from Venice. André Marie Chénier (1762–94), a poet of the revolutionary period, was born in Constantinople to a Greek mother. Poet Ioannis A. Papadiamantopoulos (1856–1910, Fr. Jean Moréas) was the author of the 1886 Symbolist Manifesto. Historian Henry Houssaye (1848–1911) was the author of numerous works on Greek antiquity. Jean-Jacques Rousseau (1712–78), Henri-Benjamin Constant de Rebecque (1767–1830), and Anne Louise Germaine de Staël-Holstein (1766–1817) were all descendants of Huguenot families who had found refuge in Switzerland.

8. The ancestors of French revolutionary Honoré Gabriel Riqueti, comte de Mirabeau (1749–91), emigrated from Italy. Literary critic Charles Augustin Sainte-Beuve (1804–69), an important influence on young Brandes, was of partial English ancestry.

9. Aleksandr Sergeevich Pushkin (1799–1837) was a descendant on his mother's side of Abram Petrovich Gannibal (1696–1781), an African-born slave emancipated and raised by Peter the Great. Alexandre Dumas (1802–70) was the son of Thomas-Alexandre Dumas Davy de la Pailleterie (1762–1806), a French general of Afro-Haitian descent.

Sweden's most national poet, Bellmann, descends from Bremen; its greatest sculptor Sergel's parents were German immigrants.[10] In Denmark Thorvaldsen was halfway Icelandic, Oehlenschläger German on both his father's and mother's side, the composers Kuhlau, Weyse, and the Hartmann family of German origin.[11] The father of Danish literature, Holberg, was not Danish; Norway's greatest poet, Henrik Ibsen, descends from a Danish seafaring family, which for the last four generations has been mixed with German, Scotch, German, and so again German blood.[12] He has himself said in a biography he has sanctioned that not a single drop of Norwegian blood has directly contributed to the development of his temperament.[13]

The nationalist movement in modern Europe, whether as in France especially directed against the Protestants, or as in Germany, Austria, Romania, and Russia especially directed against the Jews—is everywhere markedly "antisemitic." It asserts that men and women of *presumed* Jewish descent—for where is the certainty?—always continue to be foreign and can only exercise an *illegitimate influence* on a people of Latin, Germanic, or Slavic extraction.

This assertion awakens special astonishment when it comes from the mouth of men who gladly and with warmth and passion define themselves as *Christian.*

The fact that no ideas like the Judeo-Christian ideas that in their day appeared in Palestine have taken hold in Europe for nearly 2,000 years, in America since the discovery of that part of the world, demonstrates the unreasonableness and the effrontery of this assertion.

In most cases the doctrine will furthermore be disproven by the facts, by the manner in which the entirely ordinary process of influence actually manifests itself. Rachel and Sarah Bernhardt have always been viewed as representative of French stage artistry, Johanne Louise Heiberg of Danish.[14]

---

10. Both Carl Michael Bellman (1740–95) and Johan Tobias Sergel (1740–1814) were of German descent.

11. Sculptor Bertel Thorvaldsen (1770–1844) was the son of Icelander Gottskálk Þorvaldsson. Adam Gottlob Oehlenschläger (1779–1850) introduced German Romanticism to Denmark. Friedrich Daniel Rudolf Kuhlau (1786–1832) was born in Lower Saxony, Christoph Ernst Friedrich Weyse (1774–1842) in Holstein, and while born in Copenhagen, Johan Peter Emilius Hartmann (1805–1900) was also of German ancestry.

12. Ludvig Holberg (1684–1754), father of the Nordic Enlightenment, is properly referred to as a Dano-Norwegian writer.

13. The degree of "Norwegian blood" in Henrik Ibsen has been a subject of debate since Henrik Jæger, his first biographer, made this rather dubious claim in 1888. See *Henrik Ibsen: A Critical Biography*, trans. William Morton Payne (Chicago: A. C. McClurg, 1901), 14–15.

14. Sarah Bernhardt (1844–1923) was the daughter of a Dutch Jewish courtesan, her teacher Rachel Félix (1821–58) was of German Jewish descent. Johanne Louise Heiberg (1812–90), for a half century the grand mistress of the Copenhagen stage, was the daughter of a Jewish mother.

Henrik Hertz belongs to Danish intellectual development as J. L. Heiberg's friend and ally.[15] A multitude of modern writers, although few are aware of it, have Jewish blood in their veins, in Danish literature, for example, Julius Fridericia, P. F. Rist, Mylius-Erichsen, and Henrik Pontoppidan.[16] The mightiest social democracy in the world, Germany, was founded by Ferdinand Lassalle and Karl Marx, two men who were of Jewish ancestry on both their father's and mother's sides.[17] Marx's ideas have moreover spread far beyond Germany's borders to the entirety of the working populations of Europe and America.

But now it is an established truth, as philosophy has so long maintained, that two heterogeneous entities can have no impact on one another. (Paul was indeed very much consistent with Luther). Yet the fact that such a collision—no matter how great the resistance from the differently minded—does occur proves the internal affinity of that which delivers the influence and that which receives it. Jakob Knudsen is in fact correct that the Danes have been intellectually conquered by a foreign race. It happened under Harald Bluetooth and through Ansgar.[18] Of course Jakob Knudsen is right. There was something of the Gypsy in the savior himself, who as a wandering preacher traveled from city to city without a place to rest, yes, without a place to hang his hat; perhaps this was due to the strangeness of his doctrine. In spite of all the efforts of Grundtivg to adapt it, Christian teaching has never seriously caught on or been followed here in Denmark.[19]

---

15. Henrik Hertz (1797–1870) was a Danish Jewish poet and dramatist.

16. Historian Julius Albert Fridericia (1849–1912), popular author Peter Frederik Rist (1844–1926), and Greenland explorer/ethnographer Ludvig Mylius-Erichsen were all born into Danish Jewish families. Jewish characters figure prominently in the work of Henrik Pontoppidan (1857–1943), winner of the Nobel Prize for Literature in 1917. According to Flemming Behrendt, rumors of his Jewish ancestry were widespread and even encouraged at times by Pontoppidan himself, although they were without foundation. See Behrendt's "Pontoppidans Jøder," a 2014 address to Pontoppidan Selskab, Henrik Pontoppidan: Portal for læsere, studerende, lærere of forskere, http://www.henrikpontoppidan.dk/text/seclit/secartikler/behrendt/pontoppidans_joeder.html.

17. German Jewish socialist Ferdinand Johann Gottlieb Lassal (1825–64, known as Ferdinand Lassalle) founded the Allgemeiner Deutscher Arbeiterverein, the first German labor party, in 1863. Brandes published a monograph in German on him in 1877. Marx was adamantly opposed to Lassalle's state socialism.

18. Harald Bluetooth Gormsson (ca. 910–ca. 987), king of Denmark and Norway, adopted Christianity in the 960s. Saint Ansgar, archbishop of Hamburg-Bremen (801–65), led the initial Christian mission to Norden.

19. Nikolaj Frederik Severin Grundtvig (1783–1872) was, among many other roles, a Danish church reformer, the founder of the Grundtvigian sect of Danish Lutheranism, to which Jakob Knudsen belonged.

Perhaps Jakob Knudsen, who is so impressionable and who does not shrink from the peculiarities of ideas, can find an explanation for the dominance that Jesus and his teaching nevertheless have exercised, even over this distinguished author himself, in the law of peculiarity, by virtue of which the men who have acquired influence in the modern states often have been of foreign descent.

As I have written earlier:

When Cesare Borgia became a renowned prince during the Italian Renaissance, it was due to the fact that he was a Spaniard.[20] Mazarin, Napoleon, and Gambetta have ruled France not in spite of their foreign descent but by virtue of it.[21] It was by virtue of the alien (Slavic) in his spirit that Bismarck had an influence on the Germans, and that Disraeli as Lord Beaconsfield, in spite of the mountain of bigotry he had to overcome, could set himself up as leader, first of England's nobility, then of the whole of Great Britain, and in our time he becomes more recognized every day.[22] Cavour had nothing in himself that indicated Piedmontese aristocracy; he was French in nature and conduct as well as in name.[23] Parnell, Ireland's uncrowned king, was not at all an Irishman, not at all a Celt, but an Englishman, even a Protestant, belonging therefore to the very people and the very society against which he led the resistance as the first man of the Catholic Irish.[24]

Jakob Knudsen, who believes that Danish intellectual life is suffocating under a kind of Manchu Dynasty, certainly does not need to look to China for examples of foreign dominance. He can find them in enormous numbers much closer, nearest of all among those who follow the prophets and apostles and evangelists upon which the Danish National Church is built.

The views he holds on the dangerousness of the Jewish tribe are shared by various Danish authors. Sven Lange, for example, has expressed them in a

---

20. The Borgia dynasty originated in Valencia.

21. Neapolitan-born cardinal Jules Raymond Mazarin (1602–81, b. Giulio Raimondo Mazzarino) followed Cardinal Richelieu as chief minister to the French monarchy from 1642 until his death.

22. The suggestion that Otto von Bismarck (1815–98) was possessed of a "Slavic spirit" is curious, although as a Prussian Junker his ancestors hailed from the eastern reaches of Germania. He was also fluent in Russian and Polish. Benjamin Disraeli (1804–81) was British prime minister in the 1870s; Brandes published a study of him in 1878.

23. The paternal ancestors of Camillo Paolo Filippo Giulio Benso, count of Cavour (1810–61), a principal architect of the Risorgimento, historically maintained strong ties to France, while his mother was a Genevan Calvinist.

24. The paternal ancestors of Irish nationalist hero Charles Stewart Parnell (1846–91) emigrated from Cheshire in the seventeenth century.

letter from Paris, which according to him loses its distinctiveness day by day *first and foremost through the Jewish invasion.*[25]

The Jewish dramatists (he cites Henri Bernstein and Henry Bataille, the latter of which is absolutely not of Jewish descent) have according to him driven out the "French spirit" from the theater.[26] He does not cite Porto-Riche, who however is greater by far, and whose plays have made such a deep impression.[27] In all likelihood Lange does not know of his origins. Lange sorely misses earlier theater critics in Paris such as Catulle Mendès and Henry Bauer.[28] He does not even think of learning of their origins. For Lange the plays of Bernstein and Bataille, as "Jewish plays," are *utterly lacking in grace, they are completely devoid of wit, they are possessed of no kind heart, no humane compassion*—their nervous fanaticism emits a particular chill of death. "And they say nothing about France, about Paris; the author's experience or observation seems strangely limited. . . . These works have only the peculiar dry glow characteristic of the race."

The Jewish tribe's most typical poet in recent times, I suppose, is Heinrich Heine.[29] Does he lack grace? Is he wanting for wit? He has, it should seem, enough thereof to divide between two million antisemites. Is it Jewish to lack humane compassion? The Jewish tribe's most famous figure is Jesus. Did he have any?

In Denmark as well as in Norway it has become the norm to define the chill of death as the peculiar trait of Jewish cultural production. Was Antokolsky as sculptor or Anton Rubenstein as tone poet cold?[30] In our time are Arthur Schnitzler, or Hugo Hoffmansthal of Austria?[31] Is Wasserman of Germany?[32]

---

25. Brandes had denounced Sven Lange's (1868–1938) "Et Brev fra Paris" in an essay from the previous year, titled "Sven Lange og Antisemitsmen."

26. Henri-Léon-Gustave-Charles Bernstein's (1876–1953) early twentieth-century plays provoked antisemitic riots in Paris. Félix-Henri Bataille (1872–1922), the premier French dramatist until the outbreak of the Great War, was of ordinary Catholic bourgeois background.

27. Georges de Porto-Riche (1849–1930) was born into a Jewish family in Bordeaux.

28. Catulle Mendès (1841–1909) was of Portuguese Jewish extraction, while Adolf François Henri Bauer (1851–1915) was the son of Alexandre Dumas and a German Jew.

29. Brandes had profiled Heine (1797–1856) in volume 6 of *Main Currents*.

30. Jewish figures are prominent in the works of Russian Jewish sculptor Mark Matveevich Antokolsky (1840–1902). Russian Jewish piano virtuoso Anton Grigorevich Rubinstein (1829–94), like so many great nineteenth-century stars of classical music, was known as a larger-than-life figure across Europe and North America.

31. Austrian Jewish author Arthur Schnitzler (1862–1931) is best known for his 1926 *Traumnovelle*, on which Stanley Kubrick based his film *Eyes Wide Shut*. I must concede that I find the works of Austrian Jewish poet and playwright Hugo Laurenz August Hofmann von Hofmannsthal (1874–1929) a little on the cold side, as much I enjoy them.

32. Jakob Wassermann (1873–1934) was a German Jewish author, best remembered for his 1928 novel *Der Fall Maurizius*.

Our good writers should be above anxiously concerning themselves with the mediocrity wrought by Jewish intellectual influence. In Norway recently there appeared a book by a fine man, Supreme Court lawyer Saxlund, which without exaggeration I dare say might be the most humorous book yet written on modern Jewry.[33] It warns poor Norway against the cruel oppression to which it will be subjected by the twenty-four Jews who at long last have gained access to the country in the nineteenth century. And a Mr. Theodor Caspari, a poet whose father as far as is known was of Jewish descent, as well as the fathers on his mother's side, a fact that however the son kept secret, made this book the object of two long and splendid articles in *Aftenposten*, in which he gently refuted the attorney, and in which, in agreement with the race theories of Jakob Knudsen and with the concept of the semitic chill of death emitting from Bernstein found in Lange's article, is found this: "Is this ice cold breath, which now for forty years has hovered over Scandinavia from the light-bringer G. B. a portent? A light dazzlingly clear enough, but without the other aspects of light: *warmth*, a kind heart, inwardness of disposition, et cetera."[34]

We ought soon to come so far as to allow the individual to bear the responsibility for his possible failings without seeking their source in a made-up imperiousness or a fictitious racial inferiority.

33. Eivind Saxlund (1858–1938) was one of young Norway's most prominent antisemites; his pamphlet *Jøder og Gojim*, a Norwegian translation of German antisemite Theodor Fritsch (1852–1933), introduced by himself, first appeared in 1910.

34. Norwegian author Theodor Caspari (1853–1948) was the son of Carl Paul Caspari (1814–92), a German Jewish-born Lutheran convert who taught Old Testament theology at Oslo.

CHAPTER 25

Conditions in Russian Poland

1914

Brandes's longtime advocacy of the Polish cause had earned him more than his share of enemies, not just among the Russian, German, and Austrian authorities but also of course among the Ruthenians. Always lurking beneath his hardly unconditional love of Poland was, however, the specter of antisemitism among its inhabitants; indeed Brandes's warm relations with the Poles had since the beginning subjected him to relentless attacks in the European Jewish press. Long mediated by the shared misery of foreign oppressive rule (particularly in Russian Congress Poland), relations between Poland's Catholics and Jews began to deteriorate after the 1912 Duma election in Warsaw. The outbreak of the war two years later, as described in painful detail below, exacerbated the Polish antipathy toward its considerable Jewish minority, resulting in a widespread outbreak of pogroms large and small. The present essay of October 1914 (as well as an addendum from February 1915) represents Brandes at his most heartbroken, as after years of silence he is compelled to speak out against the failings of the one people he has loved more than any other.

~

I. An Introduction

This war that rages both inside and outside Europe does not provide the veteran commentator with an occasion for hope. The immense calamities it instigates on a daily basis are certain enough. The good things that presumably will come of it, about which the various peoples dream differently, are so uncertain that it is still impossible to anticipate them. Among these possible outcomes there has appeared, to those who have felt sympathy for the deep national misfortune of the thrice-divided Poles, a shadow image of its people liberated and reunited with ample self-rule, presumably under the protection and supervision of one of the great powers.

Originally published in *Politiken*, parts I and II, on October 25 and 26, 1914, and part III on February 28, 1915. Translated from the versions published in *Verdenskrigen*.

For the present this is a long way off. Poles fight under compulsion in the Prussian, Austrian, and Russian armies, and therefore against one another. Not even the weakest attempt at secession has occurred in Prussian Posen, nor in the Russian "kingdom," nor in Austrian Galicia. Moreover, it can be said that the sundering of the Poles at this moment runs deeper than ever before, insofar as it further divides the various sects.

The only fact that might hint at a coming reunification is the proclamation to the Polish people delivered by the Russian commander in chief, Grand Duke Nikolai, in the middle of August.[1] It began: "Poles! The time has now come in which the dreams of your fathers and grandfathers can be realized. . . . Let the borders that cut the Polish people into pieces be dissolved! Let the Polish people be united in brotherhood under the scepter of the czar! Under this scepter Poland will be reborn, free in religion, language, and self-rule."

And it concluded: "The dawning of a new life for you begins. In this dawn let shine the symbol of the cross, the emblem of the suffering and of the rising up of the people."

How clearly this proclamation, with its freedom-loving sensibility and its pious invocation of the cross, bears the mark of having been compelled by the conditions of the moment. And how accustomed the Poles still were to disregarding the promises of the Russian government regarding full constitutional freedom and the like, when those earlier given had hardly meant much, either in Finland or in Russia itself. The manifesto as a sign of the times was well equipped to make a large impression on the masses, who always before had heard the authorities condemn as criminal machination, as high treason, that which now suddenly from the highest places was being called "the holy dream of the fathers."

The intention of this announcement was of course first and foremost to hinder revolt in Russian Poland at the moment when enemy troops were invading. Among the Austrian Poles the manifesto seems to have failed in its impact. Since those in Galicia enjoy full self-government and for a hundred years have been witness to the roughness and cruelty with which their friends in Russian Poland have been held down, the announcement was greeted with solemn reassurances of their fidelity to the House of Habsburg, indeed all of the Sokol associations, which in peacetime (with a view toward a settlement) had trained themselves in sport and in the use of weapons, organized themselves

1. Grand Duke Nikolai Nikolaevich Romanov (1856–1929), grandson of the czar, led Russian forces on the Prussian/Austrian frontier in 1914 and as such commanded immense numbers of Polish conscripts. The "Manifesto to the Polish Nation" was issued on August 14, 1914.

now as Polish legions at the disposal of the government against the Russians.[2] And to further complicate matters, the Ruthenian inhabitants of Galicia, fully half the population, formed a Union for the Liberation of Ukraine and from August 25 onward flooded Europe with announcements and expositions that were hostile to Russia. The founders did not conceal their names: D. Donzow, W. Doroschenko, A. Skoropyss-Joluchowsky, N. Zalizniak, A. Zuk.[3]

It has also at any rate also become clear that the czar does not view East Galicia as a part of the newly proclaimed independent Poland, and does not see its inhabitants as either Poles or Ruthenians, but as Russians. The Russians were barely in Lemberg before it and the entirety of East Galicia were referred to in the army orders as old *Russian* land and its inhabitants counted as *Russians* whom their brothers had now come to liberate.

Whatever impression the imperial manifesto made in Posen can hardly be detected, since any hostile remark against Prussia would be punished as high treason.

In the meantime, the German kaiser has no less than the czar courted the goodwill of the Poles and sought to win them over with promises.

A month after the czar's manifesto a proclamation from the German lieutenant general von Morgen was issued in the provinces of Lomza and Warsaw, in which these sentences appeared: "Arise with me and drive these Russian barbarians, who would make of you slaves, out of your beautiful country, which is now receiving back its political and religious freedom. That is the will of my mighty and gracious Kaiser."[4]When we take into account the vehemence with which the Germans in Posen have driven the Poles off their lands and persecuted their language, this acknowledgment demonstrates that the German kaiser has felt it necessary to one-up the czar.

As far as is known, the czar's manifesto made a meager impression on the intellectuals of Russian Poland, who must have greeted it with not a little suspicion. The masses in Russian as in Austrian Poland had long been passionately at odds with each other, accusing each other of treason against the holy

2. Sokol is a Pan-Slavic physical fitness movement founded in Prague in the nineteenth century.

3. Brandes refers here to the pamphlet titled "To the Public Opinion of Europe," issued on August 25, 1914, by Vienna-based exiles from Ruthenian Russia.

4. It is important to note that the August 1914 manifesto was *not* in fact in the czar's name but in that of one of his subordinates. Likewise with the German counterpoint of September, signed by Curt Ernst von Morgen (1858–1928). Sean McMeekin has argued that the refusal of czar and kaiser to address directly the Polish people is indicative of bad faith. See *The Russian Origins of the First World War* (Cambridge, MA: Harvard University Press, 2011), 87–88.

cause of the fatherland, until now a new party has formed, politically the crudest of all, which precisely because of that has spread all over. Its solution is this: "we will hear of neither Russia nor Austria; we will have only one thing: a Polish state without the help or tutelage of either side." In other words: "we want what is quite impossible." The political destruction of a people for nearly a century and a half takes a toll. Political wisdom in such a people all too easily either becomes parochialism or remains in a state of innocence.

Of what use is it to join in with the cries of *Polonia farà da sè* [Poland will take care of itself]?[5] That under present conditions Poland cannot take care of itself on its own is obvious to anyone with a conception of politics.

Yet I am prepared to say this: regardless of the form that the desire for Polish independence and freedom takes at the moment, it seems that it must pass like a raging storm through all Poland. Many times before, of course, a bright future for the Poles has seemingly appeared: in 1812 when Napoleon opened the second Polish campaign, in 1830 when the Poles were borne up with the sympathy of Europe, in 1848, 1863. But hardly ever has a transformation of the established conditions appeared to be as possible, and the painful barriers standing in the way seemed so ready to fall, as during this great and terrible crisis.

Those who have been occupied with Polish and Russian relations for a lifetime can of course without difficulty imagine how many young Polish hearts now beat and glow with hope, expectation, and all the noblest intentions.

Nevertheless the circumstances in Russian Poland are at this moment more desperate than ever before during periods of war and rebellion, and not because of the stress of the conditions or the horror of the situation, but by virtue of the Poles' own complicity, by virtue of the surplus enthusiasm of national feeling that has sent its insane breath over the whole of Europe and now rustles in Polish brains, so that it drives out high-mindedness and humanity, not to mention reason, which overall has not experienced any kind of jubilee in the year 1914 in Europe.

I daresay that truthfully I have felt no more enthusiasm for any other people than I have for the Poles. I have brought to light this feeling at a time when it did not register on the order of the day, and when very few shared in it. I have expressed this for a long time, and I have done so little to bring my views to the attention of the Poles or to elicit thanks for them that the Poles only first discovered my book about them when it was ten years old and by chance had been translated to German.[6] To write in Danish is as a rule like writing in water.

---

5. This is a riff on the Risorgimento-era Italian slogan, "Italy will take care of itself."

6. Brandes's *Indtryk fra Polen* appeared in Danish in 1888, in German in 1898.

It would be ungrateful of me, on this occasion when I must speak sharp words to the Poles, not to recall the indescribable affection and goodwill they have shown me in Russian as well as Austrian Poland. Among them I have found friends altogether without equal.

For a long time now I have thus refused ever to say anything unfriendly to them, never an offending word. As early as 1898 I declined so decisively to become the spokesperson for the Ruthenians that I made of their leaders bitter enemies who never tired of attacking me, and I remained silent as a wall when shortly before his death Bjørnstjerne Bjørnson attacked the Poles at their request, fortunately for them with such unreasonable overstatement that the attack did no damage. (Bjørnson asserted that the Poles as such were nearly the devil like the Middle Ages had imagined him to be.)[7] I knew better than Bjørnson what could be said against gerrymandering and voter intimidation in Galicia, but I remained silent because I saw it as unworthy to attack a people who were so perilously positioned and who could defend various lesser injustices that had occurred as necessity. I especially saw it as impossible for me to attack the Poles, to whom I was *bound by honor* and for whom I nourished the warmest and dearest sympathy.

It is thus with no light heart that I write these lines.

The denial of human rights to Jewish subjects belongs to the very essence of Russia. Now and then Europe has become alarmed when an unusual mass murder of innocent Jews has taken place, as in Kishinev.[8] But all have known and know now that Russia packs together its Jewish population in the Polish edge of the kingdom, packs them together so closely that they can neither live nor die, denies them the freedom of movement, the freedom to study, even the right to primary and university instruction apart from a certain (all too small) percentage. Only those Jews possessed of a university degree dare reside in the capital of the kingdom; no young Jewish woman dare reside near the universities in Petersburg or Moscow unless she has signed up as a prostitute, and it has happened that the police have turned up to accuse women who have done so of deception, that she was not engaged in the profession but instead was studying learned books. For example, a man who is a lawyer dares move to Moscow. If he is married, then his wife dares to live there with him. But if the couple have a two-year-old child, the mother cannot take it with her on the train car and allow it to live with her in the capital, for the child has no right to reside there. If this right is to be acquired, they must

7. See "The Fourth Partition of Poland" in the present volume for more on Bjørnson and the Ruthenians.

8. The Kishinev Pogrom took place over the course of two days in April 1903.

send a detailed application to the governor-general, who has it in his power to grant or to deny it.

In certain cases in which the plundering and murder of a Jewish population has taken place, the culprits have in part been acquitted by virtue of the almost unfathomable ignorance of the peasantry. Maksim Kovalevsky, Russia's most famous government economist and a large landowner, has himself told me that when the elections for the electors of the first Duma were to take place, it was communicated to him that every single one of the peasants on his land had voted for himself.[9] When in surprise he asked them what their intention was and explained that in this manner none of them could be elected, they answered by asking whether or not each deputy received such and such rubles per day. "Yes," he answered, to which they responded: "and you believe that we will leave so much money to another when we could perhaps have it ourselves?"

This same prominent man has informed me that one day when he asked some of his peasants whether they really had taken part in a pogrom that had occurred in a neighboring parish—he could not believe that they had when they seemed so good-natured—they answered yes, and when he asked them the reason they answered, "you know why." They then answered that they had killed these Jews because they had murdered their savior. "But that was, as you know, such a long time ago, it wasn't them and it wasn't here." To this they again broke out in astonishment: "Was it so long ago? We thought it had been a few weeks ago." It was revealed that from the explanation of the priest they had gathered that the crucifixion had happened right there on the spot.

In such conditions no misdeed can come as a surprise. But to see anti-semitism spread in Poland, where people can read and write, that must understandably result in bewilderment. The great number of Jews in the old Polish kingdom descend of course from the days of Casimir the Great (1310–70), who out of love for his concubine Esterka opened up Jewish access to his country and gave them favorable conditions.[10] Since then the number has risen as the czar has crammed all his Jewish subjects therein, and they have suffered every possible evil, even as well to this day living in isolation and in the peculiar dress that Jews of Denmark wore in Holberg's time.[11] They have, however,

9. For more on Kovalevskii, see "The Future of Russian Poland" and "The Fourth Partition of Poland" in the present volume.

10. The union of Casimir and Esterka did indeed result in mutually beneficial relations between Polish Catholics and Jews for centuries.

11. Ludvig Holberg (1684–1754) was the "Father of the Nordic Enlightenment." Hilarity ensues when a gentile character dresses as an Orthodox Jew in his 1724 play *The Masquerade*.

felt and suffered like friends of the Polish fatherland. As early as 1794 a Jewish regiment of volunteers fought under Kościuszko; their colonel fell in 1809.[12] In 1830 the provisional Polish national government refused the appeal of the Jews to be allowed to enlist in the army.[13] When they then ventured to apply for access to Polish popular education, Nicholas I punished them by having 36,000 families sent off to the South Russian steppe, where they suffered child conscription.[14] All the small boys from six years on were sent under the guard of the Cossacks to Archangel to be trained as sailors. They died in great numbers on the way.

The misfortunes that struck Poland's inhabitants of all faiths for a long time helped hold down the antisemitism that always lurked beneath the surface among the masses. The great men of Poland hindered its arousal. Poland's greatest poet, Adam Mickiewicz, went so far as to include a Jewish tavern-keeper among the most sympathetic characters in his greatest work, Poland's national epic *Pan Tadeusz* (1834). He is introduced in the fourth song as a musical genius, as the great master of the national instrument, the cymbal, and Mickiewicz allows his poem to culminate and conclude when Jankiel plays the "Dombrowski March" for Dombrowski himself, which indeed symbolizes the entirety of Polish history from 1791 through 1812, the year in which the poem takes place, the year of Napoleon.[15]

By the year 1860 in Warsaw the equality of Jews and Catholics was a reality, and when in February 1861 the masses who gathered in two of the city's squares to sing the national song ("Z dymem pożarów") were shot down by the Russians, the Jews felt the need to declare their national sentiment in an unmistakable acknowledgment. They accompanied their rabbis en masse into the

12. Andrzej Tadeusz Bonawentura Kościuszko (1746–1817) was the leader of the 1794 Polish-Lithuanian uprising against occupying Russian forces. Earlier in life he had served with distinction in the American Revolution. Colonel Berek Joselewicz (1764–1809) raised and commanded the Jewish volunteer force during the uprising, and was also a hero at the 1809 Battle of Kock.

13. Polish Jews did eventually receive permission to serve in the 1830–31 Russo-Polish War.

14. Brandes overstates the role of the request of Poland's Jews for access to Polish schooling in provoking the mass deportations of the 1830s; Nicholas I's "resettlement" program was motivated by a host of factors.

15. Jan Henryk Dąbrowski (1755–1818, German Dombrowski) served with distinction in the Kościuszko Uprising of 1794 and under Napoleon as commander of the Polish Legions. He figures prominently in Poland's national anthem, often referred to as "Dąbrowski's Mazurka."

Catholic churches, just as the Christians in masses went into the synagogues to strike up the same hymn.[16]

This last episode, the procession of the two faiths into each other's churches during the singing of the same hymn, made such an impression on a great Nordic poet, Henrik Ibsen, that in conversations again and again he came back to it as among the greatest and most beautiful things he ever experienced.

And now, in the midst of the tornado of madness that nationalism has spread over Europe, all of this goodwill has gone to waste, indeed has turned from religious reconciliation into flaming racial hatred.

II. The Facts

In 1912 a deputy to the Duma was to be elected in Warsaw. The population of the city is somewhere between seven and eight hundred thousand. Since there are over three hundred thousand Jews among these, it was in their power to elect a Jewish deputy. Out of Polish national affinity they declined this opportunity, since they wished that Warsaw as the capital of the Kingdom of Poland should be represented by a man Polish not just by temperament but by descent as well. They demanded of the Polish election committee only that the chosen man must not be an enemy of the Jews. It became apparent, however, that the election committee in its arrogance would not negotiate with them at all, and it put forth a candidate, Jan Kucharzewski, who surely enough did not call himself antisemitic and would not be called so, but was viewed by the Jewish community as an enemy, since in the Duma he spoke for adscription of the Jews, was a demonstrated opponent of all Jewish nationalism, and felt that the Jews had in fact become nationalists under such severe pressure.[17]

When the Jews would not give their vote to a man in whom they saw an enemy, the earnest election committee recommended putting forth another candidate who did not seem hostile to them. This reasonable request was coarsely dismissed and Kucharzewski's candidacy upheld. As a consequence of this the Jews were compelled to seek another candidate of Polish descent who was worthy of the position and who was not hostile to them. In spite of

16. The period from 1861 through the January Uprising of 1863 constitutes the apex of Polish-Jewish unity during the modern era; later in the year, after the Russian authorities ordered all Catholic churches closed, the Jewish community responded by closing its synagogues in solidarity. See Leo Cooper, *In the Shadow of the Polish Eagle: The Poles, the Holocaust and Beyond* (New York: Palgrave Macmillan, 2000), 29–31.

17. In the fourth edition of *Verdenskrigen* (1917), Brandes adds this note: "Jan Kucharzewski has as an ally of the Germans been named the first council president of the new Polish state as of November 1917" (9). Kucharzewski (1876–1952) served as Polish premier until February 1918, after which he largely retired from politics.

numerous appeals they were not successful. When all possibilities had been exhausted, the social democrat Jagiełło declared himself at the last moment to be willing to stand as the candidate of the Jews.

In their eyes what spoke for him was that he was of pure Polish blood. Since all their leading men belonged to the upper bourgeoisie, they did not share any of his views, but the conditions forced them to support him.[18] Lord Beaconsfield in his time constantly asserted that the Jewish people by inclination were conservative, but that miserable statecraft rather than an enthusiasm for their conservative instincts forced them to make common cause with the widest array of oppositional elements.[19] That is confirmed here.

Jagiełło was chosen.

The leading men in Russian Poland, who in fact throughout the nineteenth century had fought against the Jews, albeit in secret in order not to lose the sympathy of the European intellectual aristocracy, now seized on this electoral triumph forced upon them by the Jews to cast off the mask and openly behave as their passionate enemies. The so-called cooperative movement built up over the past twelve years, which at bottom had been none other than a differently named struggle against Jewish business interests, was transformed now into a systematic and cruelly instituted *boycotting* of the Jewish community.[20] In private as well as public life the openly proclaimed solution became: do not buy from the Jews! Do not associate with the Jews!

The intelligentsia of Poland was positioned at the head of this movement, including some of its most distinguished writers, declared freethinkers such as Niemojewski, indeed even Aleksander Świętochowski.[21] The history of literature offers up many reversals, many transformations, which in their thoroughness are no less complete than those of Ovid. I can say that a lot would be required for one such as myself, who has witnessed the lack of character among writers for a half century, to be able to be surprised by such a transformation. But still I am shocked to see Aleksander Świętochowski, the most reckless opponent of nationalism, who in his youth suffered for his convictions, become a

18. The leftist parties of the Fourth Duma largely froze out Eugeniusz Jagiełło (1873–1947), not because of antisemitism but because of his perceived association with the bourgeoisie.

19. Brandes had produced a biography of British prime minister Benjamin Disraeli (1804–81), First Earl of Beaconsfield, in 1878.

20. Anti-Jewish boycotts had in fact been a feature of Central and Eastern Europe since the late nineteenth century.

21. Andrzej Niemojewski (1864–1921) was a poet and freethinker associated with the Young Poland movement. Aleksander Świętochowski (1849–1938) was a philosopher associated with Polish Positivism.

nationalist, to witness sight of the poet of *Chawa Rubin* become a chieftain of the antisemites.[22] Not only what Aleksander Świętochowski has written, but the words, the strong words that passed his lips in his salad days, rise up against him.

The entirety of the Polish press placed itself in the service of this movement. Young Polish hooligans were placed before Jewish businesses where they abused the Christian women and children who would shop there. With the help of the well-known Dmowski, the leader of the National Democratic party, a new newspaper was founded, *Dwa Groszi*, which straight out called for pogroms.[23] Suddenly it came to a bloody collision. In the little town of Wieluń peasants poured naphtha over the house of a Jew during the night and set it on fire, to which a large family succumbed.[24] Similar occurrences took place at various other places, until the Russian government halted the pogrom movement in order to prevent it from bolstering Polish nationalism.

The Polish priests in the villages incited the people from the pulpit toward boycotts and war against the Jews. After the verdict in the Beilis trial in Kiev the Polish papers were almost entirely in agreement in communicating through leaflet that although Beilis had been acquitted, the existence of ritual murder had been decisively proved (!).[25] In Poland *Beilis* is still an invective against the Jews.

Under these circumstances the Jews in Russian Poland turned to a single man whose name was so distinguished and whose character was so immaculate that his word could not be ignored.

A relative of the great Mickiewicz, Wladislaw Mickiewicz, together with other prominent men, called a large meeting in Warsaw in order to restore the internal peace.[26] In vain, and by the end in tears, he beseeched his countrymen, who indeed already had enough enemies, not to add the Jews into the bargain, they who had always been their friends. No Polish paper mentioned his speech.

All of this occurred before the war. The result at the time was the economic destruction of the Jews of Russian Poland. But now during the war the bloody

22. Świętochowski's moralistic novels, among them *Chawa Rubin* (1896), had specifically urged tolerance for foreigners and national minorities.

23. Roman Stanisław Dmowski (1864–1939), a hero to Rightist Polish nationalists, is considered by the contemporary Polish Left to have been a proto-fascist.

24. For more on the events of 1913 in Wieluń, see Phillip Jolly, *Jewish Wieluń: A Polish Shtetl* (Morrisville, NC: Lulu, 2010), 73–82.

25. The 1913 trial of Menahem Mendel Beilis (1874–1934) in Kiev is among the most notorious of blood libel cases in the history of global antisemitism. Beilis was acquitted and later became the subject of Bernard Malamud's *The Fixer*.

26. Władysław Mickiewicz (1838–1926) was a leading advocate of the Polish diaspora.

glow of antisemitism has arisen with far stronger flames, and the Russian government has up to now done nothing to constrain or put out the fire.

During the mobilization numerous Polish papers, for example *Glos Lubelski*, published in large thick type this disquieting report: *Large Pogroms in England against the Jews. The English Government does not Hinder them.* It was a deliberate lie. But it was a matter of setting an example for imitation.

When the scarcity of gold and silver began to make itself felt, the Polish newspapers blamed the Jews for hoarding precious metals. A closer investigation brought forth the insight that many non-Jewish businesspeople (for example the ultra-rich Pole Ignaszewski in Lublin) had in their possession whole sacks full of gold and silver coins, for which they were severely punished; not a single Jew was among them.

Likewise the Jews were among other things blamed for having smuggled a million and a half rubles in gold into Germany in a chest. The challenge against this accusation issued by the representatives of the Jewish congregation in Warsaw was printed in the Russian newspapers, but not in a single Polish one.

All this was preparation for pogroms. But many other preparations were carried out. The antisemites had published a proclamation drawn up in Yiddish in which the Jews called for an uprising against Russia; they saw to it that this was placed into the pockets of unwitting Jews on the streets of numerous cities; the same people who had distributed the papers gave up the Jews to the police. Everyone on whom the papers were found was shot.

Finally the Jews, just like in the Middle Ages, were accused both orally and in writing of having poisoned the wells. If some Cossacks or other Russian soldiers died, the Poles blamed the Jews of being guilty of well poisoning.

The principal accusation was, however, that of espionage, which was believed universally, and which was leveled both when Austrian troops came to a city or village and when Russian troops drove away the Austrians. The result was the same. A similar number of Jews were scrupulously shot down by the Russians and by the Austrians. Lists of those who have in fact been unmasked as spies have, however, been provided. A Potocki was found among them and must pay with his life, but no Jewish name is found on this list.[27]

The legend of Judas can without exaggeration be counted as one of the most imbecilic legends antiquity has left us; that it has been believed is one piece of evidence among thousands of humanity's indescribable simplemindedness. Few legends bear the mark of their untruth upon their countenances

27. The House of Potocki is among the most blue-blooded of Polish aristocratic families. The accusation is nevertheless believed since the Jews have been characterized as Judases for nearly two thousand years.

like this one, and few legends have for millennium after millennium inflicted such a sum of misfortunes and horrors. It has martyred and murdered hundreds of thousands.

According to its own assumptions the story is impossible. The assumptions are that a person with supernatural characteristics, a god or demigod, day in and day out traveled around and spoke in a city and its environs under the open sky. He concealed his movements so little that he made his entry in broad daylight and was greeted with jubilation by the people. He was known to all and everyone, to every woman and every child. He sought so little concealment that he wandered about followed by disciples, preached by day and slept by night in the midst of his disciples. And it should be necessary to bribe one of his disciples to give him up and deliver him, to *betray* him! And for the sake of effect to do so with a kiss! Indeed, if he had crawled into a hole in one or another cellar then there would be some significance to it. But the conditions are such that those who seek him need only to ask: which of you is Jesus? He would not try and deny his name.

Judas then is not just more superfluous than the fifth wheel of a carriage, but an absurdity, born of the need to posit a dark evildoer against the white hero of light and in that way awaken antisemitism among the first Christians converted from heathenism, who gradually came to forget that not just this straw man, this Judas, but Jesus and all the apostles, all the disciples, all the evangelists, were Jews.

Nevertheless over the course of the centuries this Judas—as the name indicates—has become in the imagination of the unwashed masses the Jew, the typical Jew, the evildoer, the spy.

Even as late as the previous century's final decade, Captain Alfred Dreyfus fell as a sacrifice to this silly old tale.

Now it has come to a boil against the Jews in Russian Poland.

By virtue of this Judas accusation and many other dreadful charges the pogroms have spread out over a large part of Russian Poland where they continue to gain ground, while Galicia as well as Posen have proved unreceptive to such incitements, which have not been lacking. Many hundreds of innocent people have fallen as sacrifices.

Here are few among many examples:

In the city of Bychawa, which was conquered by the Austrians, the Polish leaders appealed to the Austrian commander and accused the Jews of having secret connections to the Russian army.[28] As a consequence the Austrians

28. All of Brandes's examples in the following paragraphs are taken from small cities and towns in the Lublin district of Eastern Poland, a traditional heartland of Hasidic Judaism.

killed a sixty-seven-year-old man by the name of Wallstein as well as his seventeen-year-old son. Shortly after the Austrians were driven out, the same men appealed to the Russian commander, accusing the Jews in the city of having relations with the Austrians and having delivered to them all the foodstuffs with the intention of denying them to the Russians. As a consequence many Jews were shot and their houses burned down.

In the cities of Janow and Krasnik the Jews were accused of having laid mines in the path of the Russians. The Jews, many children among them, were hanged from telegraph poles and the two cities destroyed.

The city of Zamosc was conquered by Austrian Sokol troops, those handsome and athletic people who no one who has seen them train in the capital of Galicia can forget. When they were driven off by the Russian army, the Poles accused the Jews of having been in collusion with the Austrians. Twelve Jews were arrested. When they denied the charges they were executed. Five of them were hanged. In the middle of the execution a Russian priest with an image of the Madonna in his hand came forward and with his hand on the icon took an oath that the Jews were innocent and that the whole affair was a result of Polish antisemitism. He demonstrated that the Poles themselves had supported the Austrians and that there was even a telephone connection to Lemberg. The remaining seven Jews were set free—the other five *were* hanged.

In the city of Juzefow the Jews were accused of having poisoned the well, by which hundreds of Cossacks were said to have lost their lives. Seventy-eight Jews were killed, many women raped, houses and shops plundered.

Similar episodes took place and take place still daily in the hundreds. In this way smaller and larger pogroms with murder, rape, and plunder have taken place in the provinces of Warsaw, Radom, Piotrków, and Kielce.

Only a few Russian governors, like Korff in Warsaw, Kelepowski in Lublin, as well as the governors of Vilna, Piotrków, and Grodno have (albeit too late) spoken out against the pogroms; but neither the government nor the Poles take these admonitions seriously.[29]

Eyewitnesses have told me of Jewish soldiers in various camp hospitals who have been driven insane not by the unavoidable horrors of the war but because of the pogroms they have witnessed in the cities through which they have marched. They conflate the victims of murder and murder/rape with their own relatives, believe they have seen their own mothers or sisters or lovers in that situation. Their delusions constantly turn on the same thing.

---

29. Brandes here refers to Warsaw governor general Georgi Skalon (see "The Future of Russian Poland," note 2) by the family name of his wife, Baroness Marie von Korff. Arkadiusz Kelepowski (1870–1925) was governor general of Lublin from 1912 to 1914.

The persecution of the Jews by the antisemites of Russian Poland under these circumstances is all the more odious because 400,000 Jewish soldiers, among them many volunteers, serve in the Russian army, and the willingness of the Jews to sacrifice themselves for the army and for the Red Cross has up to now known no boundaries. In the large congregations special hospitals for Russian soldiers—regardless of faith—have been established by Jews with Jewish funds. Not a few Jews have already earned the highest military decoration, indeed several have received them from Commander in Chief Rennenkampf himself, who otherwise is an enthusiastic antisemite, as the Russian imperial court is by and large passionately antisemitic. The proclamation from the czar, "To My Dear Jewish Subjects," which has been published in French newspapers, has never been other than parody.[30]

While the standing accusation against the Jews in Russian Poland has been that they sympathize with the Russians—something they have no particular reason to do—a complaint was recently leveled at them in *Politiken* by a certain A. Warinski, according to which the German attempts to win over the Poles "only had the desired impact on the Russian and Polish Jews, since these elements *because of their psychological affinity with the Prussians feel the impulse to side with Germany*." This complaint and its reasoning ought to be seen as the climax. The Jews shall and must be Judas. If it does not work in the one manner, then try it in the opposite. Mr. Warinski does not grant a single word to how many Jews have willingly gone to war out of enthusiasm for Poland. They have not been able to believe, as I for my part cannot believe, that this latest outbreak of nationalism in Russian Poland is anything other or more than a passing epidemic.

How could the Russian Poles in the long run be unfaithful to the only forces to which they have been able to appeal, the forces that alone showed them any interest? How can those who fight for their freedom after years of abuse want to seize an opportunity to abuse the only people who (to their misfortune) are within their power! The only people who have suffered far more and for twenty times as long as they themselves! In addition to that the only people who are much too strong to be wiped out by any kind of abuse. How can the Poles, who in their time lost their state due to the treachery of the Targowica Confederation, want to hurl accusations of treachery against a tribe that has never betrayed itself and even in its deepest humiliation has

30. For more on the czar's much-pilloried "Jewish Manifesto," as well as its German response, see Zosa Szajkowski, "The German Appeal to the Jews of Poland, August 1914," *Jewish Quarterly Review* 59, no. 4 (April 1969): 311–20.

never betrayed the only Slavic tribe that in the Middle Ages provided its children a refuge![31]

Presumably it will be brought to bear against my appeal to the Poles that I who never allowed myself to be compelled by the Ruthenians to attack them, now because of my descent speak for a cause that is unpleasant in their ears. My personal descent has so little influenced my behavior and manner of thinking that during the entirety of my public life I have been the object of unceasing attacks in Jewish nationalist journals and newspapers, such as the one that refused to acknowledge my common descent and presumably common faith.

Moreover, in the spring of this year during my stay in America I was unceasingly attacked in the Jewish American newspapers as an inveterate denier of the Jews. It was hogwash like most of what is published, yet at least it reveals that it is not because of my blood but my intellect that on this occasion I take up the pen. My sympathy for the Jews is not due to my being a Jew but to their being an oppressed and abused people.

I am the one who a lifetime ago wrote: "One loves Poland not like one loves Germany or France or England, but like one loves freedom. For what is it to love Poland than to love freedom, to have deep sympathy for the misfortune and to admire the courage and the cantankerous enthusiasm! Poland is a mental image of all that which the best in humanity have loved and have fought for."[32]

These were my words, and I have up to now stood by them.

Shall I be ashamed at having written them, now that Poland's future is to be determined?

III. Incitement to Pogroms

Now that the incitement of national hatred against one another has succeeded in turning Europe into an insane asylum, a house of mourning, a field hospital, a graveyard, and a bankrupt estate, one should believe that at least a kind of peace has been preserved within the borders of the various countries who participate in the war.

As I have demonstrated in numerous articles, this does not apply to the Russian kingdom. While France and England have necessarily communicated to Europe that the Russian government like their own is fighting for justice

31. The Targowica Confederation of 1792, in which Polish and Lithuanian nobility allied with Russia against the forces of Polish republicanism, constitutes in fact the worst betrayal of Polish history.

32. Brandes, *Samlede Skrifter*, 10:47.

and freedom, this government has suppressed the labor press, dissolved labor organizations, imprisoned five social democratic members of the Duma, sent Finland's most significant statesman to Siberia, held the Poles in check with a vague promise offered not by the czar himself but by a field general whose word binds no one, and set in motion a persecution of the Russian Jews that is worse than any prior campaign.[33] While the number of Jewish soldiers who fight in the Russian army is reckoned at between a quarter million and 400,000, the government meticulously maintains the rightlessness of the Jews and watches over them, so that they dare not leave the area in which they are alone permitted to live. It is precisely this area in which the war is taking place in Poland and in certain Lithuanian provinces. When boundless misery and hunger forces the Jews to abandon their assigned places of residence they are driven back by patrols or by swarms of Cossacks. When Jewish soldiers, more or less recovered from their wounds yet still unfit for immediate service, are discharged from the hospital, they are immediately sent back to the "homeland," as uninhabitable as it is. Indeed it has happened that a Russian volunteer nineteen years of age who had gotten half his face blown off and was to be operated on by Professor Hirschmann was thrown out of his hotel and forced to leave the city, because he was Jewish or was descended from Jews. This is just as crazy: anyone whose father or grandfather was of the Jewish faith is denied admission to the officers' schools that have been established for the duration of the war.

In Poland itself a long series of pogroms have taken place since the beginning of the war. The Jewish population has been plundered, cruelly abused, in many places murdered. Additionally, this population has been cast out from a host of cities in which it has up to now had permission to live, driven out with twenty-four hours' warning, as some 1,500 families were driven out on the country road from Grodzisk, a city in the vicinity of Warsaw, which I know quite well, while everything left in the houses was robbed and plundered. In this way the Jews have been expelled from eight cities, wherefrom they stream into the capital, which cannot possibly house them. This happens at the same time that a host of young Jews who have distinguished themselves in the war receive medals of courage and decorations, and while the government press praises the Jews for their contributions to the care of the wounded and the abandoned, their establishment of hospitals and the like.

---

33. Pehr Evind Svinhufvud (1861–1944) was exiled in in 1914 for refusing to obey Russian orders; after the fall of the czar, he returned in triumph and was named chair of the Finnish Senate.

That now the rabble in Russian Poland is incensed, like in other places in Europe, with hatred of the Jews, does not come as a surprise, and it will certainly bring a writer who perhaps more vehemently than any non-Polish person alive has expressed his affection for the Polish people, to level a complaint against the Poles. If it was the rabble who was responsible for the pogroms then there would be nothing to say about it. Then the case of Poland would be the same as in Kishinev and in other places in Russia proper.

But that which has brought me to take up the pen is the immense difference in the circumstances in Russia and in Russian Poland, namely that *while in Russia all of the country's distinguished writers*, a Vladimir Korolenko, a Leonid Andrejev, a Maxim Gorky, all of the intellectuals by and large, *concern themselves with the misfortune of the Jews and view the incitement to pogroms as a shame and a scandal, the men of the Polish intelligentsia such as Niemojewski and Swientochowski place themselves at the head of the movement against the Jews and thereby reveal how far the Polish intelligentsia is behind that of Russia in genuine culture.*[34] It is this that is the main point and for which there can be no remedy. To be sure, the troubles have already occurred, and this is not written in the wind but in the most complete and justified seriousness. For this rests upon human lives and human existences in the thousands. They are destroyed as sacrifices for medieval prejudice, as if it were the task of the intellectual nobility to cut down rather than to raise up.

The Ukrainian press has to the best of its ability ridiculed me because I have written that I was aware of Polish gerrymandering in Galicia but did not consider it worthy of repeal; this press does not realize that long before Bjørnson I spoke out on the cause of the Ruthenians with great warmth (see volume 17 of my collected works), and in all likelihood these same Ruthenians, who for seventeen years have persecuted me, because I would not attack the Poles on behalf of the Ruthenians, naturally enough now explain that it is my *fellow tribe* whose side I take; regarding other nationalities my conscience is *capacious.*[35] Even a Ruthenian may however be able to understand that there is a difference between an injustice committed against a people in which they did not get all of the representatives to which they had a right into a parliament, and an injustice committed against a people in which its men and women are plundered, murdered, violated, hanged, and burned.

---

34. Vladimir Galaktionovich Korolenko's (1853–1921) opposition to Russian antisemitism began before the war, specifically during the Beilis trial of 1913. Leonid Nikolaevich Andreev (1871–1919) introduced Expressionism to Russian literature. The works of the great socialist realist Aleksei Maksimovich Peshkov (1868–1936, known as Maxim Gorky) were long championed by Brandes.

35. See "The Ruthenians," published in 1904, in the present volume.

Incidentally the following circular has been issued from Poland: "The Polish press has already many times raised the question of why the union of Polish writers and journalists has not answered Georg Brandes's articles. The union has decided in its most recent meeting not to respond, because it views the replies in the individual organs of the Polish press as sufficient. The union declines to make a collective protest."

It would have been more successful if the Polish union of writers and journalists had decided to do its part in hindering pogroms rather than sending out this vacuous communiqué, which hardly impresses anyone, in any event not me.

CHAPTER 26

Poland

1915

Following his dismayed chastisement of rising Polish antisemitism published the previous year ("Conditions in Russian Poland" in the present volume), Brandes returns to the Polish question with a much more sympathetic treatment, occasioned by the pending visit of Polish independence advocate Julia Ledóchowska. Brandes is also motivated here by the drastic change of fortune on the Eastern Front in 1915, when German and Austrian forces completed the conquest of Russian Poland. His hopes once again raised, Brandes here considers the vague German promises of a reconstituted Poland first suggested by German chancellor Theobald von Bethmann-Hollweg. The ensuing puppet Regency Kingdom of Poland would after the armistice be incorporated into the newly founded Second Polish Republic.

~

Countess Julia Ledóchowska, who will speak in the great hall of the Koncertpalæ on the sad fate of her fatherland during the world war, is a lady who has served her country and people every day of her life.[1] Like so many of Poland's distinguished women she is Polish to the core, all the more passionately so the weaker her people become. She belongs to one of the notable families of Polish history. Her uncle was the famous cardinal Ledóchowski, who as archbishop of Posen-Gnesen refused to submit to Bismarck's May Laws. He had been made an archbishop in 1866 in the hope that he would hold down the nationalist agitation in Posen, but Bismarck's campaign against the Catholic Church called him to lead the opposition party, for which he had to pass the years

---

Originally published in *Politiken*, November 23, 1915. Translated from the version published in *Verdenskrigen*.

1. Saint Julia Ledóchowska (1836–1939, known after taking the habit in 1887 as Maria Ursula of Jesus), founded Ursuline girls' schools across the Russian Empire and in Scandinavia. She was also an energetic supporter of the Polish cause, speaking regularly on the issue in the Nordic countries. She was formally canonized in 2003.

1874–76 in prison.[2] In 1875 Pius IX, who was very fond of him, made Ledóchowski a cardinal.

In reality the countess is not entirely Polish. On her mother's side she descends from the old Swiss noble family Graubünden, which has many branches, one of which provided a highly regarded officer for the French monarch's Swiss Guard during the revolution. But the ability to reconcile half-foreignness with national enthusiasm, which is striking among the Polish people as it is in the Hungarians and the Americans, has run through Countess *Ledóchowska*, who through and through feels herself to be Polish and nothing else.

Her family also has a prominent name in the Catholic world of our time. Her brother is himself superior-general of the Jesuits.[3]

What the countess will dwell on, as far as is known, is the unheard-of sufferings, the need, and the misery that the world war has brought down on Austrian and Russian Poland, which have provided the battlefields for the struggle in the East. Her hope is to move her listeners to active participation in some form of remedy for the misfortunes that have been visited upon the population for sixteen months now.

She has hardly led the unproductive life typical of a fine lady. First in Galicia, later in Russia, after her exile from Russia in Finland, after her exile from Finland in Sweden, she has dedicated her entire life to the education of young Polish girls, and she is imbued with a most singularly worthy idealism, that of the practical, and sees the conditions in Poland not politically but from the profoundly human side.

Beyond the languages she has by virtue of her upbringing always been able to speak, Polish, Russian, French, German, English, and Italian, she has in recent years learned to speak Finnish and Swedish; and it is in Swedish that she will address the Danish audience.

As said, it is from this profoundly human side that Countess Ledóchowska sees conditions in her fatherland, in other words she who herself is good, speaks in the name of the good and appeals to goodness.

Herein is found, as remarkable as it sounds, something extremely rare in our age.

---

2. Mieczysław Halka-Ledóchowski (1822–1902) was made a cardinal in 1875 while still incarcerated, after which he was released and banished by the Prussian authorities.

3. Very Rev. Wlodimir Ledóchowski, SJ (1866–1942) led the Society of Jesus from 1915 until his death. Brandes's invocation of him is, sadly enough, unfortunate, as the cardinal would eventually emerge as a leader of the antisemitic faction in the Vatican. See David I. Kertzer, *The Pope and Mussolini: The Secret History of Pius XI and the Rise of Fascism in Europe* (New York: Random House, 2014), 210–11.

He who has observed over the last sixteen months how all of the belligerent peoples are convinced they are fighting for the good cause, for justice and truth against lies and coercion, while at the same time they massacre each other with the most dreadful of means, gets the impression that the guardian spirit of humanity is an infinitely more subtle devil than that which Goethe in his time described in *Faust* with the famous words:

> Ein Theil von jener Kraft,
> Die stets das Böse will und stets das Gute schafft.[4]

The guardian spirit of humanity in our time is diametrically the opposite and thus terrifying in a different way. They are parts of the same force:

> Die stets das Gute will und stets Böse schafft.

For all of our age's statesmen, field generals, officers, and common soldiers, all politicians in the countries as well as generals and admirals, battalion commanders and ship captains, everyone without exception want, day in and day out, to do good. But this noble will expresses itself, day in and day out, as an uninterrupted calling forth of horrors, as cruelties without number, murders on a scale the earth has not known before, so that the entire struggle in the service of the good has as its only certain impact the doing of abominable evil, which would seem to have been occasioned by a wild and hateful rage of destruction.

Since, however, the conditions in Poland have a human side as well as a political dimension, the latter about which it would not be difficult to write volumes, the impulse to bring in certain political observations is never far from the countess's human perspective.

As is known the campaign of the Russian field general Grand Prince Nikolai Nikolaevich opened with a proclamation to the Poles of Russian Poland that promised them the fulfillment of their national dream in the form of a not-well-defined *autonomy*.[5] What should be understood by this self-rule, which boundaries it should have, et cetera, was uncertain. That it was not seriously meant was apparent after the occupation of Lemberg, which was treated as "old Russian land." But the proclamation served temporarily to divide the Poles. While in Galicia Polish legions were immediately formed, which throughout the war have fought with heroism and distinguished themselves in many ways

4. "Part of that force which would / Do evil evermore, and yet creates the good." Johann Wolfgang von Goethe, *Faust I*, trans. Walter Kauffman (New York: Anchor, 1963), ll. 1335–36.

5. See note 1 in "Conditions in Russian Poland" in the present volume.

in the Austrian army, in the Kingdom of Poland there was a party that hoped for the liberation of the whole of Polish territory through Russian arms, and that in any case *sounded* like it had full confidence in the proclamation and thereby took the Russians at their word. This party felt itself to be not just Polish, but Slavic in general. And there was also a large party that, barring other options, in the end preferred Russian dominance to Prussian. Russian dominance was certainly more barbaric, but less systematic. It always had lacunae, holes, through which one could breathe, because in its essence it was inconsistent. And it had the great advantage that the pressure could be alleviated through abundant bribery, while the Prussian bureaucrat is an incorruptible, deeply honest government automaton as immune to human weaknesses as he is to human virtues.

With the development of events this cleft between the Poles who hoped for national unity through the help of Russia and those who hoped to achieve it through Austria's protection and the victory of Austro-German arms has temporarily receded.

Yet there are cleavages enough left over. Poles fight against each other in the armies of the dominant powers, but since the Russians were driven out of Galicia and since the occupation of the Kingdom of Poland, the question of the Russian "orientation," as it is called, has altogether been dropped. The Central Powers and those Poles who support the Central Powers are the only ones who have a voice in the matter.

And they make use of this voice. The big weekly journal *Polen* is published exclusively in German, as well as the thrice-monthly shorter journal *Polnische Blätter* and a host of further polemical writings and pamphlets.

It thus seems that it should not be difficult to gather a comprehensive and impartial sense of what is going on politically and what is being prepared.

And yet this is quite difficult and for a simple reason, the same reason that at the moment makes it nearly impossible to get at the truth of the conditions in the various countries.

The majority of what is made public is official accounts, and the little that may not be called official from the point of view of one side or another is published under censorship and thus written with a restrained pen. Europe overall has indeed for the moment gleefully returned to Russian conditions as far as the free press is concerned. Neither emotional nor intellectual life is expressed freely. Not even that which is referred to as historical fact can be relied upon by the reader. There is lying, silencing, misinformation, effacement, fabrication, and hypocrisy all in the service of various political ends.

Since Galicia is the only province of partitioned Poland in which the population has been able to lead a life worthy of human dignity, it was tempting to imagine Galicia as the kernel of the new Poland expected to reemerge. Like in Galicia, the Poles in the kingdom and in Prussian Poland should thus also come to enjoy self-rule and independence. Early on a plan was discussed to quickly unite Galicia and the kingdom under one or another Austrian archduke as the Polish monarch. One was even chosen.[6] Yet soon this project slid out of discussion. It was sensed that Prussia, unless it changed its own treatment of the Poles, would never permit a free Polish state as its neighbor.

Then followed the German chancellor's speech in August of this year, in which he provided a kind of program for the future politics of the German kingdom, of which two points in particular deserve attention.[7] The first is that Germany is "the guardian and the steward of the freedom of the smaller nations," the second that the German occupation of Poland indicated "the beginning of a development that would banish the old opposition between German and Pole from the world and lead that country that now had been liberated from the Russian yoke toward a happy future, in which it could cultivate and unfold its national character."

The words were carefully chosen and spoke to a desire not to commit prematurely. Yet they were remarkable enough, and if they were seriously meant and the chancellor stood behind them, they betokened no less than a complete reversal in German, especially Prussian politics.

In the case that Germany should in the future become the guardian of the small nations, what light would fall over its previous persecution of the Danish and Polish national sentiment within its own environs!

If Germany intended to allow the Poles now liberated from Russian dominance to develop their national characteristics freely, then it would be a regular impossibility to be able to deny the Poles in Posen, Silesia, West and East Prussia the same courtesy.

Still this demands an explanation of why such a change of course was thinkable, when it indeed was at odds with all habit and custom. Furthermore, there is still the problem that while the kingdom is entirely Polish and Galicia somewhat evenly divided between Poles and Ruthenians, a third of inhabitants of Posen itself are German, and there are in the Prussian state as a whole four million Poles intermixed with eight million Germans. The Polish people

6. Archduke Charles Stephen (1860–1933) was fluent in Polish and a resident of Galicia.

7. Chancellor Theobald von Bethmann-Hollweg's (1856–1921) speech of August 19, 1915, amounted to a significant softening of the hard line he had developed in the previous year's *Septemberprogramm*; yet as argued by Jesse Kauffman, the vague and noncommittal promises were motivated by a desire for Polish manpower in the war against Russia. See *Elusive Alliance: The German Occupation of Poland in World War I* (Cambridge, MA: Harvard University Press, 2015), 72.

do not want to be removed from their homes, and if Poland is reestablished without any resettlement, it would be difficult to pacify them, let alone reconcile them to their situation.

In the interim the conquerors of Poland are silent regarding the political future of the country. They are occupied with helping the devastated country materially. There is still nothing that suggests their intention is to grant the desire of the people for political union, but there is much that demonstrates the German and Austrian authorities' sincere intent to grant the Polish language every right that earlier was withheld, in the universities, the schools, and on the stage. The authorities have furthermore called for Polish cooperation on many sensible measures.

Before the outcome the Great War is known it is of course hardly possible to make decisions or make definitive promises for the future, and economically there is more than enough to do before the political aspect may be addressed.

The traditions of 1812, which like idées fixes have governed Russia during the war, so that in all seriousness it has been said that the Russian withdrawal from Galicia and the kingdom of Poland is a strategic dodge in the manner of the retreats a hundred years ago, have led to the Russians' meaningless, almost insane destruction of every city and every locality they have abandoned, indeed, their driving off of the whole population, so that Polish Catholics and Jews in the millions have in the most barbaric manner been herded into inner Russia or sent by rail all the way to Siberia. Three or four days in a row unlucky people have been confined and packed into cargo and livestock cars without coming out and without nourishment. Every day many die from this treatment. The bodies are thrown out of the cars in transit so that they lay along the rails. Sometimes they remain laying in the cars at the stations, where the living are confined without being allowed to exit. Surely enough the Jewish population, which by virtue of a two-thousand-year hatred has been despised and abused, suffered the most under this brutality, but alongside of that the Poles have suffered inhumanly, and they have earned entirely the sympathy that their misfortune demands.

Never have the inhabitants of Polish territory endured such a sum of sufferings as precisely now, when the possibility of Poland's reemergence has revealed itself before the eyes of the Poles as apparently not so distant and uncertain. In 1886 I wrote that "as much hope as there still is within the Polish temperament, the hopelessness of their situation, at least in the eyes of mere men, hangs over their minds like a nightmare. There is no other prospect of coming out of their current predicament in sight than the extremely uncertain possibilities that a war between Russia on the one side and Germany and Austria on the other could open up."[8]

That which I expressed almost a lifetime ago, full of presentiment but uncertainly, has at last come to pass.

But in the interim, as I have written above, the entire struggle in the service of the good has found its only certain impact in an uninterrupted series of disasters and a long chain of horrors.

8. Brandes, *Samlede Skrifter*, 10:91.

CHAPTER 27

The Great Era

1915

In spite of the carnage wrought in the initial engagements of the Great War, the universal enthusiasm with which its outbreak had been greeted in the belligerent countries had not entirely dissipated by the spring of 1915; still to come were the even greater horrors of Verdun and the Somme in the West and of Russian collapse in the East. In this brief essay Brandes attempts to undermine whatever remained of the initial war fever of August 1914, with special emphasis, as always, on the small countries who found themselves in the crosshairs of the imperial ambitions of the great powers.

~

A common opinion holds that the era we are now experiencing is an era of greatness, that the years 1914–15 signify the largest event in the recent history of humanity, since never before has a war been conducted in which such great masses of people have been brought into the field, and in which the destruction of human lives and values has been so comprehensive. It occurs to me that events such as the invention of the steamship, the locomotive, the telegraph wire, and then the wireless telegraph, events such as the invention of the bicycle, the electric motor, electrical lighting, or airplanes are great and decisive events. But it is impossible for me to view the uninterrupted mass murder occasioned by the incitement of steadily more intense national passions as a great event deserving of the designation of a great era, in the sense that "great" is understood as *valuable*. Against this it will be asserted that the greatness of the era we are now experiencing is found not in the greatness of the damage that is dispensed but in the greatness of the ideas for which we fight.

Wars have been conducted for which the principal reasons were idealistic, for example, Napoleon III's war against Austria in 1859, which had as its goal

Originally published in *Verden og Vi*, May 14, 1915. Translated from the version published in *Verdenskrigen*.

the liberation of the Italian provinces under foreign domination.[1] As a rule, however, wars are not undertaken for ideas, but for interests. Economic competition is continued by other means, and the fighting, universally understood, is over power, over supremacy.[2] Each of the belligerent powers has at all times been convinced of having right on its side; those who in every country have led public opinion of course provide this as justification. Each of the belligerent states' inhabitants sincerely believe in this, and rarely doubt whether the heavens should therefore grant them victory. Each of them is incensed to an equal degree against the neutrals who are not prepared to see all the right on one side. People who see themselves in mortal danger do not take to deliberation, and it is a waste of time to answer their attacks.[3]

Among the countries that have been impacted by the war there are three that have been tested especially severely: Belgium, Poland, and Armenia. Belgium's ordeal has awakened the consciousness of justice in Europe and America. With good reason her fate has been found to be in conflict with all conceptions of justice, in that guarantees of her neutrality granted by one of the great powers in particular has revealed itself to furnish not even the most meager security, and in that an assertion of this neutrality, which according to international law and the law of honor, a body of law that is even by the enemy *theoretically* acknowledged, was necessarily a duty, has brought about all of the war's abominations in forms that civilized peoples imagine to have left behind.[4] It is not for the sake of Belgium that England fights the war, as it is said. On August 2, 1914, Sir Edward Grey promised M. Cambon that if the German navy entered the channel or operated against the French coast, the British navy would offer all the assistance of which it was capable.[5] This was

1. Napoleon III committed large numbers of French forces in support of Cavour in the 1859 Second War of Italian Independence, although the question of whether this was motivated principally by idealism is subject to debate.

2. Brandes here paraphrases Carl von Clausewitz's famous maxim that "war is the continuation of politics by other means."

3. This is a bit disingenuous, as Brandes would devote much of the war years to defending his position on Danish neutrality against the vigorous attacks of his old friend Clemenceau and later his British colleague, the translator and Scandinavianist William Archer.

4. At the 1830 London Conference, Britain, France, Russia, Austria, and crucially, Prussia, had agreed to respect the neutrality of newly independent Belgium. German violation of the 1830 agreement was employed as the legal and ethical justification for Allied actions throughout the course of the war.

5. Sir Edward Grey (1862–1933), British foreign secretary from 1905 to 1916, at the behest of the British cabinet, made this promise to Paul Cambon (1843–1924), French ambassador to England from 1898 to 1920. Germany declared war on France the following day, prompting Grey's famous utterance that "the lamps are going out all over Europe."

a genuine threat made against Germany, before Belgian soil was violated by German troops.

But Belgium, which had up to then been divided between two populations, the French-speaking Walloons and the Flemish, whose language is not very distinct from Dutch or Low German, has because of misfortune necessarily been united as one. While the Walloons previously had felt themselves linguistically and spiritually in kinship with the French, the Flemish had previously viewed themselves to be in kinship with the Low Germans. No one yet knows whether the Germans succeeded at the outbreak of the war in establishing a significant presence in Belgium or near Antwerp, but everyone can see that whatever previous Belgian sympathy for Germany there was has been forfeited. And the Belgians are a hard-knuckled people, unconquerable by compulsion. The Spanish in their time came to understand this.[6] Belgium's two greatest poets, Maeterlinck and Verhaeren, who before the war were both close to Germany, had been celebrated in both Berlin and Vienna; indeed the latter had been called the greatest living poet by his German translator Stefan Zweig, have in concert turned against Germany with extreme violence.[7]

From the beginning of the war the Allies have possessed a program. They understood it as a matter of course that they fought for *justice*. But the actual program was motivated by a desire to check Germany's power-mad quest for supremacy and to get back all the territory it had seized up to then. France should have Alsace-Lorraine back, Denmark North Schleswig; the unlucky, tri-partitioned Poland should be united and enjoy self-rule under Russian supervision. That last promise was openly expressed in a proclamation from the Russian commander in chief, although not backed up by the government or the czar.[8]

All that has in actuality come to pass is that unhappy Poland, which after its partition at the end of the eighteenth century suffered a severe fate, has since the declaration of war suffered as it has not done since 1846 in Galicia and since 1863 in Russian Poland.[9] Poland has been transformed into an immense

6. Flemish and Walloon troops had played a central role in the long struggle for Dutch independence from Spanish rule, known as the Eighty Years' War (1568–1648).

7. Maurice Polydore Marie Bernard Maeterlinck (1862–1949) and Emile Adolphe Gustave Verhaeren (1855–1916) were Flemish-born Symbolist poets who wrote in French. Maeterlinck attempted to join the French Foreign Legion after the outbreak of the war, while the pacifist Verhaeren fled to England.

8. See note 1 in "Conditions in Russian Poland."

9. Brandes here refers to the Austro-Prussian suppression of the 1846 Wielkopolska Uprising and the Russian suppression of the 1863 January Uprising.

battlefield on which Austria and Germany fight against the Russian army. Eastern Galicia, which under Austrian rule was free, now is under the yoke. The Ruthenians, who (oppressed in Russia) were free in Galicia, witness themselves deprived of the right to write in their own language by their Russian liberators. They are thirty-six million and yet not viewed as a people in their own right.[10]

Russian Poland, which ought to form the core of the new kingdom, is occupied by a German army. During the flight of those threatened or occupied by the enemy there have been innumerable cases of husbands and wives, brothers and sisters, mothers and children separated from one another and not reunited.

At the same time, Russian Poles are compelled to participate in a life-and-death struggle against German and Austrian Poles, since although they are countrymen they are dressed in the uniforms of the enemy.

But in that unhappy country is also found the earth's most unlucky people, the Jews, in numbers of five to six million, abused by all the warring parties. They constitute an immense proletariat that Russian barbarism has pressed together in a narrow stretch of land in which they cannot acquire the necessities of life and where from the first day of the war they have been singled out as the victims of religious and racial hatred in concert. They have no human rights, and whatever evil is inflicted upon them is viewed as deserved because of a two-thousand-year-old offense. The Jewish tribe has not endured a worse period since the conquest of Jerusalem.

And while that is unfolding, a Christian people on Turkish ground, the Armenians, are being exterminated through deportation to the desert, by saber and by bullet. No less than 800,000 have been eliminated.[11]

The great era in which we live is therefore an era in which all the old prejudices, all the old racial and national hatreds have not just been brought out in the open but have in fact become universal. Everything that is bestial in human nature stretches outward and spreads itself. Under the cruelest mass murder by day and by night the European and Asiatic peoples weaken each other, in that they exterminate their male youth and allow those remaining at home to suffer sorrow, loss, and hunger.

This is the twentieth-century result of Christendom's imperative to "love your neighbor as yourself."

---

10. See "The Ruthenians" in the present volume for Brandes's commentary on Russian repression of the Ukrainian language, which after the Russian seizure of Galicia was extended to Ruthenians formerly enjoying much less repressive Austrian rule.

11. See the 1917 essay "The Armenians" for Brandes's commentary on the Armenian Genocide.

It is completely natural that those young enough never to have experienced war and who have been taught that something good comes out of everything, even the worst, look forward to what may be accomplished in a peace settlement.

For my part I am convinced that our descendants will look back on this great era as we now look back on the age of witch trials and burnings at the stake.

CHAPTER 28

The Great Nations' Concern for the Small

1915

The outbreak of the Great War moved Brandes to return to rights advocacy after a decade or so of relatively little activity. Much of 1914 and 1915 were consumed by a heated debate in the French press with wartime premier and former close friend Georges Clemenceau over the issue of Danish neutrality; the year 1916 would witness a similar feud with another old friend, the Scottish critic and Ibsen translator William Archer. Brandes would eventually collect his writings on the war in his 1916 volume *Verdenskrigen*, issued in English translation the following year as *The World at War*. The present volume includes new translations of only those essays that specifically touch on the fate of the small countries who found themselves in the crosshairs of the belligerent powers. In the present selection, prompted by the receipt of a pseudonymous letter from a French colonial official in Sudan, Brandes critiques the spurious claims of the belligerents that they are conducting the war on behalf of the small countries whose territories they had transformed into killing fields.

~

I

In every one of the belligerent countries the people are convinced that their own country is in the right while the enemy is in the wrong. When a writer from a neutral country does not make use of these significations derived from morality and jurisprudence, but divulges the view that the whole immense war transgresses beyond right and wrong, then it can happen that an incensed and impatient politician from one of the war-making countries—in order to expose the writer's indecision and "excessive cultivation"—shouts out to him: Just answer the question! Which side is in the right?

The right! As if that word belonged at home in the boundless misery that this contest of the states for supremacy, brought on by the imprudence of

Originally published in *Tilskueren*, October 1915. Translated from the version published in *Verdenskrigen*.

political dilettantes and the short-sightedness and servility of an inflamed press, has spread over the earth!

The French and the English have most naturally taken their point of departure for the establishment of a moral viewpoint in two events that were shocking not just in an immediate sense: Austria-Hungary's invasion of a much weaker Serbia, which after the presentation of the ultimatum had done its utmost to head off war, and Germany's violation of Belgian neutrality, a wrong that was conceded at the time even by the German chancellor and that became still more frightening with the atrocities it had as a consequence.[1]

Because of this double attack, which was treated by the Allies as if it was unmotivated and did not have a long and painful prehistory, the following general view emerged: Neither France nor England wanted war, and they came to the fight solely in defense of the sanctity of treaties and the rights of small nations. This came as a surprise and a bafflement to those who know something about the recent history of Europe and the larger world and who also did not upon the outbreak of the war resign the ability to think.

And then there is the fact that Germany, despite its poor and foolish treatment of its Polish, Danish, and French subjects, also for its part asserted that it fights for the right of the small nations to independence. Namely they fight the war against Russia, which (with still less respect for solemnly given promises than Germany itself) has allowed the Finnish people to feel its wrath and in the Kingdom of Poland has kept the Poles and still more the Jews who live there in a wretched state without rights. Germany fights the war against Russia and England in union, whose collective obliteration of the independence of unfortunate Persia and collective repeal of its constitution is one of the more instructive events of recent times, in that it demonstrates the attitude of the great powers toward a weaker state.[2] Without exaggeration it can be claimed that when two modern great powers conclude a properly bilateral and sincere union, whether it be called an alliance or an understanding, the true aim is always to deprive a smaller state of its independence. All the old

1. In a Reichstag speech of August 4, 1914, German chancellor Theobald von Bethmann-Hollweg (1856–1921) confessed that the invasion of Belgium was in contravention of the law of nations but defended it as a matter of national survival. German atrocities early in the war, called by the Allied press "the Rape of Belgium," were the result of the German practice of collective punishment for individual acts of resistance and sabotage.

2. Persian republicans had compelled Mozaffar ad-Din Shah Qajar (1853–1907) to submit to constitutional rule in 1906, but his successor, Mohammad Ali Shah Qajar (1872–1925), with extensive Russian and British support, annulled it upon his accession. Continued republican agitation would result in Russian occupation of much of the country after 1911, while British forces would occupy the remainder after the outbreak of the war.

warmth between Germany and Russia has functioned to this end in Poland.[3] The last union between Prussia and Austria impacted Denmark.[4] The warm understanding between England and France impacted Morocco.[5]

The assertion of Germany's concern for the small nationalities, despite its apparent sincere intent, has almost the character of a joke. Yet the concern of the British World Kingdom for the small nationalities is also of a recent vintage. It is hardly necessary to recall the English people's seven-hundred-year rooting out of ancient Irish culture. And as is well known it was for sound political reasons that had little to do with right and wrong that England at the beginning of the nineteenth century laid waste to neutral Denmark in entirety, bombarding Copenhagen while the Danish army was in Holstein to defend the neutrality of the country, making off with the Danish navy, and delivering Norway to Bernadotte as reward for his break with Napoleon.[6]

Just in the last twelve years five smaller states have been deprived of their independence. England and France did not protest for good reason. The republics of Transvaal and Orange lost their independence when England seized their territory, which they of course incidentally have since then governed in an exemplary fashion.[7]

Persia lost its independence through what even in England has been called a robber's pact between Russia and Great Britain.[8] Morocco was divided into

---

3. The Third Partition of Poland divided the Polish-Lithuanian Commonwealth into Prussian, Russian, and Austrian sectors; Prussia and Austria would remain at peace with Russia until 1914.

4. The nineteenth-century rivalry between Austria and Prussia, expressed in the debates between advocates of a Catholic Grossdeutschland (all thirty-seven German states united under Austria) and of a Protestant Kleindeustchland (only the north German states united under Prussia), figured prominently in both the First Schleswig War of 1848 and the Second of 1864.

5. The Entente Cordiale of 1904 permitted France a free hand in Morocco in exchange for British license in Egypt.

6. Indeed Denmark only formally allied with Napoleon *after* the 1807 British bombardment of the capital, which was intended to wreck the Danish fleet so that it would not fall into French hands. Marshal Jean Bernadotte (1763–1844) was installed as regent of Sweden in 1810, becoming King Karl Johan in 1818. As punishment for its alliance with Napoleon, Norway was transferred from Danish to Swedish rule in 1814; the transfer was also compensation for Karl Johan's 1813 alliance with the Allies and subsequent support in the wars against his former emperor.

7. See "Transvaal" in the present volume for Brandes's commentary on the Anglo-Boer conflict.

8. The Anglo-Russian Convention of 1907 divided Persia into British and Russian spheres, nullifying the constitutional revolution of the previous year.

two unequal parts between France and Spain, in return for England getting a freer hand in Egypt and permission to break its promises to quit the country.[9]

Korea's condition recalls that which threatens Belgium.[10] Korea's independence and neutrality were guaranteed by Japan, Russia, England, and France with the signatures of all these powers on treaties. Korea's queen was murdered by the Japanese, as Austria-Hungary's heir was by Serbs.[11] Shortly thereafter Japan flooded Korea and forced the Koreans to participate side by side with them in the war against Russia.

Both Russia and Korea registered protest and called on England and France for help. But neither of the powers could be moved to intervene. Neither took the thorough guarantee of neutrality and independence to heart. Korea's independence lay on its deathbed and is now no more.

Now it is Europe itself that lays on the sickbed, or perhaps it is a deathbed. Preferably one keeps quiet near a deathbed. In any case one approaches the sickbed of Europe cautiously and with reserve, as one does when approaching that of a single individual.

II

I have received the following letter, signed with the pseudonym M. Georges Dauville, from Senegal in West Africa:

> Far away from the battlefield, in Sudan, where the mobilization has come as a surprise to me and has further kept me in Africa, I experienced in the *Mercure de France* of May 1915 your polemic with Clemenceau, which details the Nordic people's view of France's stance in the war.[12]
>
> From the distance at which I write to you it is difficult to be urgent. Will you allow me briefly to develop for you the truth regarding the nature of politics, will, and heart in France before and now? It is surprising that no foreigner has been able to enter fully enough into French intellectual life and politics in order to guess at certain fundamental truths. Surely enough no French newspaper can allow itself to publish what I have to say, just as no

9. The 1912 Treaty of Fez partitioned Morocco; see note 5 for more on Britain's role.

10. Japan signed its first treaty with Korea in 1876, Britain following in 1883, Russia in 1884, and finally France in 1886.

11. Because of her interest in countering Japanese influence in Korea by increasing ties to Russia, Empress Myeongseong (1851–95) was killed by Japanese mercenaries at the behest of a rival pro-Japanese faction. The Japanese presence in Korea increased steadily thereafter; in 1905 Korea was made a Japanese protectorate and then formally annexed in 1910.

12. The public feud between Brandes and Clemenceau is recounted in full in Brandes, *The World at War*.

known French author could submit this to a foreign paper. This enforced silence is the cause of the misunderstanding between us, you, and the Scandinavian people.

The simple truth is this:

In the first place: there is a profound difference between French culture and German culture—perhaps it goes all the way down to the life principles of the two races. Between them neither blending nor common understanding nor common admixture is possible. Here mutual non-understanding reigns unconditionally and eternally. Never after all would one have waged war against the other or have dreamed of waging war on the basis of the fact that one did not understand the other and never would come to do so.

In the next place: economically speaking the Germans have flooded France as they were in the process of flooding all the countries of the world. (I do not take aim at espionage, which is a military question and not anything economic). In spite of the manner in which the Germans have bored their way in everywhere, let us concede that it has not been proved that this has resulted in the diminishment of the public wealth of France or in any increase in the misery that among us is rare and nearly always dependent on laziness or drink. We sought to organize a struggle against the German attempt to dominate us in the economic sphere, but never has France meant that it ought to wage a war to protect business and industry.

In other words: neither racial differences nor economic competition made us see the German as a war enemy, however incomprehensible and incompatible he was.

Furthermore, since 1871 there has never been a real political rivalry between France and Germany. In spite of the semblance of a suggestion otherwise, this rivalry existed neither in Morocco nor in Turkey nor Antwerp nor the Mediterranean nor the Far East. At no place on the globe. This is a fact that the Germans stated openly when they accused us of being England's henchmen and fools in relation to them.

They were right, but with this caveat, that we consciously and with full consent behaved in this manner, indeed even engendered this optical illusion.

But would it not be objected that the Germans are the hereditary enemy? In no manner. The first generation of Frenchmen who were enemies of Germany are still alive.[13] That is the generation that fought the Germans in 1870. That enemy with whom we have clashed, without interruption for a thousand years, and still recently in Sudan, is the Englishman. You can hardly imagine how often among Frenchmen down here these words are exchanged: "During the

13. Dauville's elision of the Napoleonic Wars is telling.

Fashoda Incident someone ought to have informed us that the English would eventually fight side by side with us on French ground in 1914."[14] And many foreign travelers will recall the raucous enthusiasm that greeted Commandant Marchand in Marseille, Lyon, and Paris.[15]

It is quite a long time since Frenchmen harbored any hatred toward the English. Yet after all Clemenceau's career was derailed because of his English sympathies.[16] The Englishman is in no way our enemy by virtue of his culture or race, but he is from the historical-political point of view very much so. He has at all times resisted our national desire for expansion, and we know quite well that he would have done so in Morocco in 1905 if an agreement had not been reached.

As for the Russian, he is also quite unknown to us. For the masses the Russian is the good-natured giant like those who appear in fairy tales. He is the giant who will do us well. For the educated public the Russian exists in two images. First there is the ally with numberless troops to whom billions have been lent, in order to ensure equilibrium with the Germans, with their steadily increasing population and us with our stagnant number of inhabitants. Therefore the journalists, from the day the war broke out, designated the Russians as the crushing steamroller. The other image is the state in which the Russian people exist, oppressed as they are by the upper class and the czar's officials. But those conditions are of no consequence to the alliance. The great majority of the French do not as a rule deign to speak of that kind of thing. Only the vehement socialists break with the attitude of propriety. All in all the alliance was, with the help of billions in loans, a political necessity against a Germany bristling with bayonets.

To conclude: what cannot be smoothed out between France and Germany is simply Alsace-Lorraine, and that is not a political but an anatomical question.

Before the revolution treaties were entered into and dissolved like one changes clothes: every tenth or twentieth year the border posts were moved. The populations on the borders changed princes without complaint, submitted to their fate, took the decisions as fate. Then in the nineteenth century it was revealed that the revolution had brought about something deep and true, by which one was pierced as by a new principle, the principle of nationality. It

14. British and French colonial forces nearly came to blows in Fashoda, now known as Kodok, in 1898.

15. Jean-Baptiste Marchand (1863–1934), the commander of the French forces at Fashoda, became a national hero for his role in the crisis.

16. Clemenceau, who preferred an Anglo-French alliance, lost his seat in the National Assembly in 1893 due to his opposition to the Franco-Russian Alliance.

took root, grew, became a power that would no longer allow itself to be impeded. The unification of Germany is a consequence thereof. But even in that moment in which Germany achieved its national unity and in which every country, including Alsace-Lorraine, asserted its nationality, Bismarck grabbed us by the throat and took away that land. Unlike the earlier regular shifting of the border posts, the year 1871 signifies to us the amputation of a limb.

Over the course of time, an attacker who has sunk his teeth into you may be forgiven, but if one has had his hand severed, then he is compelled to live constantly with the loss of that hand. Add into the bargain the fact that the severed hand remained alive and always made its silent pain felt. Add to that the fact that the enemy had the cruelty to twist the fingers before the eyes of the mutilated and to rip the nails out of them. Add to it that he yelled: "Come then and try and take back from me what I have seized; since I am seventy millions and you only forty, you'll see some fun and games!"

Alsace-Lorraine is for France the severed hand, and the war is waged only for its sake. For thirty years our alliances, our agreements, our finance laws, our repeated humiliations, everything has been subordinated to this one cause. We felt it as our responsibility to suffer patiently, to pretend to be small until the Russian giant grew up and now for its part could say to the German: "Yes then, you are 70 millions, but I am 150; now we shall see some fun and games."

I can provide proof that what I have presented here is the truth for us French.

If there had been within German culture, which may precisely be defined as "stupid intelligence," a prince, a statesman, a true politician, perhaps a true successor to Bismarck, who after our cementing of the Russian alliance had at some point said to us: "I am giving Alsace-Lorraine back to you, break the alliance!" then we would have broken it on the spot and would have remained neutral during every German-Russian or German-English collision.

At any time in the last thirty years Germany could have received all our colonies save Algeria in exchange for Alsace-Lorraine, and a good deal of money to boot.

At the time of the Fashoda Incident and immediately thereafter Germany could have had us as an alliance partner and thus proceeded to destroy England.

I venture the assertion that even in July 1914 the offer of Alsace-Lorraine would have brought us to give up the Russians and all our billions in unpaid debt. Yes, Germany could have taken by violence the mouth of the Rhine and Antwerp without thereby moving us any more than the United States.

The "stupid intelligence" chose otherwise.

When the kaiser sent us at intervals his famous "Dry-Powder Ultimatum," "I am seventy millions, you are forty," Europe found it amusing, grinned, and saw in us braggarts and nutcases who could never get over the thought of our severed hand. But what were we to do? Stay silent, stay watchful, and cultivate the alliance with Russia. If the world does not now see that in half a year we have forged and organized a war machine of the same rank as that which the Germans took thirty years to produce, does not perceive the revanchism, in our science and our nerves, this extraordinary French production, which has been carried out while the country has in part been occupied by the enemy—then German culture understands how to fabricate especially powerful blinders!

Be assured of my full high esteem, et cetera.

III

It is, it seems to me, of particular interest to follow a young, gifted Frenchman's presentation of how according to his own persuasion and experience the manners of thinking and of feeling have evolved in his fatherland among the recent generation.

A few contrary observations are, however, in order here.

It has became a dogma among many young Frenchman that a mutual fertilization of French and German intellectual life is an impossibility, much the same as it is impossible that an animal of horse descent and another of ox descent can crossbreed. This principle, from which M. Dauville proceeds, is a remarkable delusion. The whole intellectual life of Alsace is proof of the opposite. Alsatian authors in the French language have for many years blended French and German characteristics. One of the most distinguished could be named as an example, the biblical scholar Reuss, who was professor of theology at the University of Strasbourg.[17] Before the war of 1870 he wrote his works in German, after the war only in French, but German learning and French form constitute a unity. In our time the French Swiss writers Cherbuliez and Rod were German-influenced.[18] From an earlier age could be named the descendants of exiled French Huguenots in Germany, especially in Berlin, whose singular rationalism has a French element. A multitude of these families with French names such as Fontane or du Bois-Reymond have had among their descendants writers and scientists with pronounced Prussian patriotism,

17. Édouard Guillaume Eugène Reuss (1804–91) in fact published in both French and German before and after the war.

18. Charles Victor Cherbuliez (1829–99) published a number of books on German politics, literature, and culture in the 1870s. Édouard Rod (1857–1910) studied in Berlin in the 1870s.

but in whose diction a French element yet appears.[19] Later there was an emigrant like Adelbert von Chamisso, who wanted to be German and wrote only in German, and yet who was of pure French blood, and this is certainly sensed in more than his masterful German translations of French poems.[20]

In general, it can be said that French intellectual life has not been indebted to Germany over the course of centuries. This is because of France's immense head start in culture. By the conclusion of the twelfth century influence had already traveled from France to Germany, but the stream never turned back toward its source. The authors of the German epic poems such as Heinrich von Veldecke, Hartmann von Aue, and Gottfried von Strassburg are only translators and adaptors of French.[21] Chretien de Troyes dominates Hartmann von der Aue completely. Even Wolfram von Eschenbach formed his taste through the study of Chretien.[22]

It is only in the nineteenth century that German influence makes itself felt in French literature, as when Charles Nodier is influenced by Goethe and E. T. A. Hoffman, Alexandre Dumas pére by Schiller.[23] The German influence is most clearly traced in Quinet, whose manner of feeling is German, in Taine, who has learned from Hegel as well as Goethe, enjoyed Heinrich Heine and lived with Beethoven, and finally in Renan, who has been seized by Herder and is completely run through with German science, but has recast it in the most exquisite French form.[24] In our day Romain Rolland, influenced by Germany,

19. Notable German Huguenots include the novelist Theodor Fontane (1819–98), the physician Emil du Bois-Reymond (1818–96), and the mathematician Paul David Gustav du Bois-Reymond (1831–89).

20. Adelbert von Chamisso (1781–1838) was born Louis Charles Adélaïde de Chamissot; after his family's exile to Prussia during the revolution he never returned to France, and indeed served in the Prussian army against Napoleon.

21. Heinrich von Veldecke (ca. 1150–84, Dutch Hendrik van Veldeke), the first vernacular writer of the Low Countries, based his *Eneas Romance* on French sources. Hartmann von Aue's (ca. 1160s–1210s) Arthurian poems are adaptations of Chrétien de Troyes's (ca. 1135–85) French originals. Gottfried von Strassburg's (d. ca. 1210) monumental *Tristan* was based on English and French sources.

22. Wolfram von Eschenbach's (ca. 1160s–1220) *Parzival* was based on Chretien.

23. Jean Charles Emmanuel Nodier (1780–1844) was a novelist and bibliophile who introduced the idea of the fantastic to French Romanticism; Brandes had profiled him in the first volume of *Main Currents*. Before turning to the historical novel, Alexandre Dumas pére (1802–70) was a successful playwright in the mold of Friedrich Schiller.

24. Historian Edgar Quinet (1803–75) translated Johann Gottfried Herder into French. Literary critic and theorist Hippolyte Adolphe Taine (1828–93), an important influence on young Brandes, was throughout the nineteenth century an important bridge figure between French and German thought; at the end of his life he corresponded with Nietzsche. Joseph Ernest Renan (1823–92), also a significant mentor to young Brandes, systematically studied German philosophy as a student in the 1840s.

has demonstrated himself capable of the most comprehensive understanding and critique of German being.[25]

In the course of a great people's intellectual history, however, this late and scattered German influence does not amount to much, even though in certain areas like music it has been quite considerable.

But when we look at the intellectual history of Germany, the reality of fusion and the full measure of French influence on the German mind is amply demonstrated. As the legends of Floris and Blanchefour, of Tristan and Isolde came from France, in this way later on Rabelais was imitated by Fischart, in this way Gottsched represented French classicism and Frederick the Great Voltaire.[26] Voltaire and Rousseau have each for his part dominated the German manner of thinking and feeling for lengthy periods.[27] Much later Victor Hugo influenced Freiligrath, and even Zola and Maupassant have had numerous German disciples.[28]

The allegedly undeniable heterogeneity of French and German existence is therefore no more potent than that it allows itself to be overcome, and to desire a return to racial difference, Latin versus Germanic, is almost comical, since Frenchmen and Germans have each emerged from the mixing of blood, since Gauls were Celts, not Latin, and actually in our day Frenchmen, who as the name reveals, are in part descended from the Franks, further from Burgundians, Alemanni, Normans, and Flemish, purely Germanic peoples, are more German in blood than today's Germans. The ancient Germans, those who were

---

25. Romain Rolland (1866–1944), winner of the 1915 Nobel Prize, was among the very few French intellectuals who maintained a stance of pacifist neutrality throughout the Great War; as such he is in kinship with Brandes. His 1915 *Au-dessus de la mêlée*, written from Swiss exile, is a kind of French counterpart to Brandes's *Verdenskrigen*.

26. It should be noted that only the first written versions of the Floris and Blanchefour and Tristan and Isolde legends appear in French; their ultimate origins in the oral tradition are of course unknowable. François Rabelais (ca. 1483–1553), author of *Gargantua and Pantagruel*, was among the most preeminent French Renaissance humanists. Protestant publicist Johann Baptist Fischart (ca. 1545–91) was well versed in English and Italian as well as French literature. Johann Christoph Gottsched (1700–1766) enforced the strictures of the French neoclassical school on German literature for decades. Frederick II of Prussia famously invited his friend Voltaire to Berlin in 1750, where he was appointed chamberlain for a rather stormy three-year period.

27. Voltaire in fact invited Rousseau to join him in Berlin, as Frederik greatly admired the Genevan philosopher as well.

28. Ferdinand Freiligrath (1810–76), a poet associated with the Young Germany movement, translated Hugo into German. Guy de Maupassant (1850–93) was the great master of the French short story. The principal exponent of naturalism in German literature was Gerhart Johann Robert Hauptmann (1862–1946).

ruled by Ariovistus, those with whom Caesar fought, were a Celtic people.[29] In later ages authentic Germans had their seat around the Baltic Sea, but came across Celts in southern Germany and Slavs in the southeast. The broad belt that now constitutes Germany is inhabited by a heterogeneous people without a distinguishing type.

The next point, that no one in France thought of waging war against Germany for economic reasons, certainly deserves full credit. France's trade had for a long time already failed to rise as Germany's had, and it was indeed impossible to repair this relationship through a war. Such a hopeless measure was furthermore superfluous, since France's national wealth was increased through thrift as Germany's was through the spirit of enterprise.

Regarding the next assertion, M. Dauville's account provides nothing that is new or unfamiliar to me. More than once, already before Fashoda, around the year 1896, I have encountered in France the view that England, not Germany, was the hereditary enemy. France's attitude toward the two countries was explained to me in precisely these words by a well-known and highly gifted Frenchman who had then just resigned from the diplomatic service.[30]

This ill will toward England passionately came into the open when France was compelled to give up Fashoda in 1898 under threat of war: it revealed itself during the entire Boer War, when collections for the warring Boer Republics found sympathy in France, Kruger was received with enthusiasm, and Edward VII was caricatured in the French humor newspapers.[31] The ill will again came into the open at the World Exposition in 1900, when Scottish workers, who with support from their homeland were taken in quite large flocks to Paris to gather knowledge from the exhibited machines and goods, were insulted so thoroughly that they had to clear out.[32]

M. Dauville is of course correct in his account of French motives in entering into the Russian alliance, purchased at such a steep price, and almost pitiably accurate in his description of the French masses' ignorance of the actual system of rule in Russia, the leadership of which they became patriotically obliged

29. Ariovistus's tribe, the Suebi, are generally today believed to have been a Germanic people.

30. In the 1916 book version of the essay, Brandes notes that this was the writer Paul Hervieu, who died in 1915.

31. Exiled Transvaal president Stephanus Johannes Paulus Kruger (1825–1904) received a rapturous welcome in Marseille in November 1900.

32. Anglo-French tensions often came out in the open at the World's Fairs; indeed, French enthusiasm for them (Paris hosted expositions in 1855, 1867, 1878, and 1889 in addition to 1900) may be traced to a strong desire to one-up the British, who had inaugurated the institution with the overwhelming success of the Crystal Palace Exhibition of 1851.

to glorify. He employs an exceedingly gentle phrase in this sentence: "only the vehement socialists break with the attitude of propriety."[33] This attitude, which surely has lasted more than a score of years, resulted in terrible sorrow and disappointment among the Poles, who for a century had looked to France as the power that should be their guardian against Russian dominance no less than Prussian.[34] This attitude made it possible for Russian despotism to assert itself in spite of the efforts of its despairing populace to rise up against it. The Prussian and Russian absolute monarchies had always maintained a close friendship; they had reached out to each other and given each other assistance each time the Poles and the Russian people rose against the czardom, but now French gold and French enthusiasm became forces that simultaneously propped up the Russian ruling party and placed the glory of freedom around it. The world historical irony was palpable in Czar Alexander III listening to the Marseillaise played by a Russian military band. It was still a more bitter irony that French democracy functioned as a barrier to the establishment of a freethinking government in Russia.

IV

The English share responsibility with the French here.

The deepest wellsprings of the current war have been the opposition between Russia and the Central Powers, the hatred between Slavs and Germans, Russia's struggle against Austria for control of the Balkan states. France was only attacked by Germany because it was Russia's ally. Germany would have preferred to fight out its dispute with Russia without any dustup with the French. The agreement that Great Britain openly entered into with Russia, but that *without the knowledge of parliament* transformed itself into a military alliance, has been an immense hindrance for the development of Russian freedom.[35]

Russia has always and continues to be unconditionally dependent on the financial markets of the Western powers. It needs loans. It requires credit. So that the bankers may show themselves to be obliging, the capitalist must exhibit patience toward the power that would borrow. As long as Russia constituted for the English depositor an enemy power, a danger to England, or an

33. Brandes does not mention here that the most vocal critic of the Franco-Russian alliance was Clemenceau, due of course to the fact that the two old friends were at the time engaged in the polemic over Danish neutrality.

34. The failure of the 1830 November Uprising against Russian rule resulted in what the Poles call the Great Emigration, in which many of the leading lights of Polish society, most famously Frédéric Chopin, found refuge and hope in France.

35. The Anglo-Russian Convention of 1907 dealt only with colonial conflicts between the two powers, principally in Persia.

insecure despotism threatened by revolution, the Russian government turned to the English financiers in vain. But from the moment King Edward visited the czar in Reval and the czar King Edward on the Isle of Wight, the English newspapers went along with portraying Russia as a friendly minded power in steady progress toward constitutional freedom.[36] And the English capitalist pulled out his wallet, quite like in France, where the press, politicians, and upper class entered into a tacit plot to praise the Russian government and explain away its despotic essence.

In no way did Russia approach England as a freethinking power, anymore than it had approached the French Republic. Its outreach to England was the result of having borrowed such immense sums from France that the French financiers became hesitant after the unsuccessful war with Japan, and thus Russia desired London's assistance.

The negotiations had already begun in 1905, under Lord Lansdowne.[37] But it was his successor Sir Edward Grey who really pushed them through, and the foundation for the alliance was already laid by the spring of 1906.[38]

As is known, the czar was compelled to grant a constitution in October 1905.[39] Under immense tension a vote for the first Duma took place, while the forces of reaction in the provinces maintained the full measure of their ruthless power. In the meantime, a great hope had emerged among the Russian people. The new Duma revealed an overwhelming majority of progressives. The constitutional democrats (called the Cadets) controlled the assembly. They had to fight against a reactionary ministry and against a court that regretted the concessions it had been forced to grant under threat of insurrection.

The Duma could have defied the absolute monarchy, if it had been capable of issuing the following challenge to a despised and bankrupt government: "Your treasury is empty, your credit is used up. We however have Russia and Europe behind us. If you acknowledge our authority and our right to introduce accountability to the ministries, then we will agree on taxes and make good your loans. If you deny us our rights, then we will guarantee that you will find the funds to continue your politics of oppression neither in London

36. Edward VII visited Nicholas II in Reval (now Tallinn) in June 1908; in turn Nicholas met with Edward in August 1909.

37. Henry Charles Keith Petty-Fitzmaurice, Marquess of Lansdowne (1845–1927), served as British foreign secretary from 1900 to 1905.

38. Edward Grey (1862–1933) was foreign secretary from 1905 to 1916, and as such oversaw the Anglo-Russian Convention of 1907.

39. Nicholas II signed the constitutionalist October Manifesto on October 30; the new constitution was put into effect the following May, the day before the First Duma convened.

nor Paris." The Duma could not muster up any such language, for in March 1906 the large loan was concluded in London and Paris, and when the Duma convened in May the government's treasury was full.

If only Russia's freethinkers had beseeched Europe's free states not to seal the defeat of Russia's freedom! After less than three months the first Duma was dissolved, and the rest of the year Stolypin ruled without parliament, while the war tribunals proclaimed and set in motion the death penalty over all the land.[40] The second Duma convened in 1907 and showed itself to be still more radical than the first.[41]

Stolypin engineered the accusation that the social democrats, the most influential party in the Duma, were guilty of plotting against the state with the goal of revolution in the military.[42]

The committee chosen from all the parties reported to the Third Duma that it unanimously had found the socialists innocent.[43] During the coup thirty-five of them were secretly brought before a special court, of which seventeen were sentenced to four to five years hard labor and ten to permanent exile in Siberia. Two of them died in prison, one lost his mind, and a fourth, the party's foremost spokesperson, got consumption. All of them were treated like common criminals, placed in chains, and whipped.

With the dissolution of the second Duma the experiment in Russian freedom was in fact at an end. In his 1909 *The Terror in Russia*, Kropotkin has shown that the number of political prisoners in the Russian prisons during the time of nominal freedom rose from a daily average of 85,000 to the figure of 181,000 in 1909.[44] He has told of the horrible sicknesses that afflicted the overfilled prisons and how widespread the use of torture was there. In 1909 the war tribunals hanged an average of three political criminals per day. The number of political exiles to distant villages in northern Russia and Siberia had reached 74,000 by this point, according to official statements.

---

40. Petr Arkad'evich Stolypin (1862–1911) was appointed Russian prime minister in July 1906 and oversaw the dissolution of the First Duma. In response to repeated assassination attempts, he instituted a draconian system of courts martial to combat insurrection.

41. The Second Duma, convened in February 1907, included the Bolsheviks and Mensheviks in addition to more moderate parties.

42. The charges against fifty-five socialist deputies were rejected by the Duma, resulting in "Stolypin's Coup" of June 1907, in which the Second Duma was dissolved.

43. The Third Duma, popularly derided as the "Duma of Lords and Lackeys," was convened in November 1907; it was structured to ensure a strong majority of conservative-leaning monarchists.

44. Curiously, Brandes does not mention that Kropotkin's book was subtitled *An Appeal to the British Nation*.

Without the cooperation of France and England this result would have been an impossibility.

Among the dreadful clichés that have spread in order to pull the wool over the eyes of the reading public is the one according to which the alliance with England and France moves the Russian government in a freethinking direction, so that the war makes Russia into a power that fights for freedom. At the outbreak of the war the well-known Russian revolutionary Burtsev publicly expressed his belief in this myth, and to back up his belief with action, he promised to serve the Russian government and journeyed back there. As soon as he was over the border he was arrested and sentenced to life in Siberian exile.[45]

The reactionary forces during the war, as was expected, have conducted themselves more daringly than ever before. Although the law assures Duma members immunity, five social democratic members of the present Duma were jailed under the accusation of high treason. One of these men, by the name of Adamovich, was sentenced to hard labor for life for founding a trade union for sailors.

V

The next and decisive point in M. Dauville's account is the indispensability of Alsace-Lorraine for France, the pain and the humiliation France suffered with the cession and has suffered from German rule there, the unbearable privation of the loss, for whose reacquisition they were ready to make the utmost sacrifices, of colonies, of alliances and ententes, and for whose reacquisition alone they now wage war. In order to demonstrate the immensity of the loss he refers to the analogy of the severed hand, which however does not fit well here, since after forty-four years of trying no severed hand has been permitted to once more take root, and still less immediately after the amputation. Furthermore it is awkwardly imagined that someone is torturing the severed hand.

Whether the analogy more or less hits home is however quite trifling. But what is not trifling, and on the contrary is surprising, is that a scientifically trained Frenchman, even one who preferably thinks politically, is so ignorant of Denmark's recent history that he goes to great lengths to explain to a Dane how unspeakably painful it is for a country to have lost a region that linguistically and historically belongs to it. He seems never to have heard talk of

45. Vladimir L'vovich Burtsev (1862–1942) had already been imprisoned in Britain for anti-czarist activities in the 1890s; he was later arrested on Lev Trotsky's orders for opposition to the Bolsheviks.

Denmark's war for Schleswig, never to have given Denmark's attitude to north Schleswig a thought. Neither does he know that whereas Alsace became French under Louis XIV, Schleswig had been Danish from ancient times. We know that Frenchmen are better at their own country's history than that of other countries, but still an ignorance such as this comes as a surprise.

On a subordinate point regarding the cession of Alsace-Lorraine, M. Dauville is incorrect. That is when he uses this expression: "Bismarck grabbed us by the throat." Bismarck was as guiltless in the annexation of Alsace-Lorraine as he was in Denmark's loss of north Schleswig. As his now-forgotten letter to Blixen-Finecke suggests, it was evidently his intention, should Blixen be made foreign minister, to resolve the question of the duchies without war and in such a way that Denmark did not lose any Danish-speaking territory.[46] Still at the London Conference Denmark could have gotten north Schleswig, if it had not rejected the proposal in hope of better conditions.[47] As for Alsace-Lorraine, Bismarck put up a similar hard-knuckled resistance to Moltke and the military party, with all their lust for conquest, after the defeat of France as well as earlier, Austria.[48]

At the Peace of Prague he succeeded in asserting his will, so that no part of Austria and no part of Bavaria was transferred to Prussia.[49] After the Franco-Prussian War he passionately argued that the cession of Alsace-Lorraine to the German Reich must be feared to lead to new war in the course of a half century, but here he did not succeed in getting the kaiser on his side, since Moltke and the other war leaders declaimed against the pen giving over to the enemy what the sword had wrested from him.

The loss of Alsace-Lorraine has from the start most certainly been felt as a sorrow and a national weakening, but also as a symbol of France's fall from the dominant position on the European mainland. Meanwhile M. Dauville overlooks the fact that the great colonial empire France has acquired since 1871 remedies some of that loss, and that there was a time when even that deep wound was no longer felt by the younger generation, except as a scar.

---

46. Carl Frederik Axel Bror von Blixen-Finecke (1822–73), grandfather of Isak Dinesen's husband, Bror Blixen, was an old friend of Bismarck from his student days in Germany. In October 1863 he and the chancellor corresponded in an effort to seek a diplomatic solution to the Schleswig-Holstein question.

47. The London Conference of 1864, which met from April to June, was a vain attempt to negotiate a ceasefire between Denmark and Prussia/Austria.

48. Helmuth von Moltke the Elder (1800–1891) was Prussian (later German imperial) chief of staff from 1857 to 1888; as such he was the supreme commander of Prussian forces in the wars of 1864, 1866, and 1870–71.

49. The Peace of Prague concluded the Austro-Prussian War of 1866.

The proof of this is found in a survey taken by *Mercure de France* in 1898 that revealed that only the elderly who had been born before 1870 or had even participated in the war looked on the lost provinces with a still burning loss.[50]

The distinguished French thinker *Clémence Royer*, Darwin's translator, wrote:[51]

> Alsace and Lorraine have been taken from us, as we have taken them, by the right of war. We can take them back. Then they would be wrested from us again. It becomes endless. What else do the provinces gain thereby than to be ravaged by war again and again? And can we not in this case lean on commonality in descent or tradition? From Roman times onward Alsace was a German country. Never once was it occupied by the Franks. Under the Merovingians it made up a part of Alamannia or Swabia, whose tongue it has preserved.

G. Montorgueil:[52]

> The day after defeat the thought of retaliation is noble and lovely, and contributes to rehabilitation; after a quarter of a century this aggressive stance is only a pose, more laughable than great. The war for the reconquest of Alsace and Lorraine is desirable to certain crazy people and is called for by numerous hypocrites. The people will not hear of it; they would declare this straight out, if they had not already been scared off. But they betray what they do not openly express.

That younger authors from around that time agree is surprising.

The brothers *Paul* and *Victor Margueritte* (whose father was mortally wounded at Sedan and about whom Paul has published the passionate book *Contre les barbares*):[53]

> Among those who have experienced the fever days of the war the memory will hold; among others it will be blurred. Already with certainty the moment can be

---

50. All citations below are taken from Brandes's own translations, originally published in his 1898 essay "Frankrig og Elsass-Lothringen" ("France and Alsace-Lorraine"), available in his *Samlede Skrifter*, 16:232–38.

51. Clémence Royer's (1830–1902) translation of Darwin's *On the Origin of Species* appeared in 1862.

52. Journalist Octave Lebesgue (1857–1933), who wrote under the pseudonym Georges Montorgueil, was a principal chronicler of the Parisian fin de siècle.

53. Paul (1860–1918) and Victor (1866–1942) Margueritte were the sons of General Jean Auguste Margueritte; Paul in fact produced two memoirs about his father, *Mon Père* (1884) and *Contre les barbares* (1915).

foreseen when Sedan and Metz will not stir up the mind any more than Waterloo or the conquest of Paris by the allied armies in 1814.

Ferdinand Herold:[54]

In order for a Franco-German war to break out something unreasonable must happen, such as Alsace-Lorraine rising up in rebellion against the kaiser. And even then how should the French government logically be able to intervene, when it has maintained Abdul Hamid in Armenia and Spanish rule in Cuba?

Francis Jammes (already then a highly respected lyric poet):[55]

It is not the French peasant who thinks of reconquering Alsace. The bourgeoisie will not fight. The artist would only be disturbed by the war. The only one who gladly went along is the altogether miserable and run-down worker, who afflicted by tuberculosis and alcohol slouches off in the dawn cold to the workplace, the demands of the capitalist, the reproaches of the overseer, and the fall from the ladder that awaits him.

André Lebey:[56]

Since we have been defeated, and that after we ourselves had declared war, so we are compelled to find ourselves subject to the conditions imposed by the victor. One responds immediately to a slap in the face. Two days later it is too late. We always think of Alsace; we even moan; at dessert we solemnly lift our champagne glasses in its honor; at sporting events we gladly adorn the festival speaker's poem with the black hatband. But that is all.

Remy de Gourmont (cofounder of the new *Mercure de France*, highly respected author and poet):[57]

The reconciliation is evident. The German is no longer the enemy. The stupidity of calling Germany the hereditary enemy is now found only in newspapers that

---

54. André Jules Ferdinand Hérold (1865–1940) was a French modernist poet of Alsatian descent.

55. Francis Jammes (1868–1938) was a poet from the French Basque territory.

56. André Lebey (1877–1938) was an author and socialist politician.

57. Symbolist pioneer Remy de Gourmont (1858–1915) published numerous works by Brandes in his *Mercure de France*.

believe public opinion will thereby be in their favor. But public opinion is not with them.

Camille Mauclair (highly respected author and journalist):[58]

> Revanche is now only an empty electoral promise, for it lost all esteem when Boulangism misfired due to the incompetence of the leaders and the generals' lack of authority.[59] We writers detest the insipid literature nationalism has produced.

Henri de Regnier (now acknowledged as the leader of the young poets and a member of the Academy):[60]

> I believe that the question of Alsace-Lorraine affects especially our national vanity. The incorporation of the two provinces into Germany is a demonstration of our momentary inferiority at that time, and the memory thus pains us. The wounds would be treated without any return of the lands, if national pride only rehabilitated itself in another way.

Seventeen years ago I added to the translation of these statements various considerations. I knew that these commentaries would come as no surprise to any watchful observer of French intellectual life. In the July 22, 1898, edition of *Le Journal*, the universally esteemed François Coppée described the conditions of need that a series of storms had brought about in Alsace. In moving words he appealed to the French people's filial sensibility to contribute to a relief fund, but altogether nothing came in.[61] Precisely this was the occasion for *Mercure de France*'s survey; they sought the reason that Coppeé's patriotic appeal had ended up as such a complete fiasco. Hatred of England had furthermore at that time, in the year of Fashoda, grown so strong that it had nearly replaced hatred of Germany. And for my part, I had already emphasized the selfsame words M. Dauville now employs, that in the higher circles these words were regularly heard: "Not Germany but England is the hereditary

58. Séverin Faust (1872–1945), who wrote under the pseudonym Camille Mauclair, was the art critic at the *Mercure de France*.

59. The Boulangist orientation in Third Republic Politics, named after its most vocal proponent, Georges Ernest Boulanger (1837–1891), was aggressively nationalist and advocated the retaking of Alsace-Lorraine.

60. Symbolist Henri-François-Joseph de Régnier (1864–1936) was elected to the Académie Française in 1911.

61. Brandes here cites a figure of the nationalist, anti-Dreyfusard Right, poet François Edouard Joachim Coppée (1842–1908).

enemy." The rivalry in Africa and Asia, especially the conditions in Egypt and on the Niger kept France's bitterness toward England alive. The working class at that time, whether socialist or anarchist, would hear nothing of national hatred for Germany, but viewed the German worker as a brother. Next I wrote that "furthermore it has been striking to every single observant traveler how a strange fondness and enthusiasm for Germany is so often to be found among the educated of France. The fanaticism for Richard Wagner, which in France is stronger than in any other country, has served as an immense propagator of Germanness. The desire of young people who learned German to use it, for example, is striking."[62]

At that last sentence I thought especially of Léon Daudet, now the most fuming chauvinist in France, who a few years prior grabbed every opportunity to speak German in his father's house.[63] Most often he addressed me in German but was answered in French. Now he has scolded me as insufficiently French.

Nor is it forgotten that all through the Dreyfus trial the French generals, without exception and with the support of the entire nationalist press, belligerently opposed the prospect of war with Germany, likening the idea of leading the French army against the German to the leading of a calf toward the butcher's block. During that severe internal conflict, in which "nationalism" at least apparently was subdued, the thought of revanche was resisted, and for the majority of the French a figure like Déroulède, its spokesman, gradually came to seem as a half or entirely comic figure.[64] It is only after his death that he has become a national hero.

It is really only in recent years that nationalism has regularly visited France. It could be sensed how rising confidence in the army awakened the thought of the reconquest of the lost provinces as a possibility and even as a responsibility. Nationalism, which previously had been overcome, was in reality triumphant all along the line; the neo-Catholic movement merged together with the national movement, and the newfound youthful enthusiasm received a lovely and moving expression in Ernest Psichari's *L'Appel aux armes*.[65]

It was not many years ago that Madame Adam in her memoirs derided Gambetta and his successors for giving up the idea of revanche.[66] Now this

62. Brandes, *Samlede Skrifter*, 16:237.

63. Léon Daudet (1867–1942) was founder of the nationalist journal *Action Française*; curiously, he would eventually end up a supporter of the Vichy government.

64. Paul Déroulède (1846–1914) was cofounder of the revanchist Ligue des patriotes.

65. Ernest Psichari's (1883–1914) novel *L'Appel aux armes*, widely read by nationalist youth, appeared in 1913; the following year he was killed in action in Belgium.

66. Feminist author Juliette Adam's (1836–1936) *Mes premières armes littéraires et politiques* was published in 1904; she was among Bismarck's most vehement critics. Léon Gambetta

variety of opinion is in the air, and with some surprise I have read in the *Mercure de France* of May 1915, as M. Dauville likely has as well, a denial by an M. P. G. La Chesnais that a warlike spirit has reigned in France as well as Germany in recent years.[67]

How strongly I have felt that awakening is demonstrated by what I wrote in 1912 after having been present at Henri Regnier's admission to the French Academy:[68]

> Nationalism . . . is at the moment *practically* speaking decidedly triumphant in France, triumphant as in England and Germany and Italy, but in a more striking manner. A breath of nationalist, warlike madness blows over Europe, in spite of all the electoral victories for socialists. Nationalism received a fresh and mighty wind in its sails at Algeciras.[69] Yet since the German ship was sent to Agadir, France has not just considered war, but—under governments that have done everything to prevent it—in reality has decided on war, has been consumed with hope for war.[70] Such a thing cannot be felt or assessed at a distance. But discussions with people of all stripes, from the most divergent and mutually exclusive circles, and just as much as impressions from the official sources of opinion, agree in convincing me of this war fever.

VI

That overheated nationalism is not exclusively on the German side is demonstrated in the selfsame issue of the previously mentioned French journal. Therein M. Léon Bloy has published his essay "Jeanne d'Arc et l'Allemagne."[71] With good reason the French, English, and Belgians have felt indignant at the most recent German demand to rank German culture as the equivalent of

(1838–82) was among the most powerful politicians during the war of 1870–71 and the initial decade of the Third Republic.

67. Pierre Georget La Chesnais (1865–1948) was the French translator of Ibsen and Hans Christian Andersen.

68. Brandes cites from the essay "Optagelse i det franske Akademi," published in his *Fugleperspektiv* (Copenhagen: Gyldendal, 1913), 463.

69. The Algeciras Conference of 1906 resolved the First Moroccan Crisis, in which Kaiser Wilhelm had attempted to disrupt the French annexation of the still independent kingdom; it was a humiliating defeat for Germany.

70. The Second Moroccan Crisis of 1911 was also initiated by the kaiser, who sent a German gunboat to Agadir in July as a show of force against French military intervention in the kingdom. The crisis was ultimately resolved by the Treaty of Fez the following year, in which Germany acknowledged French hegemony over Morocco in exchange for territorial concessions elsewhere on the continent.

71. Léon Bloy (1846–1917) was a Catholic novelist and pamphleteer.

civilization overall and above all other civilizations. But which German writer has gone farther in praising his fatherland than Mr. Léon Bloy has in praising France?"

For example, his treatise contains the following:

> After Israel, whose inhabitants were called God's people by a famous prerogative, there has never been any people on Earth whom God has loved as highly as the French. Anybody can explain it. To designate this nation as the most beautiful or the most magnanimous of all nations—which incidentally it indisputably is—says nothing, since these divine advantages must precisely be the reward of the chosen. God's love can only be justified at his whim, which is all the way through and in an adorable manner unexplored. The French are in this degree the first among all peoples. All the others, no matter who they are, must consider their fate tolerable only if they receive permission to eat its dog biscuits . . .
>
> A unified, homogeneous France, whose geography remained the same for three hundred years, was necessary for God, because without it he would not have been and would not be God in a complete manner. No matter France's infidelities or crimes, no matter how dreadful the expiation of them shall be, God cannot allow France to go down, since he has use for it in his own honor, and the sordid Lutherans, who as recently as a half-century ago injured it, will be weighed down with a severity that no one can imagine.

It is a given that no German professor's megalomania has reached such heights as to suggest that Europe's nations ought to consider their fate to be good and tolerable if they are allowed to share the crumbs of Germany's dogs.

The nations of our age have much about which to boast but little capacity to listen to one another. Each constitutes for itself Europe's most outstanding people, and if only God knew his responsibilities he would give them their victory. If he does not do so immediately, it is apparently due to the fact that the people have sinned against him, and as a severe yet loving father he has need of punishing them for some time. Seen through French lenses he hates German barbarism, seen through German eyes he loves German culture and especially protects the House of Hohenzollern. France as well as Germany are in the consciousness of their spokespeople his chosen lands, incarnations of his being on Earth. In order to show himself ungracious toward one of them he acts against them and awakens doubt about his almightiness or even his existence. He cannot at the same time favor both, and for some time he must listen to outcries from many sides, which move from bitter denunciation to tactless attack.

An ordinary mortal ought not then complain that it goes badly for him, since in the judgment of the belligerent states he is an ordinary human being.

But he has permission to demonstrate his discontent and assert how groundless the attacks are, or more properly what ignorance lies at the base of them. After M. Clemenceau insultingly cut off his political discussion with me, the big newspaper *Le Temps* took up his dismissal and in an irritated article found my being to be "incoherent."[72] I myself have not read this article; but the number of *Mercure de France* that has given M. Dauville the occasion for his letter has informed me that the newspaper "simply has denigrated me for having neither love of the truth nor the courage to speak it." M. La Chesnais adds to this citation: "If a newspaper article managed to affect him in such a way as to make him an enemy of France, then one could not better set about reaching that result."

My love of France runs too deep to be affected by foolish newspaper articles; after all it is hard enough, when one has in fact exhibited a lifelong and hardly ordinary insight into the historical and artistic conditions of a people, and when one has for a half century been a spokesperson for that people every time they were put down or unjustly attacked, to see oneself the object of hatred everywhere among that land's great public, which lacks every condition necessary to judge itself. And so much of this by trusted and reliable friends who have twisted innocent and heartfelt words into the meaning opposite their intention.

Although M. La Chesnais's goodwill is conditional and he quite wrongly reports that what I have written on France is less voluminous than what I have written on England and Germany, it is however for me a satisfaction that he has had the honest willingness to understand. Still more grateful am I to M. Edouard Herriot, the noted mayor of Lyon, because he has expressed his certainty that in this critical time I have not been unfaithful to myself or my ideals.[73]

When the representatives of the European press visited Denmark some years ago, they took each other by the hand in Skodsborg and danced in a ring around Hr. Alberti, while the assembled "world press" sang with enthusiasm the apt words: *he is a jolly good fellow*. It was symbolic of something.[74] The world press on this occasion revealed all the psychological insight it customarily displays, whether in praise or in censure, when commenting on Nordic personalities and circumstances.

---

72. The Brandes-Clemenceau feud was winding down by May 1915; the following year, however, would bring new attacks, this time from William Archer, Scottish translator of Ibsen; see "A Response to Mr. William Archer" in the present volume.

73. Longtime Brandes ally Édouard Marie Herriot (1872–1957) later briefly served as French premier in the 1920s and 1930s; he was among the very few French intellectuals who did not denounce Brandes during the war.

74. Peter Adler Alberti (1851–1932) served as Danish minister of justice from 1900 until 1908, when he was convicted on multiple counts of embezzlement and sentenced to an eight-year prison term.

CHAPTER 29

Introductory Words for the Polish Evening in Copenhagen

1916

The following remarks, delivered at one of the many public forums held in Denmark to express solidarity with the suffering of the Polish people during the war, turned out to be Brandes's final statement on the Polish question. Absent here are the stern words of rebuke that had characterized his "Conditions in Russian Poland," published shortly after the outbreak of the war amid the rising tide of antisemitism across all of partitioned Poland. In spite of the immeasurable suffering of the Poles—forced to fight against each other under openly hostile foreign command, their traditional lands serving as a battlefield for the Great War—Brandes here maintains a palpable sense of optimism regarding the possibility of a free and independent Poland upon the conclusion of hostilities; much to his delight and of course even more so to the Polish people themselves, this dream would indeed be realized after two more years of struggle.

~

Those peoples who have not been ravaged by the storm of the war that rages over the old world and all the seas of the globe follow with bated breath the course of the universal and reciprocal destruction.

That these peoples daily experience horrors that please the victors and dismember or destroy the sacrificed is the only certainty amid the ignorance of what is really happening, which is due in part to the belligerent powers' truth-killing censorship and in part to the fanatical articles of the ignorant journalists. There is killing at the front; there is hatred in the papers.

But with the deepest unease it is everywhere asked: how long can this go on? How long can the mutual destruction and systematic mass murder continue to harry the earth?

We see sorrow over the suffering, sorrow over the loss, we envelop Europe in a profusion of sorrow.

Speech delivered on March 13, 1916. Originally published in *Politiken*, March 19, 1916. Translated from the version published in *Verdenskrigen*.

We see destitution, hunger, agony, despair in gigantic forms spread themselves across Europe's expanses, dancing ghostlike a ring dance like the witches on the heath in *Macbeth*.

We look out over Europe: there are hundreds of battlefields, thousands of graveyards, thousands of hospitals, an immense bankrupt estate, and a single great insane asylum.

The participants in the struggle and the observers of its immense tragedy have from early childhood learned that everything that happens has a goal foreordained by a supernatural wisdom, so that everything, even that which is in our eyes most sorrowful, is heading toward the best outcome. Yet they ask in profound tension: what good will and can come of this?

Theologians and philosophers have provided the answers:

Like this: from this unceasing murder on the earth, on the sea, and in the air shall emerge a lasting peace.

Or like this: from these losses and sacrifices there emerges a new age, a heroic age, in which courage replaces indulgence.

Or finally like this: from all the din of the weapons and the thunder of the cannon, from all the grenades that explode, the mines that detonate, the machines that spit fire or spread poison gas over what was before called our fellow humans, now the enemy, there shall emerge a historical justice, the just division of power, justice's reconquered dominion.

Most believe it, because the philosophers no less than the priests and poets have taught them to believe it.

And the youth who will crest the heights of the age feel it to be *modern* to agree with the optimists.

Few are those who know that humanity is more worthy than nationality. Few are those who know that where hatred is sown there can never be anything harvested other than hatred.

Few are those who feel what is expressed in this little Swedish verse I have read:

I saw innocence trod underfoot,
I heard violence admired,
Truth smeared.
Then my blood boiled.
Now I have all but given up on admiring,
when everything simply runs against sound sense.
I know, that justice is being tread underfoot,
however much praying and wailing there is,
I know, that the laws of life are cold and not good.

And yet—given that amid the current reign of horrors our gaze seeks a point of light when it can be glimpsed—however uncertain and flickering—our thoughts are directed at the future of unhappy Poland. Certainly not when our attention is directed at its present, for in few places on the globe as currently in Russian Poland and in Galicia is misery "the misery of the entirety of humanity," as Faust said.

In the first place these lands have been harried by that impersonal thing called the war, by the three million soldiers of the superpowers warring against each other, in a struggle that has swept back and forth across these areas, leaving behind corpses, epidemics, the crippled, and the abused—the three true superpowers: hunger, sickness, and sorrow.

In the next place everything that is most personal, what is called human cruelty, conscious inhumanity, has contributed to each of the three populations, the Polish, the Jewish, and the Ukrainian, being driven into misery, but has also unfortunately driven the national majority into the persecution of its minority, so that hatred and crudeness here as everywhere has triumphed.

The war as the cultural force it constitutes has had the consequence that everything has been impoverished and immiserated, that everything has been brutalized, militarized, clericalized, and nationalized the world over.

And yet—for the first time in a hundred years, before our very eyes, the contours of Poland, which for so long was only an image of fantasy, now seem to be a real figure—an independent Poland, certainly not of the scope occupied by the kingdom in its salad days, but still a Poland, in which the kingdom and Galicia, at least western Galicia, are united in as much independence as contemporary smaller states have.

Surely enough there is no one present in this hall who is old enough to recall the enthusiasm that seized the Danes during the uprising in Russian Poland in 1863, or the passion that overtook not just the young but the elderly, not just women but men, when the Polish-chartered steamship arrived that time in Copenhagen, and the band of young warriors that hoped to reach Poland spent a few weeks here to refit and resupply.

I see them before me in the old student union, young, brave, and glowing as they were, see the most admired and most elegant of them all, Stefan Poles, who in spite of his leadership ability and rashness later did not prove worthy of his position.[1] To observe these young men and speak with them was

1. Stefan Poles (1841–75, born Raphael Tugenhold) was a principal organizer of the 1863 Polish émigré naval expedition to Lithuania in support of the insurgent forces of the January Uprising. The failure of the mission was largely blamed on Poles, who was accused of being a Russian spy, although he maintained his innocence until his death. See Adam

surely for the youth at that time an initiation into the love of freedom and daring.

And there were individuals who a lifetime later preserved and demonstrated their love of Poland and the Poles.

It occurred to me one day in 1886 while on a visit in Warsaw to the painter Koloszinski, who spread out his collection of old Polish gold and silver silk scarves before me, that by the careful inspection of a single such scarf the glorious civilization of the Polish nobility of the seventeenth and eighteenth centuries stood alive before my gaze.[2]

I saw before me the higher *szlachta*, the brotherhood as it was called, of voivodes, hetmen, castellans, bishops, all these magnates in their *sukmana* and *kontusze* of velvet and silk with the deep red stockings and broad scarves, and felt how all the glimmer reflected the proud and wild joie de vivre and glamour of this independent noble class.[3] He who has worn such a gold brocaded scarf that runs many times round the midsection has had a constant impression of beauty, vigor, and well-being. And to the acute sense of beauty in this brotherhood corresponds the boundless hospitality of the nobility, its propensity for luxuriousness in food and drink, its gentleman's morality.

I saw before me the delicate elegance of its women, the exuberant Catholic culture that was like a champagne punch prepared with a little holy water. And as the women were raised up to high-mindedness and delicacy, so were the men to heroic courage. From birth onward they had a love of freedom, a cultivation of the right of the individual that led to the political madness called *Liberum Veto*.[4] One voice alone was enough to hinder every collective decision.

This civilization, from which a Copernicus would give us the foundation of our image of the world, and under which Sobieski heroically fought the Turks and thereby saved Vienna and Europe, gleamed even in its decline under August the Strong of Saxony, who recalls the drunken and debauched

---

Lesniewski, "A Certain Fiasco or the Role of Stefan Poles in the Polish Uprising of 1863," *Polish Review* 24, no. 4 (1978): 18–38.

2. It is very likely Brandes is referring to Wojciech Kolasiński (1852–1916), a minor Polish painter better known as an art restorer, collector, and antiquarian. Thank you to Michalina Petelska of Gdansk University for meticulous research into this largely forgotten figure.

3. The *szlachta* are the traditional aristocratic class of Poland, established during the fourteenth-century reign of Casimir the Great; the hetman was a high-ranking military official in Poland-Lithuania. The *sukmana* is the traditional coat of the Polish commoner, the *kontuz* of the aristocracy.

4. The practice of the *Liberum Veto* permitted any single member of the *Sejm*, the parliamentary body of the Polish-Lithuanian Commonwealth, to end debate and nullify any current legislative proposal.

Hercules in the Greek satyr play.[5] It reached its modern high point in Chopin, whose music is at once Polish and pan-European.

Polish dress during peacetime was lovely and rich. But war was also a festival in old Poland. In war the Polish knights had great wings on their cuirasses. They understood that the plume must never be wanting.

In Cherbuliez's *Ladislas Bolski*, which is meant as a depiction of the typical Pole in his recklessness and weakness, the glamorous principle of glory is expressed in the love of the son for his father's red and white plume, which he always carries with him in his case.[6]

It is deeply instructive that one of Poland's foremost poets, Julius Slowacki, provides in his poem *Beniowski* this definition of God's being: he is not the God of the serpents or the beasts that crawl. He provides the great birds their flight and gives the charging horse its bridle.[7] He is the ardent feather on the proud helm.

No one who is not Polish could manage to define God in this way.

When the politics of Catherine II and Poland's decline led to the First Partition of Poland the plume sank and vanished in the din of battle.[8]

The diluted and corrupted aristocratic republic of thirteen million, of which nearly one million belonged to the *szlachta*, was left with only 30,000 fully independent magnates. On these the lower nobility was quite dependent, and still more the enserfed peasantry. In Poland, like in other states of antiquity, or like in Iceland and or in France under the ancien régime, the gentlemen dispensed their civilization over a population of impoverished, overtaxed subjects, serfs, and slaves.

After the first partition the Poles collected themselves. The best in their midst came forward. They had been compelled to give up a population of five million. But Poland was still not lost.

In 1789, the same year as the French Revolution, the Poles decided to change their constitution. The rule of the elective king with the notable and amateurish *Liberum Veto* vanished and was replaced by a hereditary monarchy. The anarchy was succeeded by a bicameral system, by religious freedom, by

---

5. Jan III Sobieski (1629–96), king of Poland-Lithuania from 1674 until his death, defeated the Turks at the Battle of Vienna in 1683. Augustus II the Strong (1670–1733) succeeded Sobieski, unsuccessfully leading the Commonwealth against Russia in the Great Northern War.

6. Swiss-born Charles Victor Cherbuliez (1829–99), of whom Brandes was a great admirer, published *L'Aventure de Ladislas Bolski* in 1869.

7. Juliusz Słowacki (1809–49) published the long poem *Beniowski* in 1841.

8. The First Partition, which divided Poland-Lithuania into Austrian, Prussian, and Russian sectors, occurred in 1772.

the enfranchisement of the free classes, majority rule, an independent judiciary, the relative protection of the peasantry against the arbitrariness of the landowners. The constitution of May 3, 1791, reveals the Poles' honorable desire to establish a modern state.

Poland's star rose again.

Great English statesmen of the opposition like Burke and Fox have called this constitution a work with which the friends of freedom in all countries should be pleased.[9]

Then it happened that Catherine II intervened. Russia would not tolerate a strong and free Poland. Friedrich Wilhelm II of Prussia, who originally had approved of the constitution, went back on his word and united with Russia for a new partition. Treacherous Poles of the upper nobility such as Feliks Potocki and Ksawery Branicki formed the Targowica Confederation in order to preserve the *Liberum Veto* and thus delivered their fatherland to the partitioning powers.[10]

Then followed Kosciuszko's brave revolution, and after its bloody suppression the Third Partition of Poland.[11]

A new hope appeared for the Poles in Napoleon's campaigns of 1806 and 1812. The first approaches from their side to Bonaparte were poorly rewarded. Although in 1797 Polish legions fought alongside the soldiers of the French Republic in the Italian campaign, and Dombrowski took many a pounding for the French, Bonaparte treated his Polish allies poorly. Nevertheless they formed new legions and participated during the Consulate in the battles on the Danube and in Italy. It was in the latter that the famous national song "Jeszcse Polska" by Dombrowski's soldier Wybicki came into being: "Poland is still not done. March! March! Dombrowski!"[12] No one has shown such fidelity to Napoleon as the Poles. When it came to the most extreme situations, the most desperate attacks, or the personal protection of the Emperor, the Polish lancers came forward.

On Napoleon's lonely sled ride during the retreat from Russia he was accompanied from Smorgoni in a frigid chill by hundreds of Polish lancers, who

9. The Polish constitution pleased both classical conservatives such as Edmund Burke (1730–97) and radicals like Charles James Fox (1749–1806).

10. The loyalist Targowica Confederation, under Count Stanisław Szczęsny Feliks Potocki (1751–1805) and Franciszek Ksawery Branicki (1730–1819), with extensive Russian assistance, defeated Commonwealth forces in the Polish-Russian War of 1792.

11. For more on the Kościuszko Uprising of 1794, see note 12 to "Conditions in Russian Poland" in the present volume.

12. For more on "Dąbrowski Mazurka," see note 15 to "Conditions in Russian Poland" in the present volume.

during the evening willingly offered to follow along as a screen and of whom only thirty-six were left in the morning. When Moreau in 1814 began the sad process of surrendering the fortress of Soissons, the garrison's seven hundred Poles were in the process of fighting against a besieging army of 50,000 and would have held the fortress until Napoleon's arrival the next day if Moreau had not suffered a lapse in judgment and allowed himself to be duped.[13]

When Europe was reminded of Poland later in the nineteenth century it was due to the great uprisings of 1830 and 1863.[14] It is still not forgotten how much enthusiasm the rebellion of 1830 awakened in all European countries, perhaps strongest in France, the country that the Polish emigrants of the time sought out as their second homeland, and where Poland's greatest poet, Adam Mickiewicz, was posted at the Collège de France and worked for the cause of his country.

In Germany as well the revolution of 1830 awakened a powerful echo. I would recall here Börne's Paris letters and Herwegh's poems "For Poland" and "Poland to Europe," the four lovely poems of Moritz Hartmann, and the whole collection of August v. Platen's *Polenlieder*:

Die Lüfte wehn so schaurig.
Wir ziehn dahin so traurig
Nach ungewissem Ziel.
Kaum leuchten uns die Sterne,
Europa sieht von Ferne
Das grosse Trauerspiel.[15]

In Norway Welhaven wrote his unforgettable poem, "At the barrier of the city there lies a little humble café," in which a Polish man arises among the boisterous Parisian students who drink to Poland's freedom, baring his chest: "You fools, it is the mark of Ostrolenka,—have you understood, how it aches?"[16]

---

13. Indeed, General Jean-Claude Moreau (1755–1828) was arrested on the orders of Napoleon for the surrender of the city.

14. Brandes is referring to the November Uprising of 1830 and the January Uprising of 1863.

15. "The air was so frightening / We moved through it so sorrowfully / Toward an uncertain destination. / As soon as the stars shine / Europe gazes far afield / At the great tragedy." Karl Ludwig Börne (1786–1837), Georg Friedrich Rudolph Theodor Herwegh (1817–75), Moritz Hartmann (1821–72), and Karl August Georg Maximilian Graf von Platen-Hallermünde (1796–1835) were all associated with the Young Germany Movement, which Brandes chronicled in the sixth and final volume of his *Main Currents*.

16. Brandes's citation of Johan Sebastian Welhaven (1807–73), hardly a friend of nationalist causes, seems out of place here. His 1832 poem "Republikanerne" is really more a rebuke

In Denmark Hauch and Aarestrup speak to how much sympathy was awakened, Hauch with his thousand-times sung, "Why does the Vistula Swell?" and Aarestrup with his "A Polish Mother."[17] She lifts her child into the air when his father is to be shot:

Cast your eyes on him
with the power and the ability,
which death alone can provide,
and consecrate him to revenge!

The uprising of 1863, which I began by touching on, also brought forth worthy Nordic poetry, first and foremost Carl Snoilsky's half dozen poems, of which the most gripping is certainly the poem "At Poland's Grave," about the desolate patch on Europe's bosom Poland occupies:

Och stode världen som en rosengård,
Där idel bäcker utaf honung flöte,
Han syntes dock, vanärans minnesvård,
Den öde fläcken i Europas sköte.[18]

No one knows what the outcome will be of this war that spreads over the earth. But with some truthfulness it can be foreseen that in one form or another Poland will be reestablished.

Yet Poland certainly remains the desolate patch of earth upon Europe's bosom.

It has been during the war that the presses of the belligerent kingdoms have succeeded in fomenting to previously unknown heights that most reprehensible

---

to revolutionary enthusiasm, the wounded Polish veteran of Ostrolenka serving as a reminder of the costs of the struggle for freedom.

17. Johannes Carsten Hauch (1790–1872) and Carl Ludvig Emil Aarestrup (1800–1856) were poets of the long Romantic era in Denmark; Hauch's "Hvorfor svulmer Weichsfloden" appeared in his 1839 novel *En polsk Familie*. Aarestrup's "En polsk moder" is from 1834; his single, highly influential collection exerted a profound influence on a young Brandes. See Claus Elholm Andersen, "Exile and Naturalism: Reading Georg Brandes Reading Emil Aarestrup," *Scandinavian Studies* 78, no. 4 (Winter 2006): 419–28.

18. "And though the world was a rose garden, / Through which pure streams of honey flowed, / It seems however, that a monument to shame, / Occupies the desolate patch in Europe's bosom." Carl Johan Gustaf Snoilsky (1841–1903) composed his Polish poems during his initial burst of creativity in the early 1860s; "På Polens Graf" and several other Polish tributes are printed in the first volume of his *Samlade Dikter* (Stockholm: H. Geber, 1903).

power, national hatred, that hatred that is not grounded in humanity's vices or crimes, but touches on his descent and his place of birth, that imbecilic racial and national hatred. That hatred is at the moment a factor even in politics and hinders the peace.

But behind and above the nations stand humanity and humaneness.

It is humaneness that seeks to alleviate the agonies that national hatred has brought about and to heal the wounds it has inflicted.

It is in the name of the love of humanity and in its service that we have gathered this evening.

CHAPTER 30

An Appeal

1916

As spring arrived in 1916, no end to the ever-expanding Great War appeared on the horizon. In the West the bloodletting at Verdun continued unabated while the British, for their part, concluded final preparations for their summer offensive on the Somme; in the East, Brusilov planned the great offensive that would come to bear his name and would ultimately result in the collapse of the czardom. Nowhere was there serious talk of a ceasefire, Henry Ford's rather quixotic Peace Ship mission of the previous December having concluded in abject failure. In spite of overwhelming opposition to peace in the belligerent and neutral countries alike, Brandes and his allies nevertheless released the appeal below, which appeared in Danish in *Politiken* and was then promptly distributed in the hundreds of millions in French and German translation. The absence of a British version is of course conspicuous, since a partial English version was published in the still neutral United States. This is most certainly due at least in part to the efforts of William Archer, the Scottish critic, Ibsen translator, and longtime Brandes ally and collaborator, who had in fact joined the secret British propaganda bureau known as Wellington House.[1] Archer, who had initially opposed the war on grounds similar to those of Brandes, had by late 1915 come to see it as a necessity, and was indeed so alarmed by his old friend's appeal for peace that later in the year he issued a formal denunciation of Brandes, a fifty-four-page pamphlet titled *Colour-Blind Neutrality: An Open Letter to Dr. George Brandes.* Never one to shrink from such challenges, Brandes would respond with a series of essays, including those in the present collection on Belgium and Persia, effectively rehashing his debate with Clemenceau of the previous year.

~

Originally published in Danish in *Politiken*, May 17, 1916. Translated from the version published in *Verdenskrigen.*

1. For a superb account of Brandes's wartime activities, including his feuds with both Clemenceau and Archer, see Bjarne S. Bendtsen, "Colour-Blind or Clear-Sighted Neutrality: Georg Brandes and the First World War," in *Caught in the Middle: Neutrals, Neutrality*

Each of the belligerent great powers asserts that the war they are conducting is a war of self-defense. Each is the one who has been attacked, each fights for its existence. For all concerned mass murder is a matter of self-defense, just as all lies are lies of self-defense. But since none of the powers have sought out the war, let them conclude the peace!

After nearly twenty-two months of war, however, the peace seems farther off than ever before. This applies to all the belligerent powers. Each of them must first lead its civilization to victory, the civilization that is deemed to be spiritually superior or just or free or governed by the civil spirit as opposed to the militaristic.

Civilization! The first fruit of this civilization has been that the truth-murdering spirit of the Russian censors has spread over the earth. The next is that we have returned to the era of human sacrifice, only that in barbaric antiquity four or five prisoners of war were murdered every year to appease a fearsome god, while we now sacrifice four or five million people to the idols we worship.

Lammenais has written: "Satan suggested a devilish thought to the oppressors of peoples. He said to them: 'Take from each family the most powerful man and give him a weapon! I shall give them two idols that they shall call honor and fidelity, and a law that they shall call adherence to duty. They shall worship these idols and blindly subject themselves to this law.'"[2]

We follow this struggle against militarism during which the compulsion of militarism has spread to the only state that had held itself free of it, and during which everywhere civilian authority has been set aside—this civilian power and spirit for whose superiority over the military we have spent a century fighting.[3]

We follow this struggle for freedom during which every ship's cargo is seized and every letter opened, even every private letter between two neutrals, by the spokesmen of freedom as well as the idolaters of power.

We follow this struggle for a higher culture during which Germany has trampled Belgium underfoot, Austria-Hungary Serbia, England Greece, Russia East Prussia and Poland—this struggle for justice during which justice everywhere has been replaced by state interest—this struggle for the independence of the smaller states during which this independence is trampled by both sides, set aside, dismissed.

---

and the First World War, ed. Johan den Hertog and Samuël Kruizinga (Amsterdam: Aksant, 2011), 121–38.

2. Hugues-Félicité Robert de Lamennais (1782–1854) was the founder of Social Catholicism. Brandes cites from his 1834 *Paroles d'un croyant*, verse 35.

3. The United Kingdom introduced military conscription for the first time in 1916.

In the war-making countries the armies naturally desire first and foremost victory, but most strongly they desire peace. The civilian population everywhere groans for peace. The governments who sit high in the saddle kick the spurs into the weary horse's flanks.

The desire for peace dare not be spoken.

In the neutral countries public opinion does not feel entitled to speak out for peace. Public opinion mostly accords with the point of view of the seamstress, "siding with" one or the other warring parties and thereby forgetting to come down on the side of peace.

Among the neutral powers there is one that has greater significance than all the others together. Do the American free states prefer to serve the dollar rather than employ their influence for peace?[4] Is there altogether no one who is for peace save sound reason and sound feeling?

The cries for peace that soon shall arise in all states are called cowardly. But if the people keep silent then the stones will speak. Everywhere the ruins scream for peace, not for revenge. And where the stones remain silent, the fields and the meadows, drenched in blood and strewn with corpses, cry out.

The entire earth is now under the dominance of Schadenfreude. The only joy is to inflict evil in the interest of self-preservation. Torpedoing thrives.[5] Bombing produces remarkable results. A single pilot shoots down his twentieth airplane. And there is rejoicing. If anyone asks how there can be rejoicing the response is a phrase that has been judged as Jesuitical, as devilish: the ends justify the means.

Cruelty has become duty, sympathy treachery.

The Germans endure hunger and need. The Allies enjoy it. The Belgians and the Serbs are cowed and crushed. The Germans and Austrians enjoy it.

The Poles go hungry, the Jews are sunken into immeasurable misery. The belligerents are incapable of providing relief.

All the war-makers are proud of the courage and heroic fortitude of their brave men. Both parties assert that among their opponents the lowest passions have been set loose, and both are unfortunately right.

The Central Powers declare that they want peace. But it is not apparent that they will sacrifice anything for it. They would paralyze their enemies, so that the peace will be lasting.

The Allies want nothing in the way of peace until the "definitive victory" has been won, that is, not before they have accomplished what they have in vain desired for almost two years, and what they now seem no closer to achieving.

4. The United States would declare war on Germany the following April.

5. Germany had introduced unrestricted submarine warfare in 1915.

But they would also paralyze the enemy before the peace is concluded. Whatever happens, whatever battle is won or lost, however valuable a ship is sunk, whichever airships are shot down, however many of the belligerent powers' men are killed or wounded or captured, one single thing is certain: everything must end with a cease-fire and negotiations.

Why not then begin to negotiate now? It is not as if there is anything to be gained by further murder. Peace is the Sibyl whose books, that is to say whose treasures, must be purchased, but these become less valuable and more expensive with each day that passes.

We are all familiar with this: we must first await the crushing of the enemy. But nothing comes of this crushing, only more mass murder. Neither of the warring parties will allow itself to be crushed.

And if it is said that we would not crush Germany, only its militarism, then it is like wanting not to damage the porcupine, only rip out its quills.

Both the parties will hold out to "the bitter end." Every day it becomes bitterer. Whatever can be won by entering into peace negotiations is lost many times over by the continuance of the war.

It is as if there is no other resolution to human conflict possible than that gathered from mines and grenades.

How will the future judge this? That in our day not a single statesman was to be found in the whole of Europe. Had there been one great statesman on each side then the world war would never have broken out. With one great statesman on one of the sides it would not have lasted a year. Thus the generals took the power away from the statesmen.

The future will say that this age viewed the prior age of religious wars as barbaric, yet failed to understand that national wars are far worse. That this age viewed cabinet wars as old-fashioned, yet failed to grasp that wars of financial interests are still more awful. The history of the religious wars was a farce. The history of the world war is a singular tragedy.

Preferably the war should come to an end without any severe humiliation for any of the warring parties. Otherwise the humiliation will only lead to the next war.[6] And it ought to be remembered that humiliation inflicted on the enemy replaces none of the lives that have been lost.

Every human life is of value. But humans are, however, not always in agreement. It is no consolation that we lost only a thousand men when the enemy lost ten thousand. No one knows whether among the thousand there was one who would have been the honor of his country and the benefactor of all humanity through the ages.

---

6. The Treaty of Versailles, as is all too well known, failed to heed Brandes's words.

There could have been a Shakespeare or a Newton, a Kant or a Goethe, a Molière or a Pasteur, a Copernicus, a Rubens, a Tolstoy among the hundreds of thousands of twenty-year-old Englishmen, Germans, Frenchmen, Poles, Belgians, Russians who have fallen.

What does it mean to move a border or capture a province against the loss of such a personality! The capture is temporary, the loss irrevocable. The capture belongs to a single state, the loss to all humanity.

Everyone sees how the fortunes of humanity dwindle during the war, so that in the end no one will be able to pay its costs. But the loss of human value, the most serious impoverishment, is still not accounted for.

What we are experiencing is that the white race is destroying its sense of superiority over the black, brown, and yellow races. The white race has asked for their assistance in the murder and has rewarded them for participating. How can this not come back on us?

Europe commits hara-kiri for the entertainment of Japan, and the quick-to-learn and heavy-handed forward-looking people of Asia evidently observe the suicidal madness of Europe with various admiration and no small measure of satisfaction.

The press in the belligerent countries has understood its task as that of inflaming the bitterness and thereby the enthusiasm. It ought to consider that the destructive hatred it has in this way called forth will long outlive the war and by necessity will birth new wars. The longer the war lasts, the shorter the coming peace will last.

CHAPTER 31

A Response to Mr. William Archer

1916

The publication of Brandes's "An Appeal" moved his old friend and ally William Archer to publish a fifty-four-page rebuttal, *Colour-Blind Neutrality: An Open Letter to Dr. George Brandes*, which appeared the following year. While significantly less aggressive in its tone than Clemenceau's denunciations of the previous year, Brandes was nevertheless motivated to produce a point-by-point counter-rebuttal. The full text of Brandes's response has previously appeared in English in Catherine Groth's *The World at War*; for the present volume, I have provided new translations of only the material most pertinent to its theme, namely the commentaries on the neutral countries most victimized by the war, Belgium and Persia.

~

Belgium

I

There is hardly any disagreement between Mr. Archer and myself regarding the feelings that the regrettable fate of Belgium inspires. I am familiar with Captain de Gerlache's book and sympathize with that people whom misfortune has rained down upon.[1]

When considering the indignation that the plight of Belgium has awakened in Europe and America, it is suggested that the Germans would have acted not only more honorably, but more wisely, if they had begun to march on Verdun rather than taking upon themselves the odium that an attack on a

Originally published in *Politiken* in two parts, June 28 and 29, 1916. Translated from the versions published in *Verdenskrigen*.

1. Baron Adrien Victor Joseph de Gerlache de Gomery (1866–1934) was a captain in the Belgian navy; he achieved fame for leading the Belgian Antarctic Expedition of 1897–99. Upon the outbreak of the war in 1914, de Gerlache fled to Norway, where he would plead the cause of his beleaguered country in the Scandinavian press. His 1915 *Le pays qui ne veut pas mourir*, initially published in Norwegian and Swedish editions, sold widely and helped raise awareness of the plight of his people.

neutral state calls forth, and in addition a state whose neutrality they themselves had guaranteed.[2]

And such cards they had to play in partially winning over Belgium! The continuous bitter conflict between the Walloons and the Flemish, in which the advocates of the rights of the Flemish language could hardly do other than support the related Low German people and language! Instead, now after the subjection of Belgium the Germans have quite fruitlessly tried to win over the Flemish by offering them the establishment of the Flemish university in Ghent for which they have long fought.[3] German support for this goal, in a move that speaks to the meagerness of their practical psychology as conquerors, was undermined by their response to local opposition to the plan. Professor *Paul Fredericq*, the foremost man in Ghent, as well his colleague *Henri Pirenne*, were shipped off to a prison camp in Germany.[4]

One would almost think that the German authorities were not aware that Paul Fredericq, as French as this irresistibly charming and knowledgeable sociologist is in his attitude and style, is also the most widely known figure at the Dutch congresses in which Flemish and Hollanders meet.[5] It is miserable politics to allow the Prussian garrison to take such a man hostage and thereafter let him toil as a prisoner in Germany. The bitterness over this conduct is no less severe in Holland than in Belgium, as is attested in the weekly newspapers of Holland. Regarding the neutrals *oderint, dum metuant* [let them hate, so long as they fear] should, however, no longer be the solution.

II

It is only natural that England and France, who are indebted to Belgium for the sacrifices they themselves brought on, place all the weight on Belgian courage and raise up the country into the clouds, as opposed to the other powers who have in Mr. Archer's words confined themselves to the "comforts

2. The Kingdom of Prussia, as a member of the Concert of Europe, had signed the 1839 Treaty of London, thereby committing itself to the defense of Belgian independence. The violation of this agreement by the German Reich in 1914 was a pillar of the Anglo-French justification of their war efforts.

3. Ghent University, established in 1817 as a French-speaking institution, would switch to Flemish in 1930.

4. Paul Fredericq (1850–1920) and Henri Pirenne (1862–1935) were historians at Ghent; both were imprisoned in Germany in 1916 for encouraging nonviolent resistance against the German occupation.

5. In spite of his Walloon ancestry, Fredericq was among the most prominent advocates of the Flemish language in Belgium.

of neutrality"—comforts that, however, bitterly offend, especially England's effort to starve Germany by starving the neutrals as well.[6]

In the meantime, the cause of Belgium is not only sentimental but also political. And as far as the political goes, it hardly seems evident to me that Great Britain has done its duty.

As is generally known England had in alliance with the other great powers guaranteed Belgium's neutrality in 1839. They had guaranteed this neutrality without, however, expressly promising that England would offer protection in the case of a land war, a promise that the kingdom was not capable of making for the good reason that this promise could not be kept. Belgium's neutrality could only be secured with masses of troops that would not be at England's disposal at the outbreak of such a war.[7]

Now the case was such that the likelihood of a war between Germany and France had for many years occupied the minds and captured the thinking of general staffs in the various countries of Europe. The most important eventualities of the war were discussed beforehand in the military journals of most of the countries, and those in the know everywhere had been in agreement in the belief that Germany would, in order to hit France quickly, go through Belgium, since the French border was so heavily fortified that only with the greatest difficulty could it be forced. In other words, the military writers of the various countries saw the only prospect of a German victory in its march through Belgium. And everyone also knew that Germany had stretched its military rail line to the Belgian border. In September 1914 Lord Winston Churchill said in Parliament that he had been aware of the German plan for three years. As early as February 1914 a layman such as the author of these words said publicly in a lecture that this was the plan.

The only power that seems to have never sensed the plan was France, which surprisingly enough took no measures to counter it.[8] Yet what Mr. Archer and I are speaking about is not the position of France, but of England.

---

6. The British blockade of the North Sea from 1914 to 1918, which included foodstuffs in its list of embargoed goods, affected not only the Central Powers but the Nordic countries as well.

7. British ground forces in August 1914 amounted to less than a half million soldiers, more than half of which were stationed abroad in the Empire; Germany, in contrast, mobilized nearly four million men in the opening weeks of the conflict. The United Kingdom, which waited until January 1916 to introduce conscription, only made its presence felt in earnest on the Western Front later that year, when its massive "Kitchener's Army" opened the Somme campaign.

8. Unlike the British, the French were able to mobilize an army in the millions in 1914, but the war preparations, outlined in the notorious Plan 17, focused on the German rather than the Belgian frontier.

Under these circumstances what did England do to hinder the trampling of the rights and the borders of Belgium? Did it threaten anyone who crossed the border with an English intervention?

If England was not prepared to defend Belgium by force of arms, then at the very least it owed the little, severely exposed country a bit of sensible and disinterested advice. Belgium should have been warned, should have been informed of the unlikelihood of English troops being transported to Belgium in time to provide Belgian troops with meaningful support, and of the unlikelihood of the French army, ill-prepared as it was, quickly being able to provide relief.

If this heads up had been given, and if Belgium had still decided on engaging in a conflict with vastly superior masses of troops rather than under protest bending before the force majeure and permitting the transit of their country that they could in no way prevent—then England could have remained idle and Belgium might have avoided the misfortunes its proud stance has brought down upon it.

But Belgium seems in part to have counted on more effective English support than the handful of troops who at the last moment turned up in Antwerp, and in part to have wavered with respect to what course was wisest to follow. As late as August 3 the British minister in Brussels telegraphed the foreign ministry that the French government had offered the Belgians the support of five army corps, but had received the following answer: "We are genuinely grateful to the French government for the prospective offer of support. Under present circumstances we have, however, no intention of appealing to the guarantees of the powers. The Belgian government will later decide on which course of action it sees as necessary."

As late as the eleventh hour, as far as one can tell, Belgium was therefore willing to take up the attitude of the enforcedly neutral onlooker. Had Belgium bent before the superior force and been content with the compensation package offered, which they could have demanded to be increased to cover all the damage done by the German troops, then Belgium would certainly enough have surrendered the glorious valor it has now attained; but it would have avoided destruction and much greater humiliation, and no reasonable person would be able to declare its decisions to have been without honor or even without reason. Now unlucky Belgium has certainly enough earned the praise of the Allies, but has moreover served as the whipping boy of England and France.

III

In the eloquent brochure Mr. Archer has published against me, he is all too much the *gentleman* to direct accusations of a personal nature against me.

At the same time, I can only be poorly served by the portrait he has painted of me for his countrymen, since he (like my German, my French, and my Russian attackers) concedes that while my abilities might be good enough, I lack a sense of the right, I hover between truth and lies, between justice and outrage, I am incapable of feeling the indignation that leads a man to take a side passionately and decisively.

If in this world war I have not simply taken a side like each of the citizens of the powers and many of the citizens of the neutrals have, then this is due precisely to the opposite, that my indignation is too severe for that, my pessimism too deep, my suspicion too well grounded, my idealism too unshakable for any of the warring parties to correspond to my conceptions of right and of honesty, of impartiality and of high-mindedness, of a manner of action for the well-being of humanity. Again and again in polemical articles and brochures I am referred to with the derogative term *neutral.* At one point Mr. Archer says to me: the manner of thinking that leads to neutrality is so base that "whatever sorrow the war might have or will bring him—he will not for all the world be *neutral.*"

How remarkable it is that the worthiness of neutrality changes in the life of the peoples! When I was twenty-two years old I did not sense the possibility that I should live to see Denmark mocked by England and France because it remains neutral. At that time Denmark fought entirely alone against Prussia and Austria, the two great powers against whom Russia, England, France, Italy, Serbia, Belgium, Montenegro, Portugal, Japan, and the United States (as the arsenal) have now been united for nearly three years, and against whom they seek *new* allies.[9] At that time all these powers were *neutral.* None of them lifted a finger for Denmark against the two central powers, and that in spite of the fact that Denmark among other things had entered into the war relying on the express promises of the English government: "Denmark will not come to stand alone, et cetera."

Now Denmark is ridiculed as *neutral* not just by Germany, who back then plundered us and now lets us know that nothing is so contemptible as neutrality, but in its reduced and weakened position also by the same peoples, Englishmen and Frenchmen, who with unforgivably poor foresight for their own concerns stubbornly remained neutral at that time when Denmark with its two million people alone gave battle against the two powers against whom England and France have now set the entire world in motion in the possibility of overcoming.

~

9. Brandes refers to the Second Schleswig War of 1864.

Persia

Persia is Asia's name for Belgium.

It has for a long time found itself to be in decline, and since its ruling house and its upper nobility have been among the most corrupt of the Orient, its independence was always on shaky ground.[10] The old rivalry between Russia and England impacted the country, where due to England's preoccupation with the Boer War at the turn of the century Russia's position was strengthened.

In the year 1906, after Russia's defeat in the war with Japan, a great reform movement broke out. It percolated everywhere in the Far as well as the Near East. China became a republic, Turkey got a parliament; in Persia the movement opposed the tyranny of the shah and the court's dependence on Russia.[11]

The tipping point was a general work stoppage in midsummer, during which no less than 12,000 Persians sought refuge in the English consulate in Tehran.[12] The shah conceded, was compelled to grant a constitution, and the population considered England's previously unknown participation to have played just as large a role in this victory as their own efforts.

Persia's first parliament (Majlis) convened in 1906; the esteem of England in this ancient land of culture was never higher. Then it happened that Sir Edward Grey, without consulting Persia, entered into an agreement with Russia.[13] To the painful surprise of the people it was revealed that Persia constituted for Great Britain as well as Russia only a stretch of land, a field, from which concessions could be gathered, as well as a market for trade. Both powers committed themselves to honoring Persia's independence and preserving it from partition. Then they divided it among themselves, as Poland was in its time.

From the north Russia took more than half of Persia, all the fertile and populated land with the three large cities of Tehran, Tabriz, and Isfahan; England took the small stretch in the southwest that was thinly populated and barren. Between them there remained a neutral zone of desert and mountain terrain.

The more that England has been celebrated as the land of political freedom, as the land of free trade, as the only country in Europe to which the small

10. The Qajar dynasty ruled the Sublime State of Persia from 1785 to 1925.

11. Under the corrupt rule of Mozaffar ad-Din Shah Qajar (1853–1907), many of the Sublime State's assets were pawned to imperial Russia.

12. During the "Great Bast" of July and August 1906, Persian protest leaders conducted open-air debates on constitutionalism in the gardens of the British embassy.

13. The Anglo-Russian Convention of 1907 was negotiated by British foreign secretary Edward Grey (1862–1933) and Russian ambassador to Britain Count Aleksandr Konstantinovich Benkendorf (Benckendorff) (1849–1917).

nations could reliably look as a potential protector, the greater the pain and the disappointment has been to see it in Persia betray its past, its principles, indeed even its true, deeper interests.

At the time the agreement was concluded, Russia was a defeated and impoverished power, whose army was in a state of dissolution and whose population was in rebellion. When England joined with it in Persia, it could not have meant anything other than *the purchase of Russia's goodwill and support in a coming war between Great Britain and the German kingdom.*[14]

Sir Edward Grey purchased it at great expense. The agreement was bitterly critiqued by the Englishmen who knew what conditions were in India, like former viceroy Lord Curzon, former viceroy in India. It was an old truism of England's politics that Persia's independence must be maintained because Persia was the buffer between Great Britain and Russia.[15] Sir Edward Grey evidently counted on the pact between the two powers lasting into eternity. The agreement shortened Russia's route to India; one of its first effects was England's consent for a Russian railway to be built from Baku through Tehran to Bombay.

The agreement was signed on August 31, 1907. In order to minimize and soften Persian indignation, the English minister issued an explanatory proclamation that spoke for both of the great powers:

They stood united for Persia's independence and inviolability; they would avoid any interference in Persian affairs, and even less would they do any violence against the persons or the property of their subjects. The agreement would permit Persia to focus all its powers on internal progress. All the rumors regarding England and Russia's plans for the country were groundless. Neither of the two great powers would allow any form of interference in Persian affairs under the pretext of national interests that must be preserved.

In this manner, the agreement acquired the character of a promise from the English side to be willing to hinder Russian encroachment.

A new shah, who both as heir apparent and as prince had pledged support for the constitution, had in the meantime ascended the throne, and promptly suspended the constitution he himself had issued.[16] The parliament had already intended to exile him as too unreliable in July 1908, but then both the Russian

14. Brandes is entirely correct here; the fate of Persia was an afterthought in the negotiations of 1907, which were motivated by a desire to resolve all outstanding Anglo-Russian disputes in preparation for war with Germany.

15. Brandes frequently cites George Nathaniel Curzon, 1st Marquess Curzon of Kedleston (1859–1925), who served as viceroy of India from 1899 to 1905, as a European authority on Asian affairs. His two-volume *Persia and the Persian Question* (1892) was for decades the principal English-language source of knowledge of the ancient kingdom.

16. Mohammad Ali Shah Qajar (1872–1925) ascended the throne in January 1907.

minister and the English chargé d'affaires let the Persian foreign ministry know that the shah's unseating would not be tolerated, thereby initiating Russian intervention; the Persians preferred the tyranny of one of their own rather than foreign subjugation.

The shah could then carry out his coup in Tehran. The Russian colonel Liakhov encountered only weak resistance when at the head of his Russian-Persian brigade he shelled the parliament building, while the shah executed the leading members of parliament and the publishers who had tried to seek refuge in the British legation.[17] Yet while Tehran submitted, the people of Tabriz defeated the shah's army and withstood a nine-month siege. When at last it was revealed that the residents of the city were nearly starved, and that the few Europeans to be found there were in mortal danger, a Russian army moved into Tabriz in April 1909.

Sir Edward Grey sanctioned this step and promised that the occupation of the city would be temporary. The Russian garrison has however still not departed.

Encouraged by the brave defense of Tabriz, a Persian army marched in the meantime toward the city from north and from south, defeated Liakhov and his Cossacks and deposed the shah. A regent was chosen as guardian of the shah's eleven-year-old son, and a new parliament was elected to take up the work interrupted by Liakhov.[18]

For the next two years Persia was at peace and its chief concerns financial. The state treasury was empty, since Persia's wealthy elite has avoided paying taxes by enlisting itself under Russian protection. Thievery, carried out by the former shah's supporters, was a national plague and served as a pretext for Russian occupation.[19]

Persia had to take on debt, and the two great powers offered a common loan in exchange for permission to take control of disbursements. In order to avoid such dependence Persia arranged a loan in London with one of the great banking houses, but the English foreign ministry refused permission, demanding that Persia should allow English officers to run the police in the south and threatening otherwise to dispatch an Indian army.

In the meantime, in May 1911 a remarkable diplomat from North America arrived, Morgan Shuster, who was on loan from the US government to Persia

17. Colonel Vladimir Platonovitch Liakhov (1869–1919), the commander of the Persian Cossack Brigade, which consisted of ethnic Caucasians and Persians under the command of Russian officers, ordered the shelling of the Majlis on June 23, 1908.

18. Ahmad Shah Qajar (1898–1930), the last of the dynasty, reined from July 1909 until deposed in December 1925.

19. Mohammad Ali Shah Qajar did not concede to his removal from power, and actively fomented unrest in the kingdom from exile in Russia.

in order to reorganize the state's finances. He displayed rare strength of character and ability to negotiate, inspiring in parliament such confidence that they gave him the powers nearly of an absolute monarch.[20] Morgan Shuster engaged an English major who spoke Persian and knew the country well to establish a gendarme corps that could collect the taxes. The Persian government therefore acquired the property that belonged to a brother of the deposed shah because he had sided with the former leader who was now raiding the country.[21] The Persian government placed Morgan Shuster in this brother's palace in Tehran. But his gendarmes were killed by Russian Cossacks and Russian troops marched on the capital.

Sir Edward Grey intervened, counseling the Persians toward compliance, and maintained that the Russian army would hold back if they gave in to its ultimatum, which was this: Morgan Shuster should be immediately dismissed, Russia and England should have a veto over all future appointments of foreigners in Persian service, and compensation should be paid to Russia.

When parliament stood faithfully by Shuster's side it was dissolved, and with that Persian independence came to an end. All of Russia's demands were met, and when the Russian press screamed for revenge it was taken in Tabriz, where a handful of volunteers had attacked Russian troops. A military tribunal was established, which hanged twenty-six of the leading men.[22] The highest clerical figure of the province was hanged on the Persian calendar's holiest day. As an English author remarked, this was like if the Germans had hanged the archbishop of Mechelen on Good Friday.[23]

Since then Persia has lain thunderstruck. The two great powers have brought about total anarchy. The British government, through the establishment of the Anglo-Persian Oil Company, has gained control of Persia's valuable oil fields; Persia will in the future provide the largest part of the petroleum the Royal

20. William Morgan Shuster (1877–1960), one of the very few genuine heroes of the present volume, served the Persian constitutional government loyally until his expulsion by the Russians in December 1911. His 1912 account of his brief tenure in the kingdom, *The Strangling of Persia*, is among the most powerful indictments of European imperialism produced by a Western author.

21. The seizure of the property of the Russian-aligned Shu'a al-Saltaneh was used as the formal pretext for the Russian intervention of 1911.

22. As noted by Shuster himself, the executions on the Tenth of Muharram were followed by more generalized reprisals all over Tabriz; thousands were murdered in a horrific manner. See *The Strangling of Persia* (New York: Century, 1912), 219–23.

23. Brandes refers to the nationalist cleric Mirza Ali-Aqa Tabriz (1861–1911), referred to as Seqat-ol-Eslam Tabrizi. Désiré-Félicien-François-Joseph Mercier (1851–1926) was archbishop of Mechelen during World War I and an advocate of nonviolent resistance to the occupying Germans.

Navy uses. Russia acquired not only fertile lands for its colonists to settle, but also a stretch of land, Persia's northwestern corner, that is related to Turkey and Russia in the same way Belgium is to France and Germany. In vain the Persians declared themselves neutral. A Russian forced passed through Persia to Van.[24] The only difference is that Russia was defeated.

Sir Edward Grey did not go to war to protect Persia's neutrality. The solemn promises to respect the neutrality of Asia's Belgium were broken like Prussia's solemn promises to respect the European Belgium.

All those who have celebrated and admired England as freedom's great power have suffered through witnessing her, in alliance with Russia, overwhelm a weak people precisely at that moment in its history in which it has begun to assert self-rule, quite like Poland was overwhelmed when it had given itself the remarkable constitution of May 3, 1791.[25]

In order to avoid the misunderstanding that I have, in my presentation of the situation, made myself into a spokesperson for a point of view informed by German sources, I shall expressly note that I have never seen any German writings regarding this matter, but have exclusively followed the English sources, just as in my previous articles I have had only the English materials before me. It is a testament to the greatness of the English people that many Englishmen preserve their political judgment from the influence of compulsory nationalism and partisan passion. E. D. Morel is a fine example, C. H. Norman another.[26] E. D. Morel, who ten years ago was equally adored in France and Great Britain, and who has the undeniable mark of the great personality, can comfortably accept that he has lost his position in parliament and his popularity in France; he is far superior to his opponents.

As far as I know he has not spoken out on Persia, but no one can be in doubt of where he stands.[27]

---

24. Brandes here refers to the Russian seizure of Van in May 1915, an event that played a crucial role in the beginning of the Armenian Genocide.

25. The defeat of Polish constitutionalists in 1795 resulted in the Third Partition of Poland.

26. Edmund Dene Morel (1873–1924) was the foremost advocate of British neutrality in the years before the outbreak of the war; he resigned his candidacy for Parliament due to increasing war fever, instead cofounding the pacifist pressure group Union for Democratic Control. In 1917 he served a six-month prison sentence for false allegations of treason. Clarence Harvey Norman (1886–1974) was an activist for various progressive causes in the years before the war; in June 1916 he was arrested for his anti-conscription activities, spending the remainder of the war in prison.

27. Morel was among the most prominent anti-imperial activists of the Belle Epoque, concerned particularly with African affairs; in 1904 with Roger Casement he founded the Congo Reform Association.

If the relationship between Great Britain and Persia has unfolded in the manner described here, then how is it possible that Mr. Archer could continue to view the world war in these simplistic, ethical-juridical terms:

Truth versus lies, good versus evil!

The relationship, however, is by no means unique. England has, in spite of much that is right in its behavior, no monopoly over the right. And in spite of its fundamental love of freedom, it has been far from principled as the defender of freedom against the representatives of despotism.

The very concept of *right* does not mean much politically, or as Lassalle in his *Assisen-Rede* expressed it:[28]

In the life of a people the idea of the right is a wrongheaded concept, for the law is only the expression of the will of society and never its master. And he speaks of the "rickety crutch" provided by the idea of the right.

When in 1674 Louis XIV occupied the ten imperial cities of Alsace and then in 1681 deprived Strasbourg of its rights, Alsace became French by the dubious right of conquest. When in 1871 Alsace was demanded back by Germany with the justification that the old injustice should be set right, there was universal sentiment in Europe that a bloody *injustice* had been done to France, even though in the Peace of Frankfurt the country *by law* became part of the German empire.[29]

The Danish people were in their time entirely convinced that the Augustenborgs were *in the wrong* in their claim to the Danish throne, which led to the duchy's revolt against Denmark, and not a single person in Denmark doubted that here was a matter of "truth versus lies, good versus evil."[30] In our time a Danish historian of the caliber of Professor Erslev has come to the conclusion that it was the Augustenborgs who were *in the right*—a matter that instructively

28. Ferdinand Lassalle (1825–64) was the principal founder of German social democracy. Brandes deeply admired the German Jewish philosopher and activist, profiling him in an 1877 German-language monograph. In 1848 Lassalle was arrested and tried for his actions in support of the popular uprisings of that year; his speech in his defense was published in 1849 as *Meine Assisen-Rede*.

29. Brandes addresses the Alsace-Lorraine conflict, so central to the outbreak of the Great War, in his essay "The Great Nations' Concern for the Small" in the present volume.

30. The Ducal House of Augustenborg was a cadet branch of the Danish royal House of Oldenburg. The death in 1863 of King Frederick VII, who had failed to produce a male heir, produced a succession crisis in Denmark; Duke Frederick Christian August of the Augustenborg line promptly proclaimed himself ruler of Schleswig-Holstein, setting the stage for the Dano-Prussian War of 1864.

enough has not made the most meager impression on Danish national opinion.[31] The national view has remained the same.

Everyone is in agreement that the concept of the right is of no concern to the German industrialists and bankers who demand annexations and who essentially view Belgium and Northern France as a source of *coal*. It should also be agreed that the English foreign ministry, which essentially views Persia as *petroleum* to be had, is itself not concerned with the right.

In both cases material considerations have been elevated above the right.

It is hardly correct to attack the neutrals for their lack of a sense of right and then insist on a struggle for the right.

An epigram of Goethe goes like this:

> Goats, to the left with you! the judge one day will ordain.
> And you, little sheep, stand quietly here on my right!
> Fair enough; but it is to be hoped that he will say one more thing, namely:
> As for you, stand right opposite me, you men of sense![32]

There will be no crowds forming opposite the judge.

31. Kristian Sophus August Erslev (1852–1930) was the father of modern Danish historiography.

32. Brandes cites Goethe's "Venezianische Epigramme XLVIII," trans. David Luke, in *Goethe: Selected Verse* (New York: Penguin, 1986), 117.

CHAPTER 32

Persia

1916

Following up his earlier remarks on Persia in "A Response to Mr. William Archer," Brandes published the much more comprehensive essay below later in the year. Notable as one of only two engagements with Asian affairs (the other being his essays on the Boxer Rebellion in China), the article is also important in that it addresses the more subtle form of colonial penetration known at the time as *une pénétration pacifique* (peaceful penetration). In his seminal 1922 Christiania address on imperialism, Brandes would return to this practice in its New World iteration, critiquing the US method of employing debt peonage and gunboat diplomacy as a means of soft conquest in Latin America.

~

For Sayyid Hasan Taqizadeh[1]

1. The most recent past

I

English foreign policy has never dared to reveal itself to be as weak and as miserable as it has been in its relations with Persia under Viscount Edward Grey.[2]

Originally published in *Politiken* in two parts, November 29 and December 1, 1916. Translated from the versions published in *Verdenskrigen.*

1. Sayyid Hasan Taqizadeh (1878–1970) was among the foremost advocates of Western Enlightenment ideals in Persia/Iran, as well as perhaps its most influential politician of the twentieth century. A leader of the constitutionalist movement and a deputy in the First Majles, he spent nearly two decades in exile after the coup of Mohammed Ali Shah in 1908. He supported Germany during the Great War as a foil against Anglo-Russian imperial ambitions, and was also a lifelong proponent of Persian literature and culture abroad, serving as editor and publisher of the Berlin-based journal *Kaveh* during his years in exile.

2. Edward Grey, 1st Viscount Grey of Fallodon (1862–1933), served as British foreign secretary from 1905 to 1916 and thus oversaw the signing of the Anglo-Russian Entente of 1907.

No longer is there an independent state as a buffer zone between the Caucasus and the southwestern border of India. The land route to India is no longer secure against Russia. The seventy-two million Mohammedans in India, who have always constituted a neutralizing force between the British government and the Hindus, have as a result of England's alliance with various so-called Christian states who have attacked Mohammedan countries (Morocco, Tripoli, Persia) set aside a good portion of their warm feelings for the government in London.[3] For the first time the Mohammedans have sent representatives to a Hindu congress, which they had previously refused to attend.[4]

Of lesser significance in the eyes of the world today is the fact that England, in eradicating Persian independence with the help of Russia, has not accomplished anything pleasant or good or worthy of praise. With respect to morality Europe has thrown in the towel. But a political act must, if it is not moral, at the very least be successful. Viscount Edward Grey's Persian policy has been neither.

One of the British statesmen who knows Asia best, Lord Curzon, said this about Persia during debate in the upper house on March 22, 1911: "I am convinced that the independence and inviolability of Persia, which *was guaranteed* by His Majesty's government in the prologue of the agreement of 1907, has no more enthusiastic champion than His Majesty's government."[5]

The honorable lord spoke here with a naïveté that would put a five-year-old child to shame.

Morgan Shuster has in one place or other said these fitting words regarding the English foreign minister:

> Sir Edward Grey is a man of good family, good manners, and splendid classical education. He would make an excellent foreign minister for a country like Switzerland. . . . The British Empire, however, is a different affair. Its interests extend beyond Europe, and beyond the grasp of a decidedly provincial gentleman whose longest sea voyage was across the English Channel and whose most tangible accomplishment during a lengthy public career is an authoritative treatise on dry fly-fishing. More than half of the British Empire lies in Asia, and Sir

3. Brandes refers to British alliances with France (which had annexed much of Morocco in 1904), Italy (which seized Tripoli in 1911), and Russia (which had in partnership with Britain partitioned Persia in 1907).

4. Warming relations between Hindus and Muslims in the Raj would soon result in the Lucknow Pact, signed by representatives of the Indian National Congress and the Muslim League in December 1916.

5. Brandes often cites George Nathaniel Curzon, 1st Marquess Curzon of Kedleston (1859–1925), viceroy of India from 1899 to 1905, as an authority on Asian affairs.

Edward Grey is not accused by even his most ardent supporters of having an Oriental conception or imagination.[6]

It is sweet to admire. It is painful to feel incapable of admiring statesmen who, in the commanding posts of the immense footprint that a great power leaves, have the gaze of the entire world fixed upon them every day that passes, and who capture the attention of everyone.

It is not because I believe that my admiration has any significance, but because of pure love of the truth and in order to state my opposition to the conventional wisdom of a thousand newspapers, that I will remark that in my understanding no statesman of the twentieth century has demonstrated such mastery of the craft as the American private citizen W. Morgan Shuster. And this man has been forced to retire from his profession and return to private life by conscienceless diplomats and the weak, narrow-minded ministers who support them.

If any proof were required to demonstrate how the powers who rule the earth are constituted, here it is.

I feel compelled once and for all to publicly declare my respect and profound sympathy for Morgan Shuster. It is baroque that a politician like Edward Grey has had the power as well as the weakness to allow Russia to remove this man from his post.

II

Persia's two so-called protectors, Russia and England, entered into an agreement in 1907 on "the Persian question" without consulting the country itself or advising it on what they were undertaking. Their plan sought to weaken the country by the most practical and effective means, what in diplomatic speak is called *une pénétration pacifique*. They began by destroying Persia's finances.[7] They attempted by every conceivable means to turn Persia's financial situation into chaos and bring the government of the country into the pitiable state of living from hand to mouth. The poor government was soon brought to such a degree of debasement that it had to bend its knee before the powers in order to obtain funds for the most essential and urgent expenditures, for sums such as a half million kroner or even less. It was necessary to beseech the two powers

6. Brandes cites from Morgan Shuster's *The Strangling of Persia*, 251–52. For Brandes's detailed profile of Shuster, who was removed from his post serving the Persian constitutionalist state because of Anglo-Russian demands, see "A Response to William Archer" in the present volume.

7. Shuster's removal had in fact been motivated by his efforts to establish a modern tax collection scheme in the kingdom.

for so little a sum, when need compelled it, and the two powers, who to the best of their abilities took advantage of the government's painfully difficult position, demanded allowances from it, political agreements, strategic treaties, and economic allowances that in a more severe sense are called *concessions* at the same time that the powers set the most severe conditions regarding rents, guarantees, and terms of payment. They demanded, under the threatened collapse of the entire machinery of state, and eventually received, such unheard-of rents as 7, 9, 12, 15, 18, indeed even 24 percent, sometimes with extremely short terms of repayment such as a single year, sometimes without any fixed terms. The running debt of the latter variety, repayment of which could at any moment be demanded, was a new tool in the kit of the two powers, since thereby they could without warning force their victim to accept any kind of proposal.

It is sad that the same states that pride themselves in having practiced usury by providing the natives with loans on miserable terms in places such as Egypt have, with the assistance of two simple institutions, the Russian and British banks, taken control of all Persian banking through the establishment of the Imperial Bank of Persia.[8] They led Persia into financial slavery and in an ignominious manner compelled it to sign over all of its natural resources, its rights, and its independence just so that it could survive from day to day.

It will likely be objected that Persia could have easily secured funds elsewhere, at the European and American exchanges. It could also without difficulty have acquired immense sums for the purpose of the management and development of productive official works, since Persia is a large country, three times the size of France, and with rich, as yet undeveloped natural resources.

But the country's two civilized neighbors have beforehand done everything within their power to close the door to that possibility and to make the kingdom economically as well as politically a prisoner, bound by thousands of fine, strong links and incapable of more than merely breathing. They have by every means, most often with threat of war, made every course of action impossible for Persia, deprived it of every form of freedom.

III

The Russian minister in Tehran, Prince Dolgorukov, had in 1890 under threat extracted a promise from the government not to build a railroad in Persia, nor within the next four years to give such a concession to any foreigner to carry out such a treacherous act, as detrimental to progress and civilization as

8. The Imperial Bank of Persia was founded in 1889 and served as the kingdom's state banking institution until 1929.

railroads are.[9] When the four years expired the agreement was renewed with the ban extending until 1910, when the last term ran out.[10]

At this point Persia (which had just then undergone a revolution and acquired a parliament) was, as is understandable, not very willing to give in to threats. Thus Russia and England together sent a declaration on April 7, 1910, to the Persian government to inform it that Persia dare never provide any kind of foreigner, individual or corporation, any kind of concession that would hinder any of the two powers' "political and strategic interests."[11]

The Persian government responded by asking which specific concessions were forbidden. The two powers then sent a second note on May 4 that explained their demands at great length, forbidding Persian concessions in the areas of telegraphy, harbors, and means of transport (railroads, highways, navigation, omnibuses, et cetera). At the same time the writers of the two countries and their presses added in defense of their behavior that Persia was "a half-barbaric country" without railroads or modern harbors. Last year Persia was still being referred to as a "half-barbaric country" by Mr. William Archer.[12]

One of the conditions Russia placed on the shah's initial loan of 22.5 million rubles in 1900 was that Persia would not be allowed to take on any foreign loan in the future without Russia's approval, as long as the final payment of this first loan had not been made—this with the intention of making Russia Persia's only creditor for the next seventy-five years. Another condition tied to the same loan was that Persia did not have the right to free itself from the loan before ten years had elapsed. The loan was as said for seventy-five years with 5 percent interest and a 15 percent premium.

As a condition for this loan Russia had next demanded that all the customs houses in Persia—with the exception of those on the Persian Gulf—should provide security for repayment, and that all income from the houses should

9. Russian interest in preventing Persia from establishing a modern rail system was in fact motivated by the British-sponsored establishment of the Imperial Bank of Persia in 1889. See Rose Greaves, "Iranian Relations with Great Britain and British India, 1798–1921," in *The Cambridge History of Iran*, ed. Steven Avery, Gavin Hambly, and Charles Melville (Cambridge: Cambridge University Press, 1991), 7:407.

10. Prince Nikolai Sergeevich Dolgorukov (1840–1913) aggressively promoted Russian interests against Britain during his tenure in Tehran.

11. The "April Note" of 1910 was motivated by fears of German efforts to secure railroad concessions in the kingdom, made possible by the expiry of the railroad ban that month. See Li-Chiao Chen, "British Policy on the Margins and Centre of Iran in the Context of Great Power Rivalry 1908–1914" (PhD diss., University of London, 2015), 125–26.

12. Brandes refers here to Archer's *Colour-Blind Neutrality: An Open Letter to Dr. George Brandes*. Brandes responded in detail on the Persian Question in his "A Response to Mr. William Archer."

go directly to the Russian *banque d'escompte* [bank of discount], an affiliate of the Russian state bank in Persia. The bank would then, after deducting the amounts for the loan (which constituted a third of all customs income), remit the remainder back to the Persian government or hold it in escrow at the disposal of the government, as it would reconcile the account every six months. In reality the bank withheld every sum Russia demanded for lost mail, expenditures for the Cossack brigade, et cetera.

When in this manner Russia placed the first chains around the neck of Persia there followed soon after a second loan of ten million rubles in 1902, with the same conditions. Each time Russia placed circumstances on the loan such that nearly half of the nominal amount was consumed on the first day.

England followed in Russia's path in 1904 and 1905, concluding two loans totaling 290,000 pounds or 5,200,000 kroner. Great Britain demanded as security for the rents the Persian fisheries on the Caspian Sea, the income of all telegraph offices in Persia, and all the income of the customs houses on the Persian Gulf—all this was intended to wreck politically the Persian state, whose income constituted more than ten times the small yearly payment of 23,000 English pounds that would be due.

IV

Thereafter began the system of small loans. The two banks, the Russian and the English, from then on maintained a running account with the Persian government, as from time to time after political torture they gave it small sums, such as 50,000, 20,000, or 10,000 pounds with usurious rates.

When then a revolution broke out in 1906 and a constitution was adopted, it was revealed that more than half a million pounds had piled up in the running account with the British bank and more than twice that in the Russian.

It would be too long a story to relate how these two banks came to Persia and monopolized the financial markets. The British bank obtained the exclusive right to issue paper currency in exchange for the promise to loan the Persian government a fifth of its capital at 9 percent interest when it was requested.[13] The Russian bank came to Russia with a capitalization of thirty million rubles with the goal of opening what was called "a political line of credit," and without the least concern for the creditworthiness of the loan recipient, dispensed to it sixteen million of its capital in Tehran and ten in the provinces in order to support influential reactionaries, certain landowners, a few corrupt priests, and the worst of the shah's hangers-on.

13. The currency monopoly was obtained in the establishment of the Imperial Bank in 1889.

With a nod from the Russian legation this bank was always prepared to hound and to compel any one of its debtors who did not intend to be subjected to this or to the new demands of the Russian government. The two banks worked systematically and crookedly to reach the point at which the majority of Persian banks and native firms went bankrupt. With this intention they employed every legal and illegal means, thus destroying the effectiveness and eventually the existence of native businesses. Persia tried to sell its crown jewels.[14] The two powers intervened and prevented it.

Russia and England eventually had concessions over everything imaginable, on all of Persia's telegraphy, on the mines in the richest districts, on the petroleum fields, on the fisheries in the Caspian Sea, on the timber rights from the great Caspian forests, on the trams and on the shipping on the sea, on the highways and the roads, and a concession to raise a Persian Cossack brigade in Tehran under Russian officers. And these concessions were always acquired by means in conflict with Persian law.

When the constitution was adopted it was hoped that the parliament, which now had supreme authority, would not allow the government to bend before threats, but offer resistance to any further plundering of the rights of the natives. In reality the parliament did even more than expected, exerting such power that everyone saw it was capable of rescuing the country, and at least not permitting the addition of new forms of bondage to the innumerable forms that had already been placed around the freedom of the country.

But now began Russia's covert efforts to overthrow the representative government by any means possible. They left behind nothing of Persia's constitution. And when it was apparent that the people supported the parliament so heartily that no subterfuge could sap its courage or make it unpopular, Russia openly encouraged the shah to dissolve it. The shah then overthrew the parliament with the help of the Russian officers of the Cossack brigade and with the financial support of the Russian bank.[15]

This is the event that led to the revolution. After a year's struggle with the reactionary troops of the shah, who were supported by Russia, the revolution was triumphant. The shah was deposed and a new popular government

14. Persian efforts during the war to secure an American loan using its immensely valuable crown jewels as collateral were ultimately blocked by Anglo-Russian interference. See Mohammed Gholi Majd, *The Great Famine and Genocide in Iran: 1917–1919*, 2nd ed. (Lanham, MD: University Press of America, 2013), 124–27.

15. Mohammed Ali Shah dissolved the First Majlis and annulled the constitution in 1908; in June Colonel Vladimir Platonovitch Liakhov (1869–1919), commander of the Persian Cossack Brigade, shelled the Majlis building.

established.[16] The new parliament (the second), which had the whole nation behind it, all of the leading men of the people and the Mohammedan clergy, immediately proceeded to institute all kinds of reforms and to reorganize the various areas of administration, especially the financial.

V

The British government as well as the Russian was now seized with a great impatience. Russia fomented a long series of troubles, provocations, and counterrevolutions, and did what it could to bring about anarchy. Russian officers and agents tried to break the resistance of the Persian people and weaken the authority of the government. Yet the new government overcame all difficulties. Its most ingenious step was to request from the American government a man who could be placed at the head of Persia's finances, receiving the brilliant selection of W. Morgan Shuster, whose effectiveness in foreign countries under the most difficult conditions ought to be viewed as the most admirable example of administration and energy our century has witnessed from a single individual.

It is not necessary to describe the Russian intrigues in Persia in detail, since there is no small number of writings on these, published by the Persia Committee in London, which consists of both freethinking members of the English Parliament and other leading men.[17]

When Russia at last set loose the former shah, one of the most depraved individuals the East has ever produced, allowing him to once again set foot on Persian land, the intention was to topple the parliament and destroy Morgan Shuster's work of renewal.[18] It was a hard time for Persia and its reform party, since it had to fear that the reaction would once again be triumphant. Yet by virtue of the power of the people's instinctive decisiveness and the energy of the leadership the effort was stalled, and the former shah's troops neutralized.

The moment had arrived in which Russia, if it was to dominate Persia, must demonstrate reckless energy. It sent an ultimatum in December 1911, marched its troops to Qazvin in the vicinity of Tehran and had Morgan Shuster ousted, the parliament dissolved, and every nationalist movement suppressed.

Following the coup a period of reprisals ensued in Tabriz, Resht, Mashhad, and other cities. In Tabriz alone more than a hundred distinguished patriots,

---

16. Mohammed Ali Shah was deposed in July 1909; the Second Majlis convened in November.

17. The Persia Committee was formed in 1908 to oppose Edward Grey's Persian policy.

18. Mohammad Ali Shah attempted to retake the throne in 1911.

among them the highest-ranking Mohammedan priest, national leaders, and members of the provincial parliament, were subjected to torture, dismemberment, and hanging.[19] The Russians appointed as governor in the important province of Azerbaijan a known bandit chieftain, who with the sanction of his bosses inflicted unheard-of barbarisms for three years upon the unlucky province.[20] He had one of the nationalist volunteers cut in half and then had the two parts of his body strung up in different parts of the city. He had another of the leaders, a priest, dismembered alive and then had his eyes poked out. Professor Edward Browne of Cambridge, the foremost European scholar of modern Persia, has published a whole little book with instructive photographs of the activities of a single regiment in Tabriz in 1912.[21]

2. The Present

When Russia and England had done away with the Persian parliament and with Morgan Shuster and had set up a new Persian government, they began to demand everything they could want, in part by applying financial pressure of the most severe kind and in part by threat of war; the Russian troops billeted in Qazvin could with a nod occupy the capital Tehran. In this way they obtained concessions of the railroad from Sulfa via the border of the Caucasus to Tabriz and further beyond, and from Muhammarah on the Persian Gulf to Khorramabad in central Persia.[22] Indeed they forced the Persian government into an official acknowledgement of the Anglo-Russian Entente of 1907, which every Persian ministry had up to then refused to do.

They compelled the government to promise not to establish a national army without first consulting the two powers. One by one they deprived Persia of all the rights of a sovereign nation. They brought the state finances into such a state of hopeless ruin that they could obtain compliance on every point by threatening to cut off the tap for a month.

Russian subjects as well as those persons under Russian protection, who every day became more numerable, were exempted from paying taxes. After long negotiations Russia finally conceded that they would have to pay, but only to the Russian consulate, which would then transfer the revenue to the Persian government through the Russian bank. In this manner the Russians

19. For more on the Tabriz atrocities, see note 22 in "A Response to Mr. William Archer."

20. As noted by Richard W. Cottam, Shoja al-Doleh, widely known as an agent of imperial Russia, was among the most hated men in the kingdom. See *Nationalism in Iran: Updated through 1978* (Pittsburgh: University of Pittsburgh Press, 1979), 176–77.

21. Cambridge Orientalist Edward Browne (1862–1926), a prominent member of the Persia Committee, published *The Reign of Terror at Tabriz: England's Responsibility* in 1912.

22. Mohammerah is now known as Khorramshahr.

got their hands on roughly one-third of Persian property taxes, which were the country's most important source of income. From these funds they withheld every sum they asserted Persia had to pay to Russian subjects, either in pensions or as compensation or for other reasons.

Persia was therefore in a state of miserable suffering when the European war broke out. Within the Persian soul there was vehement hatred for and such inflamed passion against their tyrants that there is hardly any embitterment between two European peoples that measures up to that of the Persians toward Russia. The Shiite high priest of Mesopotamia had already agreed with the Turkish sultan on the declaration of holy war.[23] The impact of the new murders in Tabriz, the sight of the hanged leaders, and especially the shelling of the most sacred shrine of the Shiites, that of Imam Reza in Mashhad, had incensed the people to the utmost so that they dreamed only of revenge. Nevertheless the Persian government understandably refrained from exhibiting any inclination to take advantage of the difficulties Russia faced. Persia declared itself neutral and the government did everything in its power to keep the people peaceful. They succeeded completely, and it was their original intent to remain neutral in the true sense of the word.

Russia however immediately violated Persia's neutrality in the first months of the war by arresting the Turkish and Austrian consuls in Tabriz. England followed this example by arresting the Turkish consul in Bashir (on the Persian Gulf). Thereafter followed a whole series of outrageous violations of neutrality in spite of the numerous protests of the Persian government.[24]

In November 1915, Russian troops finally marched on Tehran under the pretext of the danger to which they were exposed by the spread of German learning there. This march brought about the emigration of all nationalists, all members of the earlier parliament, all journalists, as well as all the ministers and subjects of the Central Powers. The Persian leaders, with the memory of the atrocities in Tabriz in mind, fled to the provinces of central Persia; the German subjects sought to reach the Turkish border. The government and the young shah were also planning to flee Tehran, when at the last minute the shah was persuaded by the British and Russian ministers to remain in the capital. In part they reassured him that the Russian troops would remain outside Tehran and in part they threatened that he would lose his throne if he left the capital.

23. The jihad against Russia, Britain, and France was ultimately declared by Sheikh ul-Islam, the Ottoman supreme religious official, on November 14, 1914, three days after the Ottoman Empire had formally entered the war. As a nominally independent state with a large Shia majority, Persia was not subject to it.

24. Most egregiously, a Russian army transited northern Persia en route to Van in the eastern Ottoman Empire.

The representatives of the two great powers gave their word of honor that the Russian troops would not set foot in Tehran. This word was kept if one does not count the fact that from time to time small groups began quietly slipping into the city, so that there are a good many Russian soldiers and officers there. But officially none have entered.

But later, when the unavoidable conflict between Persian volunteers and the Russians in the provinces broke out, the Russians poured in under the pretext of fighting the nationalists from central to western Persia all the way to Isfahan. Gradually they occupied more than half of the country with the intention of attacking the Turks in the flank from Persian territory. Now the fate of Persia is in the hands of the war gods, and this rarely turns out well, even less so with respect to justice.

The Persian tragedy is doubtless no less dreadful than that of Belgium; Persia is just as innocent, and none of the pretexts that have been claimed as an excuse for all the misery that has rained down on unhappy Belgium can be employed as an excuse for the damage done to Persia.

European governments have, without opposition from the peoples they rule, simply deprived the Persian nation the right to exist, because they are an Eastern people. Modern European barbarism has forgotten how much Europe owes Persia's ancient civilization, all the way back to the time when persecuted thinkers from Rome and Byzantium found refuge with Khosrow the Great, when German literature through Goethe sought renewal among Hafez and Saadi, through Nietzsche's seeking support from Zarathustra and English literature through Fitzgerald's seeking of joie de vivre in Omar Khayyam.[25]

The talents and the powers that the people still possess today are evidenced not only by the energy with which they carried out a revolution, but by the unanimity with which they established a parliament and with the brilliant eye with which they chose a statesman like Morgan Shuster, to whom such highly regarded foreign ministers as Edward Grey and premiers such as Aristide Briand cannot compare.[26]

---

25. Khosrow I (501–79) is often referred to as the "Persian Philosopher King"; his capital served as a refuge for Greco-Roman learned scholars fleeing the oppression of Justinian I. Medieval Persian poets Khwāja Shams-ud-Dīn Muḥammad Ḥāfeẓ-e Shīrāzī (1315–90, pen name Hafez) and Abū-Muhammad Muslih al-Dīn bin Abdallāh Shīrāzī (ca. 1208–ca. 1291–94, pen name Saadi) were the inspiration for Goethe's *West-östlicher Divan*. Nietzsche's famous Zarathustra is of course based on the Persian prophet Zoroaster. Edward Fitzgerald (1809–83) first published his translation of Omar Khayyam's (1048–1131) *Rubáiyát* in 1859.

26. Aristide Briand (1862–1932) served eleven terms as French prime minister, including a year and a half during the Great War (October 1915 to March 1917).

Such a people have claim to better treatment and greater interest than they have received from our age's half-civilized Europeans, who are most occupied with slaughtering each other and spreading their Mongoloid civilization to a purely Aryan people like the Persians, who have so ably avoided mass murder. These people are the inheritors of an ancient culture compared to which that of their oppressors emerged only the day before yesterday.

Such irony that these European peoples who fight for ideals—one cannot recall offhand which one, but always it is elevated and eternal—have allowed matters in Persia to go this way, even though (for a half century) everything went to hell under the leadership of despotic shahs not even of Persian heritage, who lived only to amuse themselves at the expense of the people and who led the country into deepest ruin.[27] When Persia's neighbors had leave to suck the blood of the people and gnaw away at the roots of the country, they tolerated every act of lawlessness and tyranny, and found it only natural and reasonable that the country lay in darkness and that corruption spread.

But as soon as the Persian people showed themselves to be so lively and spirited that they wanted to recapture the prerogative of Western peoples, wanted to build railroads and harbors, provide themselves a constitution, establish a parliament, a modern government, so that the surviving system of plunder by concessions, by usurious loans and the resulting slavery began to encounter insurmountable hindrances, then Russia, with Viscount Edward Grey in tow, intervened, suspended the constitution, cracked down. As long as the state finances were dissolute everything was fine. But when Persia awakened, when it would have a strikingly honest system of management instituted and gave the only man who in our age has demonstrated surprising abilities of state, Morgan Shuster, the power, when the nation in other words drove out the wretched powers that be, who sucked its marrow and sold off its riches, then the powers cowardly, crushingly intervened, drove out the worthy ones, introduced European justice, freedom, civilization, and raised up gallows for the leaders, for the best among them, foremost of all the gallows that loomed high over the little people, by which Persia itself was strangulated.

Entirely peacefully the old religious fanaticism of this country had exchanged places with a new spirit of tolerance, so that the constitution granted equal rights to the adherents of the different religions. How worthy it is that this constitution was dissolved by Europe at the butt of a machine gun!

Even during the revolution Persia demonstrated its high level of civilization, for even in the midst of a civil war not a single foreigner was affronted or

27. The Qajars were in fact of Turkic descent.

abused. Every European in Persia during this time of uproar was treated with the same hospitality in which individual Persians take such pride. Is there any other country about which it can with truth be said that during a revolution and civil war not a single foreigner—and a foreigner of a different religion at that—has in the least manner been victimized?

In antiquity during its great power days (558–330 BCE), Persia was a mighty kingdom with an elevated civilization and beautiful architecture, whose fate was remarkably tied to that of Greece. All children to this day read about Cyrus the Great, about Cambyses, about wise and powerful Darius.[28] It was the son-in-law of the king, Mardonius, who suffered the defeat at Marathon, where Aeschylus fought as a soldier.[29] Every child still knows of Xerxes's defeat, knows that Alcibiades turned to the king of Persia to save Athens from Sparta, that Xenophon went into Persian military service and led his ten thousand Greeks back when the younger Cyrus was slain.[30] Everyone knows that Alexander the Great tried to merge the Persian and Greek peoples into one people, even went about in Persian dress, and married Darius's daughter Stateira.[31]

At the time when all of this took place, Europe's Western as well as Eastern powers still did not exist as states and had still not yet appeared on the horizon of civilization. They lived, like we ourselves still live, as civilized people upon the foundation laid by Plato and by Aristotle, the teacher of Alexander, who made Persia and Greece into one kingdom, by men like Aeschylus, Sophocles, Euripides, Aristophanes, and all the others who are forgotten.

How curious is the course of fate! Two thousand years passed during which Persia and Greece had their own fates, differentiated without parallel until now in the great year of 1916, in which so many remarkable and surprising events have taken place, when their fates meet again. Both had sunk from their peaks

---

28. Cyrus II (c. 600–530) was the founder of the first or "Achaemenid" Persian Empire; he is of course particularly revered in the Jewish tradition, having secured the return of the Jews from the Babylonian exile. He was followed by Cambyses (d. 522 BCE) and then by Darius I (ca. 550–486), under whom the empire reached its apex.

29. Brandes is in error here; Mardonius (d. 479 BCE), was in fact relieved by Darius prior to Marathon.

30. Xerxes I (518–465 BCE) succeeded Darius I; he is of course best remembered today as the initiator of the failed second Persian invasion of Greece. Aeschylus (ca. 525–445 BCE), the father of Greek tragedy, was the author of *The Persians*, based on the second Persian invasion. Alcibiades (ca. 450–404 BCE), a recurring figure in the *Dialogues* of Plato, served as an adviser to the Persian satrap Tissaphernes from 412 to 411 BCE, attempting, according to Thucydides, to enlist the Persians on the Athenian side against Sparta. Xenophon (ca. 430–354 BCE) served as a leader of the Greek mercenary band the Ten Thousand in Cyrus the Younger's campaign against Artaxerxes II.

31. Stateira II (d. 323 BCE) married Alexander in 324 BCE.

in antiquity, and now we witness how Europe's Western powers and its Eastern in unison have administered to Persia and Greece the healing and strengthening European medicine. Both Persia and Greece avoided taking this bitter drink for as long as possible, much like children in their ignorance refuse bitter medicine.[32] But in no instance here does dear mother help! The hands of both Persia and Greece are tied, and now they reluctantly enjoy European civilization in large, ill-tasting, handy spoonfuls.

32. The efforts of the young Greek state to remain neutral in the Great War ended with the landing of French and British troops at Thessaloniki in the fall of 1915.

CHAPTER 33

The Armenians

1917

The formal occasion for Brandes's final essay on Armenia was the appearance in 1917 of Inga Nalbandian's (1879–1929) *The Great Misery*, the first in a trilogy of volumes describing the atrocities of 1915 and 1916. A scion of one of Copenhagen's most prominent literary families—her grandfather Jonas Collin had been the principal sponsor of a young Hans Christian Andersen—Nalbandian was herself a survivor of the genocide, having narrowly escaped Constantinople in 1916 after the death of her Armenian husband. The trilogy, which has been newly published in English (*Your Brother's Blood Cries Out*, Gomidas, 2007), is among the very first attempts to depict the catastrophe for a European audience. While Brandes here pushes back forcefully against the negative Armenian stereotypes circulating in Europe, the essay is distinguished from his earlier writings in that Brandes is much more evenhanded in his portrayal of the Armenian people, in particular lamenting a perceived tendency toward extreme factionalism.

~

I

A young Danish lady, the widow of a prominent Armenian, has written a book titled *The Great Misery*, in which, in about a dozen brief and compelling stories that stay close to reality, she has managed to provide a presentation of the martyrdom that one of the world's oldest civilized nations has suffered during the world war. Although Jews and Poles, Belgians and Frenchmen have endured immeasurable suffering during the war, no people has been martyred and murdered as has occurred in the extermination of the Armenian people.

Mrs. Inga Nalbandian's book provides a not unwelcome occasion for one who has been absorbed with the fate of the Armenian people for more than twenty years to collect his impressions on their ways and their activities.

Originally published in *Politiken*, May 17, 1917. Translated from the versions published in *Verdenskrigen*.

Immediately before the desperate Armenian uprising against the Turks and Kurds began, of which the first terrible massacre of the Armenians in Turkey was a consequence, Holger Drachmann gave expression to the vulgar European view of Armenia in his *Renaissance*, in that he has his character Tintoretto say: "The one Christian cheerfully screws the other; a Jew readily screws five Christians; but an Armenian screws ten Jews."[1] This was the kind of proverb that revealed just about the sum total of what Europe thought and knew about Armenians in 1894. A young German lady, Ilse Frapan, who was descended from a Huguenot family and was married to an Armenian, encountered this view, which was current at the time, and was likewise incensed and unhappy that the German kingdom, which was Abdul Hamid's protector, did not make any effort to hinder the horror.[2]

Pierre Quillard, who knew the Armenians intimately and for years published the journal *Pro Armenia* in their defense and their honor, aptly wrote this after a three-year stay in Constantinople: "From the fact that the majority of the *saraf* (money changers) are Armenians, Europeans conclude all too quickly that all the Armenians are money changers. That the honesty of the brokers in the bazaar is doubtful is true whether they are Greeks, Armenians, Jews, or Levantines; but who judges a people according to the failings of an individual, when these failings belong more properly to the profession than to the race!"[3]

Since the great mass of Armenians are agriculturalists, and since those who have acquired higher education have evinced particular artistic, industrial, and warlike talents, it does not pass muster to try and limit their capacities to cunning in business affairs.

In Turkey the development of industry and business is due in large part to them. Turkish fabrics, embroidery, and rugs are exported by them; Turkish jewelry is in fact Armenian. The loveliest buildings in Constantinople, the Mosque of Suleiman, the Beylerbeyi Palace, the Çırağan and the Dolmabahçe, indeed even the Yildiz Kiosk were built by Armenian architects.[4]

1. Holger Drachmann (1846–1908), an early disciple of Brandes, here voices the disturbing European tendency to ascribe antisemitic tropes to the Armenians, a phenomenon that first began to crystallize in reporting on the Hamidian Massacres of 1894–96.

2. Ilsa Frapan-Akunian (1849–1908) was, like Inga Nalbandian, one of the many European authors who came to Armenian activism through marriage.

3. French Symbolist poet Pierre Quillard (1864–1912) was an energetic Dreyfusard as well as the most prominent defender of Armenia at the turn of the twentieth century.

4. As first evinced in his 1900 essay "Armenia," Brandes tends to overestimate the role of the Armenians in the flowering of Ottoman culture and economy, while at the same time unfairly downplaying the role of the Turks.

As everyone rapidly comes to know, the Armenians are distinguished by their industriousness, their hard-knuckled perseverance, and by the civility that invariably is testament to an old culture.

For my part I have never seen other than goodwill in those with whom I have come into contact. Naturally they have failings, and how can these failings possibly help but have developed among a people who are divided between three powers, and who (if not completely poorly treated in Russia and Persia) have been subjected to indescribable abuse in Turkey, where their old homeland lies? The Armenians have and continue to suffer, just as the Jews have in Russia and Romania.

But when I have often heard words of praise for the Turks and their tolerance, when it has been observed that the Greeks, who just as much as the Armenians are Christians, have not in our time had cause to complain about Turkish dominance, then it is understandable that all around Europe it has been asked how it is that the Armenians alone among the Turk's non-Mohammedan subjects have set their masters into a bloodthirsty rage.

The answer is not easily found. In general, one is hated most vehemently for his successes. Now and then, however, one is also hated for his failings.

One characteristic that has struck me as particularly pronounced among the Armenians is their passionate partisanship and their therefore no less passionate internal disunity and ill will. Danes do not hate each other as thoroughly as Armenians hate each other. At the beginning of the century I was sought out by many Armenians unknown to me while in Paris; they came willingly in the morning around the same time. If I had an Armenian visitor and allowed another to deliver his visiting card, as a rule I would ask: "Perhaps you do not wish to meet with this gentleman?" and show the card. Without a single exception the answer was: "gladly not!," at which point I would just as invariably say: "I will ask you to go down the stairs, while I allow your countryman to take the elevator." In this way every awkward encounter was avoided.

With respect to politics the Armenians have long persisted in the state of a primitive people. Disagreement manifested itself in murder and attempted murder, which was met with blood revenge. Newspaper readers may perhaps recall how around the year 1903 two Armenian leaders were shot down while on a walk outside London by a third Armenian, who had traveled to England only to commit the murder.[5] I myself have experienced the following: a highly distinguished Armenian whom I had long known was around that time attacked

5. The 1903 murders of Agram Grigorian and Sigran Szmician followed shortly after the killing of Sagatel Sagouni, president of the Armenian Revolutionary Society. All three men were attending a convention in London on the Armenian question.

while he was on an evening stroll with his fiancée, a young Armenian lady, in a little Swiss town. The murderer who walked behind him stuck him twice in the back with his dagger and escaped while the victim fell bleeding. He hovered a long time between life and death, more or less coming to after half a year.

A year after the attempted assassination I received in Copenhagen a visit from a rich Armenian factory owner from Cairo. When I spoke with disapproval of the political passions within his people that could call forth such an assassination attempt, I received this answer: "You must not forget that this assassination attempt was a well-earned punishment." "For what offense?" "Because the victim had had two Armenians murdered, while they were traveling in the Caucasus." When I refused to believe the correctness of this explanation, the factory owner ended our conversation at that point in this manner: "There is no doubt about it. The murder was committed, and in his pocket there was still the letter from your friend, which engaged the man to carry out the assassination."

Such extreme political hate and lust for revenge still tore apart this people at the beginning of the present century, this people who were continually subjected to massacres by the enemy.

Another characteristic has struck me about the Armenians that corresponds to their hard-knuckled pursuit of their enemies: their knowledge of each other's private relations and their partisanship in this. By a twist of fate one of my Armenian acquaintances, who had a splendid wife, fell passionately in love with his cousin, a young Armenian girl whom he only then had gotten to know. He abandoned his wife in order to live near the other woman. For half a year the Armenian colonies in London as well as Paris spoke of nothing else. Without fail this would be said when his name came up: "you know, he is in love with his cousin," and a passionate condemnation would follow. The Armenians boycotted him wherever they could. He then left London, where he had lived for many years, and sought me out in Paris in order to ask me to encourage Pierre Quillard to give him permission to write for *Pro Armenia*. By chance I met Quillard that same day on the plaza outside my hotel, stopped, and put forward my request. Quillard answered me: "Perhaps you don't know that he is in love with his cousin." Yes, I answered, that seems to be of world historical significance, but it can't really prevent him from writing for *Pro Armenia*. "Unfortunately it does," was the answer. "I'd have all the Armenians here at my throat if I took him on as a collaborator. It is necessary for me to decline."[6]

6. Brandes refers here to Avetis Nazarbekian (1866–1939), former husband to Mariam Vardanian (1864–1941); it was the Nazarbekians who introduced Brandes to the Armenian cause in 1900.

That partisanship is highly developed among the Armenians could come as a surprise, insofar as they do not have a state. When in the year 1903 I arrived in Berlin to speak on the cause of Armenia at the request of the Armenian Student Union in Europe, which had its base in Geneva, I was met at the train station by nine young students.[7] I jokingly asked them how many different parties they belonged to, and they answered without a blink "nine, in part political, in part religious." It ought to be added that they nevertheless did appear to be the best of comrades. But in the most remarkable manner their sorrow over the unfortunate fate of their countrymen was paired with a southern and youthful joie de vivre. The Armenian evening at which I was to give my speech on the horrors committed against them in Turkey (the description of which was so gruesome that no small number of ladies got up and left the hall) was according to the plan of the students followed by a reading of various poems and concluded, to my great surprise, with a lively dance.

It is no mere coincidence that Lord Byron, the defender of the oppressed Italians, the spokesman of the rebellious Greeks, came to occupy himself with the language and the ways of the Armenians.[8] If he did not play the main role in the Armenian grammar that was published with his and his Armenian teacher's names on the title page, then he has, in San Lazzaro near Venice, where the book was produced with pride, studied the history of the Armenians and provided the people with this warm testimony: "It would be difficult, perhaps, to find the annals of a nation less stained with crimes than those of the Armenians, whose virtues have been those of peace, and their vices those of compulsion."

There are few peoples with more knowledge of languages than the Armenians. Like the Phoenicians in antiquity they have conducted trade with the Mediterranean countries and can speak their languages. Outside of Armenian they speak as a rule Russian, Turkish, and Persian, as well as French, English, and German. It is not rare that the numerous Armenians who are educated in Russian schools speak Russian among themselves.

The most educated among them are in possession of a thoroughly European culture. The monks in San Lazzaro who belong to their Roman Catholic minority are naïvely convinced that all the misfortunes of the Armenians are due to the fact that they have held onto their old, Gregorian form of Christianity.[9] If they had become Catholic, then the pope and the Catholic powers would have protected them.

---

7. See "Armenia and Europe" in the present volume.

8. Byron studied Armenian under the tutelage of scholar-monks of the Mekhitarist order in Italy.

9. Brandes here refers to the monastic order of the Mekhitarists in Italy, founded by Mkhitar Sebastatsi (1676–1749).

In our time the Armenians have upheld their old reputation as poets and artists. Arshag Chobanian, who with never-ceasing enthusiasm has translated Armenia's folksongs into French and who himself has written lovely poems, has made Europe aware of the poetry of his fatherland.[10] Edgar Chahine, who like Chobanian lives in Paris, has deservedly won himself a great name as a painter and etcher.[11] Anyone who has visited his atelier and enjoyed his company knows that he is an outstanding individual as well as an original and independent painter. The painter Makhokian who a few years ago visited Denmark had made such an impression in Germany that the kaiser felt the urge to purchase one of his paintings.[12]

A whole series of Russia's best generals during its earlier campaigns in Asia, Loris-Melikov, Lazarev, and many others, were Armenians.[13] Nubar Pasha, who liberated Egypt from Turkish dominance and introduced a European-style administration to the country, was also an Armenian.[14]

As long as Abdul Hamid governed, people blamed the "Red Sultan" for all the murderous acts against the Armenian population, which in the years 1894–96 and at intervals since have been committed against this richly talented tribe, so that by the conclusion of the previous century 300,000 had been wiped out. The revolution of the Young Turks was thus greeted with great expectations.[15] Now European civilization had come to the helm, now universal tolerance was proclaimed; the Armenians would finally be able to breathe freely.

And so in recent years the unarmed Armenian people have been cut down, to an extent that hardly anything in the current age may correspond. The number of the murdered exceeds one million by several hundred thousand.[16]

With respect to public opinion in Europe, which, however, only provokes intervention when the country in which the opinion thrives stands to benefit therefrom, Turkish legations found it correct and wise to send out portfolios with Turkish, German, French, and English text, whose pictures—photographs

10. Arshag Chobanian (1872–1954) was one of the principal figures of modern Armenian literature, as well as a dedicated activist on behalf of his people.

11. Edgar Chahine (1874–1947) was a French Armenian painter and engraver.

12. Vartan Makhokian (1869–1937) was an Armenian painter who studied in Berlin and later achieved fame in France.

13. Mikhail Loris-Melikov (1826–88) and Ivan Davidovich Lazarev (1820–79) served with distinction in the Russo-Turkish War of 1877–78.

14. Nubar Nubarian Pasha (1825–99) was the first prime minister of Egypt.

15. The Young Turk movement overthrew the sultan in July 1908, inaugurating the Second Constitutional Era of the Ottoman Empire.

16. While the death toll of 1915 remains among the most disputed figures in modern history, Brandes's figure is well within the conventional range of estimates.

of armed men and weapons and emblems from 1895—give an impression of the dangers that threatened the Turkish kingdom from the Armenian minority, and also to send out a Russian (with French translation) report from General Mayevsky, which in sensible and restrained expression describes the revolutionary movement that in the middle and end of the 1890s (apparently with powerful encouragement from the English consulate) broke out in Armenian territory. But everything that was therefore brought to the attention of the reader has absolutely no relation to the horrors that have taken place during the world war. Any defense of them has still not been offered. Will the Armenian people rise again now after this most recent, terrible bloodbath?

Arshag Chobanian has provided the answer, in his book on Armenian folksongs from 1903 in which he refers to Henrik Ibsen's poem on the eider duck, applying to the Armenian nation what is said therein about the repeatedly abused bird and its plundered nest.[17] The fisherman plunders the nest down to the last scrap:

If the fisherman is cruel, then the bird is warm;
he plucks again his own breast.
And when he is plundered again, he builds
his nest anew in a well-hidden corner.

Unfortunately, a nation cannot like the bird spread its wings outward and with bloody breast take flight. But even those who are devoid of hopeful expectations dare dream that the coming peace will secure Armenia's future differently and better than earlier agreements and peace treaties have managed.

II

Those who would know how humanity is faring at the moment ought to read Mrs. Inga Nalbandian's book. It looks at reality straight on, describes grippingly, without revealing any feeling or indignation, conditions as they were and are.

It is a woman's book, and therefore has its strength in portraying the passive, the forms of suffering of existence; it is not a book about action, but about agonies. In a way, it is an answer to another outstanding book, a German volume that has appeared in translation, *The Aviator of Tsingtao*, which is sheer manliness, sheer captivating action, while this other book is sheer womanliness, humanity and resignation.[18]

---

17. Ibsen's "Ederfuglen" was composed in 1851.

18. Brandes here refers to a 1916 best-selling adventure memoir, Gunther Plüschow's (1886–1931) *Die Abenteuer des Fliegers von Tsingtau.*

The Turks have lately sent out a pamphlet: *Response a la Presse Française* (*Dementies, opposes par le clergé superieur de la Syrie et de la Paléstine aux mensonges des journaux français*) [Response to the French press (The lies of the French newspapers denied and opposed by the higher clergy of Syria and Palestine)], which under current conditions leaves a purely dreadful impression.[19] The obsequious addresses from the bishops and patriarchs of the Christian congregations in Asia Minor were of course produced under compulsion, but they nevertheless provide an unusually depressing testimony of priestly servility and are at any rate authentic.

These worthies do not even hint at the violent extermination of upward of a half million Christian Armenians, a barbarism more shocking and on a larger scale than anything witnessed during the darkest days of the Middle Ages. What can be said about this exceeds every expectation of human mendacity and baseness.

As is known the murders of the Armenians took place under cover of the lovely military-political designation of *evacuation*. This year *the evacuation* has been extended to the Jews of Jaffa.[20]

And it is the very same Djemal Pasha, who has been lauded as the good angel of Asia Minor by the archbishops, who has ordered this.[21]

Insofar as the reports coming in can be relied upon, on April 1 he gave the order that the Jews of Jaffa as well as those from numerous colonies the Zionists had established in Palestine at such great cost should be expelled, and that with only forty-eight hours warning, without the possibility of transport or for the expelled to get permission to take their provisions with them. Their homes, like those of the Armenians, were plundered, even before they had left them, and within sight of the Turkish authorities. Now he has ordered that all young Jews of military age who reside in Jerusalem shall be expelled.

In the addresses to Djemal, the source of all these horrors, from the patriarch of Antioch, Gregory IV, from the Maronite patriarch, Elias Peter Hoyek, and from the Greek Catholic kaimakam, Dimitrios Cady, is found this:

> With respect to the care, the fatherly solicitude, the exemplary humanity that our esteemed government displays for every want of the people, no one is more

19. Published in 1916, the pamphlet was one of several Turkish attempts to control the press narrative in Europe.

20. Jaffa and Tel Aviv were forcibly evacuated by the Ottoman authorities in 1917; the Jewish population of each city was not permitted to return until after British victory in 1918.

21. Ahmed Djemal Pasha (1872–1922) was governor of the Ottoman province of Syria during the war.

> prominent than is his excellence, the figure of General Ahmed Djemal Pasha, who is well known for his acumen and delicacy. The arrival of his excellence in these parts must flat-out be viewed as a boon and as a demonstration of grace on the part of the Supreme Being, since He during these critical circumstances has understood the need to create beings necessary for the consolation of the people. That speaks to the truth, which must be demonstrated after a vigorous investigation into conditions has disproved all of the rumors that the French press has falsely put into circulation.

It is in this manner that the official version of history is written.

However, in *The Great Misery* is stated this: "At the head of the Army of the Caucasus, which now is en route to Erzurum, 50,000 Armenians are fighting willingly, a volunteer corps outfitted and armed by rich Armenians. . . . And all as one wear the black uniform, the color of sorrow, and a single word alights over their foreheads on the brims of their caps. . . . This word, whose flame guides their arms and gives their weapons victory and their minds a deep contempt for death, is this single word: *revenge*."[22]

In other words, this is to say that in the year 1915 the Armenians took bloody and reckless revenge for twenty-year-old scandalous acts by committing scandalous acts against Turkish men and women, adults and children, who were unconditionally innocent of every misdeed carried out in 1895. It is of course in this manner that human and divine justice are delivered.

In *Mercure de France* for May 1917 M. Pierre La Chesnais objects that "*I believe in the bestial cruelty of all sides.*"[23]

For the millions who believe what they have been led to believe this is of course shocking talk.

The bloody crimes the Turks committed against the Armenians twenty years ago and are now committing again are known of everywhere. But now the public reads as a contrast the pamphlet *The Armenian Horrors*, just released by the Turkish legation in Copenhagen, which through sworn testimony provides a view of the unheard-of cruelties the Armenian-Russian advance guard of the Russian army inflicted upon the villages and cities of Asia Minor against the defenseless Turkish population.[24] Here is found testimony confirmed under

---

22. Nalbandian here refers to the acts of revenge carried out by the Armenian battalions of the Russian Army of the Caucasus.

23. Pierre Georget La Chesnais (1865–1948) was a French scholar of Scandinavian literature. Much like his British equivalent, William Archer, Chesnais turned on Brandes with a vengeance because of his defense of Danish neutrality in the war.

24. The Ottoman state published such pamphlets in all the major European capitals in the effort to depict the Turks not as perpetrators but as victims.

oath from around sixty localities, and every Armenian who has committed cruelties is here named.

If even half of this is true, then the tiger is a lamb in comparison to these bandits, the Marquis de Sade is a miserable dilettante in comparison with these Armenians and Cossacks, when it comes to the lust for cruelty and perversely demented brutality.[25] Here there is burning alive, martyring, murdering, blinding, dismembering, spearing, here there is the systematic rape and desecration in every Turkish village. The horrors in Dante are pale and insignificant in comparison with these; his Hell is a pleasure park compared to Bitlis and to Van when the Armenians and Russians move in; the delirium of the lust for cruelty reaches here a peak unknown even during the Thirty Years' War.

From the beginning onward the belligerent powers have as a rule sought to hinder or strongly curtail the consumption of alcohol. In place of this the soldiers have become drunk on blood, as the worst instincts of the human race are appealed to. Indifference to extending sympathy to others has become a virtue and a responsibility. Constantly to be aware of the danger of loss of life and limb has called forth the lowest and rawest desire to enjoy the moment.

Blood drunk humanity reels and babbles, babbles in its blood-intoxicated constant chorus: victory for civilization, down with militarism! Rejuvenated Germanism, salvific Romanism, redeeming Britainism, purifying Americanism, democratizing Slavism! Freedom, progress, lasting peace!

—

All of the Armenian physiognomies that appear in *The Great Misery*, those that show up en face as well as those glimpsed only in half profile, are tenderhearted and emotional human countenances. Those among them that are not gentle but harsh are made so by insufferable injustices, so that the illness of revenge is necessarily awakened. It is a fine stroke that the most thorough account of the horrors is found in the words of a twelve-year-old boy, the only one to escape. We read what Humàjak reports to Garekin on the forced surrender of weapons in Trebizond, on the rounding up of the Armenians, on the expulsion from plundered homes, and on how the progress of the march was helped along with whips and goads.[26] The women were raped and sold off, the food stolen from the expelled, thereafter their footwear and lastly their

25. Donatien Alponse François, Marquis de Sade (1740–1814), author of *The 120 Days of Sodom*, is of course the source of the term "sadism."

26. Humàjak's account of the atrocities at Trebizond (now Trabzon), among the very worst of the cataclysm, is found in Nalbandian's *The Great Misery*.

clothing, until on the third day the killing began with axes, clubs, knives, bayonets, and bullets.

What has happened from the Turkish side regarding the little world that the Armenian hospital in Constantinople constitutes mirrors the approach that altogether has been applied to the Armenian population.[27] It was a menacing portent for the Armenian hospital that according to orders all the Turkish wounded were to be taken away from there. Meal and fuel were laid in together. Flour and fuel were requisitioned. This was the flour that the allies had doused with petroleum before abandoning Gallipoli. All the precious surgical equipment that had been acquired by the hospital at great expense was at once seized. Preparations were made to move the Armenians who had found refuge there and have them suffer their collective fate.

An unfortunate fate such as that of the Armenians calls forth all the more sympathy, since it does not come from blind natural forces but from human evil. The most terrifying thing is perhaps that this evil is also as blind and deaf and dumb as an earthquake or a foamy sea.

The frivolous optimism that has been implanted in us from childhood has convinced us that even the worst and basest murders were good for something, served some purpose, "world history or the world's judgment" and other idiotic absurdities. The world war has, like the hound of Hell Cerberus, three heads: the intellectual, which is that of an idiot; the ethical, which is that of a criminal; and the sensitive, which is that of a Medusa. In other respects what is fought for is that named above, for the right, for civilization, for the well-being of the small peoples and the small states, for freedom and progress and world peace.

27. The Armenian Hospital in Constantinople served as a refuge for Armenian orphans from all over the empire. Brandes again cites the account of Nalbandian, who herself had taken refuge in the hospital before her escape to Denmark.

CHAPTER 34

Imperialism

1922

Brandes had turned eighty years old in February 1922, and having devoted an immense amount of his energy to his ultimately unsuccessful campaign to bring the Great War to an earlier end, largely returned to his literary work; the final decade of his long life would see the publication of monographs on Julius Caesar (1918), Homer (1921), Michelangelo (1921), the historical Jesus (1925), and Saint Peter (1926). His single-minded defense of Danish neutrality during the war had, understandably enough, resulted in the diminishment of his international stature, particularly in Britain, and even more so in France, although he could find consolation in the fact that this stand had brought about a powerful reconciliation with his own people, who had overwhelmingly opposed involvement in the war. He was however not entirely silent on international rights issues in the 1920s, producing the 1922 speech below as well as a final essay, "Europe Now," in 1925. It should be noted that many of the issues he had addressed in his prewar and wartime writings had, for whatever it is worth, been to an extent "resolved" by the mass bloodletting of the world war: each of Europe's great continental empires was in ruins, Poland was at long last free, the Armenian people were relatively safe under Soviet rule, the Danish population of North Schleswig had been permitted to rejoin Denmark, and so on. Yet Brandes was far too acute an observer to be persuaded that the newfound freedom of so many oppressed peoples was in any manner secure; his commentary on the Versailles Treaty that closes the lecture, while hardly unusual for the time, is however remarkably prescient in anticipating the next phase of what Hobsbawm famously came to call the Thirty-One Years' War. Perhaps even more so, the lecture has value in that it provides the essential link between the issues that defined his prewar and wartime writings and the set of concerns that would come to the fore in the ensuing decades, namely the long struggle of the colonized peoples of the globe for national independence. While Brandes would not live to witness the stunning series of victories garnered by the global

---

Speech delivered on November 29, 1922. Originally published in *Samtiden* (Oslo), volume 1, 1923. Translated from the version published in *Kulturbilleder*.

movement for decolonization in the years following World War II, he should be commended for anticipating this immense struggle, and for being among the very few European men of letters who saw through the friendly façade of European colonialism. The speech is also significant, finally, in that Brandes acknowledges that his life's work, both as the principal exponent of literary radicalism in 1870s and 1880s and as an advocate for oppressed peoples, would continue after his death, that new "spires" of radical thought were emerging even in an age of profound cultural pessimism. In the year immediately following the war, a new generation of activist intellectuals sought Brandes out, as noted in the brief reference to Guglielmo Lucidi's Unione Italiana del Controllo Popolare and even more so to Henri Barbusse's Clarté group, which in 1925 would establish a chapter in Denmark. Thus Brandes could rest assured that his grand project would continue, in the able hands of "cultural radicals" like Hartvig Frisch, Poul Henningsen, Otto Gelsted, and Hans Kirk.

~

In February 1914 here in Christiania I gave a lecture titled "The Tension between England and Germany." Among other things I said at that time:

> We see that over the course of the centuries England has destroyed every foreign sea power that could either threaten it or be used against it. In this way it has neutralized the Spanish, the Dutch, the French, and the Danish navies. . . . In Germany the enormous army is essentially defensive, it is necessary to secure the kingdom's extensive borders against France and Russia. Its large navy however is not necessary for coastal defense; it is essentially a weapon of attack.[1]
>
> No doubt the prospect of a German landing in England is a nightmare scenario that is only set forth by English nationalists. No sensible person in Germany thinks of that. Yet there is a far greater danger to England than a German invasion, from which very likely no participant would come back alive. An incursion by the German army through Belgium into France, and in the case of success the annexation of Flemish Belgium, would be a deathblow for England as a world power.

I continued:

> England proposes a limitation on armaments, which is to say that Germany shall acknowledge England's mastery of the sea. Germany answers: are power

1. Brandes gave a series of lectures all over Norway in February 1914; here he cites from his address in the capital on February 9.

> relations written in a law that providence has declared? England says once again: such a superiority is necessary for the nourishment of the people and the greatness of the kingdom. Germany answers: what do the nourishment and the greatness of England have to do with us?
>
> For the time being it is proclaimed—for the sake of the press and the public—that there is agreement on the ratio of eight to five. But even though Germany, out of a love of peace, agreed to such a limitation of armaments, how then should it be practically enacted? It depends not just on the number of ships but their battle worthiness. It can, however, not forbid Germany from building still more dreadful ships of war.

My conclusion was that the future looked pitch-dark. "The old ideals," I said lastly, "must be replaced with new ones."

In the nine years since that February day, the German navy has, as I expected, been destroyed, and the German army, as I foresaw, made incursion into France through Belgium.

But the wish I had expressed in my final sentence, that "the old ideals must be replaced with new ones," has by no means come true. The old ideal, imperialism as the expression of nationalism, is at the moment dominant in all the countries whose attitude means something for the population of the world, the unfortunate mass of humanity.

In order to provide an idea of how imperialism dominates everywhere, I will begin by naming the only country that we once viewed as able to serve as a powerful counterweight against all imperialism, the United States. The states had been republics for more than one hundred years and together were taken to be a democracy. They took part in the Great War with the watchword of making the world safe for democracy.

When in May 1914 I went to New York a mob of reporters came aboard long before we reached the city, as is the custom there. Among other things they asked me what I thought about Bartholdi's immense Statue of Liberty, and whether it did not impress me in its scope.[2] For fun I answered that the Americans had probably expended all of the freedom they had in its erection; this shortly thereafter appeared in all the American papers.

It sounded like a joke, but it was serious. I meant and mean that in no place in the world is social freedom more meager than in the United States . . . At an intimate faculty luncheon at Columbia University a prayer by a clergyman was offered, like in Scotland. Recall that when Gorky and Mrs. Andreyeva

2. Frédéric Auguste Bartholdi's (1834–1904) *Liberty Enlightening the World* was dedicated in 1886.

traveled to America after thirteen years of living together but without being formally married, because Russian law at that time was against it, no hotel in New York would take them.[3]

Just cast a glance at America's attitude to the Central and South American republics: Haiti, the Dominican Republic, Nicaragua, Panama, Peru, Bolivia.

Their collected population is hardly more than eleven million, but their geographic area is half that of the American mainland.

And their abundance of forests, minerals, and oil is immense.

The little Republic of Panama, for the benefit of the Panama Canal, was carved away from Colombia through a revolt arranged by the States.[4] Then after the declaration of independence its subjugation was ensured as always in such instances by a loan from America's banks. Before the Great War Panama's 400,000 inhabitants had a debt of 5,000 dollars, now it is seven million, and a new loan of ten million is under consideration. It usually begins with the United States seizing the customs authorities of the small republics; from there a military dictatorship is developed.[5]

In 1909 the United States organized and financed a revolution in Nicaragua, driving out the president.[6] In the meantime a new president was elected, who was by no means suitable for the American elite's interests.[7] Thus the American secretary of war, under the pretext that two North American adventurers had fallen in the rebellion, sent 2,300 marines in to install a new president who would serve the interest of the States.[8] But the Nicaraguan congress

3. Aleksei Maksimovich Peshkov (1868–1936, known as Maxim Gorky) and his common-law wife, Maria Fedorovna Andreeva (1868–1953), scandalized New York high society during a 1906 visit.

4. The Republic of Panama, with US backing, declared its independence from Colombia in 1903.

5. Constitutional rule, albeit largely under the control of the commercial oligarchy, would survive until the military coup of 1968. The military junta would rule until the US overthrow of Manuel Noriega in 1989.

6. Nicaraguan president José Santos Zelaya López (1853–1919) alienated the United States by discussing the possibility of a rival canal with Germany and Japan. In response, the United States began offering support to anti-Zelaya rebels and mercenaries in October 1909. Zelaya was ultimately overthrown through a US naval intervention in November and December.

7. In defiance of US interests, new president José Madriz Rodriguez (1867–1911) continued the campaign against the US-backed rebels; he was overthrown as well in August 1910.

8. Brandes condenses the complex events of 1910–11 considerably. Juan José Estrada Morales (1872–1947), with American approval, succeeded Madriz but was ousted by a rival, General Luis Mena Vad, who installed Estrada's vice president, Adolfo Díaz Recinos (1875–1964), in May 1911. The new National Assembly then voted to elect Mena himself as president in October, but Díaz refused to step down, requesting the intervention of US marines

refused to acknowledge this straw man. The congress was then dissolved with the help of the worthy American sailor boys, and Nicaragua's independence passed into history as a memory.

Before the United States began its interference, Nicaragua's public debt was 2.5 million. When the States had restored law and order, the country was on the hook for fifteen million dollars to the North American bankers, and Nicaragua's custom authorities, railroads, and finances were under the management of the trustees of these bankers.[9] Oddly enough the unthankful inhabitants felt no love at all for their northern benefactors.[10]

Roosevelt and Taft introduced North America's imperialist attitude to the residents of Central and South America. But it was the pious Wilson, the pacifist, the idealist, who put an end to the independence of Haiti and the Dominican Republic. From 1905 North America had control of the Dominican Republic's finances. In 1916 the constitution was suspended and an admiral of the US Navy became governor with naval officers as public officials.[11] Also the poor negro republic of Haiti has since 1916 been a United States "protectorate."[12]

This occurred as Wilson powerfully declaimed against the imperialism of the German kingdom. As is well known, it has long been proclaimed that the United States will pull out of the islands as soon as the natives have fulfilled certain necessary conditions, that is to say all customs have been impounded; a loan of 6.5 million dollars is forced on the Dominican Republic, a loan of 40 million is forced on Haiti. The United States possesses the countries themselves as ample security for this money.

In this way the North American bankers, with the politicians as willing helpers, have gathered for themselves interests in a large part of South America. They employ the same approach as the British imperialists in their time did in Egypt, the Russian imperialists did in Persia; they allow the one loan to follow the other under military dictatorship until the occupied state becomes completely dependent and helpless.

---

to put down a Mena-led rebellion. The marines would remain in Nicaragua almost continuously until 1933.

9. The sell-off of state assets was formalized in the Knox-Castrillo Treaty, ratified by the US Senate in 1912.

10. Indeed, only five years later the Nicaraguan people would rise again, under the leadership of Augusto C. Sandino (1895–1934), from whom the contemporary Sandinista Party takes its name.

11. Rear Admiral Harry Shepard Knapp (1856–1923) became military governor of the Dominican Republic in November 1916; the US occupation would last until 1924.

12. The US occupation of Haiti lasted from July 1915 through 1934.

Perhaps it might be asked: is there not in the United States a press that is the upholder of the august traditions of freedom from the age of the War of Independence, the traditions that the fathers laid out in a renowned constitution?

The answer is that the press in North America is assuredly a power. Before the war in the United States there were in circulation, day in and day out, forty million copies of daily newspapers, and weekly and monthly magazines reached nearly two hundred million copies annually. But the whole of this mass is firmly in the service of the elite interests, with only three weeklies as exceptions, the *Nation*, the *New Republic*, and the *Freeman*, which are superbly edited but without political influence—they have only between fifteen and forty thousand subscribers.[13]

Upton Sinclair has taken a severe look at America's journalists in *The Brass Check*.[14]

The journalist himself is as a rule an exceedingly good-natured fellow, which cannot be said of the newspaper barons, least of all the recently deceased Lord Northcliffe.[15] The journalist is mostly anonymous. It is the power that stands behind him and that uses him that is responsible. William James, the philosopher, wrote in a letter: "As for our yellow papers—every country has its criminal classes, and with us and in France, they have simply got into journalism as part of their professional evolution."[16] The words are bitter. James seems to want to say: ignorance and lack of conscience have now found a voice in literature.

From the American journalist the boss demands diligence in tracking down the facts, clarity in expression, and the ability to capture interest from everything "that makes a story." The boss naturally does not allow the journalist to name and to praise anything or anyone the moneymen who stand behind the paper do not want named or praised. Otherwise he can say what he likes. But the paper does not live off subscriptions, which provide a negligible sum in relation to the expenses, but off the advertisements, and when the text

13. Brandes here is likely critiquing the practice of "yellow journalism," which had first come to prominence in the outrageous reporting on the Spanish-American War in the dailies of Joseph Pulitzer and William Randolph Hearst. The *Nation*, in contrast, should be commended for its consistent and vigorous opposition to American imperial adventures from the end of the nineteenth century up to the present.

14. Sinclair's powerful exposé of yellow journalism first appeared in 1919.

15. Alfred Charles William Harmsworth, 1st Viscount Northcliffe (1865–1922), the Rupert Murdoch of the Belle Epoque, founded the *Daily Mail* among many other tabloid newspapers.

16. Brandes cites from an April 12, 1900, letter to Miss Frances R. Morse, published in *The Letters of William James*, ed. Henry James (Boston: Atlantic Monthly, 1920), 2:126.

should be eye-catching and entertaining it is so because it should direct attention to the advertisements about where the best razor or automobile can be had.

With the French press the relationship is different. It is powerful because it is subsidized. At one time it was subsidized by the Boers, and then by the English, after the Boers' money was used up. As a natural illustration I will just name the now-published correspondence between Isvolsky and Sazonov. In nearly every letter Isvolsky, as envoy in Paris, must remind Sazonov that he must have still more money at his disposal to move the French press to express itself in agreement with the czar's desires, and so as not to receive a dismissive answer he cites the "results" the Austrian envoy in Paris achieved when Bosnia and Herzegovina were incorporated into the empire.[17] Calmette, who was killed by Mrs. Caillaux, was a man without means when he became the director of *Le Figaro*, but died not many years after an immensely rich man.[18]

In reality—as I have tried to show in my unfortunately unnoticed book from 1911—the death of Armand Carrel from Emile de Girandin's pistol shot marks the transformation of the French press from tribune to marketplace, from the struggle for ideas to a promising business.[19]

The fact that France, which was the most eager power to fight German imperialism, now stands as the most pronounced representative of imperialism is denied warmly and passionately by the French envoys in every country. Whether it is also denied by others I will let stand. I will not mention what every daily reports on the struggles of the moment, for example England's fruitless attempts to save the patriotic Greek ministers who have served its politics against France.[20] I will not compete with the daily newspapers.

I will cite the conditions on Africa's north coast, and I will refrain from mentioning any fact that is not already criticized by certain members of the French intelligentsia, who have sought remedy through the establishment of

17. Count Aleksandr Petrovich Izvolskii (1856–1919) served as Russian ambassador to France from 1910 until the February Revolution of 1917. Sergei Dmitrievich Sazonov (1860–1927) was Russian foreign minister from 1910 to 1916. Izvolskii had earlier been involved in the Austro-Russian negotiations regarding the Austrian annexation of Bosnia-Herzegovina in 1908.

18. Gaston Calmette (1858–1914) was murdered by Henriette Caillaux (1874–1943), wife of French finance minister Joseph-Marie-Auguste Caillaux (1863–1944), on March 16, 1914. Calmette up to his death had been leading a vigorous press campaign against the finance minister.

19. Jean-Baptiste Nicolas Armand Carrel (1800–1836) was an editor of the pro-democracy journal *Le National* from 1830 until his death in a duel with Émile de Girardin (1802–81), the inaugurator of penny press journalism in France. Brandes had profiled Carrel in a 1911 monograph.

20. Brandes refers to the negotiations to conclude the Greco-Turkish War of 1919–22.

the *Comité d-action française-musulman*, founded in May 1916 by deputies and university professors under the presidency of my revered friend Édouard Herriot, senator and mayor of the city of Lyon for more than twenty years.[21]

In Lyon he is all but omnipotent. He does not boast. But when once a dozen years ago I said to him: "you want it, but will it happen?" he answered: "In Lyon what I want happens."

Outside of Lyon this is unfortunately not the case.

Permit me here the necessary insertion, that when I speak out against the raging nationalism, the imperialist system in North America or in France, it is not due to any ill will toward the United States or the French people, still less to any enthusiasm for the moral purity of the Germans or their political delightfulness. It is due to a sense of justice that will not ingratiate itself to abuse. It is necessary that now and then one must do the crude work of speaking the truth. We can of course not live forever off the political slime that is poured down our throats. As early as 1830 Tocqueville would draw attention to the fact that no absolute monarch has ever wanted to be flattered like a so-called democratic majority. All peoples live today in constant worship of themselves.

One can quite well prefer Voltaire over Klopstock and Washington over Wilhelm II and yet feel disheartened by the lack of freethinking in the United States government and by the reactionary tendencies in Poincaré.[22] When I speak of France my sources are without a single exception French sources. But the whole system of government in North Africa is built on injustice and terror. In every attempt at remedying these evils the French colonists who live there, a handful of rich and influential men, set heaven and earth in motion, and everything stays the same.

The natives have no citizenship rights, are subjected to the violence and the arbitrariness of the administration, are worse off than the population was in the czar's Russia. The natives have no representatives in the French parliament. In Tunis the conditions are such that if there is a legal dispute between an Arab and a Frenchman, the case regardless of the law is not referred to a French court but instead decided administratively to the detriment of the Arab.

---

21. Radical politician Édouard Herriot (1872–1957) served as mayor of Lyon for a half century, as well as three terms as prime minister. He was among the most prominent advocates for the rights of France's Muslim citizens and colonial subjects; the committee he cofounded, among other projects, assisted in the campaign for construction of the first mosque in Paris. See Naomi Davidson, *Only Muslim: Embodying Islam in Twentieth-Century France* (Ithaca, NY: Cornell University Press, 2012), 41.

22. German poet Friedrich Gottlieb Klopstock (1724–1803) served as court poet to Danish king Frederik V from 1751 to 1770. Raymond Nicolas Landry Poincaré (1860–1934) had begun his second term as French prime minister in January 1916.

The Tunisians are forbidden from exporting grain; the government has ordained that all the fruits of the soil shall be sold by the military quartermaster at prices that are fixed by the administration.

At a congress held in 1917 in Paris by *La Ligue des Droits de l'Homme*, Moutet said of the conditions in Algeria: "We keep the country in a state of bondage and oppression. There is no equality before the law."[23] And Aulard, the famous historian of the French Revolution, exclaimed unchallenged: "We are less liberal than the Grand Turk. Be certain of that! He provides us in his attitude an example of freethinking."

When the political weather vane Gustave Hervé sought to bring these conditions to light and wrote that France, which so bitterly had complained of the oppression of Alsace and Lorraine by Germany, could not be said to have oppressed North Africa far more severely, he added as an excuse that Alsace in 1871 had a powerful feeling of independence, while the Arabs in North Africa were an undeveloped mass without national consciousness.[24]

To this the Arab-French press answered with good reason: "Algeria and Tunisia have always constituted a country, they have seven million inhabitants of the same race, same language, same religion. Both had full self-rule under Ottoman dominion." "In 1830 France began the conquest of Algeria. For twenty-four years we fought under Abdelkader until we bowed down to the enemy's superiority.[25] The enemy then instituted a regime of injustice, violence, humiliation, and constant terrorism."

After nearly a century Algeria is still treated like a conquered country, must to this day pay war indemnities to the victors, has no legal safeguards, no justice, no freedom, yet by contrast has responsibilities enough, among them military service.

In 1881 French troops, hardly making a show of a pretext, marched into Tunisia, halting a half mile from Bardo on the order of the feeble yet seemingly menacing Minister Barthélémy. The French emissary proceeded to present

23. The La Ligue des Droits de l'Homme (LDH) was founded by Dreyfusards in 1898; during the Algerian War of Independence it was among the leading organizations opposed to French colonial policy. Socialist politician Marius Moutet (1876–1968) was an expert on French colonial affairs, devoting much of his career to bettering the treatment of France's colonial subjects. François Victor Alphonse Aulard (1849–1928), the founding figure of modern French historiography, first published his four-volume history of the revolution in 1901. Both were lifelong members of the LDH.

24. Gustave Hervé (1871–1944) was a founder of the French iteration of national socialism.

25. Abdelkader ibn Muhieddine (1808–83, known as Emir Abdelkader) united many of the tribes of Algeria, leading the resistance against the French until his surrender in 1847.

the bey an ultimatum, which in comparison to Austria's to Serbia is humane: a treaty of subjection was presented, which if not signed within two hours would result in the bombardment of Tunis.[26] The bey signed. The people took up arms, the country was conquered.

On the boulevard in the city of Tunis something that appeals to the emotions appears: a French boy kindly teaches an Arab boy to read. This must constitute an amiable joke. It has never taken place in reality. The Arabic language is suppressed everywhere: in the central administration, police, medical establishment. With the exception of a few interpreters all of the officials in Tunisia are French.

Here every European child has free schooling, but no Arab child. Of 150,000 pupils only 3,500 are instructed free of charge.[27]

Of the country's entire population only 2 percent receive free elementary instruction in French. In the time of independence elementary education was in Arabic and free to all natives. In this way the higher education at Sadiki College was free.[28] After the introduction of the protectorate foreign languages with the exception of French have been shut out of the program.

Everywhere the native population has been stripped of its lands, which have been handed over to the colonists, in accordance with their varying degrees of influential connections. It is terrible to read the French Chamber of Deputies' debate about this from the twenty-fourth of November, 1911. Here the Deputy Lagrosilliére expressed without challenge: "All these injustices are crowned by the most outrageous of all: the driving back of the natives to the edge of the desert as a consequence of the expropriations."[29]

In vain the most learned in Tunisia have again and again recalled that the French government, in its answer to Russia regarding the goals of the war, stated this: to attain guarantees for the independence of peoples, the small ones as well as the large, to secure for the world from now on respect for the independence of the peoples. They have recalled that as council president

26. Jules Barthélemy-Saint-Hilaire (1805–95) was the French foreign minister from 1880 to 1881; as such he oversaw the annexation of Tunisia, imposed by the Treaty of Bardo on the bey of Tunis, Muhammad III as-Sadiq (1813–82), on May 12, 1881.

27. French colonial education policy was designed not for universal instruction but the cultivation of a loyal native elite.

28. Sadiki College was founded in 1875 by native reformers, loosely on the model of the lycée. Its alumni would eventually form the core leadership of the Tunisian independence movement.

29. Martinique-born lawyer and politician Marie-Joseph Samuel Lagrosillière (1872–1950) introduced the socialist movement to the island; he served as deputy of Martinique from 1910 to 1924 and 1932 to 1940.

Clemenceau officially declared: “France has among its demands inscribed the independence of the oppressed nations,” and he added, “their fate will be ordered according to the laws of humanity and justice, which are of a higher order than the actual.”

During the war the Algerian population had to provide nearly 300,000 combatants. The French government has long been unwilling to provide the precise number of the fallen.[30] If that has happened in the last two years I am unaware of it.

But in Tunisia they have given an account. Tunisia provided 100,000 soldiers, of which 70,000 were combatants. Of these, 30,000 are dead, that is nearly half, which is of course otherwise unheard-of.[31] One can surely deduce the Algerian losses.

As is known the non-French troops always received the order to make the first, most murderous thrusts. For the leadership of the French army they were of course less valuable than the country’s own children. The German army leadership behaved in the same way. In this manner as many North Schleswigers fell in the war as in the entire Danish army in 1864.[32] And the French however have hardly spared themselves. They have themselves reported their losses to November 18 as 1,385,000 dead or missing, 694,000 maimed, and 446,000 who are still held in captivity.

Nevertheless there is no relation between what the Arabs and the Frenchmen have lost.

At the embarkation of the African troops at Mairiet in Algeria a speech was delivered by M. L’Admiral, chair of the municipal council and bar association, which can almost be called tragicomic:[33]

> You are now departing! By the side of your French brothers-in-arms, by the side of our faithful allies, in an army where no concern is given to race or descent, you will pay France the debt of gratitude you have incurred from her.

30. Benjamin Stora estimates that 22,000 Algerian soldiers fell in the war. *Algeria, 1830–2000: A Short History*, trans. Jane Marie Todd (Ithaca, NY: Cornell University Press, 2001), 12.

31. Jacob Abadi estimates this figure at 12,000. *Tunisia since the Arab Conquest: The Saga of a Westernized Muslim State* (Reading, UK: Ithaca, 2013), 357.

32. Around 4,000 ethnic Danes died in German service during the Great War, more than twice the figure of 1864.

33. It should be noted here that Maurice L’Admiral, a Guadeloupe-born mulatto and descendent of freed slaves, was throughout his long career in the colonial justice system a vigorous defender of the rights of indigenes. See Christian Phéline, *Un Guadeloupéen à Alger: Me Maurice L’Admiral (1864–1955)* (Paris: Riveneuve, 2014).

> Soldiers! When you have done your duty, be assured that all laws of exception, all precautions owed to suspicion, everything that seems a humiliation or a debasement of your human dignity, will be annulled and removed.

This promise was kept about as much as the promise of the institution of Wilson's Fourteen Points.

It is understandable that the Arabic journal *El Maghreb*, which was published by Mohammed Bach-Hamba in Geneva and which had evaded censorship, bitterly poked fun at this spirited expression of the gratitude the Arabs in Algeria and Tunisia had to pay.[34]

Of the Moroccans' debt of gratitude we have yet to hear. But it will come.

It is not my intention in this bit of a speech to travel the world round to Japan, which abuses Korea, to Russia, which abuses Georgia and Ukraine, to demonstrate how much our age is defined by imperialism.

That Great Britain is an empire is denied by no one, least of all by Egyptians and Indians.

Italy has recently given over power to its imperialists, who, as is known, are the good folks who go by the name of fascists.[35]

I will not dwell on all of that. I chose a passive imperialism among the world's two most illustrious and mightiest republics, the lands of the Bastille stormers and of the independence declarers, the glowing hearths of the freedom of the people.

As a rule they are construed as the two most celebrated trees of freedom on the earth. And I would say: if it goes like this with the green trees, how goes it then with the barren ones?

Next let me cast a glance at that power whose imperialism was the point of departure for the world war, the German Reich, which devoted itself to kaiser-worship and in its prime made its French, Danish, and Polish subjects feel the power of German nationalism. The manner in which Alsace especially was ruled is a testimony to flat-out baffling stupidity, a stupidity that must be called monumental. Now this Reich is a republic without an army and without a navy, and unfortunately also without republicans.

---

34. Tunisian nationalist Mohamed Bach Hamba (1881–1920) was a founder of the Young Tunisians party; after his exile in 1912 he published numerous Arabic- and French-language journals from Geneva.

35. Benito Mussolini had just come to power in Italy; the following year Italian forces would begin the pacification of Libya.

I have personally known Wolfgang Kapp since his eighteenth year, he who made a clumsy attempt to overthrow the republic.[36] He was from the beginning a sound and plucky student without pronounced ability. He belonged to a distinguished family. His father, the historian and politician Friedrich Kapp, was a shining figure, highly noble to behold, a rebel from 1848 who fought on the barricades and after the triumph of the reaction had to escape to America and stay there for more than twenty years, until Bismarck gave the refugees amnesty in 1871.[37]

The son was therefore brought up in the most extreme political freethinking, while the mother, a daughter of a Prussian general, imparted to him a soldier's courage. When for his part he became a rebel, in the opposite direction, it was from hatred for those who had signed the Versailles Treaty and disarmed Germany out of fidelity to dishonorable promises made. He gave this hatred a foolish expression.

It is certainly difficult to imagine Germany as a republic.

A German socialist leader who visited me in the second year of the war found it disgraceful for the German people to overthrow the Hohenzollerns at the request of foreign powers, and added: we cannot after all forget that this dynasty has produced men like the superb electors and Frederick the Great.

This means that contemporary Germany constitutes a republic in which before its founding there were no other republicans than the socialists, and as has been seen, their republicanism was more theoretical than fanatical.

The republic has surely not been instituted with the enthusiasm with which the French and the North Americans first established theirs, or in our age that which has characterized the new Russian republic.[38] It was instituted because faith had been lost in the megalomaniacal kaiser and the little harmless kings who led the Reich to defeat, but especially because France, England, and America again and again had declared that they waged war to make the world democratic. The Germans were naïve enough to take them at their words. The Germans' political naïveté has always surpassed their political brutality. Thus Mérimée's astonishment when Bismarck in 1862 came for the first

36. Wolfgang Kapp (1858–1922) was the principal politician behind the ultranationalist "Kapp Putsch" of March 1920, in which the Weimar government was briefly overthrown.

37. During his exile in the United States, Friedrich Kapp (1824–84) was active in the abolitionist movement.

38. Brandes initially supported the overthrow of the tsardom, before becoming increasing critical of the new Soviet state in his very last years.

time to visit Napoleon III in Biarritz.[39] Mérimée wrote to his English lady friend at the time of him: *un Allemand intelligent et pas du tout naïf.* He was the exception.

The Germans childishly thought that when they became democratic their earlier enemies would in the spirit of conciliation meet them in the cultivation of the same political ideal. The Western powers had after all according to their own words fought the war against the absolutism of the kaiser and not against the German people.

The political hypocrisy that had gone into decay in the course of the nineteenth century had (without the simple Germans understanding it) experienced a real renaissance in the twentieth.

The Versailles Treaty opened up the eyes of the German democrats. It could not have gone worse if they had kept the monarchy. The kaisers had at least kept the Reich together, remedying German decentralization. With the fall of the kaiser the old cleft between north and south, Prussia and Bavaria, came forth distinctly. And French politics did everything to deepen the cleft. Since the state government in Berlin was socialist, France supported the monarchist as well as communist movements. The principal objects of France's efforts at dissolution have however been Upper Silesia in the east and the Rhineland in the west. The secession of Upper Silesia in spite of the outcome of the referendum occurred for the purpose of depriving the German Reich of coal and to favor the Poles.[40] In the Rhineland the French have installed themselves as if they never intend to leave the occupied land.[41] They of course fought the war in order to among other things oppose militarism, and now in peacetime have an army 250,000 men larger than the army the German kaiser had.

When the Germans had occupied French territory in 1871, the warmest and most polite letters were exchanged between the German commander in chief General Manteuffel and French Republic president Thiers, an old acquaintance of Manteuffel.[42] Both parties tried to make the occupation as easy as possible and managed to end it as soon as permitted. The letters of both men always conclude with the most respectful greetings to the ladies of the two

39. Prosper Mérimée (1803–70) was an author of the French Romantic school, best remembered for his novella *Carmen*, on which Georges Bizet based his famous opera; Brandes had profiled him in volume 5 of *Main Currents*.

40. In spite of the fact that ethnic Poles were a majority in the region, the population voted for Germany in the Upper Silesia plebiscite of March 20, 1921.

41. French forces did not depart until 1930.

42. Marie Joseph Louis Adolphe Thiers (1797–1877) was the first president of the Third Republic; as such he negotiated the eventual withdrawal of Prussian occupying forces, commanded by Edwin Freiherr von Manteuffel (1809–85). Manteuffel was later governor-general of newly acquired Alsace-Lorraine, where he continued to act as conciliator.

families. The five billion franc indemnity was also relatively quickly paid, and the German troops went away.[43]

At the moment, not only has all courtesy in internal communications vanished, but the relationship is so demented that the immense sums the Germans are forced to pay France go entirely to the extravagant maintenance of the unnecessary occupying army, so that nothing is left over for the rebuilding of the destroyed stretches of land, which could have been completely rehabilitated for half of what the Germans have already paid out to this unproductive end. The fact is that French industry has passionately opposed the idea that German workers should remedy the destruction in northern France with the building of houses and other means. Their own enterprises would suffer thereby, and their own workers would go without.

When it is observed how the French government allows its officers in the occupied areas to drive German families from their homes and permit the black troops to dominate, it should be believed that it had interest in awakening a fatal hatred among the vanquished.[44]

During the war there often emerged from the German side the tasteless and outright laughable observation that in Germany there was no actual hatred of France. From the French side there came the logical response: what more or what worse could you have done, if you did hate us?

But in spite of all, the observation was true as far as the German population is concerned. Among the bourgeoisie there remains an old and deep admiration for French civilization. The workers and the peasants know no national hatred. However, now after all the humiliations that have intentionally been inflicted on the German people, the hatred spreads and menacingly calls forth the next great war.

A peace is lasting when it is viewed by both warring parties as just, because it has been concluded with restraint and mercy toward the party that has been defeated. The war between England, France, and Turkey on the one side and Russia on the other, the Crimean War, which ended with the conquest of Sevastopol, left no bitterness in the minds of the Russians, although they were closed off from the Dardanelles.[45] A few years thereafter the Russians, French, and English were the best of friends.

---

43. The last payment was made in September 1873, after which all Prussian forces withdrew from French territory.

44. The presence of thousands of Senegalese tirailleurs in the occupied zone engendered the lasting hatred of Rhinelanders, and was later used effectively by Nazi propagandists.

45. The 1856 Treaty of Paris prohibited the establishment of Russian naval bases on the Black Sea; the recent Russian seizure of the Crimea from Ukraine is only the latest chapter in this centuries-long conflict.

In this way the American Civil War ended with a lasting peace. The southern states were treated in such a way that no desire for revenge appeared. Indeed, the generals of the southern states received memorials with the approval of all of North America.[46]

In this way the peace concluded between Prussia and Austria in 1866 was lasting, because Bismarck ensured that the defeated Austrians were not humiliated. They were only forced out of the German Confederation, and neither Austria nor its Confederation partner Bavaria had to give up any provinces, in spite of the powerful desire of the Prussian king.[47] Indeed, Bismarck formally forbade Wilhelm to make any appearance in Vienna. A few years later the two states were then also partners in the Confederation.[48]

Now to compare the behavior of the allies toward defeated Germany. They appear as judge, jury, and executioner all at the same time. By virtue of the fiction, which has been refuted and destroyed by a carriage-load of now-public documents (especially those found by the Bolsheviks), that Germany alone was the cause of this war, all the preparations for which had been underway in Russia, France, and England since 1905, innumerable humiliations have been pelted upon defeated Germany, and in addition to that unreasonable demands have been levied.[49] In the Versailles Treaty, which certainly is the stupidest document known to recent history, the victorious lords have inflicted physical destruction and moral ruin under the façade of instituting the reign of justice. They have called on the worst instincts of the vanquished, and they have been the dutiful servants of the worst instincts of the propertied classes among their own.

Their greed, which manifested itself in the form of a conviction, first deprived Germany of raw materials, provinces, colonies, navy, air force, artillery, and army, and then demanded thereafter sums that can only be written with *astronomical numbers*.

To the detriment of all, they managed to make the German mark like Balzac's peau de chagrin, steadily less valuable, so that in Germany conditions of need

46. As the US public has recently been reminded, Confederate monument building only began in earnest in the early twentieth century, decades after the conclusion of the war.

47. Bismarck's effort to restrain the desire of Wilhelm I to seize territory in the Austrian and Bavarian heartland was essential to securing the rapidly negotiated Peace of Prague in August 23, 1866, less than a month after the ceasefire.

48. Bavaria joined with Prussia in the 1870 war, and was thereafter a province of the German Reich. Austria-Hungary officially (although secretly) attached its fate to Germany by entering into the Triple Alliance in 1882.

49. Trotsky released the Entente's "secret treaties" in November 1917, exposing all manner of imperialist backroom maneuvering by the allied powers.

are found everywhere, and this deprivation spreads to France, which is bankrupt, and to England, which has a few million unemployed.[50]

Furthermore, they managed to bolster the German forces of reaction, the German nationalists, who preferably would reinstitute the monarchy; they therefore strengthened those against whom the allies claimed to have fought the war. Finally they managed to break down the respect for the German social democrats, who are at the helm, but constantly must give in to the demands of the enemy; they managed to compromise the only thing by which they were assured to be able to live in peace in the future.

How high Europe's political civilization stood one hundred years ago compared to now can be measured by considering that Europe had viewed the French Revolution with precisely the same unease and bitterness with which the Western powers now looked on the Russian Revolution, and as a consequence had formed coalitions against it; that they thereupon lived in a state of continual warfare during the age of Napoleon until 1815; and that they nevertheless allowed France after the fall of Napoleon to maintain its old borders without reduction. They did not set out to destroy the French economy. The people and their new government met with genuine goodwill in Europe. At the Congress of Vienna, Talleyrand was not just tolerated as the representative of France, but soon was celebrated as the centerpiece of the congress.[51]

Those who have visited Germany will have gotten the impression that the country is in a state of disintegration. The murder of one political leader follows upon another. It has become impossible to conduct industry, since there is a lack of coal, impossible to do business, when the value of the currency steadily falls. Among the thinking class despondency prevails, and among the larger population there is as a result of these conditions further despondency. The average man, who earlier was honorable and reliable, has been filled with hatred toward the bourgeoisie and is inclined to idleness and thievery, strengthened in this propensity by communistic theories. The workers cannot be bothered to toil and moil when the bounty of their work will be surrendered to the enemy. They will naturally not live as slaves of the enemy. The bureaucrats, who before the war were poor and proud, are now many times poorer and therefore necessarily much less proud; they are not as before dismissive of attempts at bribery.

---

50. Balzac's 1831 novel *Le Peau de chagrin* concerns a young man in possession of a wish-granting shagreen, which however shrinks in size upon the fulfillment of each desire.

51. Charles Maurice de Talleyrand-Périgord's (1754–1838) immense diplomatic skills were instrumental in negotiating favorable conditions for France in the 1814 Treaty of Paris and the 1815 Congress of Vienna.

The German Reich is threatened by hunger revolts, plundering of private property, economic and political chaos, and subsequently brutal reaction.

And during all of that there lives and thrives among the youth a movement of a remarkably unworldly and starry-eyed variety. Just as Russia presently produces nothing other than sects, so the German youth produce substantial fanaticisms. They are absorbed by the thought of the future, the dream of the introduction of a new religion, celebrating well-spoken and vacuous prophets, breathing most freely in the highest strata of metaphysics and theosophy, worshiping the hardly profound wisdom of Tagore and Rudolf Steiner, Dostoyevsky's repulsive joy at being humiliated, that is to say they cultivate the mysticism of Asia and pseudo-Asia, are in their art eagerly futuristic, but do not occupy themselves with how the country will be liberated from the burden of the enemy.[52] Still less do the intellectual youth begin at the beginning, which would be to reintroduce simple honesty and come up against the desperate looseness, laziness, fraud, violence, and murder.[53]

Germany is a republic in which first the republican manner of thinking must be made to flourish. A nation cannot change its manner of feeling in the course of a few years. For more than a thousand years Germany was monarchical, for a half century imperialist. It cannot expect to become a republic just because a few men wrote up a constitution on a piece of paper. We have seen how the Russians, who under the czar were under the rule of the secret police, are now under the so-called dictatorship of the proletariat, suffering further in the same manner, spied upon, at the mercy of imprisonment, torture, and arbitrary execution, only that the police apparatus, which before was called the Okhrana, is now called the Cheka.[54] The secret police have become still worse, by the way led in part by the same men. The name alone has changed.

Europe's old ideals are gone. Freedom has departed this life. I cannot travel the half hour over the sound from Helsingør to Helsingborg without a passport. In 1913 I traveled from Copenhagen to Vienna, Paris, Rome, Naples,

---

52. Bengali poet, composer, and artist Rabindranath Tagore (1861–1914), awarded the Nobel Prize for Literature in 1913, was neither vacuous nor lacking in wisdom; Brandes's regrettable comment may, if we are to be generous, in part be attributed to the misguided manner in which he was initially appropriated by European men of letters. Rudolf Steiner's (1861–1925) anthroposophy, by contrast, can come across as rather silly, although it is difficult to argue that its impact on the larger world has been anything but salutary. Brandes (largely negatively) profiled Fedor Dostoevskii (1821–81) in his *Impression from Russia* (1888).

53. Brandes's remarks here, curiously enough, closely echo his seminal 1871 Copenhagen lecture, which had condemned Danish culture as similarly mired in metaphysical and Romantic abstractions at the expense of concrete social problems.

54. As previously indicated, Brandes would become increasingly critical of the new Soviet state in the final years of his life.

Palermo, Tunis, and back without a passport. Every individual is now under police surveillance.

Neither is there anything left of the freedom to acquire. What I earn is so amply taken by state and municipality that I lose the desire and the drive to work. All too large a part of earnings go to others.

In Germany the taxes are so high that if businesspeople were completely honest with the state all business would have to cease.

There is only one power (the United States) that has preserved its equilibrium after it has emerged from the crisis. The States have not exactly preserved freedom; of that there was never particularly much in the *sweet land of liberty*, founded by the Puritans; but they have preserved and increased their well-being, and they have—after a brief eclipse—kept their sound political concepts intact.

There is for Europe no other remedy than that America, instead of leaving this unfortunate part of the world to its fate, takes economic and political leadership into its hands.

Officially there is always talk of morality in politics. Morality is the political cliché's first and last word. In reality morality is the word by which in political speech the advantage is named, rarely the true, but always the presumably advantageous.

Even the Western powers' Opium War against China around 1840, surely the most amoral of all amoral wars, was fought in the name of morality. It officially involved the forcing of China to uphold certain responsibilities, practically to force as much opium as possible down the throats of the Chinese.

In our time there is conducted in Norway and America a war against the relatively innocent poison, alcohol.[55]

There is another poison against which it is more useful to fight in the interest of the human race's peaceful future, the political cliché, which is another word for the political lie, which says *morality*, when it means *imperialism*.

Of what use is it to humanity to forbid the enjoyment of wine when it clings to the enjoyment of that hypocritical cliché?

Has anything positive been achieved by all the sorrow we have lived through? It would be unreasonable to doubt that. Germany's nearly insane arrogance is clipped.

Three examples. It is unthinkable now that in some little Polish city, as in Września, a teacher would seize children by the mouth to force them to recite

55. Norwegian voters had approved a limited policy of prohibition in a referendum of October 1919; that same month, the US congress passed the Volstead Act, inaugurating the long era of Prohibition.

their prayers in German and no longer in Polish.[56] It is unthinkable that if Germany had a dissatisfied province like Alsace under its control, the German army leadership would intervene to support the position of a lieutenant who had eaten plums and drunk beer in such abundance and with such consequences that a boy of eleven years yelled "Bettscheisser" [bedshitter] after him while the officer pursued the child with saber in hand, so that there was a European state action.[57]

It is unthinkable that such as this could be repeated: a Danish young lady by the name of Ea Dinesen had sung a song by Grieg in North Schleswig.[58] It was forbidden to sing in Danish. In vain she asserted to the interposing gendarmes that Grieg was a Norwegian. She did not even receive permission to change to everyday clothes, but with her bare shoulders exposed was transported by the gendarmes to the train and sent northward.

This stupid brutality is for good reason behind us, but as Luther said: the world is like a drunken peasant, if you lift him into the saddle on one side, he will fall off again on the other side.[59]

If one would offer consolation by teaching us, teach us to think not in decades but in centuries, rather in millennia, then we would judge the improvement according to scientific and technological progress. What we ourselves experience is however vanishingly little.

But the lot of life is fortunately such that only three or four men are needed to perfect the bicycle, so that millions can ride on it. Only a single individual need perfect the wireless telegraph so that a billion untalented people can use it.[60]

We must in the end not overlook the fact that in all countries new spires have been erected in the less concrete intellectual domains. In Italy Guglielmo Lucidi's *Rassegna Internazionale*, in France the group around Clarté and

56. See Brandes's early essays in the present volume on the Września Children's Strike of 1901–4.

57. Brandes refers here to the Zabern Affair of 1913, in which the German military, over the objection of the Reichstag, had intervened to protect a young lieutenant who had a history of antagonizing Alsatians.

58. The reference here is to Inger Benedicte Dinesen (1883–1923), sister of Karen Blixen, known to the English-speaking world as Isak Dinesen.

59. Martin Luther's image of the drunken peasant is among the most memorable in all his *Tischreden*, having been commented on by Kierkegaard and C. S. Lewis as well as many other Protestant thinkers. As always, the vehement atheist is selective in quoting the great reformer, eliding the following sentence: "He wants to belong to the devil."

60. Brandes here reveals the influence that John Stuart Mill exerted on him as a young man; despite a quarter century of advocating for the rights of entire peoples (e.g., collectivities), Brandes remains a liberal individualist at heart.

Barbusse and the other group around Romain Rolland.[61] They are still weak, but eventually will become powerful.

I believe most in the future of the United States. The decisive factor here is their practice of radical self-critique.[62] Conceit and smugness belong to the past.

Take a book like *Civilization in the United States*, a work written by thirty young Americans and three young Europeans.[63] It thoroughly criticizes every single sphere of life in the States, from first to last: law, politics, literature, art, the press, everything. It is unthinkable that in these small self-admiring countries, Norway or Denmark, such a work could come out. It is a good sign.

This ruthless self-critique is for us a pathway that leads to a better future. There comes a time when Bartholdi's Statue of Liberty once more will show us the way.

---

61. Brandes references three of the interconnected pacifist and internationalist organizations founded in the years immediately after the Great War. Guglielmo Lucidi (1885–1924) was a cofounder in 1920 of the Unione Italiana del Controllo Popolare, which was formally allied with the British Union of Democratic Control and the French Clarté group; *La Rassegna Internazionale* was the Unione's principal journal. Lucidi published several of Brandes's late writings in Italian, and the two met during a trip to Florence in 1921. See Jørgen Knudsen, *Georg Brandes: Uovervindelige taber II, 1914–27* (Copenhagen: Gyldendal, 2004), 382–83. Henri Barbusse (1873–1935) served in the trenches in 1914 and 1915, the experience of which converted him to pacifism; his 1916 war novel *Le Feu* is among the very first World War I novels as well as arguably the first collective novel. In 1919 he founded the communist and pacifist organization and journal *Clarté*; Brandes served as a member of the organizing committee. Both Lucidi and Barbusse, importantly, saw their political and literary work as a continuation of that begun by Brandes. See ibid., 379–82. Romain Rolland (1866–1944), winner of the 1915 Nobel Prize for Literature, was perhaps the most prominent war resister in France, having gone into voluntary exile in Switzerland for the duration of the conflict. A longtime friend and ally of Brandes, he was particularly attracted to Indian literature and thought, producing an influential monograph on Gandhi in 1924.

62. See "The Rights and Duties of the Weaker" in the present volume for a detailed commentary on this essential Brandesian concept.

63. This study, edited by Harold E. Stearns, appeared in 1922, and included contributions by such luminaries as H. L. Mencken and Ring Lardner.

CHAPTER 35

Europe Now

1925

It is a great sadness that the last of Brandes's works to touch on the fate of oppressed peoples, an early 1925 Berlin address published as "Europa Nu" in the Danish journal *Tilskueren*, is arguably the most pessimistic and despairing in his entire corpus of political journalism. For more than half a century, despite a manifold of historical events suggesting the contrary, Brandes had insisted that reasoned and enlightened debate in the public sphere could produce results beneficial to our species as a whole. Yet here he is, two years away from his death, seemingly consumed with hopelessness regarding the future of Europe and the larger world. While much of postwar European culture had indeed understandably taken a turn toward pessimism, this was after all the age of Oswald Spengler and of T. S. Eliot's *The Wasteland*, it must be remembered that, as Brandes briefly notes in the 1922 lecture "Imperialism," a powerful minor key of *cultural optimism* had indeed begun to emerge in the years following the Great War. Perhaps no part of Europe would come to be as attuned to this undercurrent of hopefulness as the Nordic countries, in which the movement that would come to be called "cultural radicalism" was only then beginning to establish itself; indeed, Nordic literary, aesthetic, and intellectual development, which had since Brandes's "course correction" in the 1870s more or less followed along with (and sometimes even led) that of Europe, began to depart again in the mid-1920s, as new figures such as Poul Henningsen, Hans Kirk, and Otto Gelsted came to actively reject the profound thread of cultural pessimism embedded within high modernism. Brandes's acknowledgment that "pessimism is unwelcome" is very likely a gesture toward these young radicals, who very much saw in the aging critic a model worthy of emulation, even if in the end he himself had given in to despair.

~

Europe entered the twentieth century with an unparalleled willingness to indulge in illusions.

Originally published in *Tilskueren*, February 1925. Translated from the version published in *Udvalgte Skrifter*, vol. 9.

In every country people believed what they wanted to believe.

Perhaps this can most clearly be observed among the greatest and most famous men of the major countries.

In Great Britain Herbert Spencer had developed the widely diffused doctrine that the instincts of humanity alone would bring about the golden age of peace.[1] He was enough of an optimist not to place much confidence in the atavistic war lust, and also sufficiently optimistic regarding the conviction that free trade in and of itself, the egotistical desire to earn as much money as possible, would lead to universal *fraternization.*

In Russia Tolstoy and Kropotkin, each in his own way, had preached a belief in the deep, unswerving goodness of humanity. Tolstoy argued that the ideal would be reached simply when no one offered resistance to evil.[2] He imagined that in certain sentences later written by the Evangelists, who had put into words the ideal legendary figure of Jesus, he had the universal means for the healing of all humanity's wounds. First and foremost it was a matter of not punishing anyone, dismissing all courts, meager art and science, renouncing sexuality, and idolizing the holy simplicity of the peasant. He had no interest in politics.

Kropotkin, a far more liberated and still more nobly inclined soul, who further had the advantage over Tolstoy that his way of life at every point corresponded to his ideals, was no less an optimist than the great poet, maintaining the same distaste as him for all criminal law, but seeing the redemption of humanity in the unconditional freedom of anarchy.[3] What the New Testament was for Tolstoy, the guidebook and the pathway toward the goal, revolution and anarchy were for Kropotkin. The upheaval and the introduction of a freedom without compulsion would according to Kropotkin in and of itself lead to a new and happy age. That human nature was at base good he never doubted, in spite of hundreds of bitter experiences.

At the end of the eighteenth century Schiller wrote this verse, but the poet's noble temperament now strikes us as unbelievably embarrassing, in spite of Beethoven's lovely music:

Seid umschlungen, Millionen!
Dieser Kuss der ganzen Welt!

---

1. British philosopher Herbert Spencer (1820–1903), the great exponent of Victorian optimism, produced his ten-volume overview of existing human knowledge, *Synthetic Philosophy*, between 1862 and 1893.

2. Tolstoy articulated his philosophy of nonviolence principally in *The Kingdom of God Is Within You* (1894), a work that had a powerful influence the young Gandhi.

3. Russian anarchist philosopher Petr Alekseevich Kropotkin (1842–1921) was a longtime friend and ally of Brandes; indeed, Brandes wrote the introduction for his 1899 *Memoirs of a Revolutionist.*

Brüder, überm Sternenzelt
Muss ein lieber Vater wohnen.[4]

This kiss for the entire world is impossible and unappetizing, the embrace of the millions impossible and sentimental; the tent of stars has become altogether impossible even as a comparison. It is likewise impossible for us to believe in this dear Father who should dwell over the tent. Nevertheless some of the world's greatest men at the turn of the twentieth century continued to share the feeling from which Schiller's verse was inspired, although neither Herbert Spencer nor Peter Kropotkin ever hinged their faith in the coming improved circumstances on the Father over the tent of stars.

But Europe and America have so proclaimed optimism to be a duty that very few have been able to see the conditions of humanity, even just the purely political, as they really are.

True enough that the peoples of Europe and America have a kind of culture. But at the same time they have a press. And it is extremely difficult to maintain a culture at the same time as this press exists. The various peoples were in general peace-loving, but their desires were warlike, and it was easy for the press to awaken those desires. The press did not need to be altogether bought up by the large industrial concerns and weapons manufacturers; it only needed to be patriotic, and it was that and is that everywhere. Patriotism and world peace are poorly reconciled.

In addition it became apparent that nearly all the nations had ideals that could not be realized without war.

Russia desired the occupation of Constantinople, Greece likewise, Bulgaria likewise. Turkey would hold on to Constantinople. Great Britain would dominate the Dardanelles.[5] This one example demonstrates how far Europe was from satisfaction with the existing order.

In addition to this Germany desired France's colonies, France would take back Alsace and Lorraine, and England would expand its dominion from Cairo to Cape Town.[6]

---

4. "Embrace, ye millions—Let this kiss, / Brothers, embrace the earth below! / You starry worlds that shine on this, / Our common father know." This is the first chorus of Schiller's "An die Freude," trans. Charles J. Hempel, in *Schiller's Complete Works*, vol. 1 (Philadelphia: I. Kohler, 1861), 69.

5. Imperial Russia's designs on the Ottoman capital were revealed by Trotsky's release of the "secret treaties" in November 1917. Britain had hoped to draw Greece and Bulgaria into the war on the Allied side through its Gallipoli campaign of 1915, as significant numbers of ethnic Greeks and Bulgarians were still under Ottoman rule.

6. Brandes refers to the vainglorious Cape to Cairo Railway envisioned by Cecil Rhodes.

In 1912 public opinion in France was still friendly to peace, although the influence of King Edward was present everywhere in the leading circles.[7] In 1913 these conditions were quite different. Nationalism, which had theoretically been overcome in the Dreyfus Affair, made itself felt everywhere once again; it triumphed in France, as it had triumphed in England, Germany, Italy, and Russia, only in a more conspicuous manner. A breath of warlike frenzy spread over Europe. Socialism won elections but that meant nothing, it could not prevent the world war.

The national pride that in antiquity led the Greeks, Romans, and Jews to see themselves as better than other peoples—and this pride was however not groundless—has gradually taken hold of all European peoples. Like the untold number of peoples who constantly display their imagined merits or their earlier successes, the European peoples have in these times almost without exception fallen into the tasteless habit of praising themselves. There is hardly a people, no matter how small or so insignificant, that does not see itself as the world's foremost. I have heard a little Polish boy, who had come home from school, ask his mother: "It is possible what the teacher said, that Columbus was not a Pole?" That is right, he was a Genoan. "I thought that all great men had been Poles."

From this arises the hatred of foreigners and the hatred of the foreign elements within a given people, for example the everywhere rising antisemitism. He who is old enough to have experienced the spirit of 1848 with its serene humanity and its superior sense of world citizenship cannot but be surprised at this nationalistic regression. In his time Grundtvig even got one of the world's smallest peoples, the Danes, to believe they were "God's people"—what he meant by that I confess that I know not—but it had as a consequence the fact that Grundtvig has stood before the Danish nation as the incarnation of all worthy Danishness.[8]

This self-idolization has implanted itself in America from Europe. There is hardly a schoolboy or schoolgirl in the United States who doubts for a moment that the United States has surpassed all the other kingdoms of the earth, and although no state (except perhaps Switzerland) should be less nationalist than the United States, they are well on the way toward providing Europe with a

7. Edward VII's (1841–1910) regular visits to France were instrumental in preparing the ground for the Entente Cordial of 1904, which formally ended centuries of Anglo-French rivalry.

8. Arguably no single figure has had a larger impact on modern Danish culture than theologian, poet, historian, and philologist Nikolaj Frederik Severin Grundtvig (1783–1872). While his contributions are many and varied, Brandes here refers to the manner in which Grundtvig seamlessly folded Christianity into his concept of Danish national identity.

model for xenophobia and the barring of foreigners.[9] Moreover, Protestantism is made into a compulsion, while in Europe's Catholic countries, in part the Latin and in part the Slavic like Poland, Catholicism occupies steadily more ground, also in intellectual life. Against the nationalism and clericalism that has taken the upper hand in present-day Europe the equally aimless communism situates itself. It is still held down in every manner, and the powers have as long as possible refused to grant their acknowledgment to its menacing representative, Soviet Russia.[10] But all in vain.

The nineteenth-century ideal of political freedom is nearly forgotten. In the conservatively ruled countries the freedom of the people is repressed by dictators. In revolutionary Russia and the nearby states such as Ukraine or Georgia, both of which have been subjected to violence by Soviet Russia, there is neither freedom for the individual nor for the press. The entire manner is communistic and unfriendly toward freedom.

Since pessimism is unwelcome and furthermore unfruitful, it ought to be hoped that gradually something good will come out of the twentieth century's political experiments.

9. The US Congress had passed the Emergency Immigration Act in 1921, and would soon enact the even more draconian Immigration Act of 1924.

10. Initially an enthusiastic supporter of the October Revolution, Brandes became increasingly critical of the new Soviet state in the early 1920s.

Bibliography

Aarestrup, Emil. "En Polsk Moder." In *Samlede Digte*, edited by F. L. Liebenberg, 217–20. Copenhagen: Reitzel, 1877.

Abadi, Jacob. *Tunisia since the Arab Conquest: The Saga of a Westernized Muslim State*. Reading, UK: Ithaca, 2013.

Adam, Madam. [Juliette Lamber Adam]. *Mes premières armes littéraires et politiques*. Paris: A Lemerre, 1904.

Allen, Julie K. *Icons of Danish Modernity: Georg Brandes and Asta Nielsen*. Seattle: University of Washington Press, 2012.

———. "Kampen mod Le Danemark s'efface." In *Georg Brandes og Europa*, edited by Olaf Harsløf, 319–27. Copenhagen: Museum Tusculanum, 2004.

Andersen, Claus Elholm. "Exile and Naturalism: Reading Georg Brandes Reading Emil Aarestrup." *Scandinavian Studies* 78, no. 4 (Winter 2006): 419–28.

Archer, William. *Colour-Blind Neutrality: An Open Letter to Doctor George Brandes*. London: Hodder and Stoughton, 1916.

Arendt, Hannah. "Herzl and Lazare." In *Hannah Arendt: The Jewish Writings*, edited by Jerome Kohn and Ron H. Feldman, 338–42. New York: Schocken, 2007.

Auron, Yair. *The Banality of Indifference: Zionism and the Armenian Genocide*. London: Routledge, 2017.

Balzac, Honoré de. *Le Peau de chagrin*. Paris: Gosselin, Canel, 1831.

Barbusse, Henri. *Le Feu (Journal d'une escouade)*. Paris: E. Flammarion, 1916.

Bayvel, Rachel. "The Jews Who Fought alongside the Germans." *Jewish Quarterly* 202 (Summer 2006): 25–28.

Behrendt, Flemming. "Pontoppidans Jøder." Address to the Pontopiddan Selskab, 2014. Henrik Pontoppidan: Portal for læsere, studerende, lærere of forskere. http://www.henrikpontoppidan.dk/text/seclit/secartikler/behrendt/pontoppidans_joeder.html.

Bendtsen, Bjarne S. "Colour-Blind or Clear-Sighted Neutrality: Georg Brandes and the First World War." In *Caught in the Middle: Neutrals, Neutrality and the First World War*, edited by Johan den Hertog and Samuël Kruizinga, 121–38. Amsterdam: Aksant, 2011.

Bergman, Judith. "Sweden: A Failed State?" Gatestone Institute, July 21, 2017. https://www.gatestoneinstitute.org/10605/sweden-failed-state.

Berthelsen, Sune, and Ditte Marie Egebjerg. "Europa i Danmark, Danmark i Europa: Georg Brandes som national kosmopolit." In *Det stadig moderne Gennembrud*, edited by Hans Hertel, 99–122. Copenhagen: Gyldendal, 2004.

Bildt, Carl. "Statement of Government Policy in the Parliamentary Debate on Foreign Affairs." Presented in the parliamentary debate of February 13, 2013. https://www.regeringen.se/49b754/contentassets/c1f7e438b32f4d6e995a09bd34508695/statement-of-government-policy-in-the-parliamentary-debate-on-foreign-affairs-2013.

Boell, Paul Victor. *Le protectorat des missions catholiques en Chine et la politique de la France en extrême-orient*. Paris: Institut Scientifique, 1899.

Brandes, Georg. "The 1872 Introduction to *Hovedstrømninger i det 19de. Aarhundredes Litteratur (Main Currents in Nineteenth Century Literature).*" Translated by Lynn Wilkinson. *PMLA* 132, no. 3 (May 2017): 696–705.

———. "Aristokratisk Radikalisme." *Tilskueren* 6 (August 1889): 565–613.

———. *Armand Carrel*. Copenhagen: Gyldendal, 1911.

———. *Benjamin Disraeli, Jarl of Beaconsfield: En Litterær Charakterstik*. Copenhagen: Gyldendal, 1878.

———. *Berlin som Tysk Rigshovedstad*. Copenhagen: P. G. Phillipsen, 1885.

———. "Den Hellige Alliance." *Tilskueren* 36 (March 1919): 207–25.

———. "Det store menneske: Kulturens kilde." *Tilskueren* 7 (January 1890): 1–25.

———. *Det moderne Gjennembruds Mænd: En Række Portrætter*. Copenhagen: Gyldendal, 1883.

———. *Ferdinand Lasalle: En Kritisk Fremstilling*. Copenhagen: Gyldendal, 1881.

———. *Fugleperspektiv*. Copenhagen: Gyldendal, 1913.

———. *Georg Brandes: Den mangfoldige; En antologi*. By Jørgen Knudsen. Copenhagen: Gyldendal, 2005.

———. *Hovedstrømninger i det 19de. Aarhundredes Litteratur*. 6 vols. Copenhagen: Gyldendal, 1872–90.

———. *Indtryk fra Polen*. Copenhagen: Gyldendal, 1888.

———. *Indtryk fra Rusland*. Copenhagen: Gyldendal, 1888.

———. *Kulturbilleder: Studier og Strejftog*. Copenhagen: Lindhardt og Ringhof, 1932.

———. *Main Currents in Nineteenth-Century Literature*. Translated by Diana White and Mary Morison. 6 vols. London: Heinemann, 1906.

———. *Petrus*. Copenhagen: Gyldendal, 1926.

———. *Polen*. Translated by Adele Neustädter. Paris: A. Langen, 1898.

———. *Sagnet om Jesus*. Copenhagen: Gyldendal, 1925.

———. *Samlede Skrifter*. 18 vols. Copenhagen: Gyldendal, 1899–1910.

———. *Sønderjylland under Prøjsisk Tryk*. Copenhagen: Gyldendal, 1919.

———. "Svend Lange og Antisemitismen." *Politiken*, 27, no. 207 (July 26, 1911): 4–5.

———. *Tragediens Anden Del. Fredsslutningen*. Copenhagen: Gyldendal, 1919.

———. *Udvalgte Skrifter*. 9 vols. Copenhagen: Tiderne Skifter, 1984–87.

———. *Urkristendom*. Copenhagen: Gyldendal, 1927.

———. *Verdenskrigen*. Copenhagen: Gyldendal, 1916.

———. *The World at War*. Translated by Catherine D. Groth. New York: Macmillan, 1917.

——— "World Literature." Translated by Haun Saussy. In *The Princeton Sourcebook in Comparative Literature: From the European Enlightenment to the Global Present*, edited by David Damrosch, Natalie Melas, and Mbongiseni Buthelezi, 61–66. Princeton, NJ: Princeton University Press, 2009.

———. "World Literature." Translated by William Banks. In *World Literature: A Reader*, edited by Theo d'Haen, César Domínguez, and Mads Rosendahl Thomsen, 23–27. London: Routledge, 2013.
Browne, Edward. *The Reign of Terror at Tabriz: England's Responsibility*. Manchester, UK: Taylor, Garnett, Evans, 1912.
Browning, Christopher. "Branding Nordicity: Models, Identity and the Decline of Exceptionalism." *Cooperation and Conflict* 42, no. 1 (March 2007): 27–51.
Butnaru, I. C. *The Silent Holocaust: Romania and Its Jews*. New York: Greenwood, 1992.
Cartwright, David E. *Schopenhauer: A Biography*. Cambridge: Cambridge University Press, 2010.
Cherbuliez, Charles Victor. *L'Aventure de Ladislas Bolski*. Paris: Hachette, 1869.
Clemenceau, Georges. "Ce Que Pensent Nos Marocains." *Le Bloc* 1, no. 25 (July 1901): 489–95.
Clemenceau, Georges, Elie Pécaut, Francis de Pressensé, A.-Ferdinand Hérold, Jean Jaurès, Lucien Descaves, Pierre Quillard, J. Grave, Paul Reclus, G. Séailles, Georges Yvetot, and Charles Guieysse. *La Mano Negra*. Paris: Les Temps Nouveaux, 1903.
Collière, Marcel. "La Mano Negra." *La Revue Blanche* 30 (1903): 161–73.
Cooper, Leo. *In the Shadow of the Polish Eagle: The Poles, the Holocaust and Beyond*. New York: Palgrave Macmillan, 2000.
Cooper, Sandi E. *Patriotic Pacifism: Waging War on War in Europe, 1815–1914*. Oxford: Oxford University Press, 1991.
Cottam, Richard W. *Nationalism in Iran: Updated through 1978*. Pittsburgh: University of Pittsburgh Press, 1979.
Curzon, George Nathaniel. *Persia and the Persian Question*. 2 vols. London: Longmans, Green, 1892.
Davidson, Naomi. *Only Muslim: Embodying Islam in Twentieth-Century France*. Ithaca, NY: Cornell University Press, 2012.
Drachmann, Holger. *Renæssance*. Copenhagen: Gyldendal, 1894.
Drews, Arthur. *Die Leugnung der Geschichtlichkeit Jesu in Vergangenheit und Gegenwart*. Karlsruhe: G. Braun, 1926.
Dreyfus, Robert. *La vie et les prophéties du comte de Gobineau*. Paris: Calmann-Lévy, 1905.
Evans, Martin Marix. *Encyclopedia of the Boer War*. Santa Barbara, CA: ABC-CLIO, 2000.
Fink, Troels Marstrand Trier. *Båndene bandt: Forbindelsen over Kongeåen, 1864–1914*. 2 vols. Copenhagen: Institut for Grænseregionsforskning, 1999.
Finot, Jean. *Le préjugé des races*. Paris: F. Alcan, 1905.
Gerlache de Gomery, Adrien Victor Joseph de. *Landet, som ikke vil dø*. Kristiania: Aschehoug, 1915.
———. *Le pays qui ne veut pas mourir*. Paris: Berger-Levrault, 1916.
"Germany's Grave Problems." *The World's Work* 3, no. 4 (February 1902): 1700–1701.
Giquel, Prosper Marie. *La Politique Française en Chine. Depuis les Traités de 1858 et de 1860*. Paris: Libraire de Guillaumin, 1872.
Gobineau, Arthur de. *Essai sur l'inégalité des races humaines*. 4 vols. Paris: Firmin Didot, 1853–55.
Goethe, Johann Wolfgang von. *Faust I*. Translated by Walther Kauffman. New York: Anchor, 1963.

———. "Venetian Epigram XLVIII." In *Goethe: Selected Verse*, edited and translated by David Luke, 117. New York: Penguin, 1986.

———. *West-östlicher Divan*. Stuttgart: Cotta, 1819.

Goldstein, Moritz. "Deutsch Judischer Parnass." *Kunstwart* 25, no. 11 (March 1912): 281–94.

Greaves, Rose. "Iranian Relations with Great Britain and British India, 1798–1921." In *The Cambridge History of Iran*, edited by Steven Avery, Gavin Hambly, and Charles Melville, 7:374–425. Cambridge: Cambridge University Press, 1991.

Haas, Christopher. "The Caucasus." In *Early Christianity in Contexts: An Exploration across Cultures and Continents*, edited by William Tabbernee, 116–33. Grand Rapids, MI: Baker Academic, 2014.

Hansen, Jens Bjerring. "Romantik, Modernität und Copyright. Georg Brandes auf dem deutschen Buchmarkt." In *Die skandinavische Moderne und Europa: Transmission—Exil—Soziologie*, edited by Bjerring Hansen, 121–42. Vienna: Praesens Verlag, 2016.

Harsløf, Olav. "Fra kulturpolitik til politisk journalistic." In *Den politiske Georg Brandes*, edited by Hans Hertel and Sven Møller Kristensen, 135–38. Copenhagen: Hans Reitzel, 1973.

Hauch, Carsten. *En Polsk Familie*. Copenhagen: Reitzel, 1839.

Havel, Václav. "The Power of the Powerless." In *The Power of the Powerless: Citizens against the State in Central-Eastern Europe*, edited by John Keane, translated by Steven Lukes, 10–59. London: Routledge, 2009.

Henningsen, Poul. *Kulturkritik*. Vol. 2. Edited by Carl Bay and Olav Harsløf. Copenhagen: Rhodos, 1973.

Herzl, Theodor. *Altneuland*. Leipzig: Seemann, 1902.

———. *Der Judenstaat*. Leipzig: M. Breitenstein, 1896.

Hobson, J. A. *Imperialism: A Study*. New York: J. Pott, 1902.

Holberg, Ludvig. *Peder Paars*. 4 vols. Copenhagen, 1719–20.

Hunt, Lynn. *Inventing Human Rights: A History*. New York: Norton, 2007.

Huxley, Thomas Henry. "On the Aryan Question." In *Man's Place in Nature and Other Anthropological Essays*, 272–320. New York: D. Appleton, 1899.

Ibsen, Henrik. "Ederfuglen." In *Digte*, 13. Copenhagen: Gyldendal, 1871.

Ihrig, Stefan. *Justifying Genocide: Germany and the Armenians from Bismarck to Hitler*. Cambridge, MA: Harvard University Press, 2016.

Ingebritsen, Christine. "Norm Entrepreneurs: Scandinavia's Role in World Politics." In *Small States in International Relations*, edited by Christine Ingebritsen, Ivar Neumann, Sieglinde Gstöhl, and Jessica Beyer, 273–91. Seattle: University of Washington Press, 2006.

———. *Scandinavia in World Politics*. Lanham, MD: Rowman & Littlefield, 2006.

Ishay, Micheline. *The History of Human Rights: From Ancient Times to the Globalization Era*. 2nd ed. Berkeley: University of California Press, 2008.

Jæger, Henrik. *Henrik Ibsen: A Critical Biography*. Translated by William Morton Payne. Chicago: A. C. McClurg, 1901.

James, William. "Letter to Miss Francis R. Morse." In *The Letters of William James*, edited by Henry James, 2:124–29. Boston: Atlantic Monthly, 1920.

Jolly, Philip. *Jewish Wielun: A Polish Shtetl*. Morrisville, NC: Lulu, 2010.

Kant, Immanuel. *The Critique of Judgment*. Translated by Werner S. Pluhar. Indianapolis, IN: Hackett, 1987.

Kauffman, Jesse. *Elusive Alliance: The German Occupation of Poland in World War I*. Cambridge, MA: Harvard University Press, 2015.

Kertzer, David I. *The Pope and Mussolini: The Secret History of Pius XI and the Rise of Fascism in Europe*. New York: Random House, 2014.

Khayyam, Omar. *Rubáiyát of Omar Khayyam, the Astronomer-Poet of Persia*. 1st ed. Translated by Edward Fitzgerald. London: B. Quaritch, 1859.

Knudsen, Jakob Christian Lindberg. "Georg Brandes og den danske Dannelse." *Politiken* 28, no. 49 (February 18, 1912): 9–10.

Knudsen, Jørgen. *Georg Brandes*. 5 vols. Copenhagen: Gyldendal, 1985–2004.

Kohl, Johann Georg. *Reisen in Dänemark und den Herzogthümer Schleswig und Holstein*. 2 vols. Leipzig: F. A. Brockhaus, 1846.

Kotliarevskii, Ivan. *Eneida*. Saint Petersburg: M. Parpura, 1798.

Kropotkin, Peter. *Memoirs of a Revolutionist*. 2 vols. London: Smith, Elder, 1899.

———. *The Terror in Russia: An Appeal to the British Nation*. London: Methuen, 1909.

Lamennais, Hugues-Félicité Robert. *Paroles d'un croyant*. Paris: E. Renduel, 1834.

Lange, Sven. "Et Brev fra Paris." *Illustreret Tidende* 23, no. 7 (1911): 518–19.

Larsen, Svend Erik. "The Telescope of Comparative Literature." In *The Routledge Companion to World Literature*, edited by Theo d'Haen, David Damrosch, and Djelal Kadir, 21–31. London: Routledge, 2011.

Lassalle, Ferdinand. *Meine Assisen-Rede*. Düsseldorff: Schaub, 1849.

Lastivertsi, Aristakès. *History Regarding the Sufferings Occasioned by Foreign Peoples Living around Us* (ca. 1072–79). Translated by Robert Bedrosian. New York: n.p., 1985. https://archive.org/details/AristakesLastivertsisHistory.

Lauren, Paul Gordon. *The Evolution of Human Rights: Visions Seen*. 3rd ed. Philadelphia: University of Pennsylvania Press, 2011.

Lenin, V. I. *Imperialism: The Highest Stage of Capitalism*. New York: Penguin, 2010.

Lepsius, Johannes. *Bericht über die Lage des armenischen Volkes in der Türkei*. Potsdam: Tempelverlag, 1916.

Leroy-Beaulieu, Pierre. *La Renovation de L'Asie: Siberie, Chine, Japon*. Paris: Armand Colin, 1900.

Lesniewski, Adam. "A Certain Fiasco or the Role of Stefan Poles in the Polish Uprising of 1863." *Polish Review* 23, no. 4 (1978): 18–38.

Li-Chiao, Chen. "British Policy on the Margins and Centre of Iran in the Context of Great Power Rivalry 1908–1914." PhD diss., University of London, 2015.

Lichtwark, Alfred. *Eine Sommerfahrt auf der Yacht Hamburg*. Hamburg: Lütcke & Wulff, 1904.

Link, Heinrich Friedrich. *Die Urwelt und das Alterthum, erläutert durch die Naturkunde*. Berlin: Dümmler, 1820–22.

MacFarlane, James. "The Name and Nature of Modernism." In *Modernism, 1890–1930: A Guide to European Literature*, edited by Malcolm Bradbury and James MacFarlane, 19–56. New York: Penguin, 1991.

Majd, Mohammed Gholi. *The Great Famine and Genocide in Iran: 1917–1919*. 2nd ed. Lanham, MD: University Press of America, 2013.

Malamud, Bernard. *The Fixer*. New York: Farrar, Straus and Giroux, 1966.

Margueritte, Paul. *Contre les barbares, 1914–1915*. Paris: E. Flammarion, 1915.

———. *Mon Père*. Paris: P. Schmidt, 1884.

Martensen, Hans Lassen. *Den christelige Ethik*. 3 vols. Copenhagen: Gyldendal, 1871–78.

McMeekin, Sean. *The Russian Origins of the First World War*. Cambridge, MA: Harvard University Press, 2011.

Mérimée, Prosper. *Carmen*. Paris: M. Lévy, 1846.

Monrad, Ditlev Gotthard. *Politiske Breve, Nr. 14–18: Liberalismens Gjenmæle til Biskop Martensens sociale Ethik*. 2nd ed. Copenhagen: Reitzel, 1878.

Moritzen, Jules. *Georg Brandes in Life and Letters*. Newark, NJ: D. S. Colyer, 1922.

Moyn, Samuel. "Beyond Liberal Internationalism." *Dissent* 64, no. 1 (Winter 2017): 116–22.

———. *Human Rights and the Uses of History*. 2nd ed. New York: Verso, 2017.

———. *The Last Utopia: Human Rights in History*. Cambridge, MA: Harvard University Press, 2010.

———. *Not Enough: Human Rights in an Unequal World*. Cambridge, MA: Harvard University Press, 2018.

Myrdal, Gunnar. *Beyond the Welfare State: Economic Planning and Its International Implications*. New Haven, CT: Yale University Press, 1960.

Nalbandian, Inga. *Den store Jammer*. 3 vols. Copenhagen: Aschehoug, 1917–18.

———. *Your Brother's Blood Cries Out*. Translated by Victoria Rowe. London: Gomidas, 2007.

Nazarbek, Avetis. *Through the Storm*. New York: Longmans Green, 1899.

Neumann, Ivar B., and Benjamin de Carvalho. "Introduction: Small States and Status." In *Small State Status Seeking*, edited by Benjamin de Carvalho and Ivar B. Neumann, 1–21. London: Routledge, 2015.

Newman, Ernest. *The Life of Richard Wagner*. Cambridge: Cambridge University Press, 1976.

Nietzsche, Friedrich. *Ecce Homo*. Translated by Thomas Wayne. New York: Algora, 2004.

Nord, Johan Christian. "Nordens grundtvigske Nietzsche og fritænkeriets førstemand: En historie om Jakob Knudsens morallære og møde med Georg Brandes." In *Den gode den onde: Om grundtvigianister og branditter*, edited by Katrine Frøkjær Baunvig and Michael Schelde, 73–98. Copenhagen: Eksistensen, 2017.

Nordau, Max. *Entartung*. Berlin: C. Duncker, 1893.

Nordby, Thomas. "Georg Brandes og imperialismen." In *Den politiske Georg Brandes*, edited by Hans Hertel and Sven Møller Kristensen, 139–56. Copenhagen: Reitzel, 1973.

Novosad, Paul, and Eric Werker. "Who Runs the International System? Nationality and Leadership in the United Nations Secretariat." Dartmouth College, October 2017. http://www.dartmouth.edu/~novosad/novosad-werker-un.pdf.

Owens, Kenneth N. *Empire Maker: Aleksandr Baranov and Russian Colonial Expansion into Alaska and Northern California*. Seattle: University of Washington Press, 2015.

Phéline, Christian. *Un Guadeloupéen à Alger: Me Maurice L'Admiral (1864–1955)*. Paris: Riveneuve, 2014.

Pictet, Adolphe. *Les origines indo-européennes ou les Aryas primitifs*. 2 vols. Paris: Cherbuliez, 1859–63.

Plüschow, Gunther. *Die Abenteuer des Fliegers von Tsingtau*. Berlin: Ullstein, 1916.

Preston, Diana. *The Boxer Rebellion: The Dramatic Story of China's War on Foreigners That Shook the World in the Summer of 1900*. New York: Berkley, 2000.

Psichari, Ernest. *L'Appel aux armes*. Paris: G. Oudin, 1913.

Quillard, Pierre. *Pour l'Arménie: Mémoire et dossier*. Paris: Cahiers, 1902.
Renan, Joseph Ernest. *Le judaisme comme race et comme religion*. Paris: Calmann-Lévy, 1883.
Robin, Corey. *The Reactionary Mind: Conservatism from Edmund Burke to Donald Trump*. 2nd ed. Oxford: Oxford University Press, 2018.
Rohrbach, Paul. *Vom Kaukasus zum Mittelmeer*. Leipzig: B. G. Teubner, 1903.
Rolland, Romain. *Au-dessus de la mêlée*. Paris: P. Ollendorff, 1915.
Rustavelli, Shota. *The Man in the Panther's Skin*. Translated by Marjory Scott Wardrop. London: Royal Asiatic Society, 1912.
Saxlund, Eivind. *Jøder og Gojim*. 1st ed. Christiania: J. Aass, 1910.
Schiller, Friedrich. *Complete Works*. 2 vols. Translated by Charles J. Hempel. Philadelphia: I. Kohler, 1861.
Schlegel, Friedrich. *Über die Sprache und Weisheit der Indier*. Heidelberg: Mohr und Simmer, 1808.
Schnitzler, Arthur. *Traumnovelle*. Berlin: S. Fischer, 1927.
Shaw, Albert. "Some Danish Fiction Writers of Today." *The American Monthly Review of Reviews* 31 (January 1905): 107.
———. "Georg Brandes Visits America." *American Review of Reviews* 50, no. 1 (July 1914): 98–99.
Shuster, William Morgan. *The Strangling of Persia*. New York: Century, 1912.
Sienkiewicz, Henryk. *Prusse et Pologne: Enquête internationale*. Paris: Agence Polonaise de Presse, 1909.
Silbey, David J. *The Boxer Rebellion and the Great Game*. New York: Hill and Wang, 2012.
Słowacki, Juliusz. *Beniowski*. Lipsk: U Leopolda Michelsena, 1841.
Snoilsky, Carl Johan Gustaf. "På Polens Graf." In *Samlade Dikter*, 1:59–60. Stockholm: H. Geber, 1903.
Spencer, Herbert. *A System of Synthetic Philosophy*. 10 vols. London: Williams and Norgate, 1862–93.
Stearns, Harold, ed. *Civilization in the United States: An Inquiry by Thirty Americans*. New York: Harcourt, Brace, 1922.
Stearns, Peter N. *Human Rights in World History*. London: Routledge, 2012.
Stora, Benjamin. *Algeria, 1830–2000: A Short History*. Translated by Jane Marie Todd. Ithaca, NY: Cornell University Press, 2001.
Świętochowski, Aleksander. *Chawa Rubin*. Warsaw: E. Wende i Spółka, 1905.
Szajkowski, Zosa. "The German Appeal to the Jews of Poland, August 1914." *Jewish Quarterly Review* 59, no. 4 (April 1969): 311–20.
Tarnawsky, Maxim. *The All-Encompassing Eye of Ukraine: Ivan Nechui-Levyts'kyi's Realist Prose*. Toronto: University of Toronto Press, 2015.
Tchobanian, Archag. *L'Arménie, son Historie, sa Littérature, son role en Orient—Poëms Arméniens, traduits par A. Tchobanian*. Paris: Cinquième, 1897.
Tedesco, James Patrick. "Missionaries and French Imperialism: The Role of Catholic Missionaries in French Colonial Expansion, 1880–1905." PhD diss., University of Connecticut, 1980.
Tolstoy, Leo. *The Kingdom of God Is Within You: Christianity Not as a Mystic Religion But as a New Theory of Life*. Translated by Constance Garnett. London: William Heineman, 1894.

Tylor, Edward Burnett. *Primitive Culture: Researches into the Development of Mythology, Philosophy, Religion, Art, and Custom.* 2 vols. London: John Murray, 1871.

Ular, Alexander. *A Russo-Chinese Empire.* Westminster: Archibald Constable, 1904.

Vik, Hanne Hagtvedt, Steven L. B. Jensen, Linde Lindkvist, and Johan Strang. "Histories of Human Rights in the Nordic Countries." *Nordic Journal of Human Rights* 36, no. 3 (October 2018): 189–201.

Wagner, Richard. "Das Judenthum in der Musik." *Neue Zeitschrift fur Musik* 33, no. 19 (September 3, 1850): 101–7.

Wassermann, Jakob. *Der Fall Maurizius.* Berlin: S. Fischer, 1928.

Weininger, Otto. *Geschlecht und Charakter: Eine prinzipielle Untersuchung.* Vienna: Wilhelm Braumüller, 1903.

Welhaven, Johan Sebastian. "Republikanerne." In *Samlede Skrifter*, 3:167–70. Copenhagen: Gyldendal, 1867.

Werfel, Franz. *Die vierzig Tage des Musa Dagh.* Vienna: Paul Zsolnay, 1933.

Witoszek, Nina. *The Origins of the "Regime of Goodness": Remapping the Cultural History of Norway.* Oslo: Universitetsforlaget, 2011.

Yambert, Karl A. "Paul Rohrbach." In *Modern Genocide: The Definitive Resource and Document Collection*, edited by Paul R. Bartrop and Steven Leonard Jacobs, 1:1074–75. Santa Barbara, CA: ABC-CLIO, 2015.

Yusheng, Yao. "Shanghai." *The Encyclopedia of Prostitution and Sex Work*, edited by Melissa Hope Ditmore, 338–41. Santa Barbara, CA: Greenwood, 2006.

Index of Named Persons